Systemic Parenting

Exploring the Parenting Big Picture

Systemic Parenting

Exploring the Parenting Big Picture

by

Mark Gaskill, MFT

cP

Aventine Press LLC

To Sam & Janet
For their encouragement and support

Contents

|| Forword

In the 1980s I had the opportunity to work as mental health aid in a psychiatric hospital just outside Philadelphia, Pennsylvania. This was both an enlightening and painful experience for me. It was painful from the perspective of the human suffering and misery that I witnessed up close and personal. This particular hospital treated persons suffering from the most severe and acute psychiatric conditions that are known. My workday consisted of interacting with persons who were clinically depressed and profoundly suicidal, persons who were grossly psychotic and delusional, and persons who had demonstrated themselves to have an affinity for violence and cruelty. I eventually left this position to work as a counselor in a drug and alcohol addiction treatment facility. The human conditions treated in this hospital were much different than the psychiatric facility but the pain and suffering was indistinguishable. From a professional perspective these experiences were educational and rewarding. I was exposed *en masse* to clinical challenges and sides of humanity that few people ever encounter. This experience would later prove to be a tremendous asset as I entered the field of family therapy.

Two personal revelations emerged from these early experiences that even today have a significant impact on my clinical work. The first revelation came one night on the psychiatric unit. I was working the midnight to 8:00 AM shift on a ward that treated the most profoundly ill and affected individuals. I was seated at a table completing some paperwork when, around 3:00 AM, a patient joined me. This man was about 30 years-old and suffered from chronic paranoid schizophrenia. His world consisted of delusional beliefs and relentless hallucinations. During the day he would usually isolate himself from other people and converse with the voices that existed nowhere else but in his mind. Traditional treatment and medications offered this man little relief. On this particular morning he seemed lucid and almost entirely without the symptoms that left him so debilitated. I had the great pleasure of having a 15 to 20 minute conversation with a fellow human being that, for all practical purpose, seemed quite normal at that particular moment. This man told me how much he missed his parents who were now deceased. He told me of his high school sweetheart and the joy he felt when remembering the time they spent together so many years before. He joked about the quality of the hospital food and casually smoked a cigarette. Eventually he returned to bed only to wake later that morning having reentered his world of delusions, hallucinations, and isolation.

This experience left me changed. My perception of the people being treated at this hospital, my perception of people with profound mental illness in general, had been rocked from its foundation. I hate to admit it, but prior to this experience I think I viewed the profoundly ill patients admitted to this facility as objects rather than as human beings. I viewed them merely as *patients* or *clients* rather than people afflicted with, suffering from, and being treated for disease and illness. Choosing to see that 30 year-old man as merely a *patient* allowed me to distance myself emotionally from the misery that was present in his everyday life. Seeing him as a *patient* allowed me to walk past this man while he conversed with the voices he heard in his head without giving it any thought. This raised several questions in my mind. Was I compromising any aspects of his care and treatment by distancing myself emotionally in this manner? Was I seeing the whole picture if I limited myself to working with *patients* rather than with *human beings*? This experience and these questions were the catalyst that encouraged me to evaluate my perception of mental illness as well as people who struggle with a variety of life's challenges. I try not to see a *patient* or a *client* but rather the human being behind the suffering – a human being worthy of attention and competent treatment regardless of condition, behavior, or appearance. That brief early morning conversation helped me realize that deep inside this patient was a person, an emotional being, afflicted with a condition that left him trapped in a world of confusion and perpetual disorientation. I realized that ignorance of his condition, perspective, or personal struggle by no means justified objectifying or seeing him as less worthy of attention or serious consideration. I now try to look beyond one's actions, behaviors, condition or affliction – to the person that might be trapped or hidden within. This was the first personal revelation that emerged from my early experiences.

I will present a few examples of people who have mistreated or have been cruel to others within the following pages. This first revelation has proven to be most helpful in working with the situations from which these examples were drawn. Making a concerted effort to see the *human being* behind one's actions has aided me in helping these families and individuals move forward in a healthy manner. Had I not had the pleasure of that early morning conversation, my perception of and interactions with many of the individuals and families described throughout *Systemic Parenting* would likely have been significantly different. I believe my work with these people would have been less helpful to the conditions and problems they brought to my office.

The second personal revelation to strike me during the early years of my professional career related to something commonly referred to as *the revolving door*. This is a phenomenon that I saw repeatedly in both the psychiatric and the drug and alcohol addiction treatment facilities. By the time somebody is hospitalized in these facilities their condition is usually pretty desperate. Hospitalization is typically considered to be the option of last resort. While in the hospital the symptoms that led to such a drastic intervention are usually reduced or eliminated altogether. This is where the **revolving door** concept comes into play. After the individual is stabilized and the symptoms leading to the hospitalization are reduced, the individual is discharged and returns home. Frequently I noticed that soon after being discharged, the symptoms or behaviors that originally resulted in the hospitalization seemed to reappear – resulting in a return to treatment. It did not matter what the original symptoms or behaviors were. The person returning home might have been hospitalized for any one of a number of psychiatric or substance abuse problems. Also, the family structure to which the person was returning did not seem to matter. For example, it didn't seem to matter if a child who had attempted suicide was returning home to a one or two parent household. It didn't seem to matter if a family member who had been treated for drug and alcohol addiction returned home to a privileged or less privileged household. This revolving door seemed to affect all regardless of the structure of their family, their race, their degree of religiosity, or socioeconomic status. What was causing individuals who had been stabilized in the hospital to deteriorate shortly after discharge? What conditions were missing from the family or home environment that existed in the hospital environment? It was these two questions that motivated me to return to graduate school to study family therapy. I believed the answer to these questions was to be found in how families function.

My second personal revelation was a direct result of observing this revolving door. It seemed that limiting the focus of treatment to the individual was an inadequate long-term solution to many of the problems being treated in the hospital setting. Variables external to the individual and the hospital environment always seemed to be strong determinates to the success of treatment. What variables differed between those individuals whose treatment was successful and those individual whose treatment did not seem to be helpful? What variables determined who passed through that revolving door? The answer to these questions seemed to center around the family system from which the individual emerged. My second personal revelation led me to believe that an effective therapist, mental health worker, or clinician, must be willing to consider and be knowledgeable of a larger picture. I thought it important to acquire a *systemic* understanding of the family and how families function. Treating an individual well meant treating an entire family. Several years ago this belief was not highly regarded in the mental health field. Even today many professionals struggle with the idea of broadening treatment considerations to include the larger family system. Popular beliefs held, and in some cases still hold, that therapists, psychologists, psychiatrists, and social workers should focus their clinical attention on the problematic symptoms exhibited by the individual rather than the larger systemic variables stimulating the symptoms. Popular belief also holds that mental health treatment professionals treat these symptoms with medications and send the individual on his or her way. In many instances, the medications are very effective in reducing the problematic symptoms. Unfortunately, they also serve to mask the larger systemic variables stimulating the symptoms. We are now recognizing the long-term effects of this approach to managing mental health and behavioral concerns: *the revolving door*. Many people treated in this manner just do not get better. By limiting the focus of treatment to the individual, and to his or her symptoms, the underlying issues that stimulate these symptoms are overlooked. One loses sight of the bigger picture, rendering treatment relatively ineffective.

I have attempted to incorporate these two personal revelations into my practice of family therapy. I try to look beyond one's actual behaviors or symptoms by focusing on the underlying emotions and motivations that might be stimulating the behaviors. I also try to keep sight of the larger *systemic picture*. That is, I try to keep in mind that the behaviors and symptoms that bring individuals and families to therapy do not occur without the influence of others, nor were others unaffected by these behaviors and symptoms. *Systemic Parenting* is my attempt to apply these ideas to the process of parenting. This text is intended to help parents recognize and embrace the larger, systemic, understanding of the parenting process. It is through this systemic view that many of the issues parents face regularly which might ultimately lead to problematic behaviors can be lessened or avoided altogether. A systemic understanding of parenting can help resolve problematic behaviors without dramatic interventions. I believe these ideas will become clear in the pages that follow.

Introduction

A parent once telephoned my office desperately seeking an appointment for her 14 year-old son; I am a family therapist. When asked how she thought I might be helpful, the young woman informed me that she and her husband could no longer control the boy. She told me he was *"completely out of control."* I had no idea what "out of control" meant to this woman and asked her to give me a few details. The boy was described as engaging in many destructive behaviors – ranging from belligerent, loud, insubordinate, explosive, and sometimes violent outbursts to abuse of drugs and alcohol. Mixed in with these behaviors were a myriad of other problems such as long periods in which the son isolated himself in his room, a general withdrawal from the family and family functions, declining grades, and a poorly developed social network both in and out of school. The mother told me she and her husband first noticed these changes about a year prior to making the phone call to my office. She also informed me their efforts to address the problems seemed to have had the exact opposite effect. That is, everything they tried seemed to result in further deterioration in the boy's behavior and increased conflict within the family. I was told there was a 10 year-old sibling – a sister – whom the mother was afraid might be adversely affected by the boy's behavior.

I heard enough from the boy's mother and attempted to schedule an appointment for the family. I asked when the four of them could meet in my office and was met with a long and uncomfortable silence. The next words from the mother's mouth are all too common to family therapists. *"Shouldn't you just meet with my son?"* I said, *"Why yes, I will be meeting with him. Now, how does next Wednesday evening sound?"* *"For my son?"* the mother responded hesitantly. *"Yes, and for his sister, you, and your husband,"* was my reply. The mother responded, *"I,... I don't understand. Shouldn't you first meet with my son.... alone ..... to find out what is going on?"*

Here we have an example of a very common misconception about parenting and the family – that individual problems, strengths, weaknesses, successes, and failures occur independently of the larger family system and all of its members (both living and deceased). This concerned parent was almost pleading with me to see her son alone. Essentially, she was asking me to separate her son from the family and to fix him – as a physician might treat an infection in an individual. From the mother's description this problem was far more complex. As such, it would require a "fix" that embraced more than just the son but rather the entire family system. This brings us to the subject of *systemic parenting*. What is *systemic parenting* and how might this subject be relevant to the family and circumstances just described? To understand *systemic parenting,* a little background on *systems* is in order.

We will get back to the family from the example above in a few moments, but first, let's talk about a biologist named Ludwig von Bertalanffy. He introduced a concept in the 1940s that he called *General Systems Theory.* This theory was von Bertalanffy's response to the scientific community's attempt to advance scientific understanding and knowledge by reducing everything to its most basic elements or parts. For example, a scientist may approach understanding the human body by breaking it down or reducing it to its most basic or individual parts (individual chemical reactions, individual cells, and individual organs). This reduction approach asserts that by studying the body's most basic elements individually, one could eventually gain a comprehensive understanding of the whole body. This belief held that the human body is nothing more than the sum of its multiple parts. Von Bertalanffy was concerned that in the process of breaking the body down to its most basic elements, scientists incorrectly assume all factors influencing the single chemical reaction, the single cell, or the single organ are included in this closed and limited evaluation. A great deal of information and knowledge has been gained through reductionism; however, *General Systems Theory* asserts that a cell or organ physically or intellectually separated from its surroundings cannot be fully understood. The complex interactions *between* cells and organs are crucial and should not be minimized or overlooked. A good demonstration would be to remove a single cell or organ from a living/healthy body and observe its response. The individual cell or organ will not survive for very long outside of the system which supports it and is supported by it. Furthermore, the body will be weakened by the loss of the cell or organ. There exists a crucial interdependence between the parts of the whole. These parts and their interactions are part of something called a system.

Every system is supported by a boundary. For example, our skin acts as a boundary. Boundaries do not completely isolate the system but serve to distinguish it from its environment. When we look at the environment in which a particular system exists (in this case our body) we see that it too contains many other systems that co-interact. For example, our environment provides us with nutrients and hospitable living conditions. Our environment also consists of other interacting and supportive systems – families, communities, businesses, towns/cities, governments, etc. The interactive and interdependent nature of these systems, in a manner of speaking, glue the individual elements together to form a more powerful and functional *whole*. If these systems, that is, the individual, family, community, businesses, city, and government, did not interact, the *whole* would consist of nothing more than the sum of its components. Fortunately this is not the case. They are interdependent and do interact. As a result of this interaction, we have much more than the sum of many parts. Likewise, the chemicals, cells, and organs of the body interact to form a living being with an individual personality, strengths, weaknesses, and physical characteristics. This is much greater than a mere mass of non-interacting individual cells, organs, and chemicals sitting in a bucket. Just as the body consists of interacting elements, a family consists of individuals who are interdependent and who interact. The benefits of this systemic interaction and interdependence include factors such as physical and emotional security and safety, shared division of responsibilities and resources, transfer of knowledge and experiences, and companionship. Families interact to form communities, which offer considerable benefit to the family systems that are contained within their boundaries. For example, community infrastructures – roads, utilities, religious and spiritual groups, structures that enable social and recreational opportunities, neighborhood security/support, and other entities that help define a community. Business systems further support communities by supplying many of the basic needs for survival such as housing, food, clothing, and services.

Von Bertalanffy believed the scientific community was focusing too much attention on understanding the individual components found in complex systems rather than working to understand the interactive, interdependent and supportive properties of the systems themselves.

Von Beralanffy believed one understands a person through understanding how the multiple systems (e.g. thought processes, cells, chemical reactions, and organs) within the person interact and are interdependent, as opposed to how they function separately from each other.

Western medicine and many schools of psychotherapy are largely based upon reductionism. A more systemic understanding of, or approach to, medicine would argue that reductionism misses an important point – the whole body. The emotional condition of the mind can and will interact with the condition and functioning of our body's cells and organs. For example, functioning of the stomach can be influenced in stressful situations, which in turn will interact with and influence other bodily functions. Interactions such as these are by no means simple but rather a complex network of interdependencies designed to support a greater goal – maintaining the bodily systems that interact to form the individual person. Thus, a physician treating a chronically upset stomach with medications designed to address problems occurring in the stomach and its individual cells without addressing imbalances in or stressors to the other interactive and interdependent networks, will find the treatment to be fairly ineffective or even counterproductive. A person with chronic stomach problems being treated solely with medications intended to fortify the stomach's cell lining or to reduce the production of stomach acid may eliminate the acute distress. However, if emotional or dietary issues impacting the individual are not considered and addressed this individual may later experience other stress related problems such as heart disease.

Each systemic hierarchy (the individual, the family, the community, the business, and so on) contains universal laws or rules that govern its functioning.   Furthermore, there are certain similarities or commonalties between the laws governing these diverse systems. For example, the cells and organs contained in our body require nutrients and a hospitable environment in order to grow, reproduce, and make repairs. The same holds true for other systems. The family, community, business, and governmental organization all require certain supportive environments to meet basic needs, be successful, make repairs on themselves, grow, and respond to adverse conditions. Von Bertalanffy believed it is imperative for scientists to advance knowledge by striving to identify and understand the **laws governing** these systems rather than focusing merely on the individual components of each system. He believed that analysis of the larger systemic picture would yield considerable insight and greater understanding. One may assert that any treatment designed to address ailments in a particular system (the body, the family, the community, the business, the government) will be significantly more effective if it takes into consideration the many interactive and interdependent components of the system. For example, a doctor who treats a stomach disorder with medication and then refers the patient to a dietitian, a counselor/therapist, and an exercise physiologist is less likely to see that patient again for future stomach complications or problems related to heart disease, mental health concerns such as depression or anxiety, and a myriad of other related medical problems.

The mother who called my office requesting assistance with her son was essentially asking me to isolate a single component of the family system, her son. She was asking me to fix that component without considering the interactive nature of the family system. When I am asked to see a family member alone outside of the family system, I ask several questions. In this particular case I was wondering if her son's problems developed independent of the family? Were other members of this family system affected by the son's behaviors? Will solutions designed to address the problem be successful without the involvement or consideration of the other family members?

Fortunately, the mother scheduled the appointment and arrived with her husband and their two children. It did not take long to realize that there were many variables affecting the health of this family system. The son's aberrant behaviors were, in part, a symptom of these stressful variables. During our first few sessions it was revealed that the parent's marriage was marred by significant conflict. This conflict had been around for quite some time (at least two years) and manifested itself in many ways. The husband was frequently away on business. While away, his wife would complain directly to the children about the undue burden his traveling caused the family. When the parents were together, the atmosphere was tense and heated arguments between them were frequent. There would be long periods of uncomfortable silence in the household, sometimes lasting days, following some of these arguments. In addition, the husband would often insult and verbally degrade his wife in front of the children. Quite often the wife would respond in kind. The rift between the parents was so severe that they had been considering separation and divorce.

The children in this family were always physically well cared for. They were well clothed, well fed, and had possessions worthy of envy. However, the household was by no means emotionally safe. The tension was obvious to both children, yet, they lacked the developmental abilities, the parental guidance, and an emotionally safe environment to process this tension. Each member reacted to this systemic condition in his or her own way. The parents became increasingly distant and hostile toward each other. They were also becoming increasingly unhappy, frustrated, and depressed. Both parents were beginning to look outside of the marriage to get their emotional needs met. The husband became enmeshed with his work – sometimes working 80 hours a week and opting to travel extensively. The wife became an avid and compulsive consumer – spending an incredible amount of money on items and services that were clearly excessive and by no means necessary. On the surface their daughter appeared to be the least affected. However, her mood was often down, she lacked energy and enthusiasm, and she would often quietly isolate herself as an escape. Her isolation went unnoticed in the family, and she was not thriving to her potential. The son felt emotionally trapped and powerless. He knew something was wrong, yet lacked the tools, life experiences, and safe environment in which to process his emotions, concerns and fears. His behaviors were a natural and understandable reaction to the difficult family crisis. They were symptomatic of problems within the *family system*.

In a nutshell, my work with this family consisted of helping them take the focus away from the son's destructive behaviors and assisting the parents repair the rifts in the family system. This entailed helping the parents create an environment in which both parents and children could safely express themselves emotionally. This would be an environment where the parents were able to express their own perspectives and emotions while simultaneously considering those of each other and their children. The parents were also challenged to address the problems in their marriage and to make the best possible decision regarding separation, divorce, or reconciliation. The parents were aided in developing skills that would help them openly and safely communicate the nature of their marital problems to their children. The parents soon realized how their behaviors were inadvertently drawing the children into their complex marital problems, creating extreme anxiety for the children. Neither child was at an age where they could appropriately deal with this burden. The parents developed skills that helped them be more receptive to, and supportive of, the children's fears and emotional reactions to the marital problems. This process helped the children make sense of their experiences and emotions.

In a relatively short period of time, the son's destructive behaviors abated. His experimentation with drugs and alcohol ceased and his social networks in and out of school rapidly expanded. The daughter's isolation immediately lessened. Her teachers commented that she appeared more relaxed and socially interactive in school. The parents struggled to reconcile their marital problems for some time. They separated and came very close to divorcing. Only after considerable therapy and hard work were they able to successfully address their differences and begin to have their emotional needs met within the marriage. It is important to note that the marital struggles and separation were accomplished in a manner that minimized the unhealthy impact on the children by promoting open processing of information and emotions. This provided the children with a sense of emotional safety and security during these difficult times. As a result, the children demonstrated few of the destructive reactions that were earlier observed.

This family benefited from a systemic approach to understanding their son's troubling symptoms. Had I seen the son individually, the initial symptoms might have been reduced by helping him develop coping skills and working to enhance his self-esteem. However, this approach probably would have had little impact on the underlying problems that were resulting in the troubling behaviors. Had the systemic variables influencing the son's behaviors been ignored, we would likely have seen more complex problems in his future behavior and relationships. His sister would also have been susceptible to experiencing similar problems in her later life and relationships. This would be an unfortunate and tragic consequence of limiting our work to the son's symptomatic behaviors.

As previously stated, von Bertalanffy believed every system, the family system not withstanding, contains universal laws regarding their functioning. *Systemic Parenting* identifies some of the universal laws associated with the family. More specifically, this book focuses on those laws that relate to the parenting process. *Systemic Parenting* is not a book in which you will find parenting advice or directives (*in this situation you do this, in that situation you do that*). I believe books instructing parents on "how to parent" consistently fall short of the reader's expectations when the *instructions* are implemented. Every family is influenced by an infinite number of variables and factors that make it unique from other families. These variables and factors include matters such as financial resources, religious convictions, communication skills, educational background, cultural influences, family histories, family size, external stressors, and so on. It is unlikely that any instructional manual for parenting will be able to take into consideration all the variables that impact an individual family. A suggestion or intervention that may be helpful for one family experiencing a particular problem will likely have a much different outcome with another family experiencing a similar problem. Rather than giving the reader instructions on parenting, this book presents laws that I refer to as Parenting Assumptions. In my practice I have observed the universal quality of these laws. They are just as applicable to a single mother of three surviving on public assistance as they are to a two parent, upper middle class household. These laws also equally apply to parents in sub–Sahara Africa as to Canadian parents who are of a different race and religion. Parents who familiarize themselves with these Parenting Assumptions will soon recognize a larger picture – a *systemic* understanding of the parenting process. As this understanding develops, the parent will have greater insight into parenting and family successes, conflicts, and problems. Armed with this understanding, the parent, regardless of the individual variables influencing his or her family system, will be in a much better position to remove or minimize the less helpful behaviors, reactions, and variables while developing or enhancing more helpful ones.

As previously stated, these systemic laws are presented to the reader as Parenting Assumptions. These Assumptions are best described as brief maxims or aphorisms averaging around 25 words. These Assumptions are written in a manner that highlight ideas and concepts that may initially appear completely unrelated to the parenting process. The reader is encouraged to review these Assumptions repeatedly as their relevance to parenting may initially be difficult to see. Remember, systemic relationships – relationships between variables or parts of the whole – may not be immediately apparent and are thus easily overlooked. As one's understanding of a larger systemic picture grows, these relationships will emerge with clarity. Every Parenting Assumption is followed by a brief explanation or an example from some of the families I have had the pleasure to work with. These explanations or examples are not intended to be instructions for how you act or react but rather bring to life the Assumption presented. The reader must determine how the Assumption applies to his or her unique family system.

Systemic Parenting presents 90 Assumptions. These have been categorized into 8 chapters. Each chapter builds upon the previous one, taking the reader closer to understanding a larger, systemic picture of the parenting process. These chapters are entitled Basics, History, Balance, Safety, Paradox, Fear, Skill, and Art. The significance of these titles will become apparent as we progress. Again, it is important for the reader to review the Assumptions several times to help promote familiarity. A list of the Parenting Assumptions without narration/ explanation can be found in Appendix A at the end of this text for quick and repeated reference. Enjoy your exploration of the family system and *Systemic Parenting*.

Chapter 1 Basics

*A foundation, an introduction,
elementary components of a whole*

Years ago I worked with a young married couple. This couple struggled with many problems in their relationship. After many unsuccessful attempts to address the discord themselves, they entered marital counseling. In one of our sessions the wife described a recent experience that was causing her a great deal of distress. The couple had a seven year-old son who just began playing on a local Little League baseball team. The team's coach ensured that all children playing on his team had ample time on the playing field. This was the first year many of the kids played organized baseball. The coach had them play various positions to broaden their experience and to help them identify individual talents and interests. He accomplished this by frequently rotating players in and out of each game. One particular game was against a long standing rival – a neighboring team. Many of the parents from the opposing teams knew each other and were friends. Apparently, the game between these two teams was always an exciting event. The parents were described as being filled with pride and enthusiastically encouraged their children to give it their best throughout the entire game. The children's response was obvious by their excitement, their effort, and team spirit. The couple's son had the opportunity to play several times throughout the game. However, during the last inning he was rotated into the game as a relief pitcher. The score was tied, there was one out, and the bases were loaded. He rose to the occasion by striking out his first batter. Unfortunately, the boy walked the second batter. This forced a score and the game was lost. On the way back to the car the young boy experienced a rush of several uncomfortable emotions and began to cry. I would imagine the boy probably felt embarrassed, confused, discouraged, crushed and defeated. The boy's father immediately responded to his son's tears by stating:

"Stop your crying. You remind me of a little girl...
No, a little baby girl!"[1]

According to the mother the boy suppressed the tears and went home with his head hanging low. The mother stated she was infuriated by her husband's response but had no idea how to respond. She believed her son placed great importance on the game and his own performance. When the game was lost the mother was confident her son felt he had let his team, his family, and himself down. The mother also stated she felt powerless to respond to, and was confused by, her husband's reaction to the boy's tears.

1. If you know yourself and the basic needs of childhood, you will likely be successful in your parenting.

This situation raises many questions. What are the systemic, or big picture, considerations here? Was this just a benign comment or are there larger issues to be considered? I wondered what messages the father's response conveyed to his son. How did it impact the boy's beliefs about girls and women or his understanding of emotions and intimacy? Did it meet the boy's needs at that particular time? Did the father's response bring father and son closer together? Is the boy better prepared for living after this experience? Where did the father's response come from?

The mother was offended for many reasons. First, she did not believe her husband's response was healthy for the boy. She had difficulty expressing exactly why she felt this way but was certain there were better ways to address her son's situation. Secondly, she felt insulted by her husband's inference that girls are somehow weak or inferior. The wife was able to identify with her son's situation as the husband often treated her in a similar manner – mocking her attempts to express or explore her emotions. This made discussion of emotionally charged matters relating to their marriage and parenting uncomfortable and very difficult to approach. The wife brought this issue to therapy because it seemed inapproachable at home. We spent considerable time exploring the event that followed this particular Little League baseball game and the many important issues it raised. We explored alternative ways the father might have responded to his son's tears and the potential consequences of each. We also explored the motivations behind the father's actual response to his son's tears.

When one or both parents tell a youngster that emotions are somehow bad or that they should be hidden or suppressed, the child will learn to do so without much question, out of a natural loyalty to his or her parents. This holds true even if the emotions are an appropriate reaction to the child's experiences. I imagine the boy's internal reaction to his father's response might resemble the following:

- *I let my team, myself, and my parents down by losing the game.*
- *I feel crushed, alone, defeated, discouraged, embarrassed, hurt, insecure, low, miserable, tired, useless, and weak.*
- *I think Dad is telling me these feelings are wrong, are somehow bad, and that they should be hidden or suppressed. He's telling me that I'm weak if I cannot control these emotions.*
- *These feelings are uncomfortable but they somehow feel right to me.*
- *However, Dad must be right. I don't want to disappoint him further.*
- *I probably should not trust my emotions and will try to be strong. Boy's shouldn't cry – that's for girls.*

Over time, and after many such experiences, this boy will become quite skilled at suppressing his true and just emotions. He will be strong. Or will he? If the child hears over and over again that emotions are a sign of weakness, are something to be suppressed, that the only emotions appropriate to express are the more comfortable ones (joy, elation, excitement, and so on), he will comply without question. The basic needs of childhood will not have been met, and the child's ability to thrive in later life will be affected in unhealthy and less than helpful ways.[2] A quick note, the phrase *just emotion* is frequently used throughout this book. It is important to recognize that all emotions are *just*. There is no such thing as a *bad* or *unjust* emotion. Some will certainly be experienced as *comfortable* while others will be *uncomfortable*. For example, when a baby cries he or she is expressing several uncomfortable emotions (discomfort, fear, insecurity, hunger, and so on). When a baby smiles or coos he or she is likely experiencing several more comfortable emotions (security, warmth, contentment, joy, excitement, and so on). None of these emotions are *bad* or *unjust* but rather serve an important function. They help us interpret our surroundings, our well being, and they assist us define our interacting with others.

After considerable introspection and discussion, the parents of the young Little League player arrived at a response they believed might have been healthier for their son's development than *"Stop your crying, you remind me of a little girl.... No, a little baby girl."* The response was something like:

> **Walking back to the car after the game was lost, the son becomes overwhelmed with uncomfortable emotions and begins to cry.**

Father: *You know, I think it must really feel terrible to have lost the game that way. If I were in your shoes right now I might feel like I let my team down. I might feel hurt or embarrassed. I might even feel discouraged and disappointed in myself. Are you feeling any of these right now?*

Son's likely response: *Yeah, I think so.*

Father: *Well, if you are I just want to let you know that it's all right to feel that way. I was really proud to see you out there. That was a tough situation you walked into. That took a lot of guts. Sure, you walked a batter. You also struck one out! I don't think very many people could have pulled off a win. Both you and your team did a great job out there. It was a very close game.*

Son's tears will likely decrease

Father: *Every team wins some games and they lose others. This just happens to be one that your team lost. Do you want to play catch when we get home?*

Son's likely response: *Yeah!*

2. If you know the basic needs of childhood but not yourself, parenthood will likely be a struggle.

This was not an easy response for the father to conceive or consider. In fact, he initially laughed at and openly mocked it. His discomfort with this type of interaction was obvious. When asked why he was so uncomfortable with this interaction he struggled to provide even one reason. Instead, he made statements such as *"that doesn't happen in the real world"* and *"you see that on TV, not with real parents."* Was the father correct? Was the alternative response fantasy or merely unfamiliar territory for him? I believe both are essentially correct. The second father-son interaction and all that it represents was so unfamiliar, so unknown, and so uncomfortable for the father that it represented fantasy. It was something beyond his immediate reach or comprehension. The father loved his son very much, yet had many emotional blind spots that were preventing full expression of his love. These blind spots were also starting to create problems in the parent's marriage and other aspects of their living and relating. After the father relaxed and became comfortable speaking with a therapist, he disclosed being aware of these emotional blind spots, yet he had no idea how to address them. The father did not want to feel uncomfortable expressing or processing his emotions, but the thought of making changes was overwhelming. In this regard, the alternative response merely represented unfamiliar territory for the father. It was his choice to either explore this unfamiliar territory (getting to know himself by exploring why such responses were uncomfortable, thereby moving closer to being able to freely respond in a much healthier manner) or to avoid the topic altogether. If he chose to *avoid getting to know himself* the alternative response would always remain fantasy – something you only see on TV.

If you know yourself and the basic needs of childhood you will likely be successful in your parenting. This father would benefit from acquiring a greater familiarity with himself and his son's basic developmental/emotional needs. *Familiarity with himself* would include greater access to the **emotional processes** that are crucial to healthy and productive human interactions; a greater understanding of **his own parenting** (how he was parented) and factors that influenced how he was raised; increased **empathy skills** (the ability to understand the feelings and emotions of those around him); enhanced **communication skills**; and a knowledge of common **thinking errors**. Knowing himself and the needs of childhood would move responses such as the alternative above from the realm of fantasy to being freely and frequently utilized.

3. If you know neither yourself nor the basic needs of childhood, both the child and parent will likely suffer.

After several weeks of family therapy this particular father moved from knowing little about himself and the needs of his son to having considerable insight into both. Over a period of several months, interactions with his wife and son slowly became more meaningful and rewarding. The mother began to understand why she, like her son, felt powerless to respond in a healthy way when emotions were discounted or minimized in the family. Both parents reported that understanding these *basics* was a crucial first step to improving the quality of their marital and parenting relationships.

Basics, as the word implies, serve as the foundation for all parenting. These three Parenting Assumptions are the foundation for chapters 2 through 8. That is, the Basic Assumptions serve as a foundation from which the parent is able to develop a more sophisticated systemic understanding of this most important responsibility – understanding oneself and the needs of childhood. Unfortunately, the father in the previous example knew neither himself nor the needs of his son very well. The possibility of losing his wife through divorce motivated him to learn alternative ways of relating to those around him and to seek a greater understanding of the origins of his beliefs, thoughts, and behaviors.

Chapter 2 History

An account of what has or might have happened

Our *basics* tell us we should know ourselves and the needs of childhood. Let's move forward by looking at "knowing ourselves." I would like to quote a Latin proverb that is relevant to the subject: *Historia est magister vitae.* Simply translated this means *history is the teacher of life.* Therapists, historians, philosophers, politicians, business professionals and military strategists have long explored and struggled with this concept – how to best learn from our past experiences in order to better understand and improve our present and future experiences. Few people will dispute that our present day actions and reactions are greatly influenced by our past or historical relationships. Yet, for reasons to be discussed, it is often difficult for persons wanting to improve their family relations and parenting experiences to accept the importance of their personal and family history. Every now and then the importance of *history* "clicks" for a person struggling with or wanting to improve the present. When this occurs the doors open for rapid change and healthy outcomes.

4. Although most people can see the outward and obvious aspects of parenting, few truly risk change by looking inward and backward. One of the fears associated with this task relates to the certain discomfort likely to be encountered. Both child and parent will greatly benefit from risking change and overcoming fear associated with befriending one's personal, relational, and family histories.

From time to time, therapists encounter very sad conditions within a family. One such example from my practice of family therapy involved a teenage boy who was referred to my office after it was discovered he had been sexually abused by an uncle a few years earlier. The abuse occurred several times over a period of three to four months leaving the boy severely traumatized. Unfortunately, he never disclosed the events to anybody. The abuse was only discovered after the uncle was arrested for victimizing other children outside of the family. My work with the boy was intended to help minimize the unhealthy impact the sexual abuse would have on his emotional well-being and future relationships. At first, the boy did not like the idea of working with a therapist. His secret had been secure for years. The uncomfortable feelings of shame and embarrassment were strong motivators to keep the lid tightly sealed on this secret. With time and considerable work, the young boy warmed up to the idea of therapy. This occurred after he recognized it to be a safe and non–judgmental environment in which to discuss this painful part of his history. Over a period of several weeks he realized the feelings of shame and embarrassment could be safely identified, processed, understood, and put to rest. I would routinely meet with the boy's mother to discuss his progress, explore the many ways she could support his efforts, and discuss how she had been impacted by these terrible events. The boy's father was deceased. After several meetings with the mother, it became apparent that she was falling apart emotionally as her son was beginning to heal. The boy was learning to freely discuss his feelings, explore how the abuse had impacted him, and was working hard to develop many helpful coping skills. The mother seemed to avoid the subject of the sexual abuse altogether and would often sit in my office crying uncontrollably. Ironically, as the woman's son became more prepared to face the abuse, she became less prepared to support him in this struggle. After several frustrating weeks, the mother revealed she had been raped by *"a friend of the family"* when she was a child (about her son's age). Furthermore, it was revealed that her younger sister had also been sexually abused by this perpetrator. Like her son, the mother also attempted to protected herself by keeping memories of this attack and the uncomfortable emotions associated with the abuse tucked away deep inside of her. They were never discussed, processed, or dealt with in any way. Now her son's struggle with a similar experience made it impossible for her to keep this emotional door shut. Asking the mother to support her son's progress by ensuring the home environment was safe for him to process the emotions connected with the abuse, I inadvertently threatened the emotional defenses she had spent a lifetime developing and maintaining. Essentially these defenses required the mother to suppress or shut off uncomfortable emotions.

My request that she remain open to exploring and processing her son's emotions represented a huge threat. She was faced with a very uncomfortable dilemma – how to help her son with his struggles without compromising her own defenses. She initially attempted to do both and her defenses began to crumble in a relatively short period of time. At one point she stated it felt as if her world was falling apart around here. She was experiencing problems interacting with others at work; she could not sleep well; she was feeling increasingly depressed, and was isolating herself from friends and family. Fortunately, she kept coming back to therapy.

The mother's revelation added a new, but not surprising, dimension to my work with the family. For the mother to be truly supportive of her son's growth and development, she would be challenged to risk change by looking inward and backward. This thought was terrifying for her as many uncomfortable emotions and experiences would surely require open and honest exploration. With time and considerable support, she was able to discuss the unfortunate events from her past. The mother was encouraged to explore how these traumatic events, and her reactions to them, impacted her ability to relate to others – including her son. She was also encouraged to explore how the sexual abuse had impacted her views of herself, her self-esteem, her feelings of self-worth, her understanding of intimacy, and her ability to relate to others with empathy. This process was intended to reduce the less healthy impact the past sexual abuse was having on her present relations and living. As it happened, she had had a series of troubled relationships with men, struggled with occasional bouts of severe depression, was not fulfilled by her career accomplishments or social activities, and was struggling with her parenting responsibilities. She also explored the structure of family relationships that had made prior disclosure of the abuse difficult. Why was it emotionally unsafe for her to talk about the abuse with her parents immediately after it occurred? Why had it been emotionally unsafe for her son to do the same? As we explored her family history, we discovered these events were not merely coincidental. As a child, the mother's family environment was not one that encouraged its members to speak of, explore, or process emotionally charged or uncomfortable topics. Her victimization was but one of these topics.

A family history was identified in which discussion of any subject likely to elicit uncomfortable emotions was perceived as risky and to be avoided. The woman sitting before me felt safer keeping her secret hidden and suppressed. These were less helpful skills she learned as a child which she eventually and unknowingly incorporated into the parenting of her son. Consequently, the son was more comfortable keeping his victimization hidden and suppressed than bringing it to his mother's attention. Through a thorough exploration of the family's relational history, the mother was able to identify the more helpful tools and skills that had passed from generation to generation. Examples of some helpful tools included the family's strong commitment to education and its desire to care for the elder members. We were also able to identify less helpful tools and skills passing from generation to generation such as the skill of avoiding emotionally charged subjects when interacting with each other. Through this process and over a relatively short period of time, she became more open, honest, and forthright with her son, her friends, and other family members. Topics that at one time caused her great discomfort and were, for all practical purposes off limits, were becoming less capable of controlling her emotions and behaviors. The mother reported she felt free to explore relationships with men in an open, honest, and self-assured manner. She reported an improved ability to establish and enforce appropriate limits, boundaries, and consequences when parenting her son. The mother also reported that her relationship with her son had never been stronger. She even began encouraging her sister to meet with a therapist about the past abuse, a subject that had been unapproachable between them for years.

The mother stated this newfound emotional freedom left her feeling as if "*a hundred pound emotional gorilla had been removed from her back.*" With time, the past abuse became less of an issue to this family. They were too busy growing and experiencing life in healthy ways to allow these issues to control them. Occasionally, uncomfortable situations would arise that were associated with the family history of sexual abuse. When this occurred, the mother and son would deal with them in an open, honest, and confident manner. Family secrets were no longer maintained. This would not have been possible if they had chosen to avoid looking backward and inward. During my last session with this mother she stated that a nightmare from the past had been laid to rest. The mother stated one family characteristic, the need to keep secrets, had been identified and eliminated. As a result, the mother and her son were no longer vulnerable to this kind of abuse. Her final statement before leaving my office was that eliminating the need to keep family secrets was the best gift she could give her, as of yet, unborn grandchildren.

The fourth Parenting Assumption concludes by stating *"both child and parent will greatly benefit from risking change and overcoming fear associated with befriending one's personal, relational, and family histories."* When speaking about abuse of any kind – physical, sexual, emotional – the word *befriend* may seem a bit strange. Why would anybody want to *befriend* something that was traumatic and painful – such as the sexual abuse cited above? People tend to deal with uncomfortable/traumatic experiences or memories in one of two ways:

1. When a person encounters uncomfortable emotions/memories associated with a traumatic event, he or she will suppress, minimize, or attempt to forget the event stimulating the emotions.

2. When a person encounters the uncomfortable emotions/memories associated with a traumatic event he or she will identify, process, and strive to understand these emotions.

Unfortunately, the first reaction to an uncomfortable experience is selected all too often. I frequently encounter people who respond to uncomfortable or traumatic events in a manner similar to: *"If we just put the experience behind us, we can continue with our lives"* or *" Just forget about it and move on. That's water under the bridge."* Although these responses are intended to be helpful, they may only serve to complicate the situation. Our best efforts to suppress, minimize, or forget uncomfortable experiences can be likened to putting out a mattress fire. The visible flames and smoke are easily suppressed, yet, hot embers remain smoldering deep inside the mattress and out of view. These embers can remain dormant for quite some time and without notice can awaken and result in a raging and unexpected fire.

The mother in the example above had put out the emotional fire associated with her own sexual abuse by suppressing and minimizing memories of the trauma. She spoke to nobody about the abuse and never processed the emotional impact it had on her. The visible flame had been put out yet the emotional embers remained alive deep inside of her. When she failed to thrive in her later life she became frustrated by her inability to understand why. The emotional embers were still smoldering inside of her. When her son's abuse was disclosed, these embers quickly grew into a raging fire – a torrent of uncomfortable emotions – and she fell apart. Through the process of therapy this mother familiarized herself with the emotions associated with the trauma she experienced earlier in her life. She gained a greater understanding of these emotions and how they were capable of influencing other aspects of her living. By looking inward and backward she was able to gain a greater understanding of their impact on her present day thoughts, emotions, actions, reactions, and behaviors. The past trauma no longer controlled her. She had a greater understanding of it, how it affected her, and how to process the uncomfortable emotions that accompanied the memories of the unfortunate event. In a manner of speaking, by learning how to process these emotions in a healthy manner, she *befriended* a part of her personal past, albeit a painful part. Her experience of abuse was no longer the enemy within but rather a part of her history and development. She now understood the trauma and had many tools to help her move forward in helpful and healthy ways.

5. A parent examining the relationship he or she had with his or her parents, and the relationship they had with their parents, will likely be confronted with grief and enlightenment. Only then can the parent give to their children by justly replacing the less helpful with helpful.

The previous example of sexual abuse within a family is a rather dramatic presentation of the importance of the first Historical Assumption. Fortunately, most people do not find themselves in a position where they must struggle with abuse of this nature. This should not minimize the importance of overcoming fear associated with befriending one's personal, relational, and family histories, as this concept has far-reaching applications. Our personal, relational, and family histories impact everything we do – especially parenting. For example, I often encountered men and women in my practice of marriage and family therapy who find expressing their honest emotions to be a challenge. This becomes apparent when families describe problematic aspects of family life and parenting. For example, a parent who is angered by the actions of his or her child may respond by yelling. Why does this parent opt for yelling rather than expressing his or her emotions and concerns surrounding the troubling event? The two History Assumptions challenge us to look deeper into what might appear to be a natural or unconscious reaction – such as yelling at a child that angers us. In many instances this historical self-evaluation allows us to improve as individuals and parents by replacing less helpful actions and reactions with those that are likely to be more helpful and healthy.

Let's take a look at an example likely to be encountered by many parents. A child is instructed to take out the garbage. He or she is watching television and ignores the parent's instruction. After the third request goes ignored, the parent yells at the child. The child yells back, then angrily separates from the TV to take out the garbage. The child is irritated. The parent is angered. Neither has moved toward having a closer relationship. There is a lot more going on in this simple scenario than meets the eye.

A parent may respond to the child's seemingly apathetic attitude in a number of different ways. The purpose of this example is not to present the best parental reaction but rather to explore how and why the parent responds in one way or the other, in this case, by yelling at the child. By looking at some of the underlying processes influencing interactions such as this, the parent will eventually be freer to choose from a greater number of options – selecting the most helpful option for any particular circumstance. Exploring the underlying processes that influence our interactions requires us to be open to the idea of examining the origin of actions and reactions we find familiar and comfortable.

Asking a child to take out the garbage is commonly cited by parents as an example of a situation where a child "does not listen" – causing a parent to become angry. I will often role-play this situation with parents to help demonstrate several points. Below are two common scenarios relating to this garbage issue. The first role-play demonstrates how the trash scenario often plays itself out. The second role-play explores an alternative response. During these role-plays I will assume the role of the parent and the parent assumes the role of the child who is tasked with taking out the garbage. I always ask parents to tell me how they experience each role play upon its completion. That is, how did it feel from both the child's and parent's perspective?

Example 1. – Typical parent-child interaction
Parent to young son watching TV:
> *Son, it's getting late. Please take the garbage out.*

Son to parent:
> *OK*

Parent to son 10 minutes later:
> *I thought I asked you to take the garbage out. Come on, let's get going. It's late.*

Son, still watching TV
> *All right, all right. I'll get to it!*

Parent, several minutes later, yelling:
> *If you don't get off your butt and get the garbage out right now there will be hell to pay. This will be the last time you sit in front of that TV for a month.*

Son, in response, yelling as he leaves to take the garbage out:
> *All right, get off my back.*

The child leaves this interaction feeling irritated and hassled. To this child, familial responsibilities and household chores are an irritation, something to avoid and loathe. This interaction brought the child closer to this belief and, in a very subtle way, emotionally farther away from his parents. This is not a catastrophic event, as the overall impact is relatively minor. However, the cumulative effect of hundreds of similar situations becomes apparent over a relatively short period of time. Here is an alternative to the above:

Example 2. – Atypical parent-child interaction
Parent to young son watching TV:
> *Son, it's getting late. Please take the garbage out.*

Son to parent:
> *OK*

Parent to son 10 minutes later:
> (Parent turns off TV and sits next to son)

Son to parent:
> *Hey, I was watching that!*

Parent to son:
> *I know. This will only take a minute and it's important. I asked you to take out the garbage 10 minutes ago. I feel like you ignored me. Rather than getting angry and yelling I thought we should talk about it.*

Son to parent:
> *All right, I'll take it out.*

Parent to son:
> *Hold on a second. There's something I want you to hear. There are certain responsibilities we all have around here. Right*

now two of your responsibilities are to take out the garbage and to listen to your mother and I. When you don't do this I feel disappointed, frustrated, and ignored. These are not feelings I look forward to – they're very uncomfortable. It's important for me to let you know that what you do and don't do has an impact on this family. What are your thoughts?

Son to parent:

I was just into the show. I didn't mean to ignore you. I think I should get off my butt and take the garbage out.

The child in this interaction may be irritated that his TV program was interrupted to take out the garbage. However, he benefited, in a small way, by gaining a better understanding of some important lessons. First and foremost, the people around him have feelings and emotions and that his actions and reactions have an impact on them. Secondly, there are alternative and healthy ways to deal with anger and disagreements. Finally, family/household responsibilities can be an inconvenience, yet they do not have to be loathed; the entire family benefits from an individual member's contribution.

This is but one of an infinite number of alternative responses for this particular situation. When I ask parents if the above role play was uncomfortable or comfortable, most opt for the former – stating they experienced the second role play as foreign, something that just does not come naturally. Many respond to my question by stating "it's just easier to motivate the child by yelling at him/her." This discomfort or unfamiliarity is the primary focus of this Historical Assumption. Why might the first example feel familiar and comfortable to the parent and the second example feel unfamiliar and uncomfortable? The Parenting Assumptions throughout this book will demonstrate how responses such as the second example above will be helpful to the overall parenting process. Yet, until we have some understanding of why responses such as Example 2 presented above may be unfamiliar and uncomfortable, we will likely avoid them.

Why was the mother who was a victim of sexual abuse fearful of disclosing the abuse? Why did her son fail to disclose the abuse he experienced? Why do many parents shy away from interactions such as in Example 2 in favor of yelling, punishing, and increasing the emotional distance between parent and child? Historia est magister vitae – history is the teacher of life. If we take time to understand our personal and family history, questions such as these are easily answered. When attempting to explore our history, it is important to realize that family patterns – both helpful and healthy as well as the unhelpful and unhealthy – will repeat themselves from generation to generation unless there is specific intervention to identify and alter these patterns. These patterns include traits such as, how family members communicate with each other, how conflict is approached and resolved, how families deal with power and control, how families understand intimacy, values they adopt, whether or not family members abuse drugs & alcohol, and so on.

As a child grows and develops within a family structure he or she becomes familiar and comfortable with the way in which the family interacts. This familiarity and comfort holds true even when the interactions are less helpful or unhealthy. For example, a child who grows up in a family where the parents communicate in an aggressive manner, always yelling at each other and rarely, if ever, considering each other's perspectives, will find this style of interacting familiar throughout his or her later life. Less aggressive and healthier communication styles will likely be foreign and uncomfortable to the child unless there is a recognition of this pattern and specific interventions are made. Family patterns, whether healthy or unhealthy, will be repeated when they are familiar, known, and comfortable.

Many people will respond to this point by stating something similar to *"You're all wrong. I'm nothing like my father,"* or *"I couldn't be more different than my mother."* Sure, differences will certainly exist between the generations, yet hidden within those differences will be crucial commonalties. For example, let's take a look at a daughter of alcoholic parents. After witnessing firsthand the devastating effects alcoholism had on her parents and family, the daughter vows never to drink alcohol. Yet, when the daughter of alcoholic parents grows up and has children of her own, she may find it difficult to relate to them in an open and intimate manner. She is likely to find intimacy unfamiliar, unknown, and uncomfortable. The consumption of alcohol is no longer an issue, however, she is vulnerable to relating to her children in ways that are also less intimate but familiar, known and comfortable to her. An unhealthy pattern of relating continues in spite of her serious efforts to intervene by merely eliminating the alcohol. This is an unfortunate behavioral by-product that is secondary to her parent's alcoholism. The daughter may state that she is nothing like her parents, yet a similar and less healthy family trait is likely going to be passed to subsequent generations.

Most family behavioral traits can be attributed to familiarity (nurture) rather than genetic predisposition (nature). For example, the ability to relate in an emotionally safe and intimate manner, as in Example 2 above, has very little to do with genetic predisposition and everything to do with familiarity. For us to change the less helpful patterns of interacting to more helpful patterns of interacting, we must recognize the many patterns that exist in our family and how they are passed from generation to generation. We are capable of maintaining the more helpful patterns while reducing the impact of, and the probability of passing on, those that are less helpful. There are several ways one can begin this process. First and foremost, an individual must be willing to examine the relationship he or she had with his or her parents, and the relationship the parents had with their parents. When examining these relationships, pay particular attention to how family members communicate with each other, who has power and control, how is this power structure justified, how is intimacy understood and expressed, what does the family value, what topics are approachable and what topics are off limits, and what happens when a family member deviates from *normative* family functioning? A person examining these questions will likely uncover familial patterns that have existed for generations. Parents have a tremendous opportunity to give to their children by justly replacing the less helpful patterns of interacting with more helpful patterns by risking change and overcoming fear associated with exploring family history. As you review the forthcoming Parenting Assumptions, pay close attention to your emotional reaction. No Parenting Assumption in this book is unattainable or incomprehensible. If you find yourself uncomfortable with a particular Assumption this is likely the result of *history* and worthy of close personal scrutiny or examination. In some instances, one's history is so full of less helpful patterns of interacting that one can be easily overwhelmed. This is where professional counseling/ therapy will likely be helpful. Family therapists have many tools for assisting persons move forward by looking backward.

Let's briefly return to the example of the parent yelling at his or her child for not taking out the garbage. Was responding as the parent did in Example 2 physically impossible for this parent? Of course not. Would this response be familiar, comfortable, and known to many parents? Probably not. I am of the belief that when a child experiences his or her parents in a manner that resembles Example 1, more often than not, emotional distance between parent and child increases.[3]

When a child experiences his or her parents in a manner resembling Example 2, more often than not, emotional distance between parent and child decreases. Even though many parents openly agree the second example is more likely to result in a healthy and helpful outcome, they will avoid implementing similar responses into their own parenting. This paradox is most likely the result of the parent's personal discomfort and unfamiliarity with this means of relating. Again, this discomfort and unfamiliarity is typically the result of one's **history**. The Parenting Assumptions found throughout this book are by no means impossible for any parent to incorporate into their parenting. Will many of the Assumptions be uncomfortable and unfamiliar to the reader? Probably. For this reason I suggest all parents read the Assumptions more than once. Consider them, implement them, and familiarize yourself with them. Become comfortable with as many of the 90 Parenting Assumptions as possible. Most importantly, try to understand the Assumptions throughout this book with respect to your family history! Only then can you begin to replace the less helpful patterns with more helpful patterns of relating.

‖ Chapter 3 Balance

To bring into or keep in a state of equilibrium or equipoise; to bring into proportion, harmony

6. Parents need emotional alliances. To be isolated or alone in this task weakens the experience for parent and child.

Emotional alliances are very important to parenting. In addition to parenting, emotional alliances tend to be a crucial component to our overall quality of living. What are emotional alliances? Well, to help us understand this concept let's look at an example that has nothing to do with parenting. Imagine that you set a personal goal of getting a promotion at work. You put in extra hours and exceed your boss's expectations in every way. Eventually your efforts pay off and you are awarded the promotion and a substantial raise. Now imagine how you feel when you inform your friends, family, or significant other of the good news. When you first learned of the promotion you likely experienced joy associated with the news. Yet, when supportive others are brought into your circle – by sharing the news – things seem to get even better. Somehow the inclusion of others further heightens the experience. Would the promotion be as satisfying if you merely went home and kept it to yourself or had no supportive others with whom to share the news? Probably not. An emotional alliance is merely *somebody who witnesses living*. This is a relatively simple role for others as it requires they provide little input whatsoever. An emotional alliance merely requires one to be present and willing to consider another's perspective.

This example is fairly joyous – a wanted promotion. What if the promotion was awarded to somebody else? Would an emotional alliance be helpful? Somebody present to consider your perspective? The disappointment and frustration? Again, if you put yourself in this position, I think you would find having an emotional alliance witness this aspect of your life to be very helpful. Having emotional alliances around for hardships and life's challenges can help make these times bearable and more easily weathered. Somehow being overlooked for the promotion will not seem like the end of the world when others are around to witness the experience with you.

Here are a few more examples. A young woman has met what she believes is the man of her dreams. The two date for several months then the young man unexpectedly ends the relationship. She is devastated. Consider how each of the following scenarios would feel if you were in the young woman's shoes:

1. The young woman tells a close friend of the events. The friend responds with, *"What a jerk! You're better off without him. Don't worry, there are other fish in the sea. You're too good for somebody like that."*

2. The young woman goes home and keeps the news to herself. She tells nobody and spends several evenings crying.

3. The young woman tells a close friend about the break–up. The friend responds with, *"That must be incredibly painful. I wish I could do something to make everything all better for you. I'm unable to do that. I am all ears though. Tell me what happened."*

The friends in the first and third scenarios are well intentioned and attempting to help out. The young woman was in love with the man who just broke her heart. Even if this man was a *"rat,"* the friend's response in scenario number 1 is unlikely to be very helpful. This person is attempting to make everything better for the bereaving woman. Unfortunately, no words will quickly heal the pain she is experiencing. This person wants to be helpful but is trying too hard. The friend in the third scenario is fulfilling the role of an emotional alliance. This friend is merely present and considering the young woman's perspective. This will go far in helping her weather the emotional storm. The woman in the second scenario will likely weather the storm; however, the emotional discomfort will be drawn out needlessly long and may adversely affect other aspects of her living and relationships.

These three reactions can also be applied to more joyous events. What if the young couple became engaged rather than breaking up? The three reactions will have a similar effect. For example:

1. *"He's a great guy. I'm sure you're going to be so happy. Let me give you some ideas about planning a wedding."*
2. The woman goes home, makes dinner for herself and watches television.
3. *"Great! Tell me about it . . . I want to hear everything, every detail!"*

In my experience the newly engaged woman will likely find greater emotional benefit from the third scenario. Parents also need emotional alliances. *To be isolated or alone in this task weakens the experience for parent and child.* This is true in all matters of parenting – the joyous events as well as the parenting challenges. As a child passes through healthy developmental stages, emotional alliances just serve to make these events more rewarding for the parent. For example, a baby's first words, first steps, first day of school, first date, and graduations are all developmental milestones for both parent and child. Emotional alliances enhance all of these events. On the other side of the spectrum, emotional alliances help make parenting challenges survivable and bearable. Parenting challenges include events such as childhood developmental disorders, behavioral problems, sexual identity crises, disease and sickness, and drug and alcohol use and abuse.

Over the years I have had the experience of working with parents displaying a broad spectrum of disturbing symptoms. Some parents were profoundly depressed and seeking relief for their suffering. Other parents were struggling with issues of abuse, either abuse directed toward themselves – as in the case of drug and alcohol abuse, or abuse toward others – as in physical, emotional, or sexual abuse of a spouse or child. There are an infinite number of factors that contribute to these conditions and situations. As I review my notes, I find that in nearly every case the individual and/or the family system was generally void of supportive emotional alliances. Over time this general lack of emotional alliances made life and adversity very difficult to handle.

When parents enter my office complaining of depression or who present an abusive situation, the concept of emotional alliances becomes paramount. Our work usually begins with me – the therapist – acting as an alliance. I make it very clear that I am interested in, and wanting to consider, their perspective. This usually results in a great deal of relief for the individual, couple, or family. One parent spent hours telling me of the hardships she was experiencing as a result of the sleep deprivation encountered after the arrival of her newborn child. She knew the baby would eventually sleep through the night, yet when she approached her husband and family about her struggle, they became very critical of her and offered too much advice. She was becoming depressed and needed an emotional alliance. She was not looking for advice. She knew this was a temporary condition and was enjoying being a new mother, yet, she was baffled by her loneliness and feelings of isolation in the midst of *"a very well intentioned husband and family."* Eventually she asked me for input. At that time we explored how she might begin developing emotional alliances from the well intentioned people around her. This young mother learned that there is nothing wrong with asking somebody to be a sounding board. Learning how to create a balance of persons in your life that are capable of being emotional alliances and those who are not is very important. There is nothing unhealthy or unhelpful in just listening when others need to vent. Nor is there anything inappropriate in asking others to just listen and consider. Input from others is not always required, emotional alliances are if both parent and child are to benefit.

7. *The parent who is emotionally depleted, more often than not, is vulnerable as is his or her child.*

Let there be no doubt about it, parenting can be stressful and exhausting. However, there is also little doubt that the rewards from parenting a child *well,* are great. Parenting a child well requires a parent to make a considerable emotional investment in the whole process. This is crucial if the child is to be successful in his or her later life and relationships and is an important point for parents to consider. If a parent's emotional reservoirs are chronically depleted, the rewards he or she will experience as the child grows, develops, and reaches important milestones will be adversely impacted. If a parent is emotionally exhausted, more often than not, the child will lose the benefit of learning from the parent's complete attention and emotional presence.

I used the phrase *emotionally depleted* in this Assumption. What exactly does this phrase mean? How does a parent become emotionally depleted? How does an *emotionally exhausted* parent interact with a child? Presenting a detailed definition or explanation of these phrases is probably beyond the scope of this Assumption. However, as a family therapist I know it when I see it. Let me explain. A parent is called upon to introduce the world and all of its complexities to the child. As the child matures, gains experience and challenges him or herself in many ways mistakes will surely be made. These mistakes, or even the threat of these mistakes, places a great many demands upon the parents. Most parents are intuitively aware of this process and show remarkable patience as the child develops and learns. Most parents understand that an infant who loudly repeats the same word over and over again is acquiring and refining important verbal skills. Parents intuitively understand that an infant who intentionally and repeatedly throws his or her bottle to the floor is developing important cognitive skills and relational awareness. An adolescent who pushes the boundaries of acceptable dress is demonstrating an emerging drive toward individuation. The parent who is *not* emotionally depleted will respond to these and similar examples of everyday parent-child interactions without anger or personalizing the child's behavior. However, when a parent responds to the everyday challenges of parenting by personalizing the child's behaviors (e.g. *"He's doing this on purpose just to get under my skin,"* or *"She has got to stop this behavior; why is she doing this to me?"*), the intuitive connection between parent and child is showing signs of weakening. The parent is personalizing what are typically natural behaviors associated with a child's growth and development. The parent becomes less patient and flexible as he or she becomes increasingly emotionally depleted and exhausted. Essentially, the parent's emotional batteries need re–charging.

I see parents in my office all the time who are emotionally depleted. These parents do not arrive requesting help with recharging their emotional batteries. No, these parents usually arrive in my office seeking help with issues ranging from simple suggestions on basic parenting skills to treatment for issues of child neglect and abuse. More often than not the symptoms of a chronically emotionally depleted parent are clear and the consequences for both parent and child can be significant. My job as a family therapist is to assist the parent restore a sense of balance in the parent-child relationship. This usually entails helping the parent learn how to address his or her own emotional needs so that the challenging and sometimes frustrating aspects of parenting will be seen as they are – merely a natural part of the child's learning, growing, and maturing. The Parenting Assumptions to follow should be helpful in this process. *The parent who is emotionally depleted, more often than not, is vulnerable as is his or her child.*

8. Parents finding themselves short tempered are likely fatigued.

I stated in the previous Assumption that presenting an exact and all-encompassing definition of *emotional exhaustion* or *emotional depletion* would be a very difficult undertaking. We can, however, explore common signs and symptoms of this emotional state and some of the circumstances that might lead to a parent becoming exhausted. Severe symptoms of emotional exhaustion are fairly easy to recognize. These symptoms often include depression, conflict or abuse within the family, overeating, overspending, chronic inactivity, a variety of nonspecific and generalized physical ailments, and abuse of drugs and alcohol. These conditions and behaviors are usually strong indicators that an individual's emotional needs are not being routinely met in healthy ways. Their emotional batteries are not being recharged on a regular basis and various aspects of their living have begun to suffer. Luckily, in most instances symptoms of emotional depletion, exhaustion, and fatigue will be considerably less severe than those just mentioned. In fact, many of the more common symptoms will hardly be distinguishable to the untrained eye. Parenting Assumptions 8 & 9 describe the most common symptoms of early emotional exhaustion that I come across in my practice of family therapy. If these symptoms are recognized early, and steps taken to address the underlying issues, many of the more severe and complicated symptoms and behaviors can be avoided.

I stated in Parenting Assumption 7 that parenting can be stressful and exhausting. The vast majority of the stress and exhaustion associated with parenting is weathered without significant impact on the parent. This stress, and the corresponding exhaustion, is intuitively understood as being a natural part of the parenting experience and rarely adversely impacts the parent-child relationship. Yet, from time to time, parents will certainly find themselves short tempered, acting impulsively, and likely to yell at or punish their children for what are natural behaviors of childhood. For example, a child may arrive home from school and proceed to run through the house shouting, "*Mom, Mom, Mom, Mom, Mom!*" The child's actions may seem to be a desperate or panicked search for the parent but are more likely to be the actions of an excited child eager to share a school assignment that received a good grade. This child has yet to learn about tact, patience, and timing – skills that will emerge with additional parental guidance and life experience. For now, the child is full of unbridled excitement and wanting to share the good news. I can imagine an emotionally fatigued parent responding to the child's loud and persistent enthusiasm by responding with something similar to, "*What the hell do you want? My god, you'd think the world was coming to an end!*"

I'm going to refrain from dissecting this response as well as spending too much time exploring the infinite number of alternative responses available to this parent. I would rather focus attention on the factors that stimulate such a response. This parent's reaction is merely a sign of a brief emotional disconnect between parent and child. At that particular moment the mother was emotionally unprepared for her emotionally charged son. She snapped at him without considering the potential impact of her words. Now, events such as this are relatively insignificant if they only occur from time to time. The child will leave the encounter with little more than hurt feelings. However, this should not minimize the fact that these rare instances of impulsive or short-tempered reactions are rooted in emotional fatigue. The "perfect" parent, and I don't know too many of those, might first calm the child, ensure there was no emergency, listen to what the child had to say, then provide feedback about their interaction. For example "*That's great news. I'm really proud of you. It makes me happy to see you do well in school. Now, let's talk about how you approached me. All that yelling left me feeling concerned that something was wrong or that something terrible had happened. I now realize that you were just excited. How else could you have gotten my attention?*"

What prohibits parents from responding to their children in ways that are more likely to be helpful each and every time they interact? The most obvious answer to this question is that humans are fallible. We make mistakes from time to time. These mistakes are usually secondary to our lack of the knowledge, insight, or skill surrounding a particular matter. Parental fatigue also figures into this equation but is infrequently discussed. Fatigue will quickly cleave parental objectivity. The child in the previous example was acting in a completely natural and age appropriate manner. The parent might experience the child's behavior as slightly irritating but intuitively understands it to be part of a young child's behavioral repertoire. However, in this example the parent did not have the emotional reserves to muster a response that would leave the child with greater insight. The parent took *a path of least emotional resistance* – yelling or impulsively snapping at the child to find relief from the behavior.

At times, a response such as "*What the hell do you want? My god, you'd think the world was coming to an end!*" takes less emotional energy than the alternate parental reaction presented above. Unfortunately, taking a path of least emotional resistance often leads to a missed opportunity for the child to learn and grow from the interaction. The parent taking a path of least emotional resistance might find brief emotional relief but the child learns little. As a result, the child is likely to repeat the behavior at some time in the future – further draining the parent's emotional reservoir. Again, if a parent only occasionally responds to a child in a short tempered or impulsive manner, little harm is done. However, if a parent finds him or herself responding to a child in an impulsive, short, loud, or threatening manner more often than not, parental fatigue should be considered as an issue worthy of serious attention.

Addressing all the factors that contribute to parental fatigue is beyond the scope of *Systemic Parenting*. The exact causes of fatigue differ for every individual and every family. However, fatigue will affect almost all parents and all families in a similar manner. Becoming short tempered is a pretty consistent sign. Merely recognizing this as a symptom of fatigue can be helpful to the parent motivated to improve his or her parenting. If a parent chooses to monitor how he or she reacts to a child's behaviors, tremendous growth can occur. For example, it may be helpful for parents to occasionally take a brief inventory after interacting with their child. A parent might ask, "*How did I just come across to my son? Might I have come across as short tempered in that interaction? What factors were pulling my strings? What did my son walk away with? Did he learn anything? Did I learn anything from that interaction?*" Merely taking the opportunity to reflect upon one's parent-child interactions can be tremendously helpful in reducing the impact of fatigue. It will not solve the underlying issues stimulating the fatigue, but it will certainly highlight the impact these issues may have on the parent-child relationship. This realization, in itself, can be most helpful to the overall parenting process.

9. Too frequent rewards indicate that the parent is at the end of his or her emotional resources; too frequent punishments that he or she is in acute distress.

The previous Parenting Assumption highlighted *short temper* as a sign of parental fatigue. There are many others. Perhaps the second most frequent sign of fatigue that I come across falls on the opposite side of the spectrum, *too frequent rewards*. Many people have wondered why some parents spoil a child with excess. These actions are actually signs of a parent taking *a path of least emotional resistance* – in this case, utilizing excessive gifts or compliments to get a desired behavior or to gain relief from irritating behaviors. From my perspective as a therapist it is often easier to work with the parent who frequently responds with a short temper than it is to work with a parent who spoils the child. A short temper is more easily recognized as harmful than rewarding a child too frequently. However, the eventual outcome is nearly identical – missed parenting opportunities.

Excessive gifts or compliments often remove the focus from issues, problems, and challenges that stimulate parent-child interactions. For example, a child begins acting in a manner that is disturbing to a father. The child is making a lot of noise. The father can address the child's behavior in many ways. He can yell at the child (a short-tempered response). The father can offer the child a reward if he or she ceases the behavior (e.g. *"You can have a cookie if you are good and stop making so much noise."*). Or, the father can let the child know how the noise is impacting him, ask the child for input, and brainstorm for alternative activities that might be less disruptive. The first two options can be effective in getting the desired reaction (getting the child to stop making so much noise). Yet, they are examples of taking the path of least emotional resistance. Yelling at the child or offering him a cookie to stop are quick, simple, and fairly effective ways of gaining short-term relief. However, the parent is required to make little emotional investment in these responses. The third option will be just as effective but requires more of the parent's emotional resources. This investment will yield healthier long-term benefits.

Offering the child a cookie, or similar immediate rewards, to cease a certain behavior does not represent a significant problem if it occurs occasionally. However, if this becomes the normative and accepted way of influencing behavior, the child loses the opportunity to gain insight from the parent. The child's focus will eventually shift from *learning from and pleasing the parent* to *acquiring rewards*. When the child begins to expect rewards for desired behaviors, or when the child uses the threat of certain behaviors to extract rewards from the parent, we can say the child is spoiled. Again, when a parent takes a path of least emotional resistance by utilizing too frequent rewards to get a desired behavior, we see several missed parenting opportunities. The parent may gain some immediate relief, but the child gains little insight about the situation for which he or she is being rewarded.

If a parent relies upon rewarding a child too frequently to get a desired behavior, he or she is likely emotionally fatigued or at the end of his or her emotional resources. Interacting with the child in other more helpful and healthy ways might represent an overwhelming task for this parent. In these situations, shifting the focus of parenting by rewards to parenting through healthy parent-child interactions can be a difficult and emotionally taxing transition for both parent and child. This transition may result in an already emotionally fatigued parent becoming distressed and vulnerable to substituting too frequent rewards with too frequent punishments. Many of the Parenting Assumptions in *Systemic Parenting* focus on providing parents with options for improving the quality of parent-child interactions. A parent who too frequently rewards or punishes the child will find options that are more likely to be helpful and healthy in the pages to follow. Recognizing that excessive rewards might stem from emotional fatigue and that frequent punishments result from a parent's feeling distressed is important in itself. In this thought comes the realization that a parent's emotional state will impact how one parents.

10. Employment of kindness is but half of nurturance. Employment of limits and consequences is but half of discipline.

Responding to a child in an impulsive or short tempered manner was linked to being emotionally fatigued in Parenting Assumption 8. In Parenting Assumption 9, too frequent rewards and punishments were also linked to parental fatigue and distress. It would seem that maintaining a healthy balance between the demands inherent with parenting and caring for one's own emotional needs is an important part of parenting well. This particular Assumption addresses yet another aspect of balance: the complex relationship between *nurturance* and *discipline*. Unfortunately, the relationship between these two important aspects of parenting is not always apparent and tends to be overlooked. Nurturance is frequently defined or understood as *educating through kind, gentle, and embracing means*. I believe this Assumption expands this definition by inserting an additional element. For nurturance to be complete it must be accompanied by elements of discipline – *the employment of limits and consequences*. The same holds true for discipline. Discipline without elements of nurturance is incomplete;

they are inextricably linked when applied to parenting. Neither is complete without the other.

I started to notice the important connection between nurturance and discipline after working with hundreds of families that were struggling in a variety of ways and who presented a broad spectrum of clinical problems. Yet, two distinct trends emerged from these families that simply could not be overlooked. These trends were:

1. When nurturance was provides in the absence of discipline, it was experienced as disorganized and lacking important elements of emotional safety. Parent-child intimacy was not enhanced.

2. When discipline was provided in the absence of nurturance, it was often confusing, vague, unjust, and ineffective. These disciplinary actions were ineffective.

The previous observations present a pretty complex concept. The relationship between nurturance and discipline must be explored from many directions to fully understand the breadth of its importance. At this point, the main idea that I would have you take away from this paragraph is that these two aspects of parenting are intimately connected and that maintaining a healthy balance between nurturance and discipline is very important. How parents achieve this balance will be explored and expanded in later Assumptions. The chapters on Safety, Skill, and Art are all laced with discussions of, and examples highlighting, this very important subject. But for now, keep in mind that, *employment of kindness is but half of nurturance. Employment of limits and consequences is but half of discipline.*

11. Parents finding themselves in conflict with their child without the ability to reflect and flex will often feel fatigued, ineffective, and defeated.

I have had the opportunity to work with many families over the years in which constant conflict was just an everyday part of life. In these families, conflict seemed to be the normative and accepted means of interaction. When I review my notes about these families several factors consistently emerge. One is that the balance between *conflict* and *collective process* was terribly askew. That is, members of these families were not very skilled at *considering other perspectives*. Each family member interacted as though their personal perspective was the most correct and felt threatened by the thought of considering the perspective of other family members. Certainly some degree of conflict will exist in every family. To some degree, a little conflict can be healthy to family functioning. It tends to stimulate growth while highlighting developmental milestones. This will be explored in detail in later Parenting Assumptions. For now, it is important to note that maintaining a healthy balance between conflict and collective process, that is, considering the perspective of others, is important if the family is to thrive.

The second factor that I observed in families where conflict seemed to be the norm was that the parents lacked the ability, or skill, to be reflective and flexible. Concrete beliefs and patterns were the norm for these parents. The idea of being flexible and reflective was very uncomfortable to these parents. By the time these families arrived in my office, the parents were usually well on their way to being emotionally fatigued, grossly ineffective as parents, and often feeling defeated by the whole parenting experience. Large emotional gaps often existed between parent and child in these strained relationships. Maintaining a healthy balance between the beliefs and behaviors that one holds in high regard and the demands for flexibility and the ability to be reflective is probably one of the most challenging aspects of parenting well. Again, this is a very complex subject matter that cannot be adequately addressed in one Parenting Assumption. This aspect of balance will be thoroughly explored in the coming chapters. For now, keep in mind that *parents finding themselves in conflict with their child without the ability to reflect and flex will often feel fatigued, ineffective, and defeated.*

12. Parents must trust each other to make decisions that consider both parental perspectives. It is often prudent to delay action until the other parent is present on large matters of parenting. However, on small matters, waiting for the other may be likened to waiting for permission to put out a smoldering fire. When one's permission finally arrives, nothing will remain but ashes. A balance between the former and latter is essential.

A couple arrived in my office after coming to the realization that they were not working as a team when it came to raising their children.

They had four young children and a strong commitment to maintaining the marriage and family. They were concerned that if this trend were to continue, their marital and family future was in jeopardy of falling apart. After working with the couple for several weeks, many issues were identified as contributing to the problem. One of these factors stood out to me as being particularly important. The mother and father's "style" of parenting appeared to fall on opposite ends of the parenting spectrum. That is, the father essentially took on a role of *friend* and *jokester* with his children. His overall style of interacting with the children primarily consisted of jovial and light hearted interactions. He would always defer to his wife on more serious matters of parenting . That is, the father would rely upon his wife when it came time to establish and enforcing limits, boundaries, and consequences. The mother's style of interacting with the children was quite different than her husband's. Her overall style of interacting with the children consisted of providing instruction, delivering a lecture, and handing down a punishment. She assumed a more serious posture with the children and was the primary, if not the only, disciplinarian.

My job was not to criticize or judge these parents or their particular parenting style. Rather, it was my job to point out how these differing styles were beginning to impact the marriage and the children's development. I was also interested in exploring the origins of these different parenting styles and wanted to know what each parent got out of their individual methods of interaction. Let's look at a fairly typical situation from the family that highlights the crux of the problem.

The mother reported that on days her husband was "in charge" of the children, she would arrive home to a barrage of complaints and behavioral problems. Shortly after getting home the husband would provide his wife with a detailed description of all the children's misdeeds that occurred throughout the day. Most of the complaints and problems could and should have been relatively easy to address at the time of their occurrence. However, they were largely ignored and routinely deferred to the mother for later disciplinary action. The mother stated it felt as if her husband was colluding with the children. They appeared to be having a great time when she arrived home. Then, the mood would abruptly change as the bad news was delivered to *the disciplinarian*. Over time it appeared as if the children were becoming emotionally closer to their father and increasingly distanced from their mother. The parents' roles were creating discord in the family system and were clearly having an unhealthy impact. Why was the father deferring to his wife? Why was the mother accepting this in the face of deepening feelings of personal resentment? *Parents must trust each other to make decisions that consider both parental perspectives.* This was clearly not occurring in this family.

As we explored this subject, it became clear that both parents were guilty of ignoring the other's perspective. This pattern of interacting had origins that went back many years. A quick glance at the parent's family history was our first clue to the origins of this pattern. The mother's family of origin had a similar structure. The children's maternal grandmother was a strong and dominating figure in the family. The children's maternal grandfather was a good provider for the family yet was rarely involved in the day to day parenting activities. In fact, he openly admitted that parenting – all matters of parenting – were his wife's responsibility. The children's mother heard that he was merely *"the sperm donor, family bread basket and playmate"* over and over again while growing up. These words were reinforced as she experienced her father as the "fun parent" and her mother as the strong authoritarian. Over time these roles became ingrained in her understanding of family relationships: *mother is strong and competent, father is incompetent and distant.* These eventually became her expectations of marriage and family. It was not coincidental that her husband fit nicely into this roll.

The father's family of origin showed a trait that also repeated itself across several generations. It seemed that men were rarely present in the family. They would either abandon the family altogether or were emotionally uninvolved. There was a history of alcoholism and drug abuse among men in the father's family of origin, which made emotional investment in the family difficult at best. Basically, many of the men from the father's family of origin were viewed as, and were expected to be, incompetent in many aspects of parenting and family life. Even though the father deviated from this pattern by avoiding drugs and alcohol and remaining present in the family, he was more than willing to accept the role of incompetent parent. This couple did not come together by accident. Each had an understanding of family roles that fit nicely into the picture they painted in my office. This was part of their family history.

We explored the early days of the couple's parenting experience – just after the arrival of their first child. Specifically, we explored how the parents and grandparents interacted during the first few months of their son's life. I heard stories of how the father *"just could not seem to get things right."* He would hold the baby's head incorrectly; he would roll the baby the wrong way when changing diapers; the bath water was too hot or too cold; he soothed the baby's anxieties all wrong; and so on. The new mother's criticism of her husband's "incompetence" was supported by the maternal grandmother as well. The father stated that the first months after his son's arrival became very difficult. He stated that if felt as if he was "always walking on eggshells." At times he felt as if he would be criticized just for looking at the baby incorrectly. It seemed as if he was shell shocked by the relentless criticism. Was the father holding the baby's head incorrectly? Did he roll the baby the wrong way when changing diapers? Was the bath water too hot or too cold? Were his attempts to soothe the baby's anxieties all wrong? In retrospect, the father was probably doing the same thing every new parent nervously does during the first few weeks and months of parenthood – figuring things out. Unfortunately, the long established family roles provided the father with little flexibility to *get it right.* The parents never found themselves on the same page. I suspect the father was doing nothing wrong nor potentially harmful during these first months. His actions and style were merely different from his wife's and mother–in–law's style and expectations. Neither was considering the other's perspective. The father wanted to be helpful but had little experience or support. The mother wanted everything to be perfect and was vigilant in protecting the child. It would have been difficult for the father to assert himself – calling for a bit of latitude – and difficult for the mother to give him the necessary latitude. In this family, all members were vulnerable to preexisting family roles and expectations. The father simply retreated in the face of criticism and found ways of relating to his children that were acceptable to the wife. This happened to be through jovial and light hearted interactions. He became the entertainer. This worked for a while. The mother's role as primary caretaker and disciplinarian was established, and the prophecy of the "incompetent father" was fulfilled. The father was involved in a way that helped him avoid criticism and felt safe but far from fulfilling. His wife's criticism abated as he worked his way into a familiar and acceptable role – "incompetent and relatively uninvolved parent." The father gradually accepted this role. In fact, just being present for his children was a significant improvement over previous generations of fathers from his side of the family. The mother was involved in a way that was initially fulfilling but eventually became burdensome and very isolating.

So, it became very important for these parents to learn how to consider each other's perspective – even when it differed from their own. In my office we started this process by exploring the family's history and the roles that had been traveling from generation to generation. We spent a lot of time exploring each parent's thoughts and emotions relating to the roles each had assumed. The father wanted to be more involved in matters of parenting yet found this prospect overwhelming. He begrudgingly accepted the role of incompetent parent, but wanted to support his wife in the more complex aspects of parenting. Unfortunately, he felt shut out. The mother's perspective was much different. She was tired and wanted help. However, seeking support from her husband somehow felt threatening and uncomfortable. The thought of asking for his assistance on complex matters of parenting was a completely foreign concept to the mother.

As the parents became comfortable exploring these roles and the many emotions and behaviors that accompanied these roles, several strange things happened. First and foremost, they became increasingly skilled in considering each other's perspective. Both acquired a more empathetic understanding of the other's thoughts, emotions, and behaviors. They realized disagreements would occur from time to time but this should by no means get in the way of listening. Secondly, the father began identifying and enforcing limits, boundaries, and consequences when the children exhibited behaviors that were not acceptable. This occurred at the moment the behavior was observed rather than being deferred to his wife later in the day. His wife admitted to being uncomfortable with her husband's new found skill, but soon experienced significant relief when she allowed herself to accept that her husband's parenting contributions were "appropriate" and "helpful," albeit different from her own. Finally, the roles each parent played in the family eventually shifted. As the father became increasingly "competent," the mother became increasingly accepting and relaxed. Both parents described their relationship with the children and each other as being "balanced" and greatly enhanced. Indeed, *small matters of parenting*, such as failing to listen to the parent or refusing to cooperate with a sibling, were addressed immediately by the parent observing the behavior. Large matters of parenting, such as bringing home a poor report card or receiving a notice from school of a disciplinary problem, were addressed by both parents. The parents had reached a helpful and healthy balance. They were able to support and maintain this balance through open and honest discussion of their previous roles.

Finally, during one of our last sessions together, the mother reported that she arrived home to find two of their children in "timeout." The children were delighted to see her after the timeout ended. She stated it was a tremendous relief to have the support of her husband.

13. Too often parents seek outside antagonists rather than focusing inward when faced with a parental challenge. It is often familiar and comfortable to look outward rather than to evaluate one's own influence. Balance between internal and external antagonists is most important.

A devout Christian couple – parents of three sons – arrived in my office wanting to discuss *discipline and spiritual problems* they were having with their eldest son. He was 15 years-old. The parents were concerned their son was taking a destructive and immoral path. He had recently started listening to a musician that openly portrayed himself as – among other things – the anti-Christ, as transgendered, and an enemy of Christianity. The lyrics in the music spoke of suicide, violence, bizarre and unhealthy sex acts (e.g. bestiality), and aggressively challenged authority and society's mores. The parents were actively involved in parent-teacher organizations at school. They knew most of their children's friends and the parents of these friends, and they supported the children's involvement in extra-curricular activities. The parents also monitored the television programs and movies their children watched, tried to keep abreast of the music they listened to and the web sites they visited. When the eldest son become a fan of this musician, the parents were aware of it almost immediately. They quickly reacted by forbidding him from purchasing the musician's CDs, talking about the musician in the house, and quickly notifying the parents of his friends about this "moral cancer" encroaching upon their family and community. The congregational minister was also informed of the boy's emerging interests. He fully supported the parent's actions and convictions. The parents had many long discussions with their son about the evils associated with this music and expected him to fall into line. This did not occur.

As the parents asserted more pressure on their son to conform to their beliefs, the more emotionally distant and oppositional he appeared to become. He would refuse to engage in conversation with his parents. He rejected church activities and services and got into frequent arguments with his parents. The parents responded by attempting to enforce more limits, boundaries, and consequences – including grounding, counseling sessions with the church minister, withholding of allowance, prohibiting access to the internet, giving frequent lectures, and so on. Nothing seemed to work. The boy started acquiring new friends at school and securely kept the identify of these friends from his parents. The boy attempted to dress in ways the parents found offensive. He also continued to defiantly quote the lyrics and beliefs of this musician. The parents were terrified and were considering home schooling their son in an attempt to shelter him from the outside influences that were sparking these new interests. They also wanted to get politically involved, in hopes of eventually having restrictions placed on music lyrics they believed to be immoral, offensive, and dangerous. The parents believed an outside antagonist, the culture that produced this music, had taken control of their son and was destroying his moral foundation and negatively impacting the family. The parents believed that *if everything they tried was unsuccessful, there must be a larger external influence at work.* They felt powerless to produce change and believed they had lost control of their son.

I met the parents on a Thursday evening and listened to their plight. They were amongst the most motivated I had ever encountered. Rarely does a family therapist come across parents so active in their children's lives and development. Yet, I sincerely expected this to be our first and last session. I was certain the parents were unprepared to hear what I had to say. I did not believe the problem originated from the "external antagonists." The musician, the lyrics, the culture that supported this musician, the boy's new found friends, the other "less moral" persons who allowed this culture to flourish actually had little to do with the problems being described by the parents. The issues causing distress to the family were to be found in the parent's internal antagonists, certain internal beliefs and the resulting actions and reactions. I did not believe the parents would be willing and open to approach the problem from this direction. They were heavily invested in denouncing and blaming these external influences. Fortunately, I was wrong.

A Chinese military strategist and philosopher once wrote: "Know the enemy and know yourself; in a hundred battles you will never be in peril."[4] These parents were adept to living a Christian lifestyle. However, these newfound adversaries, the son's emerging beliefs, views, behaviors, and the musician and his lyrics, were completely unknown to the parents. Until this situation arose, the parents were able to effectively shield their children from influences and situations they found offensive and harmful. Now these "threats" were being courted and brought into the family by one of their children. When the parents glanced at this enemy, they experienced very uncomfortable emotions – fear, resentment, disbelief, uncertainty and insecurity. Their reaction to these uncomfortable emotions was to aggressively eliminate the adversary without process. What do I mean by *without process*? I asked the parents several questions during our first session. **Specifically, I wanted to know what they knew about the musician's personal beliefs. I wanted to know if the parents knew about this musician's family, his developmental history, and his life experiences. I also wanted to know how much the parents knew about the musician's lyrics and messages. I was interested to know if the parents knew what sparked their son's interest in this musician and what emotional benefits he was getting from championing these new messages. Finally, I wanted to know if the parents were aware of, and could verbalize, the nature of the boy's personal struggles. He appeared to be rejecting his family and religion in a very dramatic way. Why?**

The parents could not answer my questions in any depth whatsoever. They would state over and over that the music was evil and immoral but had great difficulty going any further. The parents would frequently respond to my questions with "*it just is!*" and would not take the conversation further. They confiscated one CD and a concert tee shirt from their son weeks earlier. They examined the artwork on the CD jacket and listened to one or two songs. This, in addition to the bizarre sexual images pictured on the tee shirt, was enough for the parents to take immediate and decisive action: forbidding the material altogether and closing discussion on the matter. They would not have debate on the matter as the material was too offensive and clearly contrary to their core beliefs. The parents believed further discussion would be irrelevant and destructive, and would send a message to their son that there was room for negotiation. The son's age and maturity level were such that he was capable of engaging in discussion of the previous questions. He was able to process the subject and the associated emotions with his parents. Yet, the parents were resistant to do so. My job was to open emotional process between the parents and son by promoting interactions that considered each other's emotional perspectives. I was sure the son was willing to cooperate, but were the parents? Exploration of the previously mentioned questions would have to become emotionally safe if this family was to move forward in a healthy and beneficial manner. The parents initially reacted to this idea with great resistance. At one point I believed they thought I was in bed with the devil himself.

The parents initially believed that by wanting to know more about the musician, I was working against them and colluding with their son. They felt that by inquiring into the son's interest in this music and exploring the emotional benefits he was receiving from it, I was somehow agreeing with his newfound beliefs. They felt I was being insensitive to their beliefs. On the contrary, I was attempting to open the door to their internal antagonists. The internal antagonist in this instance was a concrete set of beliefs that prevented emotional process of topics that differed from their own or were emotionally uncomfortable in any way. The parents believed that discussing or gaining an understanding of beliefs that differed from their own was an indication that they subscribed to such beliefs. At no point did I imply or suggest in any way that the music their son was listening to was appropriate. Nor did I suggest that the parents compromise their beliefs in any way. Yet, this is what the parents apparently heard. I was merely suggesting that the parents approach their son in a manner that was less concrete. I was suggesting they approach their son in a way that would engage him rather than push him away. I was asking the parents to join with their son without judgment to cooperatively learn more about this musician and what he represented. I was asking the parents to openly process what they encountered without lecturing or attempting to dissuade their son. The parents were encouraged to express their personal feelings and emotions about what they were seeing, reading, and hearing. However, they were not to criticize their son's understanding or interpretation of the material. Nor were they to quote scripture as they often did in my office.

This 15 year-old boy had certainly benefited from having parents that were actively involved in his living and development. I was confident that he was struggling and uncomfortable with his present oppositionional stance toward his parents. Yet, I believed the parents' internal antagonists were placing this adolescent in a position to martyr himself. He was not going to wake up one day and be as the parents wished. He was at a point in his life where he was capable of incorporating his own understanding of a moral foundation in his living. This is by no means easy for anybody – especially in a family with very concrete beliefs. The parents were blind to this process. Rather than supporting the son's struggle in a way that would likely result in him making helpful and healthy decisions, they were inadvertently cornering him into a position nobody was comfortable with. As a result, a natural developmental process came to a screeching halt. It was halted not by the external factors cited by the parents, but rather by their own fears, discomforts, and insecurities. An affinity for this music and the messages it carried was just a means for the son to say: *"Hey, I want to start making my own decisions about some things in my life. I think I'm ready."* The parents had to be reassured that they had done a good job raising their son and that he had likely absorbed key elements from the moral foundation established by the parents. They had to be reassured that, if their son was given support that included open processing of feelings, emotions, and information, he would be more inclined to make decisions that would be significantly less threatening and contrary to the parents' beliefs.

The parents were instructed to purchase biographies on this musician. They were asked to review the music lyrics and visit the many web sites devoted to the musician. Most importantly, the parents were asked to explore, listen to, and view this material **with their son!** The parents were asked to use this opportunity to discuss the numerous topics in a safe and supportive manner that were sure to arise.[5] No topic was to be off limits. The parents would certainly be offended, if not shocked, by the material they would be exploring with their son. I had to remind the parents over and over that if the boy was determined to access and explore this material, he would find a way. Fifteen year-olds are very resourceful. My question to the parents was: "How do you want your son to proceed? With input and direction from you or merely with input from persons unknown to you, such as his friends which you do not know and internet contacts?" The discomfort the parents were likely to encounter is simply a part of the parenting process that should not be ignored. The parents genuinely wished they could avoid this situation altogether and often questioned, *"why can't he just understand that we want the best for him?"* and "why *can't see how destructive this stuff is?"*

Reluctantly, the parents agreed to sit down with their son and let him know they disagreed with what they believed this music represents, yet they were willing to learn more. The parents were to ask their son for suggestions as to which CDs to purchase and to listen to with him. The parents were to make it a point to get on the internet with the son and search the sites devoted to this musician. They were to select a biography on this musician from an internet bookseller and begin reading about his history and life experiences. The parents agreed to pursue open discussion with their son on the subject matter. This discussion was not intended to assert one's position or to discount the other's, but rather to decrease the emotional distance that had developed between parents and son. The parents were not to hide their emotions and were asked to express them openly and without judgment of the other.

Several days after meeting with the parents, I received a phone call from a very angry minister. He insisted I meet with the parents and recant my suggestion that the parents process the material with their son. He stated their son was *"doing battle with evil"* and that my input was delaying the ultimate outcome. I listened to the minister then informed him that due to confidentiality issues, I was unable to comment on any family or individual seen in my office. The minister was informed that I would welcome a conversation with him if I had the parents' written consent. Something had apparently stirred in this family.

The next Thursday came and the parents arrived at my office. I was pleasantly surprised. They appeared excited and eager to get started. The parents stated their son was initially shocked by their shift in attitude.[6] The parents informed me that they believed several doors had been opened. In the first few evenings the parents were already able to have several open, frank, and heartfelt discussions with their son on topics such as sex, violence, religion & philosophy, civics, and so on. These discussions were stimulated by the music they listened to, the websites they had visited and the first two chapters of the musician's biography. The parents told me they were a bit overwhelmed by the graphic nature of the material, but found significant relief when they expressed the emotions they were experiencing. For example, when the mother found herself viewing offensive material on the internet she responded in the following manner:

Mother: *Oh my gosh, that picture is pretty frightening to me. I feel kind of nauseous when I look at it. It makes me want to run away from the computer. Why would anybody produce something like that? Why would anybody want to look at that?*

Son: *Well Mom, I think whoever painted this picture is probably pretty angry with the world. Maybe he's trying to express his anger the only way he can. In a way, I think he's communicating his emotions pretty well. Who knows, maybe he has a difficult time expressing himself with words. It's kind of sad.*

Father: *I think I'd prefer words.*

Son: *Well, everybody's different aren't they? Maybe he doesn't have anybody close to him that he can talk to.*

Mother: *I guess so. I still don't like it! It leaves me feeling very uncomfortable.*

Rather than turning away from these uncomfortable situations and emotions, the family was able to face them, begin to process them, and reduce the control these emotions had over their thoughts and behaviors. The subject matter was separated from the family member. That is, rather than seeing the son and his newfound interests as one and the same, the parents began to view the son and the offensive materials/beliefs as separate entities. The son began viewing his parents as separate from their position on this matter as well. As a result, both parents and son could begin seeing each other as such: "I can love my son and work toward having a closer relationship with him while recognizing that he currently has beliefs that are very uncomfortable for me," and, "I love my parents yet recognize that we are having and will continue to have different views on many subjects." This was accomplished through a process that was initially very uncomfortable for both the parents and their son. Yet, by separating the issue from the person, the family was freed from the concrete personalization that had been impacting them in unhealthy ways.

After spending considerable time on the subject, the parents and son were able to come to a consensus. He was well aware of the parents' thoughts on the music. The parents understood their son did not subscribe to all that was represented in the music, but that he was feeling trapped by his parents' beliefs and wanting to individuate. Individuation is the process whereby one starts making independent decisions, formulating unique beliefs, exploring aspects of living and relating that may differ from that of the parental or family systems. This music represented a vehicle in which he could assert independent thought. The parents heard their son say that he wanted room to individuate yet was frightened and felt insecure when he found himself so distant from them during this process. He knew that blindly accepting his parents' beliefs and thoughts was not going to work for him. He also knew that to reject them in such a dramatic way also put him in an uncomfortable place. The parents' efforts to change their focus from the external antagonists to the internal antagonists set the stage for greater emotional safety to emerge in their relationship with the son. A relationship was emerging where the son could begin exploring the boundaries of his moral beliefs and when challenged by what he found, might feel safer to seek support, input, and guidance from his parents. These issues were no longer personalized by the parents. They could now disagree with their son without becoming trapped into seeing the son and the subject of the disagreement as being one and the same.

The parents later informed me that their son would bring issues and questions to their attention that they would never have expected but were now in a position to welcome. For example, on one occasion their son approached the father and stated that he was hanging out with several of his friends and was asked if he wanted to "get high" by smoking marijuana. The boy told his father that he wanted to say yes, believing this would contribute to his feeling accepted. However, the son explained that he also knew that this would have been an unhealthy decision. He told his father that he chose not to get high but was still struggling with the subject. The father admitted that his first impulse was to ask who was asking his son to get high and to lecture to his son on the destructive nature of drugs; however, he refrained from doing so. Rather, he told his son that he was proud of his decision to say "*no*" and even happier that he felt comfortable enough to disclose the incident to him. The father went further by asking his son how he (the father) might be more helpful. The son responded that it was just good to know that he could discuss these matters with him in a safe manner. Later that evening the father told his wife what had occurred earlier that day. Both felt confident in their son's ability to handle this challenge in a healthy way and believed he would continue to say "*no*" in the future. However, the parents agreed to check in with their son on the subject from time to time. When the parents brought this incident up during one of our sessions, I asked why they chose not to demand the name of the boy who offered their son the marijuana. I was also interested as to why the parents did not respond by quoting scripture they believed to be relevant to the situation to their son as they had in the past. Both stated it felt better to have an open and trustworthy relationship by creating emotional safety than to promote emotional distance with concrete reactions. This was a struggle for these parents, yet the benefits of looking inward rather than to external antagonists was overwhelming.

Several months after our first Thursday appointment, I was again contacted by the family's minister. He stated that the son had returned to church and that he appeared to have more confidence and was never at a loss for verbalizing his thoughts and emotions. The minister stated that the young man's opinions often differed from his own but that discussion of these differences never escalated into anything destructive or disrespectful. I was also informed that the young man was taking a leadership role in several youth activities in their church as well. The minister invited me to host a workshop for the other parents in his congregation on "Creating Emotional Safety Between Parent and Children." We spoke a lot about creating a balance between internal and external antagonists at this workshop.

14. *The parent distant from the child's educational process, extracurricular opportunities / accomplishments, and peers will find himself rapidly distanced from the child and always struggling to regain a connection. The child's emotional reservoirs will be depleted attempting to engage the parent. Neither will likely excel.*

I wish this Parenting Assumption spoke for itself and required no additional comment from me. Unfortunately, I'm frequently reminded that this concept eludes many parents. It seems like a simple idea – children whose parents are involved in their living are more likely to excel and have fewer behavioral problems. Furthermore, as these children grow and mature, the parent-child relationship is less likely to be without regret. By *without regret,* I mean that several years down the line, the parent will less likely experience feelings that the parent-child relationship somehow vanished, that it failed to meet the parent's expectations, or that he or she could or should have done more.

All too frequently I meet with parents who put great effort into justifying backing away from involvement in their son's or daughter's lives. It's hard for me to imagine very many excuses or situations justifying a parent being distant from their child's education, extracurricular opportunities/accomplishments, and peers. Yet, some parents will invest considerable effort attempting to convince me that it's to the child's benefit to have a parent who is removed or distant from the child's everyday life. This belief is more common than one might imagine. It becomes evident when we look at the behaviors of many parents. As we explore this Parenting Assumption I'm going to summarize three examples of different family conditions. These examples will hopefully clarify the importance of this Assumption. Let's briefly look at (1) a wealthy family, (2) a divorced couple, (3) a summary of conditions in North Philadelphia.

The first example relates to a very wealthy family referred to my office. The father was a senior vice president of a large communications company. He was held in high esteem by the business community. His face frequently adorned the cover of business journals and trade publications. From the outside it seemed the family had everything: a large house in a prestigious neighborhood, the best clothes, nice automobiles, and frequent vacations. Money was not an issue for this family. Yet, the two eldest boys, ages 15 and 16, were abusing drugs and alcohol. They were doing poorly in school and constantly lied to their parents. The parents were confused by this situation as they believed they were doing everything "correctly." The mother was a stay-at-home mom. She maintained the household and assumed primary responsibility for raising the children. The father immersed himself in work. The father worked in New York City while the family lived in a prominent part of Philadelphia. The daily commute to and from New York, in addition to the long work hours, left little time for the father to participate in the boys' lives during the week. They had most weekends together and frequently vacationed. The parents had no idea what steps they could have taken to help prevent their sons' drug and alcohol abuse.

It's impossible to ascertain exactly what led to the boys' behaviors, but after just a few meetings with the family, I had a pretty good idea what was motivating them. During one of our sessions, the youngest boy lied to his parents. The older boy, upon recognizing his brother's lie, attempted to support his sibling by covering it up. The father was dumbfounded by the lie and the attempts to cover it up. He floundered and seemed powerless to respond in a manner that would likely be helpful. The mother intervened as her husband struggled. I immediately stopped this process and asked the father what was going on. He reluctantly admitted that he felt powerless when interacting with his sons. He felt they neither respected him nor responded to his attempts to discipline them. He considered using more forceful means of getting their attention, such as using threats of physical harm, but concluded this to be inappropriate.[7] This was incredibly frustrating for a man who wielded such authority in the business world. How could he successfully manage the efforts of several thousand employees, yet be drawn to his knees when interacting with his two sons? I believed the answer was simple. The father was away as the boys grew, matured and made achievements. He was only peripherally available to partake in many crucial parenting activities. The boys' mother did an excellent job of taking up the slack; nonetheless, the parenting responsibilities were skewed and unbalanced. I believe the boys' less healthy behaviors evolved slowly, over their entire lives. The boys were simply doing what felt natural and were unable to verbalize exactly what motivated their troubling behavior. I suspected their opposition to their father and failure to thrive in an environment with such opportunities was a pretty clear attempt to engage the father in their lives. I come across this over and over again. Children will appear to martyr themselves through self destructive behaviors to gain the attention and recognition of their parents. Eventually the children's emotional reservoirs will be depleted in attempts to engage the peripheral parent – leaving it difficult for them to thrive in other aspects of their lives.

From the outside it appeared as if this family had it all. The boys were certainly privileged. Some might say their behaviors were merely the actions of spoiled children. I did not believe this to be the case, as they appeared to be cognizant and appreciative of their privilege. On some level I believe the boys would welcome the opportunity to trade some of their privilege for greater parental involvement. They were inadvertently manipulating the situation so that the father would be forced to take a greater interest in the boys as things got out of control. Having their father present and involved in their lives would represent greater privilege to these boys even if his involvement was centered around less than desirable circumstances and destructive behaviors. By the time the family reached my office the problems had reached a critical level. The lying, manipulation, experimentation with drugs and alcohol, and declining grades required intervention. The parents were considering several options, including inpatient hospitalization or sending the boys to boarding school. **I suggested the parents merely evaluate their schedules.** There was no need to create further distance between parents and children. Inpatient treatment would likely result in the children depleting more of their emotional reservoirs in an attempt to engage the parents – by not cooperating with treatment, acting out at the treatment facility or continuing to abuse drugs and alcohol. Boarding school was not necessary and unlikely to be helpful. It would not address the underlying issues creating the problems and would likely result in further distance between parents and children.

The father was challenged with this Parenting Assumption – to involve himself, immerse himself, in his children's school, extracurricular opportunities/accomplishments and peers. Nonetheless, he rose to the occasion by restructuring his schedule. He notified his subordinates and superiors that his schedule would require additional flexibility. He began attending school sponsored activities such as parent teacher conferences. He made an effort to meet his sons' friends and took the initiative to introduce himself to their parents. He also arrived home early several evenings a week to have dinner with the family and reviewed the boys' homework assignments nightly. On several occasions the father would take one of his sons out of school for a day to accompany him to work in New York City. Remarkably and without prompting from the parents, the children began participating in school based extracurricular activities. One son took up the sport of fencing while the other started playing lacrosse. The father made it to many mid-week competitions to cheer his children's teams and each son's individual performance. The boys' social networks began to change as well. They spent less and less time with friends that routinely abused drugs and alcohol. For several months the parents had their sons tested for drug use. This practice ceased after the relationship between the parents and sons solidified. It no longer seemed necessary as the parents felt they were now able to recognize the behavioral changes that accompany drug and alcohol use. Finally, the parents felt assured they were almost always aware of the children's schedule and whereabouts. This responsibility was coordinated and shared between the parents. A healthier sense of balance had been achieved in this privileged family. As a result the children began to thrive.

The father's increased involvement worked for this particular family. Yet, when I discuss the family's success at parenting workshops, many participants animatedly state that the father's privilege and executive status allowed him to make the necessary changes in his schedule to accommodate my request. Again, it seems that some parents want to justify non-involvement and will search for reasons to support this belief. So, let's look at an example where privilege was not a factor. A divorced couple I worked with years ago immediately comes to mind. This couple had a 5 year-old daughter. Both parents worked and were struggling to make ends meet. These parents were referred to my office by their attorney. Apparently the attorney had concerns for the young child's well being. He felt the divorce would be relatively simple from a legal perspective as the couple had few financial assets to fight over. However, the attorney believed the anger and hostilities evident between the parents would adversely impact the child. They could not stand to be in the same room together nor could they have a civil conversation with each other. He offered the couple a deal whereby his legal fees would be greatly reduced if they would address the anger issues with a therapist. So I had the rare occasion to see a couple prior to their divorce specifically to work on co-parenting following the divorce.

The couple had been separated for many months by the time they visited my office. The anger and hostility, each directed toward the other, was influencing their parenting in very unhealthy ways. For example, the mother was withholding visitation or making visitation very difficult for the father. Once the father had his daughter, he frequently returned her home many hours late. The couple's anger was manifesting itself in passive-aggressive behaviors.[8] This was impacting the child in very unhealthy ways. The child always seemed sad and often started crying for no apparent reason. She did not want to leave her mother to visit with her father. Yet, once with her father, she did not want to return to her mother's house. The young girl was also having severe problems socializing with her peers at kindergarten. Many parents and professional therapists will state these behaviors are commonplace in the early months of a separation or divorce and are to be expected. I am of the belief that they may be common but are by no means necessary. I find that when conditions exist whereby the parents play tug-of-war with their children following separation and/or divorce, one of the parents will eventually tire of the hostilities and the obvious unhealthy impact it has on the child and will withdraw from parenting responsibilities. In this case, the father was about to give up by assuming a more peripheral role in raising his daughter. He could not stand to see his daughter struggle and felt it was "best" to concede. This meant withdrawing from many aspects of his child's living. This might have reduced the troubling behaviors but would have opened the door to a whole new set of eventual problems.

The couple was fortunate to have found a very insightful and compassionate divorce attorney. It only took a couple of weeks to turn the situation around. From my perspective, although it appeared as if these parents really hated each other, they had one thing in common – both loved their daughter very much. The daughter had nothing to do with her parent's hostile feelings for each other, yet she was unjustly experiencing the destructive consequences of their issues. It took a neutral and objective person to help the parents realize that if they did not cooperate on matters of co-parenting, the little girl would suffer. Cooperating did not mean conceding and withdrawing to a peripheral parenting role. My work with the couple consisted of assisting them put aside or process their anger when it came to parenting. We spent considerable time exploring how their anger toward each other was impacting if not controlling their actions and reactions in less than healthy ways (such as visitation tug-of-wars). I helped the young parents realize that the consequences of not working with each other were far greater than the difficulty of learning to work together on matters relating to their daughter. They could dislike each other to their hearts' content, but these feelings had to be put aside or preferably processed in my office when it came to matters of parenting.

The couple arrived at an arrangement that seemed to work. The father spoke to his daughter almost nightly to say goodnight. The mother supported this by ensuring the phone was available just before bedtime. The daughter kept copies of her kindergarten work and accomplishments. She would proudly review these accomplishments with her father on the weekends she stayed at his house. The girl's mother would help the little girl organize her work to help ensure the father saw everything that came home from school. The father made it a point to attend the child's kindergarten activities, such as parent–teacher meetings, as well as attending the child's appointments with her pediatrician. The mother ensured the father was informed of said appointments well in advance when possible. Finally, the mother agreed not to withhold or impede visitation in any way. The father was to stick to the schedule both agreed to. Returning his daughter late was no longer an option. The parents put aside or processed their anger when it came to parenting. When an issue arose that caused the parents consternation, I was asked to intervene, mediate, or act as referee. I was not on the mother's side. I was not on the father's side. I was on the daughter's side. My job was to help the parents understand that they both could be on the daughter's side by remaining involved.

The young girl weathered the divorce and excelled in school and other activities, including dance classes and swimming lessons. She eagerly made the goodnight calls to her father. Both parents were engaged in the parenting process. Neither withdrew, and the child's troubling behaviors ceased almost immediately.

This family had neither the privilege nor the flexibility seen in the first example. Yet, they were able to remain close to the child's educational process, extracurricular activities/accomplishments, and peers in the face of many very challenging obstacles. Lack of privilege did not matter. The efforts made by these parents were equally as great as the efforts made by the parents in the privileged family. The results turned out to be similar.

Now, let's take a look at a completely different example. Years ago I briefly worked on a research project at Temple University. We worked with parents and children residing in North Philadelphia. These families typically came from desperate neighborhoods and conditions. The environment in this particular part of Philadelphia was run-down and dangerous at best. The socioeconomic conditions and future for many of these families seemed, for all practical purposes, bleak and without promise. The research I was involved in examined how children living in such desperate and deprived conditions might find success. As previously stated, the neighborhoods where many of these children and families resided were neglected and run down. Gang and criminal activities were rampant as were drug and alcohol abuse and teenage pregnancies. There was also a high degree of dependence upon public assistance to meet one's housing and basic daily needs. As a result, a generalized sense of hopelessness and helplessness established itself among many people living in these North Philadelphia neighborhoods.

Historically, infusions of money into these areas had little effect on increasing the rate of success of children raised under these conditions. Money did not seem to significantly increase how many people graduated from high school. Money, in itself, had little impact on how many of these children avoided involvement in the criminal justice system and on finding gainful employment. This seemed counterintuitive to the conventional thought – "if a community is floundering, success can be purchased by infusing tax dollars." When the facts are evaluated, money is found to take a back seat to increased parental and community involvement. Again, this involvement relates to the child's or children's educational processes, extracurricular opportunities/accomplishments, and peers. An evaluation of a child who, against the odds and in the face of these tremendous obstacles, somehow succeeded (completed high school, pursued higher education, become financially self-sufficient, avoided teenage pregnancy and substance abuse problems) finds at least one parent or a strong parent figure who was passionately involved in his or her living. Of the children coming from these deprived communities, there are few exceptions to this rule. Furthermore, when the families were supported by parenting education and encouragement rather than mere financial assistance, success increased significantly. Finally, when children who experienced little success (children who dropped out of school, who were involved in gangs, or who were abusing drugs and alcohol) were interviewed, few had parents intimately involved in their living. Therefore, my experience leads me to believe that the child from severely disadvantaged circumstances who finds success and ultimately contributes to his or her community usually does so because he or she had a parent or parent figure deeply involved in his or her life and living.

I was moved by the commitment and dedication many North Philadelphia parents had for their children. I saw parents pick their children up from school daily to ensure they did not get involved with gang members. I saw parents form block watches to ensure the drug dealers did not encroach upon the children's play areas. I saw parents form neighborhood after school activity groups to help ensure their children were monitored and involved in healthy activities. Finally, I saw parents who were involved in all aspects of their children's educational process. These parents demanded intimate involvement in school activities and diligently monitored their children's progress. Despite a paucity of resources, these parents attended to one of the most basic needs of their children – parental involvement. This in itself helped insure their children had a much higher chance of succeeding. Upon review of the empirical data, these parents were and continue to be successful.

The conditions of the neighborhoods I worked within were initially alien to me. At times I felt I had stepped into a war zone. Many of the buildings were abandoned, burned out, or in a significant state of decay and neglect. Violence and intimidation was an everyday part of life for children living in these neighborhoods. Yet, in these conditions there were successes. The common denominator in nearly all the successes was this Parenting Assumption. Social and financial privilege was not in the vocabulary of these families. Privilege to the children who succeeded came in the form of parental involvement. This served as an important lesson for me.

15. *There are fair and unfair situations associated with living. Parent and child experience both in a similar manner.*

One of the most enjoyable aspects of being a family therapist and writer is that I have the opportunity to speak at a great many workshops and seminars. These workshops allow me to meet many parents and explore a broad spectrum of parenting issues in great detail. A very memorable experience occurred when I was asked to conduct a workshop for the University of Utah on sibling rivalries. When first presented with this opportunity, I began outlining the origins and dynamics of rivalries within the family. I immediately discovered this to be a very complex subject. The variables influencing how family members relate and interact with each other are infinite. Complicating matters further, variables that may lead to aggressive or unhealthy rivalries between siblings in one family may have little to no effect in another. I was interested in determining which systemic variables, if any, are common to most families that experience problematic rivalry issues. Where was I to begin?

One family I worked with immediately came to mind. This family sought professional assistance after their youngest son, age 12, was discovered stealing some of his older brother's, age 14, personal possessions. The personal effects being stolen had no great value nor were they of any particular use to the younger boy. The youngster was stealing things such as pictures of his brother's friends, an old pair of shoe laces, sea shells found during vacations to the beach, and so on. The younger child was also unusually aggressive toward his older brother. Seemingly small disagreements between the siblings would quickly escalate to a point where the younger boy would kick or hit his older brother. The older brother would respond by insulting and making fun of the younger sibling.

One instance described to me occurred while the family was having dinner. The younger boy asked his brother to pass the salt. The older child briefly hesitated while he finished drinking from his glass of water. This brief hesitation enraged the younger child. He began yelling at his older brother, then punched him very hard in the ribs – knocking the breath out of him. This was obviously an over reaction and very inappropriate. The parents informed me that the younger boy's reaction could have been life threatening as the older child had a severe case of asthma. I asked the parents to elaborate on the elder son's medical condition. Apparently, his asthma was a significant problem. The boy was prescribed many medications to help control the severity and frequency of the asthma attacks. Unfortunately, these medications were unable to adequately stabilize his respiratory problems. On average, the older boy and his parents found themselves in the emergency room three or four times a month seeking medical attention for an uncontrolled attack. Many of these visits resulted in hospitalization. Two of the most recent hospitalizations resulted in the boy being placed on a ventilator as an emergency life saving measure. I wondered how this hardship, this family stressor, was impacting the family's relational dynamics. Could the eldest boy's asthma be related to the youngest boy's troubling behaviors? This was worth consideration.

When a member of a family is sick or somehow suffering, other family members rarely feel comfortable exploring how that illness or condition impacts the non-ailing persons. It may seem selfish to discuss, consider, or explore the emotional impact an ailing family member's suffering has on other family members. I suspected members of this family were all profoundly affected by the eldest son's asthma. Yet, processing how each had been impacted had not occurred nor would it be an easy task. The eldest son's suffering was so severe that the painful emotions experienced by the other family members were thought of as irrelevant in comparison. Exploring these feelings might leave other family members feeling selfish or insensitive.

To help this family get to the bottom of the emerging sibling rivalry and troubling behaviors, I used a technique called *multidirected partiality*.[9] This entailed a systematic taking of sides. I assertively solicited each family member's perspective – briefly taking the side of and supporting each family member – in an attempt to gather information previously unexplored by the family. Specifically, we explored questions of fairness and unfairness within their family system. This was not an attempt to find fault or to point a finger at a victim or perpetrator, but rather to stimulate inter–member dialogue in a family that was trapped by a condition of unhealthy beliefs about fairness regarding the child's asthma. I asked each member of the family to help me understand their perspective and understanding of fairness and unfairness as it related to the eldest boy's asthma. We started with the younger son. He raised several surprising points:

- He believed that it was unfair that the family was burdened by his brother's asthma. He thought the asthma "was interfering with everything."

- The youngest son believed it was not fair that he should feel selfish by wanting to spend time with his parents, but was unable to, as they were frequently attending to his brother's medical needs.

- He believed it was not fair that he couldn't partake in activities with his older brother like other siblings (e.g. exploring a nearby wooded area and creek together).

- The younger child said he was scared that he may lose his brother and that he wanted to collect things that would be mementos of their relationship.

- He also stated he hated the pain the asthma caused the whole family. He said that at times it felt as if he hated his brother for having asthma. This left him feeling "confused," "conflicted," "small," "scared," and "selfish".

- He wished he knew how to separate feelings he had regarding the asthma and the unfair burden it placed on the family and the feelings he had for his brother. Having asthma was not his brother's choice. The younger boy knew it was not fair to hate his brother for a medical condition beyond his control. He admitted to feeling very confused about how he "blended" all of these emotions.

These were pretty complex thoughts from a 12 year-old. He had obviously given this subject a great deal of consideration but never verbalized these feelings prior to coming to our meeting. The older brother's comments were just as moving:
- The older son stated that he constantly felt embarrassed by his condition and the excessive attention the asthma generated.

- He stated that he gets irritated by his younger brother's intrusions, his stealing, and his physical assaults, yet believed they might be warranted. He felt that somehow if he let them go without much complaining, it might help "balance things out a bit." His little brother's actions also helped take the focus off his asthma. The older brother stated it was nice to be in a professional's office for something other than his medical problems.

- The older child wished his parents would not worry about him. He believed they fussed over him and his condition too much. Their attempts to restrict his activities seemed to be a response to their fears rather than the actual risks.

Again, these are pretty complex thoughts from a 14 year-old. The older son had been described as being a victim of his asthma. His comments seemed to indicate that perhaps he wanted or was ready to shed himself of this role, that being perceived as or labeled a "victim" was inappropriate.

Their son's comments left the parents speechless. Their surprise was centered around the realization that many of the problems within the family were not as closely related to the obvious pathology (the eldest son's asthma and the youngest son's aggressive behaviors), but rather the family's inability to engage in spontaneous, trusting, safe, and reciprocal relating. Together we established a goal to begin strengthen the family's interpersonal resources so that they could begin relating with each other in a more multidirected manner thereby becoming more skilled at soliciting and considering each others perspectives.

Initially, I believed the youngest boy was engaged in a sibling rivalry. Yet, upon a more detailed evaluation of the family condition, I believed any rivalry that existed was merely a symptom of other processes at work. In this particular case it was how the family dealt with the inequities associated with a chronic medical condition. Once this issue was exposed and processed, two important things happened. First, the younger child's stealing immediately ceased as did his aggressive attacks on his older brother. Secondly, the older son's asthma attacks significantly decreased in severity and number. He also spent less time making fun of and insulting his little brother. I do not believe the boy's improved medical condition was merely coincidental but was rather a physiological response to systemic shifts in the family's improved ability to relate to one another.

Earlier I stated that I was interested in finding what systemic variables might exist, if any, that are common to all families where we find problematic rivalry issues. Upon an exhaustive review of every sibling rivalry I have come across, this Parenting Assumption seems to be the most universally applicable. Where rivalries exist, I always find a skewed or limited understanding of fairness between parent and child. That is, parents tend not to believe their children are capable of understanding or processing the concept of fairness. In this case, the parents were attempting to shoulder all of the emotional responsibilities surrounding the eldest son's asthma. This included believing only they, the mother and father, should discuss the inequities that were caused by the oldest son's complex medical needs. As it turned out, the children were capable of comprehending the complexities of the problem and had very insightful and sophisticated ideas as to how it affected their family system, especially their understanding of fairness and unfairness. When the opportunity to process their ideas and thoughts was made available through multidirected partiality, the symptoms that brought this family to my office ceased to exist. I do not think this was coincidental by any means.

This Assumption regarding fairness is applicable to many other aspects of parenting and parent-child interactions. For example, children experience inequities associated with privilege and loss every day. Some families are financially well-off while others struggle. Some families live in areas where they experience varying degrees of privilege regarding race, religion, or sex. Some families remain intact while others are headed by single parents. Some families lose members to an early death while others have several generations of incredible longevity. As these situations are encountered, it is important that parents remember that *there are fair and unfair situations associated with living. Parent and child experience both in a similar manner.* The parent who recognizes that fair or unfair situations do have an impact on us, and engages the child in spontaneous, trusting, safe, and reciprocating dialogue about these situations, is giving their child a great gift.

16. If your decision is already made, it remains important to consider the child's perspective. For if the child feels his or her perspective has been considered, anger will be accompanied with respect and feelings of being cared for vis-à-vis anger and defiance if his or her perspective remain unconsidered.

A fifteen year-old girl and her parents came to see me to help them resolve a problem. The school year was about to come to an end, and the young lady wanted to spend a large part of the summer at a beach house on the New Jersey coast. She had already given a deposit for her room at this beach house. The house was being rented by several of her older friends (16 to 18 years-old). The parents heard of their daughter's plans and put an immediate stop to it. They did not know any of the other teenagers renting the house and believed their daughter to be much too young for an un-chaperoned summer at the shore with persons who were strangers to them. Normally this situation does not require the input of a therapist. However, in this case, the daughter made it very clear that she was going with or without her parents' permission. She became very secretive of the location of the beach house and the names of the other persons planning to stay at the house. The parents were firm in their decision not to give their daughter permission; however, the more entrenched they became in their decision to keep their daughter home, the more determined she became to spend the summer at the beach. The parents were becoming alarmed at the prospect of their 15 year-old daughter running away to the Jersey shore. This thought terrified the parents.

So, the three of them sat silently in my office. I was tempted to intervene with my perspective; however, this would not likely be very helpful. The daughter was not about to hear anything I had to say about the matter, especially since I believed the parents to be correct. The daughter's plans for the beach, as they were presented to me, were by no means healthy or necessarily safe. For the parents to permit their daughter to go would be irresponsible. It was the parent's job to "fix" this mess, not mine. They had already established limits and communicated their boundaries regarding the matter, yet these were not being respected by the daughter. I believed there was a very specific reason this situation was heading to a potentially destructive conclusion. *If your decision is already made, it remains important to consider the child's perspective. For if the child feels his or her perspective has been considered, anger will be accompanied with respect and feelings of being cared for vis-à-vis anger and defiance if his or her perspective remain unconsidered.*

I excused the daughter from the second session scheduled for the following week. I only wanted to meet with the parents. The second session was dedicated to this Parenting Assumption. I asked the parents two questions: "*Why do you not want your daughter to go to the shore?*" and "*Why does she want to go to the shore, to the point of disobeying you in such a dramatic way?*" Their response to the first question was to be expected: "*She's only 15 years-old; she will be exposed to drugs and alcohol; there is no adult supervision in the house; there are much older boys staying at the house. They will take advantage of her.* We don't trust her decision making skills yet; the thought of her being unsupervised for the summer is terrifying – and so on. These were definitely valid concerns. Their answer to the second question, *"Why does she want to go to the shore?"* was not so concrete. Their response was: *"She wants to experiment with drugs and alcohol, to avoid the family rules, to act irresponsibly,"* and so on.

With this said, I believed the problem would be relatively easy to address. The key here was to help these parents become more skilled in soliciting their daughter's perspective. She was a 15 year-old being defiant. Nothing new here. However, this defiance was accompanied by a great deal of anger and little respect. The parents' understanding of their daughter's perspective appeared to be somewhat limited. This is all too common in families where a child is emerging from one developmental life-cycle stage to another – in this case from *childhood* to *young adulthood.* As a result the parents found themselves making too many assumptions about their daughter's perspective without soliciting her input. It was not too long ago that these parents had to make many assumptions about their daughter's perspective as she did not have the developmental skills to communicate them well. She now possessed these abilities and skills. It was up to the parents to assist their daughter apply them. When the daughter experienced her parents as unwilling to elicit and consider her perspective she immediately resisted. This was a clear example of the daughter's emerging maturity forcing change in the family.

During our second session we explored ways the parents might gain insight into why this trip was so important to their daughter. This was crucial and appeared to be a missing piece of the equation. During the second session the parents learned how to ask probing questions so as not to sabotage the communication process. For example:

Probing Questions
"I'm not sure I completely understand what I'm hearing you say right now. What do you mean by that?"

As opposed to:

A Way to Sabotage the Communication Process
"You want to do what? No way. You're much too young. That's idiotic and out of the question."

The parents were sent on their way and instructed to return with their daughter the following week. During the third session the parents were instructed to learn as much as they could about why this summer at the beach was so important to the daughter. They were to use the entire hour for this process and then arrive at an answer for their daughter on the spot – *Yes* or *No*. The parents were to keep the conversation going by using probing questions and avoiding judgmental statements that would shut down or sabotage communications. During this hour, the parents heard and were able to consider their daughter's perspective They were amazed at the depth and maturity of her presentation. They were amazed at how calm everybody remained and how different this conversation was from previous ones on the subject. The daughter had a lot to say. More importantly, the parents heard their daughter communicate the following points:

- The parents heard their daughter state that she could begin taking care of herself. She gave the parents many real and pertinent examples of her emerging skills and maturity.

- The parents heard their daughter assure them that she had absorbed the values important to the parents. The daughter summarized these values very well for the parents. She asserted that she would not compromise these values over the summer.

- The parents heard the daughter state that she was not perfect and that she would make mistakes but that she viewed her parents as a resource. The parents heard her state that she would like to feel more comfortable coming to them for advice and input rather than specific direction.

- The parents heard their daughter state that she believed she was old enough to begin making decisions for herself as she felt capable of making ones that were well thought out. She believed her plans for the summer were well thought out.

- The parents heard their daughter state that she believed her parents still viewed her as a child. The summer at the beach house would assist the family "*break*" from this perception.

- The parents heard their daughter state that she did not feel trusted. This left her experiencing a mixture of uncomfortable emotions. The parents heard their daughter state that she didn't want this to become a wedge between them but was unable to find a resolution.

This 15 year-old was working pretty hard to get her way. Many of her comments appeared to be intended to manipulate a favorable response from her parents, *"Yes, by all means go to the shore and have a great time. Give us a call every now and then to let us know how you are doing."* I was impressed by the parents' composure during this session. They sat there, asking the occasional probing question and listened. They must have seen through their daughter's attempt to manipulate them, yet chose not to react defensively. They listened and probed for more of her *perspective*. At the end of the hour the parents gave their daughter their final answer: "No." She was pretty angry, especially after putting her thoughts and emotions on the table for everybody to see. The session ended and everybody went home.

The fourth and final week I met with the parents alone. I was told the ride home from my office the previous week was very uncomfortable, to say the least. The parents then said that within a few days the daughter began presenting them with alternative plans for the summer. The first of these plans included a stay at the New Jersey beach house but for a shorter duration. Eventually, the parents and daughter arrived at a plan everyone could accept. This plan allowed the daughter to demonstrate that she was capable of caring for herself away from the parents, she would be in a position where her values might be challenged and where mistakes could be made, but with a lot of support. The plan also allowed for the preexisting views of family roles to be challenged and broken. The daughter chose to attend a month-long outdoor survival and mountaineering course. There were young adults facilitating this course. All were strangers to the parents. Most of the daughter's time would be spent with people her own age while being challenged to develop rock climbing, kayaking, and mountaineering skills. The daughter was able to get her deposit back from the beach house and managed to pay for a significant portion of the summer trip with her savings.

Although the points made by the daughter during the third session appeared to be manipulative, they were much more than that. They were rooted in truth and were a genuine representation of her perspective. The daughter left the third session feeling as if these points were heard and considered by her parents. She was angry when the parents said *no* to the beach trip, yet this anger was accompanied by a certain amount of respect and a feeling of being cared for by the parents. These are important factors in any relationship, especially between a fifteen year-old and her parents.

Finally, what does this have to do with balance? Well, maintaining balance between sticking to one's guns while simultaneously hearing and considering another's perspective is most important. Quite often we will find that our own position is not always as firm as we initially believe it to be.

17. Anger is a just emotion. A child learns how to manage this emotion solely from the parent(s).

A man in his mid 30s entered therapy with me shortly after his girlfriend and her two children moved into his house. The couple had been dating for nearly a year when they decided it was time to share a home. The children were from the woman's first marriage. Their biological father knew of my client and, until the couple decided to cohabitate, had no problems with the relationship. However, when the children and their mother moved into the new household something changed. The children's father became hostile toward the his ex-wife and her boyfriend and the children's new living arrangements. One evening the ex-husband and a few of his friends arrived at my client's house and knocked on the door. Apparently they had been drinking, were intoxicated, and very agitated. My client opened the door and was immediately met with a barrage of verbal threats and attempts to engage him in a fight. The mother and her children were nearby and witnessed the whole event. My client did not leave the house to fight the intruders but rather responded by yelling expletives and threats of his own through a screen door. Eventually, the children's mother called the police which motivated the visitors to leave.

My client was struggling with many issues relating to this incident. On one hand, he was adjusting to the many responsibilities that accompany becoming a step-parent. On the other hand, he felt emasculated and angered by the manner in which he responded to the intruders. In the past he would have stepped out of the house to "defend his honor and home." Standing behind a screen door while these "punks" made threats left him feeling like a coward. This event seemed to unleash many issues for this man. Somehow he knew that getting into a fight with the antagonists would not serve as a healthy example for the children. Yet, responding in a more physical manner, such as fighting, seemed to be familiar and comfortable. He always dealt with "things like this" in a physical manner in the past. Without this option, he reported feeling exposed, uneasy, cowardly, and weak.

After the aggressors left the scene, my client's anger did not recede. He yelled at his girlfriend for having "such a loser ex–husband." He slammed nearly every door in the house, kicked several dining room chairs around the room and isolated himself from the other family members for the rest of the evening. Conversation at breakfast the next morning was brief and the children were eager to go to school in order to get out of the house.

My client initially asked for help identifying alternative coping strategies for similar situations. However, shortly into our first visit I started getting the impression he really wanted me to agree that leaving the house to fight the aggressors was somehow an acceptable or appropriate response. This left me wondering why this man came to therapy in the first place? What was motivating him to be here if he felt his impulse to fight was in fact his best option? Where did he learn this behavior? I asked him these questions directly. As it turned out, his girlfriend threatened to end their relationship if he did not address his "anger issues." She was pleased he chose not to fight her intoxicated ex-husband and his friends, yet, the anger he displayed following the incident left the girlfriend feeling very uncomfortable. Apparently, her ex-husband had been physically abusive to her. She wanted no part of another relationship where similar abuse was even a remote possibility. My client's reaction to this particular situation left her feeling as if he was capable of becoming abusive as well.

The exact circumstances described in this example are unlikely to be encountered by very many families. However, this example does highlight a situation that every family will encounter – a situation that elicits anger. I would probably be angry if strangers arrived at my house and threatened me in a similar manner. I might also be angry if I accidentally hit my finger with a hammer while hanging a picture. I might experience anger if one of my dogs were to destroy an expensive goose down comforter or if my spouse or children were to lie to me. How I respond to each of these situations will be determined by my understanding of anger. Unfortunately, this is a subject that is rarely discussed in many families.

This Parenting Assumption states that *"anger is a just emotion."* This means that anger is not *bad* or to be avoided but is rather an important emotional reaction to a stressor, stimuli, or situation existing in one's life or immediate environment. As we will see anger is simply **a secondary emotional *reaction* that serves as an emotional explanation point**. That is, it is an emotional reaction whose specific purpose is to bring attention to areas of our lives and relationships that require, or might benefit from, some attention. Anger is a wake up call and relatively easy to manage once its origins and purpose are understood. As previously stated, anger is a *secondary emotional reaction*. Contrary to popular belief, anger is not an emotion at all, but rather a reaction to a conglomeration of several primary or basic emotions. There are many such secondary emotional reactions that tend to be commonly mislabeled or understood as being emotions. Examples of a few other secondary emotional reactions would include jealousy, rage, and fear. Any reaction that can be broken down into many emotions should probably be considered a secondary emotional reaction. We will see why this distinction is important in the following paragraphs. The exact primary emotions culminating into a secondary emotional reaction will be completely dependant upon the condition or situation that stimulated that emotional reaction.

Confused? Let's say I hit my finger with a hammer while attempting to hang a picture. This event may leave me feeling angry – a secondary emotional reaction. Why exactly am I angry? This is a question few people ask when they nail their thumb with a hammer, but let's play along for a moment. What's going on when I hit my finger with a hammer? I probably did not hit my finger intentionally, nor did I expect to hit my finger when I decided to hang the picture. I probably would rather have avoided the whole incident. I have successfully hung hundreds of other pictures in my lifetime without experiencing a similar incident. My finger was injured and now it hurts. These are examples of just a few of the possible thoughts that might pass through one's mind immediately following this unfortunate incident. These thoughts stimulate an immediate and powerful emotional reaction consisting of many **primary** emotions. The following table presents an emotional synopsis of this event:

Event: *I hit my finger with a hammer while hanging a picture*

Thoughts that might pass through my mind immediately after the hammer impacts my finger:	Possible emotions associated with these thoughts:
• This was not intentional nor expected →	Surprised, Shocked
• I would rather have avoided the whole incident →	Embarrassed, Disappointed, Irritated
• It is painful →	Pain, Discomfort
• I have successfully hung hundreds of other pictures in my lifetime with out this happening →	Annoyed, Foolish, Enraged

Now, as anybody who has ever hit their finger with a hammer knows, these thoughts do not seem like the first thing that comes to mind. No, one usually shouts a few expletives, kicks the nearest trash can, or takes their anger out on the poor soul that happens to be close by. But these or a myriad of very similar thoughts will occur in the brief moments immediately after the hammer impacts one's finger. They come and go so fast that we may not be aware that they ever occurred. Yet, these fleeting thoughts have a dramatic impact on us. They stimulate a great number of primary emotions. These thoughts and the corresponding cascade of primary emotions are capable of overwhelming the individual. This is when the secondary emotional reactions such as anger, jealousy, rage, and fear will likely emerge. The best metaphor I can think of that might help clarify this point would be that of an avalanche. In nature almost any event can trigger an avalanche – a sound, a fallen limb, a light breeze. This simple event can initiate a nearly instantaneous release of tons of snow and ice which in turn can cause a great deal of destruction. Anger and other secondary emotional reactions work in very much the same way. A relatively simple event, such as hitting your finger with a hammer, can instantaneously trigger the release of many thoughts. These thoughts immediately stimulate a great number of primary emotions. The sudden cascade of primary emotions is very powerful and can be difficult to manage such as the tons of snow and ice that are released during an avalanche. The person experiencing the sudden cascade of primary emotions might find him/herself unable to process these emotions and will be swept away. The emergence of the secondary emotional reaction is an indicator that the individual has lost the ability to manage the situation in the most healthy and helpful manner. This process is pictured below. Please note the cascade or avalanche flow of this anger pathway:

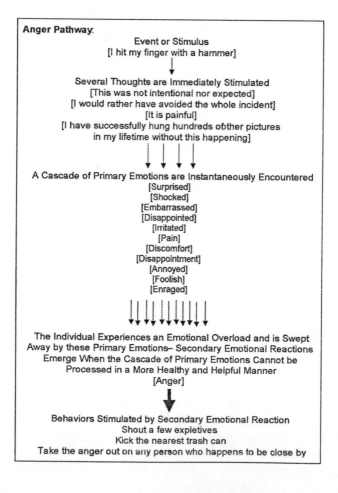

Anger Pathway:

Event or Stimulus
[I hit my finger with a hammer]

Several Thoughts are Immediately Stimulated
[This was not intentional nor expected]
[I would rather have avoided the whole incident]
[It is painful]
[I have successfully hung hundreds of other pictures
in my lifetime without this happening]

A Cascade of Primary Emotions are Instantaneously Encountered
[Surprised]
[Shocked]
[Embarrassed]
[Disappointed]
[Irritated]
[Pain]
[Discomfort]
[Disappointment]
[Annoyed]
[Foolish]
[Enraged]

The Individual Experiences an Emotional Overload and is Swept
Away by these Primary Emotions– Secondary Emotional Reactions
Emerge When the Cascade of Primary Emotions Cannot be
Processed in a More Healthy and Helpful Manner
[Anger]

Behaviors Stimulated by Secondary Emotional Reaction
Shout a few expletives
Kick the nearest trash can
Take the anger out on any person who happens to be close by

Accidentally hitting one's finger with a hammer is a pretty obvious event. It's easy to make the connection between the event and the resulting thoughts, emotions, and behavioral reactions. What about an event that is related to parenting, say, when a child lies to the parent? Many parents will find themselves angered by this sort of behavior. The anger is indicative that something in the parent-child relationship might benefit from attention. *The child's manipulative behavior along with the parents' emotional reaction is merely an explanation point highlighting an area in need of attention.* We can apply the process used to understand one's reaction to hitting a finger with a hammer to explore this situation as well.

Event: Child lies to his parent.

Possible Thoughts : *Is he really lying? Why would he lie to me? I hope this is not a trend. What are his motives? I thought he trusted me. I thought I could trust him.*

Primary Emotions: Surprise, shock, disappointment, confusion, manipulated, disbelief, concern, let down.

Secondary Emotional Reaction: Anger (Rage in extreme circumstances)

Common Behaviors: Spanking or hitting the child; yelling at the child; refusing to interact with or isolating the child (time out); not allowing the child to play with his or her friends, grounding, etc.

In this example, the child's lying initiates a cascade of events. First, the parent is instantaneously hit with a barrage of thoughts. These thoughts almost instantly stimulate a bunch of primary emotions which create a sort of emotional log jam. A secondary emotional reaction – anger – emerges from this log jam. The primary emotions are compressed into a single reaction. The secondary emotional reaction can be very difficult to process and may result in behaviors that are less healthy and helpful to the situation. In this case, hitting, spanking or yelling at the child. Actions and reactions based solely upon these secondary emotions are rarely the most healthy and helpful response available to the parent.

For some reason, this child made the decision to lie to one of his parents. The parent responded by getting angry. Perhaps the child will be disciplined or maybe the child will learn his lesson merely by seeing his parent angered. Who knows? My question is, *what did the parent learn and how did the child's understanding of anger evolve?* Remember, anger is an emotional explanation point. It brings attention to areas of our lives and relationships that might benefit from some attention. In this case, and in most cases when one becomes angry, those initial fleeting thoughts are pretty good at telling us what might benefit from attention. The child did not feel safe telling the truth? Why? *Why would he lie to me? I hope this is not a trend. What are his motives? I thought he trusted me. I thought I could trust him.* If the parent spanks the child, hits the child, yells at the child, refuses to interact with or isolates the child, have these thoughts been explored or processed in any way? Probably not. The parent will have missed an excellent opportunity to explore an area of the parent-child relationship that would probably benefit from some attention. What did the child learn after his lie had been foiled? Probably that he must try harder not to experience the parent's anger. This may mean telling the truth in the future. This may also – and more frequently – mean that the child learns to improve skills that are less likely to be foiled by the parents: Becoming a better liar. If the parent recognizes anger as a *just* emotion, captures those fleeting thoughts, and processes the issues and emotions with the child, much is gained by parent and child. This may sound complicated but when the process is understood it becomes remarkably simple.

The parent is the sole individual who will determine how the child understands anger. Does the child learn to become a better liar? Does the child learn to kick chairs around the room? Or does the child learn to capture those initial thoughts that, if missed, can begin a less healthy and helpful cascade of events? A child learns how to manage anger primarily from his or her parents. Sure, as the child interacts with other people throughout life, much is learned about anger management, but it is the parents who are by far the primary models for the child.

Let's return to the original example that opened this Parenting Assumption. What do we know about this particular family? We were informed by my client that the children's biological father may have been physically abusive to his wife. We also learned that the biological father might have a problem with drinking. These are prime indications that the father is vulnerable to working with anger in less than *just* ways. His secondary emotional reactions are probably unlikely to result in healthy and helpful outcomes. From the little I heard of the situation, it seemed as if the father was unable to explore questions, concerns, or thoughts he had about his children's new living arrangements. Examples of a few thoughts or concerns the father might have experienced would include: "*Why wasn't I consulted on this move? They're my children! I think I should have some input on where my children live. Is this a safe place for them? How will they address your new boyfriend – Dad!? How is discipline approached in this home?*" and so on. These or similar thoughts can quickly overwhelm any parent in a similar situation. In this case, they probably initiated a cascade of events that led the father to the children's new house, drunk, and making threats. The father's anger and resulting behaviors arc relatively easy to understand from this context. If the biological father were in my office, I would certainly assist him explore these questions. I would also try to find out what was prohibiting the father from identifying and exploring these concerns, thoughts, and questions himself.

Why were these initial thoughts resulting in such destructive and unhealthy behaviors? I would bet the children's biological father experienced his parents in very much the same way. Anger was probably not a *just* emotion in the father's family of origin. The children's father is probably working with anger in very much the same way his parents did. My client also approached anger from a similar perspective: kicking chairs about the room, yelling at his girlfriend, isolating himself from the other members of this family and household. These are not indicators that he identified and processed those initial fleeting thoughts. Imagine how different the situation might have been if, after the aggressors left, my client sat down with his girlfriend and attempted to capture and process some of those initial fleeting thoughts and questions. My client probably experienced thoughts similar to:

- *This is awkward and uncomfortable.*
- *What options do I have?*
- *What is this guy's problem?*
- *I'm not hurting his ex-wife or children, in fact they are probably being treated much better than when they were living with him.*
- *What does he want from me?*
- *What a jerk.*
- *He seems to have some issues. What are they?*
- *I don't what this to happen again.*
- *Do I now have to worry about being jumped when I'm away from my house?*

The mere process of capturing these thoughts will open the door to a much different conclusion. The questions raised do not necessarily require answers. The thoughts do not require a response. It is the underlying process of capturing and considering these thoughts that makes this experience *just*. A healthy and helpful by-product is that productive solutions for this problem are more likely to emerge. For example, shortly after attempting to capture these thoughts in my office, my client called the children's father and extended an invitation to discuss any concerns he had about their new living arrangements. As it turned out the phone conversation was nearly an hour long and was very productive for both parties. No threats were made and both men were amicable.

There was a missed parenting opportunity in this situation. The children witnessed the entire event. Their father was drunk and making physical threats. Their mother's boyfriend responded by yelling and making his own threats. Their mother had to call the police to bring an end to the unfortunate incident. The boyfriend became angry – he kicked chairs around, yelled at anybody that was nearby, and isolated himself from the other members of the household. Where is the missed opportunity in an event such as this? Simple, the children did not move any closer to an understanding that anger is actually a by-product of an event, several fleeting thoughts, a conglomeration of many primary emotions, and a secondary emotional response. No, they probably learned that when my client is angry, get out of the way. They also probably moved somewhat closer to understanding these type of reactions as being a normative way of dealing with problems. Eventually, these or very similar behaviors will emerge from the children as they encounter stressors in their lives.

Because my client felt his phone call to the children's father went well – he took notes during the phone call and later reviewed them with his girlfriend – he felt the matter was probably closed. Was it? I asked him about the children. Why hadn't he processed the event, specifically, his reaction to the whole mess, with them? He was unable to answer my question. This thought had completely eluded the man. Eventually, he asked me, *"What possible benefit would come from embarrassing myself that way with the children? The matter is closed. It's done and unlikely to happen again. I want to move on!"* **Anger is a *just* emotion. A child learns how to manager this emotion solely from the parents**. My client was stepping into a parental role. Almost everything he does and says will impact the growth and development of his girlfriend's children. Even several days later, a discussion with the children about those fleeting thoughts, the resulting emotions, and the emergence of anger as a secondary emotional reaction will have a helpful and healthy impact on the children.

Their understanding of why chairs were being kicked around the house will be advanced. Earlier my client asked me why would he *embarrass himself that way?* When I asked him where the embarrassment was coming from, he correctly identified the secondary emotional reaction – his anger. This was not something he wanted to focus on with the children. We spent a few minutes breaking the whole event down in a manner similar to the example where one hits their finger with a hammer. We explored how he might capture the initial thoughts and resulting emotions. We then explored how processing them will, more often than not, prevent a secondary emotional reaction and likely result in more healthy and helpful outcomes.[10] I recommended that my client and his girlfriend repeat this process with the children. This would help them make sense of this confusing and very uncomfortable situation. More importantly, this will expand their understanding of anger. It will help solidify their understanding of anger as *just.*

18. Pay heed to nourishing the child's intellect, creative forces, and spirit. Yet, in so doing, do not unnecessarily fatigue the child.

A member of my extended family was fretting about their 4 year-old daughter getting into "*the best*" pre-school. Apparently there was considerable competition for classroom space in the small town where they resided.   When the parents, particularly the child's mother, received notification that the daughter was not admitted to their first choice of pre-school programs, she became very distraught. The mother also became very aggressive and argumentative when we discussed the issue. During our conversation I suggested that getting the young girl into "the best" pre-school might not be as important to the child's overall development as the parent apparently believed. This situation is common. Many parents place too much emphasis on influences and activities outside of the family for determining how well a child will develop. This would include the schools one attends, the activities in which one participates, the church one attends, the friends and social networks one acquires, and so on. Unfortunately, this belief can come at the expense of the parent-child relationship. That is, more energy and resources are focused on ensuring the child *"get's into the best pre-school,"* or *"attends the best soccer camp,"* or *"belongs to the right church"* than on fostering a parent-child relationship that is engaging and emotionally safe and secure. This is not to say that these external factors and activities are not important and influential. They are. However, without question, they take a back seat to the quality of the parent-child relationship. What would happen if the 4 year-old girl was only accepted into the mother's third or even fourth choice for pre-school? In all likelihood the child would still emerge well prepared to transition into kindergarten and the first grade, especially if the parents were involved with her educational activities and accomplishments. I would be more concerned with the child who was excepted into "the best" pre-school yet had little parental involvement.

Upon further discussion with this mother, I discovered that her child's schedule was far more complex than my own. In addition to childhood activities such as playing, coloring, learning to ride a bike, reading with her parents, trips to the zoo, and so on, the young girl was taking child music classes once a week, dance and tumbling classes twice a week, swimming classes three times a week, art classes twice monthly, and had a date with her regular play group one afternoon a week. This child always seemed to be traveling to and from these various activities. These parents should be complimented on their dedication and resourcefulness. However, I wondered if there was a healthy balance in this child's life? Was there an adequate amount of time for the child to explore her own sense of creativity and fun? Was this child being fatigued? Was the parent-child relationship healthy? I believe these to be important questions and worthy of further exploration.

As it turned out, the mother seemed to be the primary parent and caretaker. The father traveled extensively and worked long hours. The father-daughter relationship seemed to be emotionally distant and lacking intimacy. The two always seemed to be "catching up." When the father and daughter had time together, they reviewed her accomplishments from the previous week. The father had relatively few real-time experiences with his daughter. He only heard about how she had mastered a new tumbling maneuver or how she jumped off a higher diving board. The mother's life seemed to be focused on managing her daughter's schedule and ensuring she got as many activities in as possible. These parents were at risk of fatiguing their child. If this pattern continued, she would be vulnerable to having struggles with the concept of intimacy later in life.[11] Intimacy requires considerable patience and focus. When one is emotionally fatigued by the imposition of a frantic schedule or environment, skills necessary to develop intimate relations will be slow to emerge. Indeed, this child was already beginning to show early signs of fatigue. The parents received reports that she was having a difficult time interacting well with her peers. She was not sharing and seemed to get into many disagreements and fights with the other children her age. She often played alone and isolated herself rather than engaging with others in her peer group. The young girl's peers seemed quite content leaving her alone and excluding her from group activities. The girl was only 4 years-old; however, if these early trends were not interrupted, they could easily become engrained in the girl's behaviors – adversely affecting her later abilities to thrive and relate well with others.

What recommendations would I make to these parents? First of all, parents who involve their child in such a broad spectrum of activities should be commended for their efforts to provide such nourishing experiences. Their hearts may be in the right place, however, I would recommend the parents take a breather. That is, they may want to consider reducing the number of activities in which the child was partaking. She was only 4 years-old. The young mind can absorb an incredible amount of information. However, the young mind also requires rest and downtime to organize and process that which it has absorbed. Finally, I would recommend the parents explore the concepts of balance and intimacy. The mother's entire life revolved around her child. Although a noble effort, was this healthy for the child? It appeared to be burdensome for the child. Was there a healthy balance in the mother's life? Was there balance between the parents in regard to parenting responsibilities? And finally, was there balance in the parent's relationship and marriage? They seemed to have forged an arrangement that met the logistical and financial needs of the family, but were the emotional and intimacy needs being met?

When I work with families facing struggles with balance, I will often use a chandelier metaphor to help explore the topic. I begin explaining this metaphor with a simple statement, *"Life is like a chandelier."* Imagine, if you will, a chain hanging from the ceiling in a room. Attached to the end of this chain and suspended from the ceiling is a wagon wheel. The wheel is suspended so that it is hanging flat and parallel to the floor. This is the platform for our chandelier. Now, to this platform we will attach a single light bulb on the wheel's outer rim. This single bulb does little to adequately light the room. Furthermore, the weight of the single bulb leaves the chandelier off balance and hanging in a skewed manner. It will lean to the side containing the bulb and look awkward. To address this problem, we will place a second bulb on the opposite side of the wheel. The second bulb provides additional light to fill the room and will, for a short time, balance the chandelier. However, the wheel remains vulnerable to tipping to one of the sides without a bulb. The wheel may be equally balanced but is not stable. To address this problem two additional bulbs are placed on the chandelier at equal distances from the others. The four bulbs now light the room well and leave the chandelier more evenly balanced and stable.

In the chandelier metaphor the light bulbs may represent important aspects of our living. For example, one bulb may represent one's recreational interests and activities. Another bulb may represent the resources invested into one's family relationships. Other bulbs may represent one's involvement in organized religion, one's career, the effort one invests in maintaining a home, and so on. We could easily add many bulbs to the chandelier. However, just as a chandelier has limited space for bulbs, people have finite physical and emotional resources. A chandelier with too many bulbs may become overloaded and cause an electrical circuit to blow or become too heavy and crash to the floor. The 4 year-old girl in the previous example probably had too many bulbs on her chandelier. I believe the problems she was experiencing interacting with her peers was an early sign that her internal emotional circuit breakers were becoming overloaded and about to trip. A few bulbs – activities – could easily be removed while still adequately lighting the room. The mother, on the other hand, had but one bulb on her chandelier. This bulb represented her daughter through whom she seemed to be living vicariously. Bulbs representing intimacy in her marriage, her own hobbies or recreational interests, friendships and a social support network, were missing from the mother's chandelier. As such, the mother's room was not very well lit. There was too much emphasis on parenting and too little emphasis on addressing her own emotional needs. Her chandelier was off kilter and unbalanced. The same condition existed for the child's father. His chandelier primarily consisted of one bulb – his work and career. The father's room was fairly dim as well. The father-daughter relationship was becoming increasingly distant. This was an indication that attention to balance may be indicated. *Pay heed to nourishing the child's intellect, creative forces, and spirit. Yet, in so doing, do not unnecessarily fatigue the child.*

Chapter 4 Safety

The quality or condition of being or feeling safe;
freedom from danger, injury, or damage; security;
reducing danger or harm

When we speak of safety and the parent-child relationship many things come to mind. Perhaps the most common association is with physical safety, e.g., being or feeling safe or free from physical harm, threat, or danger. Providing an environment that is safe from physical harm must be a primary responsibility for any parent. This is a daunting task for parents, as our daily lives are full of potential threats and hazards. If one considers the number of childhood injuries and deaths that occur each year secondary to poisoning, burns, falls, choking, automobile accidents, electrocutions, drowning, and crime, the importance of constant vigilance becomes quite clear.

This chapter does not focus on elements surrounding physical safety but rather on an aspect of safety that is rarely discussed in significant detail – **emotional safety**. The importance of ensuring children have an emotionally safe and secure environment is equal to that of creating a physically safe environment. I base this conclusion on years of clinical experience in which I have worked with hundreds of families seeking treatment for conditions that, in all probability, might have been avoided had the emotional aspects of safety been better understood. The conditions I'm referring to include everything from suicide to drug and alcohol abuse, teen pregnancy, and situations where a child simply fails to thrive or excel. The costs of overlooking emotional safety and security in the family system are enormous.

This chapter contains 18 Parenting Assumptions. Each explores a different aspect of emotional safety, yet all are inextricably interwoven and related. The first four Safety Assumptions (19 through 22) are essentially the foundation for the remaining 14 Assumption in this chapter. If you understand *accessibility, engagement, entrapment*, and *exposure* you will find yourself well on the way to being able to create a parent-child relationship that is emotionally safe and secure. Efforts to expand your understanding of these subjects will prove to be a great investment in your children's future.

19. *"Accessible" is when both parent and child can approach each other with near equal ease.*

Wouldn't it be nice if both parent and child could freely and comfortably approach each other to discuss any and all issues that might come to mind? For example, can you imagine confronting your child on a lie and having the child freely and without hesitation admit to the offense? How about engaging your child in a discussion surrounding body development, puberty, or sex without experiencing discomfort or anxiety? Imagine your child approaching you to explore the pros and cons of experimenting with drugs, whether or not to engage in sexual activities, or difficulties he or she may be having at school or with peers. Unfortunately, parent-child relationships with these characteristics are the exception rather than the norm.

From my experience, it seems as if the vast majority of children learn about subjects such as sex, sexuality, body development, body image, the consequences of drug and alcohol abuse, complex relational issues, ethics, and spirituality on their own and *from sources other than their parents*. When this trend is studied, we discover that children seek outside sources for guidance and information when parents fail to create an environment that is consistently emotionally safe. This is unfortunate because it represents a missed opportunity for parents to contribute to their children's lives in a very healthy and helpful manner. Children are not adverse to discussing important issues with their parents but are more often than not pushed away by the parents. This is contrary to what many parents choose to believe. Some parents will assert that factors such as peer influences or individual personality characteristics draw the child away from the parent-child relationship – somehow weakening or diminishing the parent's role in educating or guiding their children. To this I respond by stating that children are by no means predisposed to seek information and guidance outside of the family system. In fact, the exact opposite is true. Children are born with a natural loyalty to their parents. They are programmed to understand their parents as the primary educators for living. Children, if given the opportunity, will seek information and guidance from their parents throughout life unless somewhere along the way they learn – from their parents – to do otherwise.

Early in life children learn through very subtle signals and messages that a parent is either an approachable and accessible source of information and guidance or that the parent should not be approached and is inaccessible. Many of the Parenting Assumptions found throughout this text offer excellent examples of parental messages and signals that leave the child feeling as if his or her parents are approachable (safe) or inaccessible (less safe). When a child is faced with a quandary, such as having a need for information, answers, and guidance, but experiences the parent as emotionally inaccessible, he or she will naturally seek input from resources outside of the parent-child relationship. Unfortunately, the source of information and guidance ultimately found by the child may not have that child's better interests in mind.

Let's take a moment to summarize accessibility. When a child somehow feels prohibited or hindered from opening a discussion with his or her parents on any subject, or if the child feels as if he or she must guard or withhold thoughts, beliefs, or actions from the parents, we can say that accessibility is lacking in the parent-child relationship. Furthermore, when a parent feels nervous about or hesitant to open a discussion on any subject with the child, we can again say that accessibility is lacking. This is an unfortunate and unnecessary condition whenever it exists. This condition will ultimately have a less healthy impact on the parent-child relationship and the child's ability to relate to others in a healthy and open manner in his or her future. Parenting Assumptions 23 through 36 present many examples of different aspects of safety. Accessibility is a crucial element to each example, concept, and scenario presented. As you review these Assumptions ask yourself this, *"Do the parents and children discussed in these Assumptions portray relationships whereby each feels safe to approach the other with near equal ease?"* Also, as you explore this most important aspect of *Systemic Parenting,* try to hypothesize what might be getting in the way of accessibility in your parent-child relationship.

20. "Engaging" is when life perspectives are mutually considered.

Parenting Assumption 19 states that accessibility is when both parent and child *can* approach each other with near equal ease. Engaging is when they *do*. An accessible relationship is one in which barriers that might prohibit an open and honest exchange of information between parent and child have been identified and eliminated. The idea of accessibility is a core component to safety. However, a parent that is accessible may not necessarily be engaging. Engaging is when the parent communicates an interest in and takes the initiative to explore the child's perspective. Why is this important? During the course of any given day, a younger child experiences many aspects of living for the very first time. This includes exposure to new vocabulary and its usage, new visual sights, new challenges, and new problems. How these experiences are processed and interpreted by the child is very important to establishing the cognitive and reasoning skills that will be utilized throughout life. The parent who communicates an interest in and takes the initiative to explore the child's experiences and perspective is reinforcing *wonder, exploration,* and *growth.* Basically, the parent is encouraging the child to use his or her mind in new ways. The parent is also providing important validation for the child by communicating that he or she is special and *worthy* of attention. Finally, the parent is opening the door to patterns of accessibility. That is, a pattern of comfortable parent-child interactions is being established. A parent may communicate interest in and take the initiative to explore a young child's perspective in may ways. For example, the parent may:

- **Listen to what the child has to say even if it is confusing or makes little sense.**

- **Show considerable enthusiasm:**   *Wow! That's neat!*

- **Ask the child for input:**   *What's that!?*
          Tell me about that.
          What do you think?
          How do you feel about that?

Initially, parents promoting engagement must continually solicit the life perspective of the child. They must always look for opportunities to listen, show enthusiasm, and solicit input from the child. Through this process, the child learns that the parent is accessible, wanting to consider his or her perspective, and emotionally safe. Obviously, this is an unbalanced relationship as the younger child is, for the most part, dependant upon the parent and lacks the developmental capabilities to understand the parent's perspective beyond a rudimentary level. However, the child who consistently experiences the parent as accessible and engaging will eventually reverse this skewed pattern of interaction by eventually soliciting the perspective of the parent. For example, it would not be uncommon for a child who has parents that are accessible and engaging to openly ask questions such as:

* *How are boys and girls different?*
* *Why do so many adults get nervous when the topic of sex comes up?*
* *A lot of my friends are smoking marijuana. I'm struggling with what to do. What do you think?*

The process of developing an engaging relationship is best started early in a child's life, however, parents will experience similar results with children of all ages. I have worked with many parents of adult children who, after focusing on communicating accessibility and making attempts to engage their children, saw the quality of their relationship improve dramatically.

As with accessibility, engagement is another critical element to each example, concept, and scenario presented in Parenting Assumptions 23 through 36. As you review these Assumptions, ask yourself this, "*Do the parents and children discussed in these Assumptions communicate an interest in and take the initiative to explore the other's perspective? Are they engaging?*" Also, as you explore this most important aspect of *Systemic Parenting*, try to hypothesize what factors might be getting in the way of engagement in your parent-child relationship.

21. "Entrapping" is when the parent portrays accessibility yet is unprepared or unable to be consistent in this manner.

Parenting Assumption 20 states that engaging is when life perspectives are mutually considered. The parent invites engagement by communicating an interest in and taking the initiative to explore the child's experiences and perspective. When the child is young, his or her thought processes and reasoning skills are relatively simple. The parent will find communicating an interest in and taking the initiative to explore the child's experiences and perspective a relatively easy task. However, as the child matures, so will the level of sophistication of his or her thought processes. At some point in time, the child *will* conceive and present beliefs or ideas that greatly differ from, or even offend, beliefs and ideas held by the parent. This is most often recognized during adolescence, but typically can be observed much earlier. This is a very common occurrence in parent-child relationships that are both accessible and engaging – the child has both the freedom and emotional safety in which to express and explore a wide variety of developing concepts and views. Unfortunately, when a parent is faced with this situation, he or she may sacrifice safety in an attempt to embed beliefs that are held dear – beliefs that the parent would like to see perpetuated through his or her children. This may be experienced as entrapping to the child, thwarting emotional safety and healthy cognitive development. For example, imagine a scenario in which a parent and child are watching the evening news together. A story is presented that depicts considerable human suffering, such as a massive flood or an airline disaster. Following the story the child questions the existence of God or any higher power. The parent responds in a manner that leaves the child feeling attacked, put down, and shut out. For example, the parent might make a comment such as, *"Your father and I believe in God, so should you."* Or , *"You don't know what you're talking about. You're way out of line."* Essentially, the parent is demonstrating, through his or her response, that theirs is not a completely accessible relationship. The child who experiences this over and over will unlikely approach the parents on other important issues and will seek input and guidance outside of this relationship. I've seen this time and time again in my practice of family therapy. Parents will encourage their children to come to them with anything, and then are unprepared when a child confronts them with something they do not like or want to hear. It's tough being a parent. Especially when your strongly held beliefs are challenged by your own children. In these instances, the parent is presented with a great opportunity to promote growth and safety. Let's return to the scenario of a child questioning or denying the existence of God or a higher power. This belief may differ from beliefs held by the parent. Rather than compromising safety in the relationship with a either a concrete or nebulous response, imagine how the child might respond to the following:

Child: *When I see things like that on the news I find it hard to believe there's a God. If there's a God, things like that would never happen!*

Parent: (Rather than responding with something like *"You don't know what you're talking about. You're way out of line"*) *Wow, that's an interesting position. That's a lot different than what your mother and I believe. Help me understand where you're coming from. Let's talk about it.*

In this response the child is being engaged and dialogue on an important issue is safely opened. The child's cognitive and communication skills are also being stimulated, exercised and challenged. This occurred without safety in the parent-child relationship being compromised in any way. The child is more likely, versus less likely, to approach the parent when facing struggles of conscience encountered down the road. Issues that parents and children will likely disagree on from time to time may include religion, politics, sexual orientation, sports, views regarding drugs and alcohol, dress, and race relations. The parent who prepares in advance by accepting that opposing views *will* emerge from their children, and then makes every attempt to avoid entrapment, is significantly more likely to have a long and emotionally safe relationship with their children. *Entrapping is when the parent portrays accessibility yet is unprepared or unable to be consistent in this manner.*

22. A "constricted" parent limits the child's exposure to the parent's emotional self. This is a great misfortune.

This Assumption covers perhaps one of the most important aspects of parenting – that of *emotional processing*. This is discussed and presented in many forms and from many angles throughout this book. [12] How one understands and processes emotions is a skill that is most often learned directly from the parents – **through the child's exposure to the parent's emotional self.** Unfortunately, many parents seem to believe that they must be "in control of their emotions." More often than not, "in control of one's emotions" turns out to be synonymous with "suppress and hide one's emotions." I have worked with many parents who embraced a belief that showing or discussing their own emotions in the presence of their children is indicative of weakness, inappropriate, or just too uncomfortable. I consider these to be constricted parents.

A constricted parent limits the child's exposure to the broad spectrum of emotional possibilities. Constricted parents often seem to portray themselves as "in control" and "even keeled." Unfortunately, by maintaining this posture, the parent is placing a serious burden and handicap squarely on the shoulders of the child. I see this in families where anger and sometimes joy are of the few emotions ever expressed. Why is this a handicap? Well, children are dependant upon the parents to pass along the basic tools they will need to excel in life. These tools include the basics of language, self-care, many cognitive and problems solving skills, and a wide spectrum of social skills.

Emotions are crucial components of, and intimately connected to, the development of these basic tools for living. Appendix B contains a list of over 400 emotions one is capable of experiencing. Many of these words – these emotions – are absent from our children's language and understanding. Yet, children certainly experience a great number of them as they interact with others and their environment. Unfortunately, when a child experiences an emotion without having access to the language and understanding of the emotion, his or her ability to formulate sophisticated, complete, and complex thoughts will be severely limited. This is a pretty startling statement. Hopefully, bold statements such as this will help drive home the fact that intellectual and emotional processes and development are intimately connected and intertwined. They should not be separated. Each is dependant upon the other to form a complete and balanced individual. How is this related to Safety? Well, if a parent merely focuses on promoting intellectual development and ignores the emotional aspects of living, the child will be less prepared to deal with many of life's challenges. As such, the child, future adult, will feel vulnerable and ill-prepared when facing the challenging and difficult aspects of living and relationships we all encounter. Many healthy and helpful solutions for difficult situations will feel foreign, emotionally unsafe, and thus unlikely pursued.

Let's look at a brief example to help clarify this point. Suppose I discover that a colleague is talking about me behind my back. This person's actions appear to be a deliberate attempt to undermine my work and reputation. After hearing this news I will certainly experience a number of uncomfortable emotions. I could probably identify 15 to 20 individual emotions from Appendix B that would accurately describe what I might feel after learning of my colleague's actions.

This list would likely include emotions such as *alarmed, annoyed, anxious, appalled, concerned, criticized, deceived, displeased, distressed, enraged, inflamed, irate, irritated, offended, perplexed, provoked, puzzled, regretful, shocked, surprised,* and *suspicious*. Being armed with an understanding of the emotional impact and vocabulary leaves me in a position to deal with this problem in a very healthy and productive manner. I might approach my colleague and ask him if he has a few minutes to discuss an important issue. The conversation would be simple. I would let my colleague know what I heard and how it left *me* feeling. I would not attack or blame this colleague but rather ask him for *his* perspective. The key element here is to let him know how I had been impacted by his actions rather than to attack him. I would identify a few of the emotions listed above and use them in my conversation. For example, I might say something similar to, *"When I heard the news about what you said, it left me feeling puzzled, criticized, provoked, and very concerned. I'm interested in hearing your perspective. Help me understand what's going on here."* By identifying and working with the emotional components of this situation, I have taken the higher ground and have opened the door to dealing with this problem in a manner that will minimize less healthy and less helpful consequences.

Directly approaching someone to resolve conflict may not always be an easy process, however, it is a very powerful and effective tool. There is a chance that my colleague would be so intimidated by my approach that he might just shut down or break off the conversation. It is more likely that he would feel safer to communicate any differences of opinion he may have directly with me rather than behind my back. More often than not, people will attempt to resolve similar situations by taking a more aggressive approach. For instance, it would be very easy to respond to my colleague with: *"What is going on here? Why would you talk behind my back this way? Why would you attack me this way?"* I think it would also be very easy to just ignore or avoid future interactions with this colleague or to reciprocate by talking behind his back. Unfortunately, these responses are usually the first choice in situations such as this. I say "unfortunately" because these responses will always create more problems than they cure or they will leave everybody involved feeling emotionally drained.[13]

Why do we rely upon less helpful solutions to resolve difficult problems? I believe it boils down to Safety. My initial response – the one that incorporated emotional elements – tends to leave many people feeling uncomfortable, vulnerable, nervous, unsafe, or weak. This is usually consistent with an earlier theme in one's family – that one *must be in control of their emotions*. Again, this is usually synonymous with *suppress and hide one's emotions. They're not to be discussed.* If a person is rarely exposed to emotional process it will feel foreign and uncomfortable when they are called upon to resolve a problem or to interact with another in this manner.

A parent who continuously exposes the child to the broad spectrum of emotional possibilities through exposure to the parent's emotional self is preparing the child for later interactions that are direct, forthright, and absent of many unhealthy characteristics. These healthy and helpful interactions will be less likely experienced as uncomfortable, emotionally unsafe, or leaving one vulnerable. Approaching a co-worker later in life who is talking behind your back or attempting to undermine your work will be an easy task. Disagreements with family and friends tend to be resolved very quickly and in a very healthy manner when one is skilled in emotional processing. A child who has been exposed to a parent's emotional self from an early age will have a tremendous advantage later in life. In other words, laugh, cry, be sad, jovial, and embarrassed around your kids. But most importantly, talk about these emotions and expect your children to do the same. *A "constricted" parent limits the child's exposure to the parent's emotional self. This is a great misfortune.*

23. When parents become accustomed to the just role of parent they will certainly administer rewards and punishments in an enlightened manner. This is but one measure that facilitates safety.

This Assumption speaks of the *just role of parent*. To understand this concept I believe we must be willing to explore the topic of intimacy, as these subjects – *intimacy* and *just role of parent* – are closely related. I am amazed at the many misconceptions that surround the concept of intimacy. This is unfortunate, as intimacy is a crucial component to most, if not all, of our relationships. In fact, I believe that the vast majority of all the marital, family and parenting problems raised in my office are in some way related to struggles with intimacy. I also believe that nearly **all** marital and family successes – including parenting successes – can be attributed to a greater understanding of intimacy. To help us better grasp the broad topic of intimacy we, should look at some all–too–common misconceptions.

I often ask people to give me their definition of intimacy. A majority of their responses focus on some kind of physical (hugs, massage, etc.) or sexual interaction. These responses also tend to be limited to *significant other* relationships such as husbands and wives, boyfriends and girlfriends, and lovers. Rarely do people questioned in my informal polls speak of intimacy in terms of parent-child relationships, work/business relationships, same or different sex friendships, or non-sexual familial relationships. I also find that many people believe intimacy is relatively static – not moving or progressing; at rest; stationary. That is, they believe intimacy is either present or absent in a relationship and that the degree of intimacy in a relationship remains constant over time; therefore believing that varying degrees of intimacy do not exist. It is my assumption that intimacy is never static but rather very dynamic – relating to or tending toward change. **We are always moving toward or moving away from having greater intimacy in *all* of our relationships.**

Let's put some common misconceptions about intimacy to rest. We can begin this process by considering some complaints often encountered by therapists. For example, a parent may question the therapist, *"How did I become so distant from my children?"* Some parents will wonder *"Why are my children so difficult to manage?"* A couple considering separation or divorce will often report that *"Intimacy in our relationship seemed to slip away – gradually, over time."* These couples often wonder *"How did this happen?"* I believe there is a common denominator between parents and couples asking these or similar questions. Both likely have an incomplete or limited understanding of intimacy in their relationships. There are literally hundreds of definitions of intimacy. I usually like to keep things relatively simple and would like nothing more than to select and present a simple definition of intimacy. However, in regard to intimacy I cannot do this. Sorry. I'm going to complicate things quite a bit by limiting discussion of intimacy to my very complex definition. At first this definition may appear lengthy and overwhelming. Yet, as we progress I believe you will appreciate its complexity and depth.

Intimacy

Intimacy results from having the **freedom** and **tools** to honestly consider and express your own, *while simultaneously considering another's*, experiences, emotions, fears, vulnerabilities, strengths, weaknesses, needs, wants, fantasies, personal history, goals, and life-cycle position.

Freedom → Freedom requires one to ask, consider, and address several questions:

• Can I create emotional safety, and do I feel emotionally safe, in this relationship?
• Can I be non-judgmental and do I experience the other person as non-judgmental?
• Will my perspective (even if different from the other person's) be considered?
• Am I prepared to consider the other person's perspective even if it differs from my own?

Tools → The use of the word *tools* can be clarified through consideration of, and action in furtherance of, these questions:

• Do I possess the vocabulary to express my emotions?
• Am I skilled in pairing words for emotions to the emotions I am actually experiencing?
• Are these pairings congruent to the situation?**
• Does the other person in my relationship possess the same skills?
• Am I aware of my emotions, fears, vulnerabilities, strengths, weaknesses, needs, wants, fantasies, history and life-cycle position? Am I willing to explore these?
• Is the other person in my relationship willing/able to do the same?

(Note: Sex is not mentioned in this definition – at least not directly. Rather, the topic of sex is found throughout the definition. Consider for one moment the vast number of topics that make up one's needs, wants, fantasies, emotions, fears, vulnerabilities, strengths, etc. Sex, in some form, would be included in each of these areas.)

** *Congruent to the situation* – Are the emotions that I'm experiencing true to what is going on around me. For example, an individual who views a video tape of a person being violently attacked and responds with feelings of joy or excitement is responding with emotions that are incongruent to the situation. A parent who responds to a frightened child's emotions with anger is experiencing emotions incongruent to the situation.

I will often ask couples who are struggling with their relationship to read this definition out loud. I will then ask the couple if they would want a relationship where each is freely and honestly able to express their own, while considering the other's experiences, emotions, fears, vulnerabilities, strengths, weaknesses, needs, wants, fantasies, person history, goals and life-cycle position. Rarely does a couple respond with "no." In fact, most couples enthusiastically state this is exactly what they want from their relationship, yet somehow feel impeded from attaining. My job as a therapist is to help these couples determine what might be inhibiting the emergence of greater intimacy. This usually requires us to focus on establishing greater *freedom* in the relationship while simultaneously developing access to the necessary *tools* of intimacy. I must also stress that intimacy is a dynamic concept. We are always moving **toward** or moving **away** from having greater intimacy in our relationships. Intimacy never stands still.

Let's take a look at an analogy between intimacy and a marble resting on a large pane of glass to help clarify this concept. In this analogy the marble's position on the glass pane represents the level of intimacy that exists between persons. The closer the marble is to the center of the glass pane the greater the degree of intimacy. The closer the marble is to the outer edge of the glass the lesser the degree of intimacy. When two persons collectively pick up the pane of glass, by the corners, they enter into a relationship. The marble will certainly begin to move about as it is difficult for two persons to hold the glass completely steady. The marble rarely remains still for an extended period of time. Its course is determined by the input of one or both persons in this relationship. The marble will either move toward the edge of the glass pane – moving away from greater intimacy – or toward and around the center of the pane – moving toward greater intimacy.

Couples struggling in their relationship tend to gravitate away from having the *freedom* and *tools* to honestly express their own, while considering the other's, experiences, emotions, fears, vulnerabilities, strengths, weaknesses, needs, wants, fantasies, personal history, goals, and life-cycle position rather than closer to the same. By fostering *freedom* to move toward greater intimacy and always expanding one's *tools*, the couple will find this definition to be less foreign in their relationship and greater intimacy likely attainable. In our analogy this is equivalent to learning how to gently lift or lower the corners of the glass pane in order to maintain the marble in or near the center. They are working toward greater intimacy in their relationship. When both members of a couple find themselves working toward greater intimacy rather than away from greater intimacy, few challenges relating to their family and relationship will be overwhelming. Each person's needs are more likely to be identified, communicated, considered, and met.

If both persons in a relationship work toward greater intimacy, the couple will most certainly thrive. However, in many relationships both persons do not work equally to increase intimacy – only one person makes an attempt to keep the marble in or near the center of the glass pane. In these situations, it is important to keep in mind that one person alone striving to increase intimacy can have a significant influence. Keeping the marble in the center of the glass will require greater effort from the person working to increase intimacy. Quite often, a single person's efforts to appropriately enhance intimacy will not be in vein. His or her actions will often result in the other person eventually jumping on board. It is very uncomfortable to be in a relationship with a person working hard to increase emotional intimacy when the other is not. The person struggling with intimacy will likely acquire skills through close association with the other. It's hard to not provide input that keeps the marble in the center of the glass when interacting with somebody who has the tools associated with intimacy. On the other hand, if one person in a relationship is absolutely determined to continuously undermine development of intimacy, little can be done.[14] The person attempting to undermine intimacy when facing a person skilled at enhancing intimacy will likely abandon the relationship – drop the pane of glass and walk away.

This brings us back to the concept of the *just role of the parent*. The parent-child relationship is very similar to the couple relationship with respect to intimacy. Imagine the child and parent holding a pane of glass. The parent is initially responsible for making adjustments that will keep the marble in or near the center. The parent expresses his or her own, while simultaneously considering the child's, experiences, emotions, fears, vulnerabilities, strengths, weaknesses, needs, wants, fantasies, personal history, goals, and life-cycle position. The parent ensures an environment exists where there is *freedom* for the child to explore issues of intimacy while having handy access to the *tools* of intimacy. Eventually, the child begins to offer input that is in harmony with the parent's efforts. The quality and depth of the child's input is determined directly by the parent's understanding of *freedom* and willingness to utilize the *tools*. Through this process, the child learns from his or her parents how to relate to other human beings in a healthy, intimate manner. When I ask parents if they would like their son or daughter to have the skills and ability to honestly express their own, while still considering another's experiences, emotions, fears, vulnerabilities, strengths, weaknesses, needs, wants, fantasies, personal history, goals, and life-cycle position, rarely do I receive a negative response. As the child's ability to relate to his or her parents in a more intimate manner develops, few barriers between parent and child will emerge. This is a parental role, a responsibility, that I consider *the just role of the parent.*

Parent-child relationships that move toward greater intimacy will feel emotionally safe. Rewards and punishments that occur in these *safe* relationships will assume a vastly different meaning from those in *unsafe* relationships. Imagine the following scenarios. The first represents a parent-child interaction that is moving away from greater intimacy. The second represents a relationship that is moving toward greater intimacy. Take a few moments to consider how you might administer rewards and punishments if you were the parent in each scenario.

Scenario 1

Parents to teenage daughter arriving home one hour after her curfew: *You are an hour late. What do you have to say for yourself?*

Daughter (defensively): *My ride fell through. I had to wait around until somebody else decided to leave. I told them I had to get home but nobody seemed to care.*

Parents: *Why didn't you call?*

Daughter: *I didn't think to.*

Parents (feeling deceived and wondering *"are we getting the complete story?"*): *I think you will be spending next weekend grounded.*

Scenario 2:

Parents to teenage daughter arriving home one hour after her curfew: *You are an hour late. I think this is something we should talk about.*

Teenage daughter to parents upon arriving home one hour after her curfew: *Yeah, can we talk?*

Parents: *What happened?*

Daughter: *I was at [a friend's] house. I arranged to get a ride home before I got there but it fell through. I told everybody I had to get home before curfew but nobody seemed to care. I thought I worked this out but everything seemed to go wrong. I really feel bad about the whole situation.*

Parents: *Why didn't you call us?*

Daughter: *Well..... I was working pretty hard begging for rides. I would have felt really uncomfortable calling you guys. I wanted to take care of things myself. I was also pretty angry with myself for trusting somebody I thought I could trust. I don't think I would have been too pleasant on the phone. I tried to be responsible by planning ahead. I feel like I messed up and wanted to try to work it out for myself.*

Parents: *We were really concerned. When you're late and we don't hear from you all kinds of things go through our minds. We're pretty confident with your ability to take care of yourself but as parents it's our job to worry. We're not ready to turn off that worry switch quite yet. We're really uncomfortable with this whole situation. What do you think we should do about this?*

Let's take a look at how these brief scenarios differ with respect to intimacy. Consider the following questions:
• In which scenario did the parents and daughter better express their own, and consider the other's experiences, emotions, fears, vulnerabilities, strengths, weaknesses, needs, wants, fantasies, personal history, goals, and life-cycle position?

- In which scenario did the parents and daughter appear to be more emotionally safe when interacting with each other?

- In which scenario were the tools of intimacy better employed (i.e. in which scenario did the parents and daughter use more words to express their emotions? Were these words/emotions congruent to the situation? In which scenario were parents and daughter more aware of their emotions, fears, vulnerabilities, strengths, weaknesses, fantasies, history, and life cycle position?)?

- Which scenario is likely to end with all persons feeling closer and which is likely to end with all persons feeling slightly more distant from each other?

- How will parental punishments likely differ in each scenario?

Almost every interaction a parent has with his or her child should in some way guide that child toward a greater understanding of intimacy. This is a basic tenant of the *just role of parent*. The scenarios above are vastly different. Some parents will state that the second scenario is unrealistic and unlikely to occur. I beg to differ. Safe and intimate interactions can be commonplace between parent and child. I see them all the time in my office. Some parents report their child *"just won't respond as the teenager did in the second scenario."* I believe these parents would welcome an intimate and safe relationship with their child. However, they seem to place too much responsibility on the child in determining the course of the relationship. That is, the child must first experience the parent as consistently "safe" over a period of time before he or she will learn to respond in kind. Parents who do not believe the second scenario is realistic may make an occasional attempt to establish *freedom* in the relationship and, more than likely, inconsistently use some of the *tools* associated with increased intimacy. Yet, when these efforts fail to be consistent and on-going, the parent's self-fulfilling prophesy – that interactions such as these found in the second scenario are unlikely to occur – will be realized.

Intimacy will emerge in the parent-child relationship only after the child experiences the *freedom* and *tools* as established by the parents. This *freedom* and the associated *tools* must be experienced consistently and over a significant period of time. Again, imagine the parent and child holding that pane of glass. The child, by virtue of limited life experiences, will have difficulty providing input that will direct the marble closer to the center of the glass. The parent must carry the load until the child becomes comfortable with being in an intimate relationship and contributing to the relationship with greater intimacy. The *just role of parent* is a phrase that describes a process whereby the parent stands back and considers his or her overall role as parent. Does the parent see his or her role to help the child develop skills that will assist that child thrive in his or her living and relationships? Or, is the parent's role merely to get by from day to day? By understanding and incorporating the concept of intimacy as defined under this Assumption, the parent will have a valuable tool to help the child thrive in all aspects of living.

I previously mentioned some common complaints made by couples – *A couple considering separation or divorce will often report that "intimacy in our relationship seemed to slip away – gradually, over time." These couples often wonder, "How did this happen?"* Complaints such as these are important when discussing the *just role of parent* and intimacy between parent and child for several reasons. First and foremost, if the adult struggles with intimacy in adult-to-adult relationships, he or she will likely feel limited in the parent-child relationship. Also, if the parent struggles with intimacy in adult-to-adult relationships, he or she probably did not experience an intimate relationship with his or her own parents. This cycle will continue to be passed from generation to generation until the process is recognized, and someone decides to intervene. When parents arrive in my office with marital/relationship complaints, I will also, more often than not, find problems with intimacy between parent and child. Assisting the parents realize intimacy in their relationship will certainly bring the parents closer to realizing the importance of and having the tools to act upon their *just role of parent*.

24. Children act out for a variety of reasons. The artful parent will distinguish between behaviors attributed to trial and error (growth) and the child's response to unnatural, unjust, and/or incongruent situations. Discerning between the former and latter is paramount for safety.

I would like to regress to my early childhood for a few moments to expand this Parenting Assumption. I recall an event that occurred when I was about five or six years-old. Although this event occurred over 35 years ago, it remains vividly embedded in my memory. In retrospect it was not a terribly severe incident. However, at the time I thought it particularly traumatizing. When I was a child there was a candy product called Pixy Sticks. I have no idea if they are still produced, however, for those who are not familiar with the Pixy Stick, it was a paper straw filled with fruit flavored sugar and sealed at both ends. You would open one end and pour the contents into your mouth. I recall being very fond of Pixy Sticks. I also recall being very fond of Coca–Cola at that age. Thirty years ago, Coke was bottled in long neck, returnable glass bottles. One day I was exploring a room in our house that had been freshly painted by my parents. The room was empty of its contents and the walls were a brilliant white. I was drawn to the room by the smell of fresh paint and mesmerized by the clean white walls. I was probably very content, as I had a Coca–Cola in one hand and a purplish Pixy Stick in the other – two favorite foodstuffs for most six year-olds at that time. While staring at the white walls I recall having a brilliant revelation – *"Pixy Sticks and Coca-Cola, both are great by themselves. Wouldn't they be better together?"* I was particularly proud of this thought and was sure the universe would somehow be complete as soon as I introduced the sugar contents of the Pixy Stick into the bottle of Coca–Cola. Well, this six year-old was unprepared for the universal reality of these actions. The purple sugar stuff immediately reacted with the carbonated cola unleashing a cascading chain of events. The cola reacted violently to the Pixy Stick's contents and began erupting. I overcame my initial surprise and lept into action. The eruption had to be contained. The only way to do this was to place my six year-old thumb into the bottle. Again, I underestimated the power of the reaction unleashed. My thumb was an inadequate cork. The purplish brew was now spraying the freshly painted walls in a very efficient manner thanks to the nozzle created by my thumb. This is where panic set in. It's hard to remember exactly what I did or why I did it, but to an outsider the whole situation probably would have looked pretty chaotic. While still attempting to contain the reaction with my thumb, I began flailing about the room in total panic. All rationality had left my mind. Purple colored soda was now everywhere – dripping from the ceiling, traveling down the walls in long purple streaks and covering the door, window, and closet. The last thing I recall was standing in the middle of this now redecorated room, a nearly empty Coke bottle in my hands, and looking about. I felt as if my world had just crumbled. I was overwhelmed by a rush of uncomfortable emotions and just started to cry.

I do not recall exactly how my parents reacted when they saw the damage. However, the situation itself raises many questions about safety and the parents' role in creating an emotionally safe environment for the child to grow and develop. My recollection of the event leads me to believe my actions were not malicious nor an intentional act to destroy the room. The damage was an unfortunate by-product of trying something new – mixing my favorite candy with my favorite soft drink. Children learn a great deal through trial and error. Unfortunately, at times this can be quite distressful to parents. How does a parent protect their child and property through this early trial and error learning process? How does the parent recognize and support trial and error learning while preventing potentially destructive behaviors such as playing with fire?[15] Finally, how does a parent discern trial and error learning from behaviors that are stimulated by unnatural, unjust, or incongruent situations. For example, the situation would have been vastly different had I walked into the freshly painted room, placed my thumb into the Coca-Cola bottle, and started to shake the bottle so as to intentionally spray the freshly painted walls. This behavior and the resulting damage would be the result of factors other than trial and error.

I wish I could recall my parent's reaction upon entering the room. I wonder what their initial thoughts were? Were they concerned with my emotions or intent? Were they interested in whether I learned anything from the experience itself? Was their focus merely on the damage? I believe I was guilt ridden and emotionally devastated prior to my parents entering the room. Would a scolding or spanking at that moment have been helpful? I wonder what my immediate emotional needs were after all the dust settled? What would have made the situation safe for me? What parental response would have prevented emotional safety from emerging in our relationship? Take a few moments to imagine your reaction upon entering the room.

There are an infinite number of possible reactions to this situation. Some would be more helpful while others would be significantly less helpful. This Parenting Assumption calls upon the parent to be open to the child's motive. In the example above, my motives were to simply improve the taste of my Coca-Cola. However, this might be difficult for a parent entering the room to recognize for several reasons. I was likely overwhelmed with emotions and limited in my ability to articulate my thoughts and feelings very well by virtue of my age and limited life experiences. My parents were probably experiencing their own rush of uncomfortable emotions. These emotions would certainly influence their reactions.

Let's take a look at one way my parents could have made this situation safe. Upon entering the room they might have been surprised, somewhat confused, very concerned, distressed, displeased, and overwhelmed. In situations such as this, the parent would experience these uncomfortable emotions all at once. This emotional rush may compel the parent to react with a secondary emotional reactions such as anger. For example, the parent might find him/herself responding in a way similar to one of the following:

- *What the hell happened here!?*

- *What did you do in here?*

- *The room, it's ruined, you destroyed the room!*

Let's assume my actions were not malicious but merely trial and error gone awry. My initial expectations were that everything was going to work out well after I mixed the pixy stick with the cola. When the cola erupted, I was caught off guard and found myself immediately confused – *"What's happening here?"* When the bottle started to spray cola all over the room feelings of panic and being overwhelmed were added to my confusion – *"Why is this happening?"* and *"Why can't I stop it?"* When the parents enter the picture and respond with anger or aggression, the already confused, anxious, and overwhelmed six year-old will only be further confused and anxious. Little benefit will come of this. Rather than expressing this rush of emotions through anger, the parents might pursue a more helpful course by identifying and acknowledging the emotions (both the parent's and child's). For example:

Parent to Son (parent still not aware of exactly what happened in the room but seeing the aftermath and the son crying): *Oh my gosh, are you OK?* [child appears to be physically OK] *What a mess. This must be pretty scary for you.*

Son: (Continues to cry)

Parent: *I'm not quite sure what happened in here. However, I'm sure if we work together we can figure it out. What do you think?*

Son: (Nods yes)

Parent: *I know you might feel pretty bad right now. You also look like you might be pretty scared, nervous, and embarrassed by all*

this. It's OK to feel that way. I know I'm a little confused and very concerned right now. Can you help me understand what happened?
Son: *I don't know.*
Parent: *Let's start from the beginning. . . .*

The parent initially responded by trying to acknowledge emotions the child might be experiencing. This required the parent to use his or her empathy skills. The parent attempts to briefly put him/herself in the son's shoes by trying to understand the son's emotions, his perspective, and his experience. The parent also verbalized emotions that he or she was experiencing. Identifying and acknowledging emotions supports safety in several ways. By focusing on the emotional experience, emphasis is briefly taken off the troubling event. This comes as a great relief for the child. It also allows the parent to slow down the interactive process between parent and child. Less helpful, impulsive and angry reactions are minimized or eliminated altogether. In the example, the parent also sought to understand the child's perspective. The parent will find this helpful even if he or she witnessed the entire event.

The child who feels as if his or her perspective is important and taken into consideration by the parent, will experience an immense sense of safety. The child will not state that he *"made a trial and error mistake"* and that he *"learned never to do that again."* However, the child will come pretty close to this in an age appropriate manner if the parent is open to considering and works hard to solicit the child's perspective. From here, both parent and child will benefit by including the child in evaluating the situation and trying to determine how to avoid similar situations in the future. For example:

Parent: *I don't think I would want this to happen again. How about you?*
Son: *No way.*
Parent: *How do you think we can keep this from happening again?*
Son: *Don't pour my Pixy Stick into my Coke.*
Parent: *That's a really good idea. I would be real careful about pouring anything together without checking with your mom or me first. What else can you do?*
Son: *Well . . . . Don't put my thumb in the bottle. That seemed make it worse.*
Parent: *That sounds like a pretty good idea.*

Finally, the parent can enforce some *just* consequences to help reinforce the severity of the situation. It is important that these consequences do not overshadow the powerful emotions the child already experienced. Focusing on the child's own emotions is a far more effective way to redirect behaviors or to promote self-evaluation than any parental punishment. The child feels pretty rotten already. Identifying and acknowledging these feelings will have a powerful impact on the child, more so than spankings, time outs, and so on. In this case, the parent might enforce consequences in the following way:

Parent: *I think this has been pretty scary for you and that you might feel badly about the damage in here. I also think it would be a good idea if you helped clean up the mess. Do you think you should help us clean up?*
Son: *Uh huh.*
Parent: *Alright. Why don't you get some of the old towels out of that closet and we'll get to work.*

The examples above follow a specific pattern.

Create Safety
↓
Promote Insight
↓
Enforce Just Consequences
↓
Anticipate Greater Parent-Child Intimacy and Growth

Safety was initially created by identifying and processing the emotions. Insight was promoted by engaging the child in discussing ways to keep the incident from happening again. Finally, *just* consequences were enforced that did not overshadow the emotional reaction to the event. This pattern of reacting to behaviors attributed to trial and error will move the parent and child closer together with respect to intimacy and trust. In addition, the child will grow from an unfortunate incident, rather than becoming frightened of trial and error learning and intimidated and distanced by an angry parent.

This Parenting Assumption states that *children act out for a variety of reasons. The artful parent will distinguish between behaviors attributed to trial and error and the child's response to unnatural, unjust, and/or incongruent situations. Discerning between the former and latter is paramount for safety.* If the child's behavior is motivated by *unnatural, unjust, and/or incongruent situations,* the parent may approach the issues troubling the family by promoting increased emotional safety. However, these issues will likely require significantly more attention. For this, the parent should refer to other Parenting Assumptions in addition to those outlined in the Safety chapter. For example, what if I walked into the freshly painted room, placed my thumb in the Coca-Cola bottle and intentionally shook it so as to spray the walls? Most six year-olds will not initiate such malicious acts. Other factors are usually at work in these cases. I encounter similar situations almost daily in my office. Many are very complex and require professional attention. These situations are usually the result of *severe* unnatural, unjust, and incongruent situations and conditions in the family, such as such as severe conflict, neglect, physical abuse, sexual abuse, addictions, and so on. The Parenting Assumptions found throughout this book present parents with many helpful tools to address these unnatural, unjust, and incongruent situations, whether they be relatively minor or quite severe.

25. Those skilled in parenting realize the child is vulnerable in nearly every respect. The artful parent will support these vulnerabilities in a manner which leaves the child self-assured and safe.

I attended a large picnic some time ago. There were probably 50 to 60 people enjoying each other's company and the beautiful spring weather. I took my dog, an Austrian Shepherd, along for the day. He's a very friendly animal and often seems compelled to greet as many people as possible. He is particularly drawn to children and will often seek them out. I watched as he engaged a young girl in play. She was probably 4 years-old and both child and dog appeared to be at ease and very comfortable with each other. They were at play for several minutes when, without notice, a small Chihuahua darted from the parking lot and ran toward the girl. The Chihuahua could not have weighed more than a couple of pounds and stood no more than 8 inches tall, yet this dog possessed a most horrific growl. Needless to say, the young girl was terrified and immediately ran to her father crying with the little dog in hot pursuit. She jumped into his arms and out of harm's way.

I watched the father's reaction as I was certain he was about to stomp the dog out of existence. I was touched by his actual reaction. He did not focus attention on the dog nor its owner who seemed relatively unconcerned with the whole situation. The father's full attention was on his daughter. I was too far away to hear his exact words, yet I got the impression from his body language and his daughter's reaction that his entire focus was on addressing her fears and letting the girl know that she was safe and secure. He hugged her, spoke to her in a calm and gentle tone, slowly turned and walked away. There were no abrupt movements nor harsh words directed to the dog or its owner. There was no yelling or hostilities exchanged of any kind. Shortly thereafter, the child's mother arrived to find out what the commotion was all about. The father simply stated their daughter had a little fright but that everything was going to be OK. They walked away to enjoy the rest of the afternoon.

I often think back to that brief encounter and find myself admiring the little girl's father. He appeared to address his daughter's anxiety without threatening her sense of safety, security, and well being. This is easier said than done. Imagine if you will an alternative reaction. The child runs to her father's arms and out of harm's way. The father directs his attention away from his daughter's immediate needs and to the small dog or the dog's owner – by stomping on or yelling at the dog or verbally attacking the dog's owner for not restraining the animal. Whose needs are being addressed with this type of reaction? The father's or the daughter's? This reaction would likely heighten the child's anxiety rather than promoting a sense of safety, security, and well being. I imagine the father might experience a brief sense of satisfaction by focusing his attention on the dog and/or its owner. He probably would have left the encounter feeling that he had protected his daughter while simultaneously addressing the problem of an annoying animal. Isn't this what parents are supposed to do?

I believe this father recognized the animal – although a pretty frightening little dog – offered very little physical threat to his daughter or himself. I also believe he chose to focus his attention on the child and her emotional and physical needs at that particular moment rather than going on the attack himself. I believe the net gain of the father's reaction, that is, addressing the daughter's immediate needs, was far greater than if he had chosen to focus on the dog or its owner. This was obvious by the tenderness and comfort that existed between this parent and child. I believe the father's reaction was also instrumental in helping his daughter quickly recover from the fright, learn from the experience, and enjoy the remaining picnic activities.

This may appear to be a relatively simple and insignificant example. However, ask yourself these questions: Given that situation how would I react? Would I focus on my child's immediate emotional needs or would I express anger toward the dog or its owner? Would I do both? What other examples can you think of where your child might experience similar anxiety in his or her living? Adults possess a wide range of life experiences. As such, we should be skilled at differentiating between actual risk and perceived risk. Creating safety for children requires the parent to consider probable outcomes to most situations a child may likely encounter. This requires a parent to identify and communicate the wide spectrum of emotions surrounding events both parent and child are likely to encounter. For example, I spoke to the father from the example above later that day. I asked him what he said to his daughter after picking her up. He told me that the conversation went something like this:

Father: *That's a pretty scary dog, isn't it?*

Daughter: *Yeah!*

Father: *Who would think that such a dog could have such a mean bark?*

Daughter: *I know!*

Father: *It's all right to be scared........... The other dog seemed to be pretty friendly. What's his name?*

Daughter: *I don't know.*

Father: *Perhaps you and I can be formally introduced to his owner a little later. Do you think that would be a good plan?*

Daughter: *That'd be great.*

This father realized the Chihuahua's bark was far worse than its bite. The father told me he was irritated with the situation but believed there was little chance of any real harm coming from the event. He, like I, admitted that the animal had a scary bark. He was not going to ignore or minimize this when interacting with his daughter. However, he was not going to exacerbate the fright by placing an inordinate amount of attention on the dog. His efforts would be better directed to acknowledge that this was a scary situation and that there is nothing wrong with feeling frightened. This father did not want his daughter to leave this situation fearing all dogs and made an effort to introduce his child to a friendlier animal later that day. Parents are capable of drawing upon their own life experiences and the resulting emotions stemming from these experiences to introduce aspects of living to the child in manners that will foster a sense of safety and self confidence.

There are many examples from living where a child will encounter general anxiety and discomfort. The parent might benefit by recognizing that he or she will have access to an understanding of "the larger picture" associated with these situations by virtue of life experiences. For example, as the child approaches and experiences puberty and body developmental changes, he or she may encounter fear, confusion, discomfort, and anxiety. There are obvious anxieties surrounding death and illness in the family. School and early social relationships can also be source of anxiety for children as well as issues such as crime in a community and marital discord. The parent has lived through these or similar experiences and has greater insight into what might be a more helpful or less helpful action/reaction when encountering anxieties associated with life events. The child will be looking to the parent to gauge how these situations might be best handled.

The child's vulnerability is his or her lack of experience and ability to identify and process the many emotions surrounding these events. If the parent is able to access his or her vast knowledge base and communicates his or her experience and emotions in a manner that leaves the child self-assured and emotionally safe, both parent and child will benefit. Many of the Parenting Assumptions throughout this book assist the parent to recognize ways of fostering a sense of safety, security, and well being. Keep this Assumption in mind while reviewing other Assumptions.

26. The skilled parent will address the child's anxieties without threatening his or her sense of safety, security, and well being.

A friend told me about a problem he was having with his son. After hearing his story this Parenting Assumption immediately came to mind. My friend had recently separated from his wife and was in the process of getting a divorce. Both parents were approaching the divorce amicably and had worked out a fair and equitable custody arrangement.

Their son was four years-old. At first all was going well but several weeks into the separation things began to change. It seemed as if the little boy was beginning to oppose spending time with his father. For example, when the father arrived to pick up the boy he would give him excuses as to why he couldn't go. On one occasion the young boy assertively stated *"Dad, I can't go."* The father asked him why not, to which he responded *"Because I'm playing."* I asked the father if his son might have been playing when he arrived and was merely not ready to leave. Was he placing too much importance on his son's statement? The father sadly told me that his four year-old made this statement while seated at the kitchen table quietly drinking a glass of milk – his overnight bag sitting at his side.

I asked the father for additional examples of his son's behaviors. He said that he calls his son nightly to wish him goodnight. The child's mother does the same when the boy sleeps at the father's house. The father said sleepovers at his house always went well. That is, until the mother's goodnight call came. As soon as the little boy recognized his mother's voice on the phone, his mood would immediately change from being happy to being sad. He would start to cry and beg to return to the mother's house. After the phone conversation ended, the son's mood would immediately return to its previously happy state. These examples were no longer isolated events, but seemed to be emerging as the norm. The father was at a loss for what to do. He was concerned that the cooperative spirit that had been established during the early weeks of the separation would soon wear thin. The mother was starting to question the custody arrangement they had worked out. She was making comments such as *"Maybe he's too fragile right now to spend time at your house."* And, *"He seems happier when he's with me. I don't think we should traumatize him."* These comments were disturbing to the father as he believed they represented the beginning to the end of their cooperation and his ability to spend time with his son.

The behaviors exhibited by my friend's son are quite common immediately following a separation. I would also consider the mother's concerns to be a natural reaction to her son's behaviors. The father also had cause for concern as the spirit of cooperation between the parents could rapidly deteriorate. This situation is relatively complex with many variables influencing the family's emotions and behaviors. I believed a healthy and helpful way through this situation might involve the father addressing his son's underlying anxiety rather than addressing the obvious behaviors directly.[16] The father is faced with a huge challenge and a tremendous parenting opportunity.

As previously stated, the son's behaviors are very common following parental separation. His world had recently been turned upside down. Almost everything he had previously known to be safe and secure now being redefined. Seemingly overnight he went from having one bedroom in the only house he had ever know to having two houses and two bedrooms. The daily routines he had become accustomed to and which were sources of safety and security were now in turmoil. He was facing complexities that were way beyond the cognitive abilities of a four year-old. To this little boy, seeing mommy and daddy together was what he knew. That was his world. His bedroom had never been significantly changed. His toys were there and there was no reason to believe this would ever change. When the routine he knew to be *his world* was interrupted, he likely encountered a great deal of confusion. He responded to this confusion by attempting to return *his world* to its previous routine – *"If I don't go with dad, everything will be as it was before. I won't have to deal with two homes, two rooms, new and uncomfortable situations."*

The child's parents initially responded to their son's behaviors by painting a rosy and joyful picture for him. They attempted to comfort their son by reassuring him everything would be okay or better than it had been before the separation. For instance, the mother would tell her son that he was going to have a great time at his father's house. The father would ensure he had many activities planned for the time he spent with his son. These did not resonate with the four year-old. The mother's comments probably didn't make much sense. The son might wonder *"What do you mean have a good time at his house? I'm fine with having a good time at my house. Two houses are not necessary, are they!?"* The father's attempt to fill their time together with activities was also out of the norm for the little boy. This is not how he routinely spent time with dad. This deviated from his norm and probably didn't make a great deal of sense.

I believed the parents might have neglected to consider how the changes imposed upon the little boy were to likely impact him emotionally. For example, the father responded to his son's statement that he could not go with him because he was playing by saying there would be plenty of time to play at his house. He also told his son about all the great plans he made for the two of them. This helped get him out of the mother's house on that particular occasion but did little to curb similar behaviors that were to occur in the coming weeks. I suggested the father acknowledge the changes that were disrupting the child's sense of safety, security, and well being. For example,

Son: *Dad, I can't go.*

Father: *Why Not?*

Son: *Because I'm playing.*

Father: [Noticing that he was not playing, sits down next to his son] *You know, there have been a lot of changes around here lately haven't there?*

Son: [Silent]

Father: *I think it might be hard to understand all these changes. It's hard for me. It might not feel comfortable and may be scary at times. . . . . You know what?*

Son: *What?*

Father: *It's ok to feel scared and uncomfortable when things change.*

Son: *It is?*

Father: *Sure. Sometimes change is hard to understand. I hope that if you feel scared or uncomfortable as we make these changes that you will ask your mother and me to help you understand what's going on. We'll do our best to answer any questions you have.*

Son: *Ok.*

In this example, the father was more concerned with the motivation behind his son's opposition to leaving his mother's house than trying to convince him that he would have the opportunity to play at his house later. Some parents and psychologists might say this father-son interaction is too complex for a 4 year-old. I disagree with that assertion. The child easily recognizes the dramatic changes occurring around him. The child's cognitive skills are not developed enough to allow him to connect all the dots. He does the best he can with the skills and abilities he has. His oppositional behavior – an attempt to restore normalcy to his world – makes sense when viewed from a four year-old's eyes. The father's attempt to focus on addressing the child's underlying motivation in the above example will resonate with the four year-old. It might not make complete sense to the child, but the message will be well received – his anxieties are being addressed without his sense of safety, security, and well being threatened.

My friend started to have conversations with his son similar to the example above. He reported that within a very short period of time the oppositional behaviors ceased. Also, when the child's mother called to say *goodnight*, the son would happily give her a rundown of the day's activities. The crying and begging to go home also ceased.

This Parenting Assumption has a great deal of applicability to other aspects of the parent-child relationship. In the example presented above, the father–son relationship benefited by shifting focus to the son's anxiety surrounding major changes occurring within the family. This was achieved without compromising the son's sense of emotional safety. This Parenting Assumption also comes to mind when families arrive at my office seeking help for issues such as eating disorders, severe behavioral problems, and problematic communications between family members. Problems such as these tend to be symptomatic of underlying and unprocessed anxieties. When families find themselves facing complex problems, shifting focus from the problematic behaviors to the underlying anxieties will, more often than not, help establish a great deal of emotional safety within the family system. This is very helpful in creating an environment where complex problems are more likely to be resolved in a healthy manner.[17] One final note, this particular Parenting Assumption works well when considered in conjunction with others. Try to keep this in mind as you continue reading.

27. When a mistake is made and the parent responds by focusing on the negative rather than the growth aspect, the child's sense of safety has been assaulted.

I have an example from my practice that I often refer to when discussing *mistakes*. I call this my table cleaning example. Parents of a young boy were hosting several friends for dinner. After the meal was completed, they retreated from the dining room to the living room. The parents assumed their son was quietly playing in an adjoining recreation room. However, unknown to the parents the boy decided to lend a hand by clearing the dinner table. He obtained a large platter from the kitchen as he had seen his parents do on many previous occasions, and loaded it with many pieces of fine china and crystal. The child then attempted to slide the platter from the table to his waiting arms. Needless to say, the platter was much too heavy and unwieldy for the child and its contents fell to the floor. Most of the china and crystal was broken. The parents immediately rushed to the dinning room upon hearing the crash. They found their son standing motionless and crying in the middle of broken glass and china. The parents immediately removed the boy from the danger then scolded him furiously for his expensive mistake. He was sent to his room and the mess was cleaned up. The parents were very upset as the china had been a wedding gift and would be difficult, if not impossible, to replace. They felt as if they had lost something very sentimental and special to them.

The parents and I discussed this event in great detail. I didn't want to minimize or be insensitive to their loss. Yet, I was wondering what they had hoped to achieve by scolding the boy and sending him to his room. The parents stated they had not considered this question at the time of the incident and that their reaction "just seemed to occur naturally." It "seemed like what we should do at the time." I asked the parents to take a few minutes to consider exactly what they wanted their son to learn from this experience. After considerable discussion they arrived at the following:

1. They wanted their son to be better able to avoid similar catastrophes in the future

2. They wanted their son to realize there are consequences to his behaviors and that he should think before acting or reacting.

Did the way in which the parents reacted help the boy walk away from this experience better prepared to avoid similar catastrophes in the future? Did he learn there are consequences to his actions? Sure. However, I was interested to know whether the parents' reaction was the **most helpful** way to achieve these goals. In addition to the above lessons, what other messages might have been reinforced as a result of the parents' reaction?

Let's put ourselves in the boy's shoes for a few moments. What were the boy's motives? I believe he was 5 or 6 years-old at the time of this incident. His actions were unlikely a malicious act intended to hurt his parents' feelings. On the contrary, I believe his actions were probably a genuine attempt to *give to his parents*. He probably wanted to show them that he was capable of helping out around the house. In some way he was probably attempting to demonstrate to his mom

and dad that he is growing up and capable of greater contributions to
the family. These are wonderful aspects of childhood development
when recognized. Unfortunately, in this particular case the child's
physical coordination, his strength, and his past experiences were
lagging behind his desire to contribute. When things did not work out
– and his attempt to help his parents by clearing the table failed – the
boy probably found himself baffled and confused. When the parents
responded with anger and punishment, several unexpected and less
helpful messages may have been inadvertently communicated to the
boy. Remember, the son's basic thoughts and motivations were likely
well intentioned. The boy's only mistake was that he did not ask for
permission or input from his parents. Again, this can be attributed to
his young age and lack of experience.

In addition to the two conclusions or lessons cited by the parents,
the boy likely left this experience being somewhat closer to believing
the following:

- I should not take risks.

- It's risky to give to others.

- Helping out can be dangerous.

- The world is not a safe place.

- I should not trust my thoughts and emotions; they are likely wrong.

These messages are unlikely to be, in and of themselves, detrimental
to the boy. However, if he finds himself receiving these or other,
similar messages, more often than not his view of the world and
relationships will eventually be impacted in less healthy ways.

Can a parent respond to situations such as this in a manner that
minimizes attention on the negative – *the broken china and the boy's
mistake* – while simultaneously focusing on the growth aspects
– *the boy's desire to give to his parents*? Absolutely! Is this easily
accomplished? Not always. Remember, the parents were likely
startled by the incident. They were probably concerned for their son's
safety and simultaneously hurt by their loss of possessions that had
tremendous sentimental value. The boy's desire to help out could have
been dangerous. He could have sustained serious cuts. Had he chosen
to help out by removing a hot pot of coffee from the table rather than

the china, things might have been disastrous. Situations such as this are capable of eliciting very powerful and often uncomfortable emotions from parents such as fear, panic, loss, irritation, surprise, sadness, broken heartedness, and inconvenience. These emotions are also capable of stimulating impulsive reactions from the parents – clouding access to reactions that are likely to be more helpful.

What options do parents have when facing situations such as this and the accompanying uncomfortable emotions? First and foremost, the child should be removed from any danger – in this case the broken glass. This is where impulsive parental reactions are helpful and appropriate. Once the child is safe, the uncomfortable emotions will likely set in and begin to exert their influence on the parents' next reactions. In this example the parents responded with a severe scolding and sending the child to his room. Let's explore a parental reaction that might prove to be more helpful in this situation. Imagine discovering the child crying, standing motionless, with a large platter and broken china and glass strewn around his feet. You pick the child up and remove him from the glass. Then what? Let's place ourselves in the child's shoes once again. Below is an alternative parental reaction. How do you think the child might feel following this interaction?

Son: (Drops the platter resulting in broken china and crystal. The boy is overwhelmed with emotions and begins to cry).

Parent: (Rushes to the dinning room after hearing the crash, sees the child standing among broken glass and immediately removes the child).

Parent: *Are you okay?* (Comforts boy with a hug)

Son: (Continues to cry)

Parent: *Wow, this seems like a pretty scary situation. Help me understand what happened here.*

Son: (still crying*) I don't know.*

Parent: *Well. . . . It looks like you were trying to help out by clearing the table.*

Son: *Yeah.*

Parent: *Doesn't seem like it turned out exactly how you may have wanted it to.*

Son: *No, it didn't.*

Parent: *Well. . . . I'm really glad you wanted to help. That was very thoughtful of you. I'm wondering... ...what do you think went wrong here?*

Son: *It was too heavy.*

Parent: *Oh. . . . What do you think you can do the next time you want to help?*

Son: *Carry less?*

Parent: *Yes, that would probably help. Do you also think it might be helpful to ask your mother or me first?*

Son: *I wanted it to be a surprise.*

Parent: *That's a really nice thought, but sometimes things don't work out exactly how we plan them. Your mother and I were really concerned when we heard the dished break We were scared that maybe you hurt yourself. These dishes and glasses were very special to your mom and me. They were a gift from your grandmother. We're sad that they are broken. Do you think you and I could have put our heads together and come up with a safer way you could have helped?*

Son: *I guess so.*

Parent: *It might not have been a surprise if you asked us first, but it would have made us just as happy. Will you ask us the next time you want to help? It might help us avoid this from happening again.*

Son: *OK.*

Parent: *Well, I think we have mess to clean up. Do you think you could help by getting the broom from the garage and a large paper bag?*

Son: *Sure!*

Let's revisit the parents' original goals. They wanted the boy to walk away from this experience better prepared to avoid similar catastrophes in the future. They also wanted him to realize there are consequences to his actions. Did the above parental reaction meet these objectives? I believe so. The negative aspects of the boy's actions were acknowledged – the potential for injury, his mistake, and the parents' loss. This is evident when the parent stated *"It doesn't seem like it turned out exactly how you may have wanted it to. Your mother and I were really concerned when we heard the dished break We were scared that maybe you hurt yourself."* And, *"The dishes and glasses that broke were very special to your mom and me. . . . we're sad they are broken."* Simple statements such as these will likely resonate with the child. He was attempting to help by giving to his parents. When things did not work out for the child, statements such as these are much more likely to be helpful in assisting the child evaluate his thoughts, decisions, and actions than any punishment. Actions such as yelling at or scolding the child will likely shut down any possibility of introspection or emotional process – leaving the child feeling defensive, hurt, confused and emotionally distant from the parents. When a child is merely scolded, little is learned other than *"I should not take risks"* and *"Next time I will try harder not to get caught so as to avoid the punishment."*

The growth aspect associated with this incident was acknowledged when the parent in the alternative interaction stated *"I'm really glad you wanted to help. That was very thoughtful of you."* The parent's effort to focus on the boy's attempt to contribute, while in the midst of an uncomfortable situation, will be tremendously helpful. The child's level of emotional safety and security will immediately increase. This sense of safety and security will leave the child open to the parents' instructions rather than turned off to what they have to say. This will also help reduce the possibility of leaving this experience with any of the previously mentioned less helpful messages, such as *I should not take risks. It's risky to give to others. Helping can be dangerous. The world is not a safe place. I should not trust my thoughts and emotions, they are likely wrong.* Finally, the parents originally disciplined the child by sending him to his room. They wanted to give him some time alone to think about the situation while they cleaned up the mess. It would be difficult to ascertain exactly how much consideration the child gave to the situation and how much thought he gave to other distractions or less helpful thought – *I'm a failure. Mom and Dad are really mean. I was only trying to help.* By safely including the child in the clean up process – *Do you think you could help by getting the broom from the garage and a large paper bag?*, the child had the opportunity to safely experience consequences of his decisions and actions. This type of interaction promotes emotional safety between parent and child while further directing the child to evaluate his actions.

Let's return to the parents for a few moments. When I present this example to groups of parents, many believe the alternative parental reaction is unrealistic. Many assert that it is impossible to act or react in this manner when confronting a situation such as described. I am informed that the uncomfortable emotions encountered in situations such as this are far too powerful for the alternative response to emerge from the parent. I could not disagree with these parents more strongly. Yes, the parents in the example were confronted with many uncomfortable emotions. Nowhere does it require a parent experiencing a rush of uncomfortable emotions to lose control or lose the ability to access more helpful and healthy responses. In fact, these emotions – the uncomfortable emotions – may be a clear signal to the parent that he or she is faced with an opportunity to help the child grow in wonderful ways. Remember, the child learns how to identify, process, and benefit from his or her emotions, through direct interaction with the parents. When a child experiences parents as being immobilized by or reacting impulsively to uncomfortable emotions, he or she will incorporate this understanding into his or her interactions with others. This is unfortunate as this *less helpful skill* can be a tremendous handicap in later life.[18]   How can a parent move from being immobilized by uncomfortable emotions to using these emotions in a manner as depicted in the alternative response? This question is addressed in many other Parenting Assumptions. As you review the other Assumptions keep this question in mind – *"How can I use the uncomfortable emotions I experience in a manner that will be healthy and helpful?"*   This is a most important skill – one that will go far in helping to create emotional safety between parent and child.

28. Parents are the protectors of their children. If this protection is all embracing, is approached with continuity, yet provides for maneuverability, flexibility, and individuation the child will grow strong.

Let's take a look at a situation that was once described to me by a college professor. This professor assigned a failing grade to a student who had performed very poorly in his class. The student had just completed his third year of college and was probably nearing his 21st birthday. There was little doubt about the appropriateness of the student's final grade. The quality of his written assignments was poor and he failed most of the examinations and quizzes. There is nothing unusual about a student failing a class, although, the professor was certain that this student was underachieving. This happens from time to time. In most instances the student learns from the experience and works harder when and if the class is repeated. However, this particular situation differed in a very unusual way. The student's parents contacted the professor and demanded an explanation for the grade. They went so far as to petition the professor to reconsider his evaluation of their son's performance. When the parents' request was rejected, they proceeded to blame the professor for the difficulties their son was likely going to have getting into a competitive graduate school the following year. The professor informed me that the student had not at any time approached him with concerns about his grade nor had he asked for any remedial attention during the school year.

This Parenting Assumption immediately came to my mind upon hearing the professor's story. There is no doubting the importance of the protective umbrella parents provide their children during their formative years of development. Without it, a child's chances of succeeding in later life are greatly handicapped. I usually come across parents in my practice of family therapy who struggle to provide adequate protection for their children. Yet, from time to time parents will respond with too much protection. I believe this might be one such case.

Several questions immediately came to my mind upon hearing the professor's account of this incident. My first question was, why were the parents of a 21 year-old college student fighting his battles? Shouldn't the parents' concerns about their son's grade be directed to the son rather than the professor? If the student felt the grade was in any way inappropriate why did *he* not approach the professor? Was it not the student's responsibility to perform at a level that would help him gain admittance to a *competitive graduate school*? Was this the student's goal or was it the parents' goal for the student?

I think there was little question that these parents were protective of their son. However, I would question whether the parent's protection allowed for maneuverability, flexibility, and individuation. That is, was the son encouraged to make decisions for himself and to deal with the consequences of his decision and actions? Was the student becoming better prepared for life's challenges by his parents' attempt to intervene on his behalf?

As it turned out, this particular student had career and educational goals that were significantly different from what his parents desired for him. Apparently, these differences had never been resolved between the parents and their son. The parent-son relationship did not seem to allow for maneuverability, flexibility, and individuation. That is, it did not seem as if the student was being encouraged to make independent decisions, formulate unique beliefs, and to explore aspects of living and relating that may differ from that of his parents or the family system. I believe this might have been a contributing factor to the student's failure in this, as well as other, classes. Perhaps he intentionally performed poorly so as to jeopardize his chances of getting accepted into graduate programs in which he had no interest but his parents were pressuring him to attend.

I followed up with this professor some time later. As it turned out, this particular student eventually graduated from the university but he chose not to pursue graduate studies as his parents desired. Throughout his college years, the student had been taking flying lessons. Aviation had always been his passion. Following graduation, the student pursued a career as a commercial pilot and is currently flying for a small regional airline. He is apparently having the time of his life. It seemed as if the professors who failed the student did him a great service. By holding him accountable for his actions and performance they indirectly provided him the opportunity to individuate. *Parents are the protectors of their children. If this protection is all embracing, is approached with continuity, yet provides for maneuverability, flexibility, and individuation the child will grow strong.*

29. Parents who are able to unite in matters of parenting will have children who feel secure and able to develop a harmonious existence.

I hope the importance of this particular Parenting Assumption becomes clear after reading the following discussion. I stress the importance of this Assumption after having seen the devastating effects of parents who have conscripted their children as leverage in an attempt to resolve marital or relationship discord. I can recall dozens of examples where one parent withheld visitation in an effort to manipulate the other parent. I have worked with many children whose separated or divorced parents have questioned the child about the activities of the other parent. I have also encountered many situations where one parent attempted to turn children against the other parent. These situations are rarely successful in any regard other than to cause significant emotional trauma to the child or children. In therapeutic jargon, we refer to this as *triangulation.* The parent triangulates the child or children into what are issues specific to the parents. I know of few circumstances that are as destructive to a child's overall emotional well being than to be used in a relational power play between parents. I most often come across examples of parents triangulating children into their conflict during or shortly after a separation or divorce. This issue also seems to surface when step parents enter the family.

Triangulation occurs when parents become so enthralled and distracted by their marital and relationship differences that they fail to see the unhealthy, destructive, and avoidable consequences of involving their children. This is not to say that all parents who separate or divorce harm their children in this way. In fact, I can recall many examples of divorces that were handled in a manner that left the child or children feeling remarkably safe and secure. These parents, regardless of the differences leading to the divorce or separation, were able to unite on crucial areas of parenting. They realized the importance of remaining parents, albeit separated, during and after the breakup process. Let's take a brief look at an example to help us explore this idea of parents uniting in matters of parenting. This particular example presents a couple who separated and divorced. However, the important points in this example apply to all parents. It highlights many factors that have relevance to couples who separate as well as those whose relationship is intact.

In this particular example I was contacted by a father of two children. He asked that I serve as a mediator between he and his wife who were in the process of divorcing. I agreed and an appointment was scheduled. When the parents arrived in my office I was informed they had already separated and that the children had been told of their intentions to divorce. As it turned out, the parents were not exactly seeking mediation but were looking for a therapist to serve as an objective judge. It seemed that their marriage had been turbulent and filled with conflict. They saw eye-to-eye on very few issues but one, both loved their children very much. The anger and hostility each felt for the other was obvious by the manner in which they interacted. Civil conversations between the two were rare. Yet, they had the foresight to realize the contempt each held for the other would bleed into their parenting interactions during and after the divorce unless they took specific steps to prevent this from occurring. Both parents felt this to be especially true as they began to split assets and negotiated custody and visitation issues. These parents wanted a neutral and objective authority to help them separate their personal and marital issues from their parenting responsibilities. I agreed and we began the process of exploring this particular Parenting Assumption.

The parents put their heads together and came up with five areas of parenting in which they believed it imperative to find common ground, so as to minimize chances the children would be triangulated into their marital and personal discord. It is important to note that these five areas of parenting were specific to this particular family's unique circumstances. These categories are by no means universal to all families. However, the importance of identifying and exploring crucial areas of parenting, those areas in which parents must unite in order to provide children with a safe and secure structure, is universal to all parents. These particular parents arrived at the following five areas they believed were critical for them to remain united:

1. **Health** – The parents agreed that they must be cooperative, and in agreement, regarding matters of the children's health. This meant that both parents would be involved in appointments with the pediatrician. Both parents would share in the care of a sick child (e.g. the parents would alternate who picked up a child from school who had become ill). Healthcare expenses would be shared and not debated (e.g. the cost of orthodontic care and braces, medications, etc.).

2. **Education** – The parents agreed that both would remain involved in all aspects of the children's education. Both parents would attend parent-teacher meetings. Both parents would attend extracurricular events (e.g. sporting events). And, both parents would discuss the children's progress reports and would intervene together when necessary.

3. **Limits, Boundaries and Consequences** – The parents agreed to ensure the children experienced continuity in the limits, boundaries, and consequences they communicated and enforced. Each parent agreed to keep the other informed of the punishments they enforced and the reason behind the punishment.

4. **Ceremony** – The parents agreed to be involved and present for ceremonies that mark developmental and educational milestones. The parents agreed to set aside the anger each had for the other during the planning and execution of birthday parties, graduations,

religious events, and so on. Both parents would attend as many of these as possible.

5. **Emotional Safety** – The parents agreed to make every possible attempt to provide an emotionally safe and secure environment for their children. This meant that any problems one parent had regarding the other would be dealt directly with that parent. That is, the children were not to be engaged as any sort of referee, pawn, or spy between the parents. Communications between the parents regarding parenting would remain open regardless of their personal differences.

The parents agreed to set their personal differences aside when it came to interacting on these areas of parenting. When they arrived at an impasse regarding any aspect relating to these five areas, they would bring the issue to my office rather than allow it to adversely impact their parenting. The parents initially asked that I solve their differences for them by deciding who was correct. They believed that a neutral party deciding whose perspective was most correct would help ensure a sort of balance and fairness. I avoided getting pulled into this trap by returning to the father's original request for mediation. Rather than taking an authoritative stance by simply deciding whose perspective might be correct, I encouraged the parents to figure it out for themselves. These two would not always have access to a therapist to help them out of these jams. They would gain greater benefit by figuring out how to best unite on these matters for themselves.

Identifying and agreeing upon the five areas of parenting just cited was a pretty good start. This was common ground on which they could focus in the midst of their divorce. These parents would probably agree in concept with this particular Parenting Assumption. Yet, when things got a bit heated between them, the concepts underlying this assumption would probably be lost. The five areas identified by these parents were concrete and quantifiable. They helped the parents proceed with the divorce without triangulating the children into unfair and unjust situations. The five areas designated by the parents as *neutral territory* were very important. However, the specifics found in the parents list failed in comparison to the importance of the underlying process that was occurring. The parents were developing a structure for cooperation, consideration, and occasional compromise regarding their parenting activities.

It is unfortunate when the process of divorce provides parents a reason to look at the importance of working together – *uniting in matters of parenting*. This particular subject was never discussed between these two parents while they were married and the family was intact. Decisions regarding parenting were often hotly contended and very conflictual. The parents would often draw the children into their personal differences. For example, one of the children brought home a report card from school that had a *lower than usual* grade in mathematics. One parent might respond to the child's grade by assertively encouraging the child to do better, only to be interrupted by the other parent stating that the child is being pushed too hard to excel in mathematics. The question of which is best – *more* or *less* *pressure* from the parents regarding the child's efforts in the math class – is not as important as the child experiencing the parents being united on the matter. Children naturally view their parents as the primary authority figures in their lives. This natural parental authority essentially empowers a parent to parent. The child looks up to and wants to please the parents. When the primary authorities in a child's life are divided, more often than not, the child's emotional security suffers. The child is forced to pick and choose between the parents' meandering perspectives and direction. With respect to the report card matter, the child would ultimately be in a healthier place if the parents chose one or the other perspective and supported it in a unified matter. The emotional benefits from experiencing the parents as united far outweigh the benefits of a single grade in one class.

The parents in the example above were able to unite on the five critical areas of parenting they outlined. Initially, they brought many conflicts to my office for resolution, such as how much pressure should be placed on their oldest child to excel in math. We visited this Parenting Assumption over and over as the parents presented their dilemmas and differences. In a relatively short period of time, the parents' focus began to shift from arguing about these differences to discussing how they, as parents, could promote emotional security in their children's lives. These parents eventually stopped coming to my office for mediation. Before closing my files I made a final follow-up call to each parent. Both stated that they had become quite skilled at separating their personal differences from their parenting responsibilities. Both stated that their original list of five critical areas of parenting was still in the forefront of their mind and that several other areas had been added to the list. Both parents reported that their children were doing well. Both parents also stated without prompting from me that these skills would have been very helpful while their marriage was intact. Both believed that a lot of unnecessary stress could have been eliminated from their children's lives had they been *able to unite in patters of parenting.*

30. A house with fewer resources and clear structure is greater than a house with unlimited resources and loosely defined structure. The former promotes safety and confidence; the latter promotes false security and arrogance.

Years ago I met a woman who was of Native American decent. After becoming very good friends she invited me to meet her family who resided in the southwest part of the United States. This was a great experience for me. I was raised in the Northeast, just outside of Philadelphia, where life was significantly different. This woman's family had very few resources. Their house was at best modest and amenities were few. At first I felt very uncomfortable in this environment. I felt sorry for this family and struggled to see beyond their lack of material possessions.

I am fortunate that my visit was several days, as this time afforded me the opportunity to relax and see something very important. To my surprise, this family was happy, successful, and envious of nobody. This conclusion required me to question, evaluate, and redefine my understanding of success. I had been raised in a family and community much different than this. This family and their community seemed to value healthy relationships and the quality of one's character above all else. One's material possessions or financial resources were definitely less important than how one chose to live life and interact with others. The concept of status was much different than what I was accustomed. The value of one's profession was determined by job satisfaction and enjoyment, not by its title or salary. A person with means and many possessions was not viewed as either more or less worthy. Success within this family and their community seemed to be defined by one's character rather than what they possessed or had acquired.

This family frequently had lively discussions. Everybody was encouraged to present and process their opinions and perspectives, even when these differed from traditional family views or beliefs. Members of this family seemed very skilled at separating people from issues. Differences in viewpoints were not personalized nor were they barriers to their relationship with each other. For example, if one family member possessed conservative views and another possessed more liberal beliefs, these differences were simply understood in a manner such as, "She's my sister whom I love very much and who happens to have views that differ from my own." Pressures to convince others to see the world in a like manner simply did not exist in this family. This family also benefited from clearly defined structure and expectations. The parents were in charge, however, this structure and the household rules were by no means repressive. Rather, the structure seemed to promote and maintain healthy and open relations. The limits, boundaries, and consequences within the household always left room for processing one's emotions and perspective.

I did not fully appreciate the impact of meeting this family on my understanding of family systems until several years later. After completing graduate school and entering practice as a family therapist, I had the opportunity to work with many affluent families just outside of Philadelphia. Many of these families were the antithesis of the family I had met many years before. Many of these families had great resources, yet they seemed to be very unhappy. Many of these family members had troubled and unsuccessful relationships. Character was defined much differently in many of these families. There was what I would call "a need to succeed" acculturated in these affluent families and their communities. This need to succeed seemed to place little emphasis on many of the character values the family I stayed with earlier so successfully promoted.

I am by no means stating that wealth and developing healthy character are incompatible. In fact, I recently contacted the family I visited so many years ago to check in and say hello. The children, now grown up, had achieved impressive levels of financial success. The family members who had married were still together. Each family member was excelling in a career that brought them great joy and the family often met for dinner in the very humble home that I visited so long ago. I'm sure the discussions continue to be lively and that issues are still separated from the individuals. I like to visit this particular Assumption when I work with an affluent family that is struggling. Sometimes these families can benefit from some objective input regarding the benefits of simplicity. Sometimes affluence should be examined against alternative measures. Providing for one's family is not merely a financial matter. *A house with fewer resources and clear structure is greater than a house with unlimited resources and loosely defined structure. The former promotes safety and confidence; the latter promotes false security and arrogance.*

31. During the occasional uproar associated with parenting, all may seem chaotic, yet those skilled in the art of parenting will find little disorder when knowledgeable about fundamental systems.

Years ago I worked as a family therapist at an outpatient mental health clinic in Philadelphia. This clinic was affiliated with a medical school and served as a training facility for psychiatric residents and psychology interns. From time to time these students found themselves working with families that challenged their professional skills. That is, the student's work with the family was not proving to be helpful in alleviating the symptoms for which they sought treatment. Since this was a training facility, these cases were openly discussed between the students and the clinic's professional staff. From time to time, families who presented challenging problems would be referred to one of the clinic's family therapists for a consultation session. The goal of these consultation sessions was to get a second opinion regarding the issues affecting the family and to promote movement in a clinical process that had stalled.

The consultation session would occur in a specially designed room. The family and the family therapist would be seated in one room while the residents and interns observed, via close circuit television, in a nearby classroom. The family was aware that others were observing in a nearby room and had consented to this format. After the consultation session ended, the family therapist would adjourn to the classroom to discuss the experience with the students and to answer questions.

Families that were referred for one of these consultation sessions were usually struggling with a variety of very complex problems. Rarely was there a single problem or a single symptom causing distress in the family system. Rather, these families had many seemingly unrelated problems. For example, a family might have one member who was struggling with depression, where a child was doing poorly in school or was involved with the juvenile criminal justice system, and where communications between family members were less than healthy and bordering on chaotic. Often, the complexity and severity of the problems presented by these families left the residents and interns feeling frustrated, overwhelmed and ineffective as providers of mental health services.

These consultation sessions were an important part of the student's educational experience, for it was through these sessions and the discussions that followed, that they learned how to work with the family system rather than the individual symptoms they presented. Prior to observing these consultation sessions, many students would experience doubt about their abilities to address the severe and complex problems being presented. Many of the problems these families faced seemed hopeless and beyond repair. The students learned, by watching a family therapist, that the problems were not beyond repair, but that they could be addressed very effectively if the clinical focus remained on the larger systemic picture. This required the therapist to work with the interrelationships between the problems being presented rather than the problems individually. The students' frustrations were often the result of how they responded to the family's symptoms rather than the severity of the problems presented.

When a therapist works with a family he or she is presented with two basic options. The first option is to focus on the actual behaviors or symptoms that brought the family to therapy. In the case of depression, treating the symptoms might entail prescribing an antidepressant medication. Yet, when the family of the person being treated for depression also consists of a child who is doing poorly in school, treatment might include counseling intended to assist the parent schedule and enforce regular study hours. Treating each symptom separately might be an effective approach if the individual or family is struggling with a single or relatively few issues. However, this rarely turns out to be the case. Problems are most often multifaceted, involving several members of a family, and are usually interrelated. For example, communications between the person being treated for depression and his or her spouse might be strained. Their sex life might be less than fulfilling. Relations with extended family might be distant or cut off. Levels of physical activity, and physical health, as well as the quality of the diet within the family might also be contributing to the family's struggles. A therapist who focuses on identifying and treating each behavior or symptom individually might find him or herself quickly overwhelmed and rendered ineffective. The family being treated in this manner might experience some relief from the presenting symptoms, however, the relief is rarely long-term.

The second option available to therapists is to identify and explore the underlying systemic variables that result in the problematic behavior or symptoms. This second option also requires the therapist to acknowledge the symptoms and behaviors that brought the individual or family to therapy, but to treat the underlying variables that are causing the symptoms rather than the symptoms themselves. For example, say a family enters therapy complaining about conflict between its members. It is also reported that a child is doing poorly in school and that the mother is depressed. These are important symptoms, but treating each separately without exploring the systemic variables connecting the symptoms is unlikely to result in long-term and sustainable relief. There are many possible systemic variables that could produce the symptoms described in this picture. Many of these variables have or will be presented in this book. For example, some key systemic considerations include how the family understands and promotes intimacy, empathy, and emotional process. How does the family develop and promote self-esteem? How does the family define emotional safety? How open are the communication pathways between members? Exploring interrelationships between these variables is a significant step to understanding the basics of fundamental systems. This process represents the second option for treating families and its members.

Helping the psychiatric residents and psychology interns recognize the connection between the systemic variables and the symptoms they observed was the goal of the consultation sessions. However, the connection between these symptoms and the variables resulting in the symptoms is not always apparent. A therapist may have to work quite hard to identify these variables and even harder to support the family as they struggle to make healthy and helpful changes. Many of the residents and interns were focusing their attention on the symptoms rather than the systemic variables leading to the symptoms. The students were simply missing the big picture. Their interventions and clinical efforts were not resonating with the family and the behaviors that brought them to therapy continued or actually got worse.

Following the consulting session, the resident or intern would continue to work with the family. However, their focus would usually shift away from the family's presenting symptoms and to the underlying systemic variables causing the symptoms. As the resident and interns became more skilled in this process they had fewer and fewer families requiring consultation. The students were able to help the families that sought therapy in a more effective manner and without significant input from the therapists who supervised them.

Parents often find themselves in a very similar situation as the residents and interns working at that outpatient mental health clinic. Parents, like the students described above, can become frustrated, overwhelmed, and will even question their effectiveness as parents if their attention remains on their child's undesirable behaviors rather than the underlying systemic variables stimulating the behaviors. This book is full of examples that should be helpful to parents who are willing to shift their focus from problematic behaviors to the deeper aspects of the problem – the variables that are actually responsible for the undesired behavior.

When I speak before groups of parents, I am often presented with an example of a problematic behavior exhibited by a child. The parent will ask me how to best address that particular problem. I think this is an example of a misperception held by many people about therapists and mental health professionals in general; that we have simple solutions to difficult problems and situations. Parents who present a problem and then expect a brief or magical solution are failing to take into consideration the numerous systemic variables that are likely contributing to the problem. If I or any therapist were to give this parent a one or two sentence solution to the problem he or she presented, the chances that I was helping the parent and child move toward a healthier and helpful resolution are pretty remote. This would be like the students described earlier merely treating the symptoms and neglecting the underlying systemic variables. My advice for parents seeking simple, brief, and concrete solutions to parenting challenges is to continue reading. Allow yourself the opportunity to consider that an undesirable behavior, no matter how minor or severe it may be, is always influenced by systemic variables existing within the family and parent-child relationship. As a parent comes closer to this realization, skills will emerge that will promote levels of emotional safety previously unrealized.

32. Continuity in most aspects of parenting is essential for safety to emerge. However, this by no means implies that a parent should avoid evaluating and altering his or her method of relating, for this will be interpreted as honest and genuine by the child of an artful parent.

   To this point I have stated that continuity in parenting is important for emotional safety to emerge within the parent-child relationship. The concept is simple, children who know what to expect from their parents tend to feel safe. This is not to be interpreted as meaning that if one's parenting practices are inherently unhealthy, but consistently applied, that the child will feel safe. This **is** intended to mean that a child who can rely upon continuity of healthy parenting practices will experience emotional benefits of said practices. As discussed in Parenting Assumption 28 children who are raised in families where discontinuity and unpredictability tend to be the norm will feel less safe. This is painfully evident in families where one or both parents are active alcoholics. A person who abuses alcohol may respond in a healthy and appropriate manner at one point in time. Then while under the influence of alcohol, may respond in a manner that seems antagonistic or hostile to a healthy relationship. Discontinuity in the parent-child relationship such as this, if frequently experienced, will certainly impact the child in very unhealthy ways.

   Ensuring the child experiences continuity in his or her parenting does not mean the parent should be locked into concrete beliefs or parenting practices. There is significant room for flexibility. In fact, flexibility is dictated by the mere fact that we are human beings. We learn as we experience different aspects of living. We learn from our mistakes and we gain knowledge from our interactions with others. It is through this maturation process that our belief structures and skills evolve. Children can and should benefit from the parent's personal growth and maturation. From time to time, parents will be faced with situations where they must, or desire to, alter the manner in which they relate or respond to their children. For example, consider the following parent-child interaction:

Child: *Last week you let me get by with this* [referring to a particular behavior]. *Now you're telling me to stop it or I'll be punished? That's not fair.*

Parent: *You're right. I think that if I were in your shoes right now this would certainly feel unfair. I know you didn't get into trouble last week. I felt very uncomfortable after letting you off the hook. Since then I have given the subject a lot of thought. It seems as if*

this behavior is becoming a pattern. I can see that now and want to
address it.

The child will probably leave this interaction feeling somewhat
disappointed. However, the child has benefited by having a parent who
is willing to evaluate his or her method of relating to and parenting the
child. The parent did not minimize the possibility that this process
might feel unfair. Safety in the parent-child relationship allows for
flexibility, mistakes, and growth as long as the process is openly
acknowledged. The parent in the above example told the child that
he or she was aware of the problem, that he or she was uncomfortable
with it, and that a great deal of thought and consideration had gone
into the matter. The child may feel the parent's discontinuity is unfair,
however, these feelings will likely be accompanied by feelings that the
parent's actions were honest and genuine – both necessary for safety to
emerge in their relationship.

33. In parenting, trust and safety outweigh respect.

I once knew a young father who insisted his 6 year-old son address
him as "Sir." I would hear interactions such as, "Did you have a good
day as school?" "Yes Sir." "Did you finish your vegetables?" "No
Sir." I asked the father to help me understand the reasoning behind
this particular family rule. The father explained that this formality was
a sign of politeness and reinforced respect for his authority as parent.
The first few times I saw the son respond with *"Yes Sir"* or *"No Sir,"*
I thought I noticed what looked like resentment in his expression and
body language. The boy's body would become tense and he would
look away from his father ever so slightly every time he said "Sir."
I wondered if merely the act of addressing his father as "Sir" was in
itself capable of creating respect? After seeing the boy's reaction, I
began to wonder about this question. I was wondering why the father
could not see his son's physical reactions to his demand for respect. I
found myself looking back to the six years I served in the United States
military.

There is a well established hierarchy of authority in the U.S.
armed forces. Subordinates address their superior officers as "Sir"
or "Ma'am." This is to reinforce and acknowledge respect for the
authority bequeathed the officer. When a commissioned officer
addressed me or attempted to get my attention, my response would

be *"Yes Sir?"* or *"Yes Ma'am?"* When I worked with officers who possessed strong leadership skills, who were trustworthy and demonstrated sound judgment and decision making skills, using "Sir" or "Ma'am" felt genuine and appropriate. I respected these officers and was proud to address them as such. From time to time I would come across an officer who demonstrated questionable decision making or leadership skills. In these situations a "Sir" or "Ma'am" response generated a much different reaction from me. The show of respect was not genuine and left me feeling slightly resentful and irritated. I found my demonstration of respect hollow when not accompanied by trust and safety. In no situation is this point more important than in parenting – especially when a child is disciplined. When trust and safety exist between parent and child, genuine and deep respect will naturally emerge – even if accompanied by anger. However, respect through intimidation, coercion, or on demand will result in deep resentment.

I was an adult while serving in the military and had life experiences that helped me better understand the hierarchy of military authority. When faced with feelings of resentment and irritation after interacting with less skilled or poor officers, I was able to work through these feelings in a healthy and appropriate manner. I did not internalize or carry around my feelings of anger and resentment. I realized this was just a part of the military experience. Does a young child have the skills to do the same when faced with similar circumstances? This is a question all parents must ask themselves when interacting with or disciplining their child(ren). The father who insisted his son address him as "Sir" was not necessarily placing the child at tremendous emotional risk; however, let's take a moment to look at a flowchart illustrating the complex processes involved and two possible outcomes.

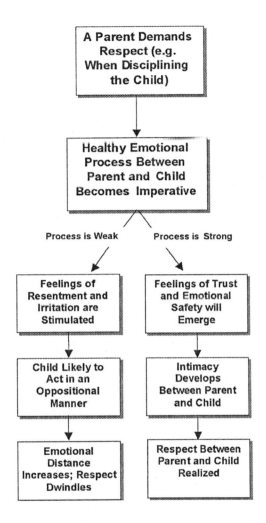

In this flowchart, the parent demands respect from his or her child(ren). This demand may take many forms. The parent may be very direct as in the example above – the father requires his son to address him as "Sir." Respect may also be demanded in many ways that are less obvious. For example, every time a parent disciplines a child he or she is seeking compliance and thus making an implicit demand for respect. When a parent instructs a child or provides direction or redirection, that parent is asking the child to do as he or she wishes. There is an implied demand for respect for his or her authority as parent. When the demand for respect is placed on a child, it is imperative to ensure emotional process occurs (emotional process is explained in detail under Parenting Assumption 56). However, in brief, *emotional process* relates to being able to consider the perspective of those with whom we interact while simultaneously communicating our own emotions, thoughts, and perspective. When emotional process between parent and child is weak and demands for respect are made, the child will foster feelings of resentment and irritation. When a child is placed in this position over and over again, these feelings will eventually result in wide variety of oppositional behaviors and attitudes, such as defiant, testing and passive-aggressive behaviors and attitudes. These behaviors will ultimately prove unhealthy for the child and likely opposite to what the parent is attempting to achieve through his or her direct or indirect demands for respect. If emotional process is strong following parental demand for respect, feelings of trust

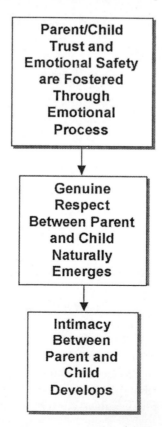

Parent/Child Trust and Emotional Safety are Fostered Through Emotional Process

Genuine Respect Between Parent and Child Naturally Emerges

Intimacy Between Parent and Child Develops

and safety will likely emerge. This will ultimately lead to increased intimacy between parent and child. Only then will respect between parent and child be realized.

Respect is an important element in the parent-child relationship. However, attempting to force respect can be a risky venture and may result in undesirable and paradoxical consequences. For this reason, I believe that *in parenting, trust and safety outweigh respect.* If the parental focus is on fostering emotional safety and developing a trusting relationship, there will be little need to consider the topic of respect. Respect between parent and child will naturally emerge. Trust and safety in the parent-child relationship lead to respect and eventually increased and appropriate intimacy between parent and child.

So, I believe the father who required his son to address him as "Sir" was taking a considerable risk. If the father's other interactions with his son did not continually promote emotional safety and trust, the father was risking creating increased emotional distance in their relationship. Judging from the boy's reaction I suspect this might have been the case. The father's need to have his son verbalize respect was achieved, yet with time, the father will likely see the son as oppositional, disrespectful, or fearful of his authority. Unfortunately, the father's focus was on respect rather than trust and safety. Both father and son will eventually suffer as a result.

34. Children experiencing their parents as accessible & engaging will feel safe. Children experiencing their parents as distant, constricted, and entrapping will feel unsafe.

A young divorced father of two, Manuel, was referred to my office. He was struggling with issues surrounding visitation with his children. The divorce was emotionally and financially devastating to both Manuel and his wife. Both left the marriage carrying a lot of resentment and anger with them. Manuel petitioned the court to have the children every weekend, a significant part of the summer, and many holidays. He was awarded far fewer visitations than he wanted and anticipated. In the months following the divorce Manuel found that the little time he had with the children was usually spent dealing with troubling behaviors. The children seemed to be angry with him all the time. He wanted to understand and process his children's anger, yet everything he tried seemed to result in the problem getting worse. Manuel stated it felt as if he was losing his children. This resulted in great feelings of frustration, overwhelming remorse, feelings of isolation and that he was without support. He also stated he felt helpless to alter the course of what was occurring in his life and relationship with his children.

One day he approached his father and asked for advice on how to best handle the children's anger during visitations. The father's immediate response was "I'm not a counselor, what do you want from me?" Several weeks later Manuel found his way to my office and presented me with the same dilemma. To be perfectly honest, I was just as concerned about the response Manuel received from his father as I was about the problems presented for counsel. I asked Manuel how he felt after hearing his father's response. He came up with the following list of descriptive emotions without hesitation:

* Let down
* Disappointed
* Alone
* Overwhelmed
* Hurt
* Insecure
* Unsafe
* Abandoned
* Angry

I found it interesting that, in spite of these very uncomfortable emotions, Manuel defended his father's response by stating that this was a complex problem and that it might have been unfair to ask his father for help. Manuel described his father as a good provider, yet when it came to emotional matters he would often come across as "*distant*" and "*elusive.*" Manuel stated that he should have anticipated his father's response and avoided asking for assistance.

I asked Manuel how he reacted to his father's response – "*I'm not a counselor, what do you want from me*" – and was told that he simply waved his father off and walked away. It was my guess that both Manuel and his father were uncomfortable leaving this matter lingering and unprocessed. Yet, neither knew how to take it in a different direction. I asked Manuel why he chose not to answer his father's question. Rather, he chose to accept the response, make excuses for his father, and walk way from a potential source of support. My inquiry was met with silence. Eventually he asked "*What do you mean?*" I was interested to know why Manuel simply did not tell his father what he wanted from him. The father's response was quite clear, "*What do you want from me?*" Manuel sat in front of me with a confused look on his face. After an uncomfortably long pause he stated "*Yes, my father did ask me what I wanted from him, but I honestly didn't think he meant it. I think he would have been as uncomfortable going further with the matter as I was in bringing it up in the first place.*"

This highlights the central core of this Parenting Assumption – children, even if they are adult children, will greatly benefit by experiencing their parent(s) as *accessible* and *engaging*. Manuel was struggling with some overwhelming problems – the divorce and repercussions stemming from the newly emerging family structure. Only after he experienced considerable distress and feeling as if he had no other options did he risk seeking input from his father. Why did Manuel consider his father to be among one of his last options for advice and support? Was Manuel's father emotionally accessible?

I believe this is an excellent example for this Parenting Assumption as the problems Manuel was having with his children were probably very similar to the problem he encountered with his father. When Manuel was confronted with his children's anger, he wanted some outside input. He approached his father and was met with a response that left him feeling unsafe and further discouraged. When the children found themselves struggling with issues surrounding the divorce, were they being met with responses that left them feeling unsafe and discouraged? When an adult is confronted with a situation such as this, there are steps he or she may take that will likely help create accessibility and promote engagement where there is little. For example, the following brief interaction was explored as a possible response to Manuel's father:

Manuel's Father (after hearing his son's predicament): *I'm not a counselor, what do you want from me?*

Manuel (possible reaction to his father's response): *Dad, I know you're not a counselor. I'm not asking you to be a counselor. You're a father, my father. I think you might have more experience dealing with things like this than I do. I might not agree with everything you say or do, but I would value your opinion and input. That's what I want from you. What do you think?*

Manuel's Father (after a pause): *It seem like you're in a difficult situation. What exactly are the kids doing? . . .*

This interaction took a much different direction than the original. Manuel's response is more likely to move this interaction in a constructive and healthy direction. Unfortunately, this response required Manuel, an adult, to take quite an emotional risk. When Manuel and I discussed this response, he told me that he simultaneously felt uncomfortable and a great sense of relief. His discomfort seemed to stem from just thinking about relating to his father in an emotionally laden manner. This was unfamiliar territory for both of them. On the other hand, his sense of relief appeared to stem from considering the possibility of being able to express thoughts and emotions that he really wanted to communicate yet had always felt constrained from doing in the past.

The process described above – attempting to engage a parent that is not perceived as emotionally accessible and engaging – is very difficult for many adults to initiate. The emotional discomfort surely to be experienced – such as Manuel described – is a strong deterrent for many adults wishing to utilize their parents as an emotional resource. When a *child* experiences a parent as emotionally inaccessible and difficult to engage, he she will simply shut down. The child may also embrace destructive "acting out" behaviors or seek input from sources less likely to be concerned about his or her healthy development and well being. Manuel's children were "acting out" through aggressive anger. Children are rarely, if ever, able to respond as Manual did in the alternative interaction above. Children simply do not possess the life experiences or skills to direct a conversation in a manner that might create accessibility and promote engagement where there is little.

Manuel and I explored how his children may have perceived him during and after the divorce as well as during recent visitations. Was he emotionally accessible to the children, and were the children able to freely engage him? Was he open to processing their fears, emotions, and questions about the newly emerged family rift in ways they perceived as accessible and engaging? Manuel had many powerful emotions surrounding the divorce. He was struggling with the fact that he no longer was able to have daily contact with his children. He stated he felt completely overwhelmed by these emotions and was concerned his ability to parent had been adversely impacted. This was the first time Manuel had considered whether he was perceived by his children as engaging and emotionally accessible. He could not rule out the possibility that this was a significant factor behind the children's anger. We spent considerable time exploring this subject, as it impacted Manuel's relationship with his children. We did this through multiple reverse role plays. I would assume the role of Manuel, and he would assume the role of his children. After each role play we would discuss how each of us was impacted by the interaction. For example, questions we always included in our discussion were:

- *Did you experience the interaction as moving in a healthy direction or did it feel like it was heading down a destructive, conflictual or unhealthy path? Why?*

- *Did you experience me as being interested in and wanting to know your perspective (and vice versa)?*

- *Were we able to be non–judgmental of each other's perspectives?*

- *Did I let you know how I was feeling?*

- *Did you experience me as being interested in how you were feeling?*

These are very important questions to consider when looking at the topic of emotional safety between parent and child. I would recommend these questions be revisited over and over again. They should be considered after your own parent-child interactions. Below is an example of just one of the many role plays Manuel and I had. Image yourself in the shoes of both parent and child. How would you answer the above questions?

Manuel to his Young Son (played by this therapist): *When I picked you up this morning I felt like you were really mad or something. What's going on?*

Son (played by Manuel): *I don't know.*

Manuel: *I know I'm struggling to figure out this whole divorce situation. It's hard to make sense of all the recent changes.*

Son: *You got that right!*

Manuel: *I think it's important for you to understand that your mother and I both love you very much and will do what we can to support you through all of this.*

Son: *Mom says you're a jerk . . . . Why did you move out?*

Manuel: *Well, when a married couple divorce they are usually pretty mad with each other. I think your mother and I might be pretty mad at each other right now. . . . . . I hope we don't do anything to*

make you feel that you are in any way responsible for the decisions
your mother and I are making right now. Again, we both love you
very much. There will probably be some issues your mother and I
will have to work out – between adults – in the next few months. My
moving out was a decision your mother and I made together. It was
tough and very painful for the both of us. We felt it was the right
decision.

Son: *It feels wrong to me.*

Manuel: *Help me understand that.*

Son: *Well. . . . Mom's always moody and crying. You're never around.*
Everything just feels different. I'm not sure what to do, what to say.
. . . It's just not right!

Manuel: *I wish I could make everything all right for you. I think*
it's going to take some time for this whole situation to work itself
out. But for right now I'm really glad you are able to tell me how
you're feeling. That takes guts. I will do everything I can do to be
completely honest and upfront with you while we figure this whole
thing out. I hope you and I can keep the lines of communication
open during all this.

Son: *I'll try.*

Manuel: *I look forward to it. We have the rest of the day together.*
What do you want to do?

Ask yourself these questions: Do you think this conversation was
being drawn in a healthy direction? Did Manuel and his son appear
to be interested in each other's perspective? Were they judgmental
of each other's perspective? Were they able to express their feelings?
Was each interested in the other's feelings?

The relationship between Manuel and his father did not reach the
point where each felt comfortable approaching and supporting each other
on big issues, such as dealing with Manual's angry children. Rather,
a relationship that exudes accessibility and engagement is developed
over time and after many small interactions. When a child approaches
a parent with a relatively small but emotionally laden issue, the parent's
reaction will, in part, determine if larger and more important issues are
processed between parent and child. I use the phrase "in part" here
because there is a cumulative effect to be considered. That is, if the child

experiences the parent as accessible more often that not – over hundreds of small issues, the larger issues – such as processing the emotions surrounding a divorce, will be more likely processed in an open manner where multiple perspectives are considered.

Let's take a look at one of the *small issues*. Manuel cited this as an example of an issue one of his children brought to him several months after the divorce.

Daughter: *I wore these shoes to school the other day and some of my friends made fun of me.*

Manuel: *How did that leave you feeling?*

Daughter: *I don't know. Not good though.*

Manuel: *How did you deal with it?*

Daughter: *Well, I got mad at first and didn't talk to [friend] until after lunch. She knew I was mad at her. Then I started thinking that sometimes I do the same thing.*

Manuel: *What do you mean?*

Daughter: *Well . . . . sometimes I make fun of other people, you know... when they wear something different.*

Manuel: *Oh?*

Daughter: *Yeah.*

Manuel: *What do you think you should do about this?*

Daughter: *I think I will give this some thought. What do they say . . . . . I got a dose of my own medicine?*

Manuel: *Sounds like a tough situation.*

Daughter: *Yeah.*

Let's revisit the questions posed earlier:

- Did Manuel attempt to move the conversation in a healthy direction? What did he do?

- Do you think Manuel was interested in his daughter's perspective?

- Was Manuel judgmental of his daughter?

- Was Manuel interested in how his daughter was feeling?

- Did the interaction appear to be occurring between persons who felt "safe" with each other?

If the daughter experiences her father as she might have in the above interaction more often than not, whom do you think she will approach for advice years later on larger issues – such as when her boyfriend begins to pressure her to have sex? Manuel was faced with tremendous opportunities. He was being challenged to create greater emotional safety in his relationship with his children by increasing his emotional accessibility. In addition, he was simultaneously challenged to move his relationship with his father in a healthier direction. Both of these situations represented profound challenges for Manuel, yet as he risked change and overcame the discomfort of these challenges, he began to view them as opportunities rather than situations to avoid. As Manuel risked change and overcame the initial discomfort experienced with risking change, the matter of the divorce took on less significance. His children's anger abated, and the time they spent together was rewarding and intimate. Manuel's relationship with his father also began to evolve in healthy ways. They were spending greater time with each other and were having conversations that neither believed possible just months before. *Children experiencing their parents as accessible and engaging will feel safe. Children experiencing their parents as distant, constricted, and entrapping will feel unsafe.*

35. When there are no consistent rules to guide children, familial disorder will prosper. This sense of disorder will be all–too–common in other aspects of the child's later life.

Very frustrated parents of a 2 ½ year-old girl arrived in my office one day. The couple complained that they were having a hard time adjusting to the baby. It seemed that since the arrival of the child, they had very little quality time together. The couple felt as if they were becoming emotionally distant from each other and were looking for advice on ways to improve their relationship. After asking just a few questions, one issue seemed to surface over and over again. It appeared as if the young child wielded too much control over the couple and the household. This was evident in many respects. For example, every room in the house was the child's playroom. Toys and baby items were found everywhere – including the dining room and parent's bedroom. Also, when I asked the parents how they occupied their evenings, after the child was put to bed, I was met with a long and uncomfortable silence. The parents eventually told me that the child goes to bed when they adjourn for the night. These parents were not *early to bed, early to rise* individuals. No, they would often go to bed after 11:00 PM and sometimes as late as 12:00 AM. The parents would usually watch TV, videos or would use their evenings to read or prepare material for work the next day. The child would always remain with the parents during these evening activities.

These parents arrived in my office wanting to improve intimacy within their relationship. Their complaints are all-too-common among new parents who struggle to find quality alone time with each other. This is especially true when faced with the never ending and always expanding parenting, work, and household responsibilities. The few hours available to parents in the evening – after the kids go to bed – are valuable for maintaining health in the parents' relationship. When young parents state they are feeling emotionally distant from each other I like to offer support by encouraging them to use these few hours to remain acquainted. That is, I recommend they use this time working toward greater intimacy rather than away from greater intimacy in their relationship. Quite frankly, this child was getting in the way. This became evident when I asked the parents what happened when the child was put to bed at a more reasonable hour – say 8:00 PM. They reported the child would immediately begin to scream. After a short period of screaming they would give in and release the young girl from her bedroom to enjoy the rest of the evening with Mom and Dad. It appeared as if this child wielded too much power in family decision making. The child was not being guided by constant rules.

This condition seemed to arise out of, or was justified by, the parents' concern that they were not spending enough time with the child. The baby was kept at day care while both parents worked. They wanted to spend as much time with her as they could. Unfortunately, this was unnecessarily fatiguing the child, placing a great burden on the couple, and adversely impacting emotional safety in the child's life. We put this issue to rest by exploring actual time spent with the child as apposed to how much time they perceived spending with the child. Even when considering the time spent at day care these parents clearly had an adequate amount of time with their daughter. Yet, they could not bring themselves to establish and enforce constant rules within the household, especially regarding bedtime.

This young couple and I spent considerable time exploring this particular Parenting Assumption. I was concerned that early patterns of less healthy behavior were becoming engrained in their daughter's life. There was little structure and even fewer constant rules that are so crucial to establishing emotional safety in the child's life. This would likely surface in a variety of undesirable ways in the girl's later life. A general lack of structure and constant rules early in one's life can significantly increase the probability that one's later relationships will be less fulfilling and healthy. This should not be interpreted as a military boot camp approach to parenting. Too many rules and repressive structure can have an equally devastating effect on a child's understanding of safety. There is a fine balance between *too much* and *too little* when establishing and enforcing rules and family structure. Many of the Parenting Assumptions throughout this book will assist the parent in determining where the healthy middle ground lies.

With considerable support and encouragement, these parents set out to establish and enforce two basic rules within the household. The first was that the baby had two play spaces in the house – her room and the family room. Her toys were only to be maintained in these spaces – unless she was actually playing with them and then they would be returned immediately after she was finished. The second rule was that bedtime was 8:00 PM sharp. We discussed how their daughter might react to these rules. Previous experience led the parents to believe she would not be at all happy with their decision. The parents freely admitted to feeling very anxious – terrified – by what was going to happen when these rules were enforced. We spent considerable time trying to predict their daughter's reactions. For example, the parents believed their daughter would scream her lungs out when they attempted to put her to bed. They believed she would destroy her room and might even go so far as to reject them. The parents were not at all thrilled with these prospects and were hesitant to implement any rules for fear of their 2 ½ year-old's wrath. These feelings, these fears, were so strong that the parents were willing to martyr intimacy in their own relationship in order to support the existing status quo – avoiding healthy change in the family structure.

Two of the parents' three predictions came true. When the 8:00 PM bedtime was set, the child screamed her lungs out while attempting to destroy her room by throwing around her toys and bedding. The little girl was, to say the least, angry with her parents – *but she did not reject them*. In fact, the exact opposite seemed to occur. Much to the parents' surprise, she was drawn closer to them. The first evening was terrifying for the parents. They described the whole process in the following manner:

When we told her it was time for bed she simply and confidently said "no." I then picked her up to carry her to the bedroom and she freaked out. She arched her back the way two year-olds tend to do and started screaming bloody murder. Her screams actually hurt our ears. We carried her to her room – she was fighting us all the way. When we placed her in bed the real fun began. She kicked, screamed, tore her bed apart and began throwing everything about the room. We shut the door and left her alone. It sounded as if there was a monster in the room. This continued – nonstop – for three hours! Who would think that a 2 year-old had so much vigor? Then, the room feel silent. Strange, this happened about the time we usually go to bed.

While she was tearing her room apart, all we could do was hold each other and cry. The impulse to open the door was overwhelming. We both knew that giving in would stop the screaming, would stop her pain and our discomfort. We just held each other, crying, and tried to get through it.

The first night we were really confused and hurting. When the screaming stopped we peaked into the room to make sure everything was OK. To our surprise, our astonishment, we saw that our daughter had reassembled her bed and was sleeping peacefully with several of her favorite stuffed animals. The next morning she was very affectionate toward us. It was like she could not get enough kisses and hugs. The second night was similar to the first with two exceptions. Our daughter's screaming and crying only lasted about an hour and a half and we only held each other. Our tears were replaced with confidence. Oh yeah, it was painful to hear our daughter cry that way but we felt as if we were moving in a healthy direction. Again, she reassembled her bed and favorite toys and was sleeping soundly. The next morning our daughter was again full of hugs and kisses.

The third night her screaming and crying lasted but half an hour. We watched a video as she cried herself to sleep. Finally, on the fourth night, our daughter went to her room without prompting. This seemed strange. She fell asleep on her floor surrounded by her stuffed animals. When I picked her up and placed her in bed there was no struggle. It was 8:00 PM. It's funny, every morning since we set the 8:00 PM bedtime rule our daughter seems much more alive. She has been infinitely more affectionate with us. She had also become more active and engaging at her day care.[19]

This couple told me they still watched videos, watched TV, or prepared material for work the next day after their daughter was put to bed. However, they reported that their undivided alone time seemed more intimate. They were now working toward greater intimacy rather than farther away from greater intimacy in their relationship.

We explored why the child seemed to become increasingly affectionate after the parents started establishing and enforcing consistent rules. Was this merely coincidental? The parents did not think so. The parents thought their daughter was simply more rested. This was probably true; however, I thought that perhaps a sense of emotional safety, previously non-existent in this family, was now present. The child was no longer burdened by having to make up all the rules. Her parents were gaining control which represented a significant relief for the child who was busy enough just being an active 2 ½ year-old. My prediction is that other aspects of this child's later life will be significantly more healthy and happy. *When there are no constant rules to guide children, familial disorder will prosper. This sense of disorder will be all-to-common in other aspects of the child's later life.*

36. An enlightened parent is cautious to avoid rash actions and reactions. In so doing, the children are made to feel secure, and trust is preserved.

Several years ago I was employed as a family therapist within an agency that offered in-home therapeutic services. The therapists in this agency made house calls. This was a great experience as it provided me with the opportunity to see families interact in their home environment and on their home turf. This seemed more natural than the artificial environment created in the office. I found myself more likely to see the families' everyday actions and reactions. Their interactions appeared significantly less scripted than what I would typically see in my office. Quite often I would come across families that appeared to be *completely out of control*. Nothing seemed to be working for these families. Much of my time was dedicated to helping these families manage the almost daily crises that seemed to plague the households. From time to time I would also come across families that seemed to *have it together*. They seemed well balanced and functioned well together. Everything fell into place for these families. They experienced relatively few crises. The rare crises that **did** occur were handled in ways that were more often than not healthy and helpful. When these two "types of families," those seemingly *out of control* and those who appeared to *have it together*, were compared, this Parenting Assumption surfaced over and over again as being an important factor contributing to the differences.

I experienced the families who *had it together* as tending to be skilled at avoiding rash actions and reactions. Impulsiveness ran rampant through the *out of control* families. Small issues or disagreements would quickly escalate into arguments with family members yelling, or angrily disengaging from each other. In contrast, small issues were just that, "small issues," for the *together families*. Problems were recognized, processed by the family, and brought to a healthy and helpful resolution. Over and over again I saw emotionally secure and trusting parent-child relationships emerging from families whose members avoided rash actions and reactions. Conversely, I would see parent-child relationships that were lacking emotional security and trust in families who tended to act or react in impulsive ways.

With this in mind, how might we begin to evaluate our styles of interacting? How can impulsive actions and reactions be minimized or avoided? How can a family move away from disagreements that quickly escalate into family members arguing, yelling, or angrily disengaging from each other? I believe these questions can be addressed by exploring four basic styles of interaction. *All* interactions with others *will* fall into or closely resemble one of these four categories. Merely improving your ability to identify these four styles of interaction can be a powerful tool for enhancing your relationships. Individuals and families who take it a bit further, going beyond merely identifying these four styles of interaction, by investing effort into shifting focus from the less helpful styles of interacting to a more helpful style, will find their ability to thrive in all aspects of living tremendously improved. A certain by-product for the parent will be the emergence of increased emotional security and trust in the parent-child relationship.

The four basic categories of interaction are as follows:

- Aggressive Interactions

- Passive Interactions

- Passive-aggressive Interactions

- Assertive Interactions

Let's define and explore these interaction styles.

Aggressive interactions are interactions between persons where one or both people attempt to get their individual desires met in such a way so as to disregard the perspective of the other. One's personal needs and perspective are viewed as more important and having more value or merit than another's. Aggressive interactions reveal themselves in many ways. One of the most common indicators of an aggressive interaction is when one person in the relationship/interaction acts or reacts in a manner so as to suppress or otherwise discourage input or alternative viewpoints. These actions and reactions may range from being very subtle and almost indistinguishable to being overt and obvious. These actions and reactions may include, but are not necessarily limited to the following:

- Terse statements such as "Yes but . . . . "

- Accusatory statements that usually begin with "You . . . . "; "You are . . . . "; "You should . . . . ";"You need to. . . . ", and so on

- Interruptions that are intended to dominate a conversation

- Escalating the interaction to yelling or using a harsh or loud voice

- Any type of intimidation, threat, or violence

- Finger pointing

- Utilizing a ridged or threatening posturing

- Refusing to listen to or consider the other's perspective.

Those who rely on aggressive interactions will go to great lengths to ensure their perspective is or remains paramount. They are usually unaware of, or not interested in, the relational consequences of their actions and reactions – that is, how the other person is impacted by their comments and behaviors. Aggressive interactions and relationships are **based upon winning** – *in order for one person to win, the other **must** lose*. Other people or their perspectives are felt to be, or are seen as, adversarial, threatening, or wrong. The only way to feel satisfied is if the other give in. The person who routinely relies upon aggressive interactions rarely gives any thought to "others" after the interaction ends.

Passive interactions are interactions between persons where one fails to present or assert his or her perspective – allowing others to transgress upon or disregard their personal perspective. Persons invested in passive interactions will often apologize or will avoid presenting their true feelings, perspective, or thoughts. Compromise is a central tenant of passive interactions. Persons who incorporate passive interactions into their relationships tend to:

- Seek agreement at all costs

- Make concessions to maintain balance or calm

- Allow others to cross or violate their personal boundaries

- Will easily change their position to accommodate those around him/ her

- Will yield to pressure and find it difficult being honest about their emotions, wants, needs, and perspective.

Passive interactions are **based upon fear, anxiety, or lack of entitlement** and ultimately result in a *lose-win conclusion*. The fear, anxiety, and lack of entitlement associated with passive interactions may be very subtle; however, it is always present. This is what prevents the person heavily invested in passive interactions from asserting or otherwise communicating their emotions, wants, needs, and perspective. A person relying upon passive interactions will often feel unheard, unfulfilled, frustrated, thwarted and anxious. Yet, there is a general belief that one's own viewpoint, if presented, would create conflict and discomfort. Therefore, one's perspective, needs, wants and thoughts are kept to oneself *for the better good*.

Passive-aggressive interactions are primarily **based upon a foundation of non–ownership, inconsistency, deception and the use of guilt.** They ultimately end in a *lose-lose* conclusion. That is, all persons touched by passive-aggressive interactions are typically adversely impacted. Persons who are heavily invested in passive-aggressive interactions will avoid direct conflict, confrontation, and assertiveness. Rather, a person invested in passive-aggressive interactions will attempt to achieve gains through a myriad of other behaviors or subtle manipulations. Some common indicators of these behaviors or subtle manipulations include, but are not limited to, statements and behaviors such as:

- *"If you loved me you would . . . . "*

- *"I guess I'm just not good,"* or, *"I guess I'm just an awful wife"* (husband, mother, father, etc.)

- *"My feelings aren't important anyway."*

- *Asking indirect questions as a means of prompting action (e.g. "Do you think the trash should be taken out right now?" vs. "I would appreciate it if you could get the trash out now rather than later." And "Are you going to put more salt in the soup?" vs. "I think the soup could use some more salt, what do you think?")*

- Rolling one's eyes when there is disagreement then denying there is a disagreement and avoiding conflict.

- Looking away, sighing, or distracting oneself as the other speaks

- Being dishonest by pretending to agree then covertly sabotaging the relationship (e.g. *talking behind one's back* or in extreme situations *secretly scratching a co-worker's automobile with your key after a disagreement.*).

- Attempting to manipulate behavior through the use of indirect questions or statements (e.g. *"I guess the bathroom will never get painted."* vs. *"I'm disappointed the bathroom hasn't been painted yet. Let's talk about it"*).

- Use of covert actions to get a desired reaction or to indirectly manipulate (e.g. placing a family member's dirty laundry in an awkward location – blocking the bathroom – to motivate action or gain their attention. vs. Making it a point to inform the family member how their neglect to take care of the dirty laundry has impacted you and the household.)

Passive-aggressive interactions may range from being very subtle and almost indistinguishable to obvious and overt. Persons heavily invested in passive-aggressive styles of interacting or relating want others to concede – as in aggressive interactions – yet act and react in a manner that is insidious or covert. The person invested in passive-aggressive interactions shy away from taking responsibility for their actions, reactions and emotions and may be skilled in getting their needs met through the use of guilt and subtle manipulations. Rarely are true emotions or personal perspectives openly processed by persons invested in passive-aggressive interactions.

Assertive interactions are interactions that are *based upon a win-win mindset.* A person skilled in assertive interactions will be able to present their perspective and emotions while remaining open to considering the perspective and emotions of the other. The person invested in assertive interactions is able to state his or her emotions, thoughts, interests, wants, and needs in an honest, forthright, and direct manner. They will not rely upon guilt, manipulation, or intimidation to "achieve a win" and are interested in achieving solutions that work for all. Persons skilled in assertive interactions will separate people from the situation or problem. Tension and uncomfortable emotions that may result from interactions with others are processed rather than personalized. For example, when having a disagreement with another person those skilled in assertive interactions will separate the disagreement from the person (e.g. *"He's my brother whom I disagree with on this matter, yet this disagreement does not mean that I have to harbour ill feeling toward him as a person. I am able to separate the issue from the person."*). Persons skilled in assertive interactions may find themselves responding to problems in ways similar to the following:

- *"When I hear you talk behind my back I find myself feeling very uncomfortable and concerned. Help me understand what is going on here?"*

- *"I feel like you are not telling me the truth here. The facts, as I see them, are not adding up. This leaves me feeling a bit irritated, frustrated, and very concerned. I would appreciate it if you would help me understand your perspective."*

- *"When I bring up this problem then hear you say "I guess I'm just a lousy wife" I feel really confused and uncomfortable. I feel like we should look at the problem and our differences. I don't think this has anything to do with us as individuals or the nature of our marriage. How do you feel? What are your thoughts? They're important to me.*"

- "*No, I don't think it matters when we get the trash out. Although it feels like you want me to do it now by asking that question.*"

The persons interacting as depicted in the above examples are taking an assertive approach to addressing the issues at hand. The problems and conflicts are being confronted in a very direct manner. Different perspectives are open for discussion and consideration. There are no tricks. No intimidation. No threats. No manipulation. No guilt. The persons above appear to be interested in achieving a solution that will work for both parties. He or she is not ignoring the problem, apologizing for their perspective, backing down, nor shutting off the other person. The people in these examples state their perspective and emotions and leave the door open for the other person's perspective. If an assertive approach is maintained, chances are these interactions will result in a *win-win* conclusion for both persons – the interaction will go in a healthy or helpful direction for all involved.

Now, consider something I call the 90/10 rule. This rule is by no means scientific nor does it represent a proven fact. It is merely something that makes sense to me and more often than not has demonstrated itself to be pretty accurate. The 90/10 rule asserts that individuals who are not thriving and families who might appear *out of control* rely upon aggressive, passive, or passive-aggressive interaction styles in 90% of their interpersonal encounters. The remaining 10% of their interactions will fall into the assertive category. This ratio is reversed for individuals who tend to thrive and families who appear to *have it together* (90% representing assertive interactions and 10% representing the sum of other three). Time and time again, this has demonstrated itself to be true. If you open yourself up to recognizing the four interaction styles, these percentages become strikingly clear. You will find families who avoid rash actions and reactions, and thus appear to be less impulsive, will, for all practical purposes, *have it together*. These families tend to produce children who appear confident, self-assured, and seem to feel safe and emotionally secure. You will likely see parent-child relationships marked with an abundance of trust.

I took the above theory and put it to test while doing in-home family therapy. I shifted the focus of my work with the *out of control* families from helping them manage the almost daily crisis they encountered to understanding these four basic categories of interacting. We then worked to shift the ratio from 90%–10% to 10%–90%. This was not always easy, yet as the ratio began to shift, so did the emotional and relational health of the family and its members. Altering our personal method of interacting with others, even if those around us choose not to, will have a tremendously helpful and healthy impact. Again, the first step in this process is to familiarize oneself with these four styles of interaction. I recommend watching how those around you – family members, co-workers, people you see in grocery stores, friends, your children – interact. Ask yourself, *are these people relying upon aggressive, passive, passive-aggressive or assertive styles of interacting*? Observe the outcomes of each style. More often than not you will see that interactions between persons that are predominantly *assertive* will move in healthy and more helpful directions. Those interactions that are marked with *aggression, passivity, passive–aggression* will rapidly move toward arguments, disengagement, and everybody involved experiencing a broad spectrum of very uncomfortable emotions and unhealthy consequences. It should be noted that one person skilled in assertive interactions can have a tremendous impact on the outcome of interactions with others not skilled in the same. The person skilled in assertive interactions being confronted by aggression, passivity, or passive–aggression will find great comfort and confidence with this healthier style of interacting. This person will likely be empowered to move the interaction in a healthier direction. Many of the Parenting Assumptions throughout this book are intended to help you develop emotional security and trust in the familial and parent-child relationships. In a roundabout way, many of the Assumptions throughout this book direct the reader toward more assertive interactions. Keep this in mind and, if you choose to shift your focus to using assertive interactions, be prepared to feel very, very empowered.

Chapter 5 Paradox

A statement, act, or belief that may seem
contradictory, unbelievable,
or absurd but that may be true in fact

37. Parents exposing a child to their emotional selves are acting from strength and taking great strides to prepare their son or daughter for adult relationships.

I find many parents resistant to the idea of exposing their *emotional selves* to their children. I've often wondered about this, as almost every parent I know who risked change and overcame the fear associated with exposing their *emotional self* benefited significantly by taking that risk. What is meant by *exposing a child to the parents' emotional selves*? Well, let's take a look at an example of parents who were struggling with their five children. The household was described by the parents as being in a constant state of chaos. The children, ages 6 to 19, were constantly misbehaving, were resistant to parental redirection, and always seemed to be fighting with each other. The eldest child moved out of the house when he was 18 years-old then returned a year later when he started experiencing financial problems. The parents welcomed the son's return and assured him that he would have their support until he got back on his feet. The parents did not re-establish house rules with this son as he was of an adult age. They expected him to behave as an adult and believed rules would leave him feeling infantilized.[20] Upon the son's return, he occupied space in the basement since his room had given to a younger sibling after he left home.

The basement previously served as a children's recreation and laundry room. The family agreed to give the young man as much privacy as possible. Several weeks passed and all appeared well until one day, the mother was doing laundry and came upon a used condom and condom wrapper on the basement floor. The mother was shocked. She informed the husband and they brought the matter to therapy. The parents suspected the eldest son had been having intercourse with his girlfriend and were unhappy with the situation. The parents had strong beliefs against premarital sex. They were also concerned that one of the younger children could have accidentally stumbled across the condom while retrieving one of the many toys stored in the basement. I asked the parents to take a few minutes to come up with five ways they could respond to this situation. The following is their list:

1. *Ignore the matter altogether. He's an adult and we should not impose our beliefs onto him.*

2. *Confront the son about the condom, then ask him to move out of the house.*

3. *Confront the son about the condom, then establish house rules which will include no sex.*

4. *Confront the son about the condom, and prohibit the girlfriend from visiting the house.*

5. *Give the young man – and his girlfriend if possible – a good scolding.*

After presenting their list, the parents eagerly awaited my input as to which option I felt would be most appropriate. They did not expect my actual response. I believed something was missing from the parents' choices; something very critical: *their emotional selves.* I asked the parents to describe how they felt when the condom was first discovered. They immediately stated that they were angry. I encouraged them to go a little deeper and to identify additional words that described their feelings about the situation. They struggled with this request for several minutes and were only able to identify two additional feelings: shock and disappointment. The parents were then given a copy of a list of possible emotions.[21] We reviewed this list word for word while the parents thought about finding the used condom. The parents were encouraged to identify additional emotions associated with this incident. They easily identified the following:

Hurt	Concerned	Anxious
Disconnected	Appalled	Disrespected
Embarrassed	Frustrated	Ill-at-Ease
Imposed upon	Inflamed	Infuriated
Let down	Injured	Offended
Overwhelmed	Startled	Surprised
Torn	Disgusted	

The parents gave me excellent descriptions of why each of these emotions struck a cord within them. For example, the mother stated she felt *startled* and *disgusted* when she saw the condom. She also admitted to feeling *embarrassed* and *uncomfortable* when she brought the matter to her husband's attention. When the father thought about one of his younger children coming across the condom he stated he felt *offended*, *infuriated* and *concerned*. Both parents stated they felt *disconnected* from their eldest son. Each emotion identified by the parents was accompanied by a similar explanation. The parents took their original list of three words – angry, shocked, and disappointed – and expanded it to 23 emotions. This list embraced the true spectrum of emotions they likely encountered. It took us about 35 minutes to review the list of emotions and to identify those that the parents experienced.

At the end of this process, and after hearing the parent's explanations for each emotion, I felt as if I understood the parent's position and how they had been impacted by the event. I had no problem empathizing with the parents, that is, I understood the parents' struggle, their emotions, and thoughts regarding this matter. I complimented the parents on giving me such a detailed description of the event and how it impacted them. I then began to conclude the session. The parents interrupted me and asked how they should deal with their son. They asked which of their five responses I thought would be most helpful. I reminded the parents that I was not living in their house, nor was I their son and that it was not my condom they came across. In spite of these facts, I was concluding the session with a very thorough and complete understanding of the situation. I really felt as if I understood how they had been impacted, how they were struggling with the issue, and how hurt they were by the whole situation. I told the parents that if I were their son, I would find it almost impossible to avoid taking a serious look at my decision to have sex in their house after hearing how they had been impacted by my behavior. It would be very hard not to consider the parents' values while living in their house, and it would be very difficult not to see myself as having an impact on those around me. I would be more cognizant of the repercussions of my future decisions. I think I would leave this conversation closer to having an adult-to-adult relationship with my parents rather than a parent to child relationship. I know that I would not leave any used condoms lying around anymore, and I would seriously think twice about having premarital intercourse under my parents' roof again. I told the parents that if I were their son I would have come to these conclusions

1. without ignoring the matter,

2. without being asked to move out of the house,

3. without developing a complex set of house rules,

4. without having my girlfriend be prohibited from visiting,

5. and without being scolded.

The parents helped me come to these conclusions by exposing me to their emotional selves. I recommended they review the list of emotions again and that they have a conversation similar to ours with their son as soon as possible. Everybody would surely benefit.

This Parenting Assumption was placed in the Paradox chapter for a very specific reason. Exposing a child to the parent's emotional self may often feel like the exact opposite reaction in many parenting interactions. The parents in the example above had little difficulty arriving at five responses to their parenting challenge that minimized aspects of their emotional selves. Their proposed responses were directive, authoritative, and unlikely to be very helpful to the situation. When challenged to consider and implement this Parenting Assumption, they were caught off guard. The parents reported that my suggestion – telling their son how they felt and how they were impacted – somehow felt incomplete and lacking the necessary directive. That is, it lacked instructions and directives from parent to son. The mother told me that my suggestion to expose their son to their emotional selves felt weak and like the exact opposite thing to do in that particular situation. Yet, when they risked change and overcame the discomfort associated with this response, they observed an immediate reaction that was both helpful and healthy. The son did not attempt to minimize the

severity of the situation. He expressed deep and sincere remorse and
surprised his parents by making no argument whatsoever. The parents
also received a telephone call from the girlfriend several hours after
the parents spoke to their son. She expressed her sincere apologies for
not respecting the parents' values and for acting irresponsibly in their
house. She assured the parents that it would not happen again and that
they – the son and his girlfriend – had given the matter considerable
thought. The parents and I discussed the paradox of the situation and
how their younger children might greatly benefit from having access to
their *emotional selves.*

**38. Parents who invest themselves by taking emotional risks
will likely experience rewarding long-term parent-child
relationships.**

   When I think of emotional risks, one particular memory comes
to mind. I was working with a man in his mid 30s. He had been
separated and divorced from his wife for several years by the time I
met him. While married this couple had two children together. After
the divorce, the father had regular contact with the children for several
months. However, the children's mother soon remarried. She, her
new husband, and the children moved away without notifying the
father of their whereabouts. Visitation with the children had been
intentionally cut off.[22] After considerable time, and at great financial
expense, the father located his ex-wife and children and attempted to
arrange visitation. Unfortunately, the children's mother and stepfather
were raising the children as their own and had gone to great lengths
to conceal the existence of the biological father. The ex-wife and her
new husband responded to the father's attempt to reenter the picture by
moving away a second time. This cat and mouse activity continued for
several years.
   Eventually the children's father was able to pin down the mother
and stepfather by successfully obtaining legal support – via court
order – for his visitation. The court ordered supervised visitation and
family therapy to facilitate a healthy reunification for the father and his
children. If the mother failed to allow visitation, she would be found
in contempt of court, arrested, and the children would be placed in
permanent custody of the father.
   The father entered my office devastated. He had not seen his
children for several years. In addition, the father was informed

by the family therapist that the kids were unaware of his existence and that they, for all practical purposes, regarded the stepfather as their biological father. As the father's first supervised reunification appointment drew near he experienced a cascade of both comfortable and uncomfortable emotions. He was at a complete loss as to how he should react upon seeing his children and was beginning to feel panicked. The children were to have had several sessions with a family therapist prior to the reunification. During these sessions the children would be made aware of the father's existence. The mother was required, with the support of the family therapist, to explain why the father was removed from the picture. This would require her to take full responsibility for her evasive and deceptive actions. The father believed his ex-wife likely felt forced into taking these actions by the courts. As a result, he felt as if she was probably resentful of the uncomfortable position she was in. He was fearful that she would comply with the court order to go to therapy then, when out of earshot of the therapist, would attempt to "poison" the children with negative talk about the father in order to justify her aberrant actions. He was wondering if it was realistic that he could develop a healthy relationship with his children under these particular circumstances.

This father entered my office wanting help to identify the "best" thing to say and do when he first encountered his children. I had both good and bad news for the father. The bad news was that the circumstances were far too complex for me or for anybody to formulate a response that would make this situation anything other than what it was – complex and very uncomfortable for all parties involved. The good news was that there was a response that was likely to be helpful and healthy to the situation. However, this response required the father to take a considerable risk. He was looking to me to give him a technical solution for this mess – *in this instance you say this; in that instance you say that*. I had several things in mind that I might say if faced with this situation. However, my response or anybody's response other than his own would ultimately prove to be less helpful to the father and his children. Rather, I encouraged the father to invest himself in this reunification process. That is, invest of himself by preparing to take an emotional risk.

I asked the father to consider the children's perspective. Specifically, I wanted the father to place himself in the children's shoes for a moment and attempt to identify some of the many emotions he believed his children might be experiencing as a result of the recent events. The father was provided a list similar to that found in Appendix B and asked to highlight any emotions he felt were relevant. He easily identified several emotions the children might be experiencing. The father's list contained both comfortable and uncomfortable emotions. When the father and I explored these emotions in greater detail, a fairly clear picture of the difficult situation these kids were facing emerged. This process unfolded in the following manner: the father would identify an emotion from the list, then explain his selection. For example, the father stated, *"The children might feel insecure when hit with such a difficult problem. That is, when they were informed that the family structure was not as they understood it, they could have been left feeling insecure. They might be feeling perplexed and confused. They are young children facing a very complex situation. I would imagine they might be very perplexed and confused as they struggle to make sense of it."* This process was initially difficult for the father. He was so heavily invested in blaming the children's mother for everything that the kids' perspective was getting lost.

After the father identified and expanded the numerous emotions he believed the children may have been experiencing, I asked him to look ahead to the day he was to see his children after being separated for so many years. I asked him to identify and describe the emotions he believed *he* might encounter as he entered the room to see his children. The father immediately teared up. It was evident that there were a great many emotions associated with this event.

The father arrived at a great many emotions. He expanded each of these emotions in the following way:

Scared: *I think my heart will be pumping a mile a minute. I'm pretty confident that I will be scared if not terrified the day I see my children again.*

Insecure: *I hope I will know what to do and say to the kids when I see them. I think I will be entering the room with a lot of insecurity.*

Awkward: *I am pretty confident in most areas of my life, yet I think I might be feeling awkward at that moment; somewhat like a newborn horse trying to take its first steps.*

Cheated: *When I see how much they've grown and changed I think I will feel cheated.*

Relieved: *This has been a long time coming. When I finally see them I'm sure I will be somewhat relieved.*

Nervous: *I think* nervousness *is probably an obvious emotion that I will be experiencing. This is probably closely tied to being pretty scared.*

Confused: *I think I will be* confused. *I guess that's why I am talking to a therapist.*

Uncertain: *As hard as I am working to arrive at the best thing to say to my children when I first see them, no matter how hard I work at it, or how prepared I feel, I think I will still be* uncertain. *I feel like I am facing a big unknown.*

Optimistic: *I have come this far. I think that as the reunification day approaches, I will, in addition to the uncomfortable emotions, feel an overwhelming sense of* optimism. *They're worth it. This is all worth it.*

I found it interesting that after reviewing both lists of emotions – the emotions the father believed the children were experiencing and those he will likely encounter – that both seemed to be on similar emotional ground. The lists were nearly identical. The reasoning behind each of the emotions found on both lists was also almost identical. Now, we do not know if the father's assumptions about the children's emotions were entirely accurate. However, I believe the father put considerable effort into considering the children's perspective and that he was probably pretty close. **Within this realization lies the answer to the father's dilemma –** *what is the best thing to say and do when he first encounters his children***?** If he enters the room to meet his children armed with nothing more than an awareness of his and the children's emotional perspective, all will likely go well. Imagine the father and children facing each other for the first time in several years; the children having little or no memory of this man. I would think this would be a truly awkward moment for all.

Which of the following responses do you think might prove to be more helpful in moving this situation in a healthier direction?

First Option	Second Option
Father facing his two silent children for the first time (his first words): *Hi boys, I'm your father how are you?*	Father facing his two silent children for the first time (his first words): *You know. . . right now I'm feeling a little scared and nervous. This feels like a pretty awkward moment. Either of you guys feeling the same?*

There are several differences between these two responses. Both establish a different foundation on which the rest of the meeting will be built. Both are likely to result in significantly different outcomes.

There is nothing wrong with the first response. It is merely less likely to be as helpful as the second. The first fails to address a very critical point – the emotional perspective of the children and the parent. There would be little denying that the children and the father are feeling awkward. Yet, to openly address what might feel obvious – the uncomfortable emotions surrounding this situation – entails most persons taking an emotional risk. In this case, the emotional risk consisted of the father identifying his own emotions and the emotions likely being experienced by his children. This process was evident in the second example. The father was very direct in the manner in which he addressed everybody's emotional perspective. In fact, he did not even say hello.

I encouraged the father to take a similar emotional risk with his children. During a follow-up session the father told me that when we first met, he thought I was completely off base when I offered the above suggestion. He was desperately wanting me to give him a scripted one-liner that he could memorize and repeat once he was face-to-face with his children. The father told me that he expected to look and feel foolish if he chose to take my advice. Luckily, he took the advice and did not look or feel foolish. When the real meeting occurred, the first words out of his mouth upon seeing his children were nearly identical to the second example above. The emotions he communicated reflected those he was experiencing at that point in time. The father stated that all tension immediately left the room. Both children let out a visible sigh of relief. The eldest responded by telling the father how terrified he was and that it was good to know that his father was such a nice guy. The first meeting between father and children lasted 90 minutes. The social worker present during the reunification session called my office the following day and stated that she had been facilitating reunification meetings for nearly 10 years. During those 10 years she had never had a first meeting in which she was *not* required to intervene or offer input. This was a first for her. She informed me the only words she had the opportunity to say during the entire 90 minutes, was that it was time to end and that she looked forward to meeting the following week. The social worker asked that I keep up the good work with the father. She seemed surprised when I told her that I was only planning to have one or two follow-up visits with the father and that our work was nearly completed. The father invested himself in the reunification process by taking an emotional risk. As such, he experienced a tremendous benefit which reinforced this Parenting Assumption. I was relatively certain the father would continue to take these risks and reap the rewards for a long time to come.

At one point the father in the above example asked me why I was "*discouraging [him] from holding [the mother] accountable for her actions.*" His question was in response to my attempts to direct him away from blaming the children's mother for the awkward situation the father and children found themselves. It was obvious these two parents have many issues between them. The parents proved, through their past actions, that they lacked the skills to resolve their issues without triangulating the children into their messy marriage, separation, and divorce. The hostilities between the parents was already impacting the children in less than healthy ways. By the time the parents – or at least the father – sought professional support, they were ready, willing, and able to martyr their children's long-term emotional well-being to affect revenge on the other parent. The mother's attempt to completely eliminate the biological father from the picture would have served no other purpose than to inflict pain on the father while simultaneously subjecting the children to great emotional harm and feelings of insecurity. The father's attempt to hold the children's mother accountable for her actions in front of the children would have had a nearly equal effect. Essentially, both parents were asking their children to be disloyal to the other parent.

When one child is asked to be emotionally loyal to one parent by siding against the other (e.g. *What your mother did was wrong. She intentionally hurt me by keeping us apart. It's her fault that we haven't seen each other in three years.*), he or she is placed in a very destructive bind. The child will try to comply with the parent seeking the child's loyalty through his or her disloyalty to the other. However, the child possesses a biological loyalty to both parents. This places the child in a bind which *will* eventually lead to significant emotional distress.

The father wanted to tell his children his side of the story. He believed the children had been exposed to their mother's side for several years and that it was his turn to attempt to restore balance. When I discouraged this, he felt I was denying him his right to correct the matter by presenting his perspective. He asked me how he should respond if one of his children were to ask him something like:

"Dad, why did mom not want us to see you?"

This is a logical question that one of the children will certainly and understandably ask at some time in the future. The father knew this to be a certainty and wanted to be prepared. He viewed this as an open door to assert his perspective of the whole situation – that the children's mother was at fault. His perspective would likely place the children in a loyalty bind. *"If I accept dad's perspective, I have to be angry with mom."* I was interested in helping this father create greater intimacy and wanted him to avoid this situation as it would only serve to create eventual distance, confusion, and distrust between parent and children. The father and I worked on a response that would avoid as many loyalty binds as possible. We arrived at an answer to the above question that resembled something similar to the following:

Child: Dad, why did mom not want us to see you?

Father: That's a tough question. I'm glad you asked it. Sometimes adults have disagreements that take them a long time to straighten out. I think this is one of those situations. Your mother and I had several big disagreements that we should try to straighten out. While we do this, it's important for you to know that your mother and I love you very much. I also want you to know that I missed you very much while we were separated. I want to do everything I can to see that you and I continue to develop the best possible relationship that we can. I'm sure your mother feels the same way about her relationship with you.

This response initially felt awkward to the father. He stated that he felt as if this response was placing him in a role as an ally with his ex-wife – leaving him feeling uncomfortable and vulnerable. The father stated he believed his wife would view this type of a response as a weakness and certainly try to take further advantage by continuing to "poison the children." The father was asked to take yet another emotional risk. The risk was to freely allow his ex-wife to attempt to convince the children of anything she wished. When confronted by the children about their mother's views, it was recommended that the father respond in a manner similar to the example above. This response does not ignore the issue but attempts to focus attention on the father's feelings for the children. It also supports the ex-wife's role as mother and does not place the children in a loyalty bind. If the children are repeatedly asked to be disloyal to their father and the father chooses not to respond *in kind* by justifying himself, emotional safety in the father/child relationship will quickly grow.

This appeared paradoxical to the father. It seemed like my suggestion was the exact opposite of what felt natural and what he initially wanted to do. If the father continued to take this advice, I would imagine that the mother – several years down the road – would be confronted with a child stating something similar to: "*Mom, if you have an issue with Dad, don't you think it would be best if you addressed it to him rather than through me? I don't have a problem with Dad. I'm uncomfortable being placed in the middle of your marital and divorce issues.*" Why was I not supporting the father's desire to explain his perspective of the mother's actions to the children? To be perfectly frank, in the long run it will be more helpful to focus on the father–child relationship. If the father focuses his attention on developing greater intimacy in his relationship with his kids, they will eventually hold the mother responsible for her actions.

I informed the father that he would experience many comfortable and uncomfortable emotions in the months ahead. I told him that it was important that he talk about the frustrations he encounters during reunification and beyond. However, frustrations centered around his ex-wife's behaviors should not be processed in the presence of his children or other relatives. Preferably, they should be processed with his ex-wife. Unfortunately, I would not expect this to occur for some time. Hopefully, these two parents will learn how to co–parent while divorced, in a manner that will enhance emotional safety and increase the children's ability to thrive in their later life. The father learned a lot about taking emotional risks. This, in itself, will prove to be helpful in developing a strong, safe, and trusting father-child relationship.

39. Before entering parenthood, prospective parents may benefit from considering the emotional resources required. If the parent's resources are depleted prior to entering this venture the child's resources will likely be exhausted attempting to fill the void. If the parent's emotional reservoirs are frequently replenished through means parallel to that of the child, the child will be better able to challenge living without unnecessary constraint.

I've heard many parents state, *"You are never completely ready to have children, but everything falls into place when the child arrives."* From the perspective of a family therapist this statement seems a bit naive. It may be true for some; however, my office is filled with families who were not so lucky. When I examine why things simply do not *fall into place* for many couples having children, I find the vast majority of the *unlucky ones* failed to consider – in advance – the emotional resources required to raise a child. Indeed, they expected everything to magically "fall into place" and were blindsided when things didn't quite work out that way. These parents describe themselves as feeling emotionally burned out, exhausted, and unable to respond well to the parenting challenges they encounter.

Children whose parents are chronically burned out and emotionally exhausted will fail to thrive and are vulnerable to having severe behavioral problems. This is unfortunate because a parent's emotional reservoir can be readily replenished. In fact, the Parenting Assumptions throughout this book, if incorporated into one's parenting and relating, will leave the parent in a much better position to address his or her emotional needs as well as the needs of his or her children. Parents who incorporate an understanding of systems – understanding the larger picture – and these Parenting Assumptions into their living, report feeling empowered and in charge of the parenting process. Some parents who find themselves exhausted, burned out, and struggling with their children will frequently seek input from a professional therapist. These parents usually arrive in the therapist's office complaining of and focusing on the child's behavioral problems. There is little mention of the parents' emotional state or their contribution to the child's behavioral problems. There is usually little thought given to the possibility that the problems exhibited by the child are centered around the parents or the parenting the child received.

Rarely do I find a child that is a "bad apple." That is, the child's troubling behaviors are unlikely to be the result of genetic factors or influences outside of the family. Rather, the troubling behaviors can usually be traced to well-defined origins within the family system. Therefore, when I'm asked to "fix a child," I will, more often than not, want to focus on the parents. I will likely find a mother and/or father whose emotional resources have been depleted. The child's troubling behaviors – those behaviors that I am tasked with fixing – are usually the result of the child filling the gap created by the parents' depleted emotional resources.

This Parenting Assumption should not be interpreted as an attempt to discourage couples from having children. Rather, this Parenting Assumption merely encourages prospective parents to explore the broad range of resources necessary to raise a child *well*. For example, parents-to-be usually prepare in advance for the financial and logistical resources required to raise a child. Soon-to-be parents tend to have an adequate supply of diapers on hand. They usually have scheduled child care if necessary and have purchased strollers, cribs, and other paraphernalia. Unfortunately, many prospective parents give little attention to the importance of exploring the emotional resources required. Let's look at two brief examples of parents who fall on opposite ends of this scale – parents who considered the emotional resources required to raise a child well and a couple who neglected this process.

The first couple was very young – ages 18 and 19. They arrived in my office during the third trimester of the pregnancy seeking information and support. The pregnancy was a surprise and unplanned. Both wanted children but planned to wait a few years. Neither knew how they would react after the birth of the child. The couple's parents were very supportive and ensured they had everything new parents would need. The baby's room was well furnished and stocked with supplies to care for the infant. Yet, when the soon-to-be parents asked their parents about subjects such as the emotional impact the child might have on the young couple's relationship and about their ability to raise the child, the parents brushed off these most important questions. They merely stated that the young couple "*will be ready when the time comes.*" I'm pretty sure the couple would have done a fine job raising this child without input from me – a family therapist – however, this particular couple did not want to leave anything to chance. We only had the opportunity to meet four of five times before the baby arrived, but were able to cover a lot of territory during these sessions.

The couple was clearly anxious about becoming parents. This anxiety was taking its toll on their relationship. They reported having frequent arguments and were both having a difficult time sleeping. The couple stated they felt isolated and alone, even with the support of family and friends. The young parents-to-be were scared of the changes that were certain to come and unsure of their ability to handle the responsibility. These are completely natural feelings that should in no way be minimized. They are emotions that required attention if the young couple was to meet the needs of the child without depleting their emotional reservoirs and burning out. The couple and I made no attempt to brush off anything they were experiencing. We did not rely upon the *"everything will fall into place when the child arrives"* approach. Rather, we spent considerable time reviewing the physical and developmental needs the child would depend upon the parents to meet. Specifically, we focused on how the parents might create an emotionally safe and secure setting while continually fostering a sense of belonging. The couple would certainly encounter surprises throughout their child's life. No amount of preparation could cover every challenge the new parents were to encounter. However, we attempted to fill in as many of the gaps regarding the technical and emotional aspects of raising a child as we could. Most importantly, we opened the door to frank discussion surrounding the parenting process and their new role as parents. This was a crucial component that seemed missing from input provided by family and friends. By taking time to view the young couple as parents and exploring this role in great detail, they became more comfortable and at ease. We explored which of their emotional resources would be taxed when facing the demands of parenthood. For example, they were the first of their peer group to have a child. The couple knew that less time would be available for the social activities than they were accustomed. How would the social stressors and feelings of isolation created by parenthood be dealt with? It was important for the couple to consider and openly process this and similar questions. If the couple's emotional needs were not being met after the arrival of the baby (e.g. if they were feeling chronically isolated and alone) their relationship and ability to parent well would certainly be affected in less than healthy ways. If the parents' emotional batteries were not being constantly recharged, fewer emotional resources would be available for the parenting process. By preparing in advance through discussion of these issues, the soon-to-be parents found themselves better prepared for the challenges to come. Their emotional reservoirs were full, and they had a better idea of how to maintain these reservoirs. They were better prepared to meet the baby's needs as well as their own emotional needs.

When the child arrived this couple was prepared. They had tools and information to parent the infant well while simultaneously taking care of their own emotional needs. Sure, this couple was challenged by the demands of having a child at such an early age. Yet, their willingness to focus on the emotional aspects of parenting left them in a wonderful position to parent well and be better prepared to enjoy the entire process.

The second example is similar only in that the couple was young. Both the mother and father were eighteen years-old when the child was conceived. This couple separated and reconciled several times during the pregnancy and first years of the child's life. Communication between these parents was poor, and their relationship was filled with conflict. The young couple's parents viewed the pregnancy as a mistake and were critical and unsupportive.

I became involved with the family years later – after the child was admitted into a drug and alcohol abuse treatment program. The boy had just turned thirteen years-old. I was a family therapist at this program and tasked with meeting with the parents of the adolescents admitted for treatment. I attempted to contact the boy's parents shortly after he arrived in treatment. To my surprise, I was informed by a co-worker at the father's place of employment that the couple left on an unplanned vacation to Hawaii immediately after dropping their son off for treatment. I met with the boy the next day and asked if he knew of his parent's whereabouts. As far as the boy knew, his parents were in town. I eventually was able to schedule an appointment after the parents returned 10 days later.

I find this situation significant for several reasons. First, having a child admitted to inpatient substance abuse treatment usually represents a crisis situation to most families – especially when the individual hospitalized is so young. What would motivate parents to secretly and abruptly leave town in the midst of such a crisis? Secondly, why is a 13 year-old abusing drugs and alcohol? Children are not predisposed to abusing substances without some sort of motivation. What role did the child's substance abuse play in this family? When I eventually met with the parents the picture became quite clear.

Having an unplanned pregnancy represented a considerable stressor on the young parent's relationship, and in retrospect, both parents admitted to harboring feelings of resentment toward the child. They freely admitted to being unprepared for the sacrifices that accompany parenthood. This couple had few people in their lives to discuss these feelings with and struggled to do the best they could with the parenting tools they had. Essentially, these parents were burned out from the start. Their emotional reservoirs were empty and their ability to replenish those reservoirs was severely limited. They were merely going through the motions of parenting, just trying to get by. Unfortunately, the result was that few emotional connections existed between the parents and between the parents and their son. They were unable to adequately develop intimate relationships from the beginning.

A child entering the world with limited opportunities to make intimate connections will by no means roll over and play dead. On the contrary, the child will expend a great deal of his or her energy and emotional resources attempting to engage the parents in an intimate relationship. This is a natural and instinctual developmental process. In this family's case, the parents had neither the emotional reservoirs, skills, or support from extended family to develop a parent-child relationship that embraced emotionally intimate interactions. This is not to say the parents did not love their son. They loved him very much. Their chronically depleted emotional reservoirs merely prevented this love from being expressed in healthy and helpful ways. They had no idea how to recognize or address this problem in a manner that was likely to be helpful. The boy experienced years of repeated failure attempting to engage his parents in an intimate relationship. He did the best he could with the limited skills he had to get his emotional needs met. These needs included having a sense of belonging, safety, and emotional security. Eventually, he came across drugs and alcohol. These chemicals instantly met these needs. They essentially anesthetized the boy. When he was high, the natural drive to find belonging and emotional safety and security no longer existed or mattered. These drives were temporarily blocked, giving the boy instantaneous, albeit, inappropriate emotional relief.

To a child who was unable to have needs met through the parent-child relationship, getting high made sense. It felt right and filled a gap that existed in his world. The 13 year-old boy told me that the first time he sneaked a drink from his parents' liquor cabinet, "*it felt right.*" This was not an instantaneous physical addiction but rather a parenting and intimacy substitute. The child's drinking and use of other drugs grew exponentially. With the increased abuse came increasingly disturbing and destructive behaviors. The parents were essentially blind to the signals and symptoms that in all likelihood would have been obvious to others. Why was this? The parents' relationship, their relationship with their son, their household, and their lives were in a constant state of crisis. Their emotional burnout perpetuated ongoing crises in the family and prevented them from recognizing the severity of their son's condition. When their son was admitted to treatment, after being arrested for drug possession, the parents saw an opportunity to recharge their own batteries by getting away for a while. As irrational as this may seem, the parents' abrupt departure made some sense.

The primary focus of therapy, if it had any hopes of being helpful to this family, was not on the 13 year-old's drinking and drug use. No, a paradoxical approach was indicated. The parents had to be encouraged to see themselves as who they were: parents. I initiated discussions that were very similar to those I had with the young couple in the first example. We explored those feelings of resentment the couple experienced, and still harbored, after discovering they were to be parents 13 years ago. We explored the inconveniences they experienced and the activities they missed out on as a result of becoming parents at such a young age. We explored the physical and developmental needs every child has and depends upon the parents to meet. We explored how, as parents, this couple could still get their emotional needs met without unnecessarily fatiguing the child. We also explored how the boy's behaviors might have been a result of his attempts to fill an emotional vacuum that existed in the family. Most importantly, we opened the door to frank discussion surrounding the parenting process and their role as parents. This took considerable pressure off their son and focused attention on the parents.

Several months into therapy that focused on the issues above, the parents stated this was the first time – after 13 years of being parents – they actually felt like parents. Their son had been drug and alcohol free for nearly 4 months when they made this statement. This was an indication that these parents were beginning to consider the emotional resources required to parent well and that they were beginning to replenish their emotional reservoirs in ways that did not leave the son vulnerable.

40. The child who acts out is often seeking safety and security. When the parent encounters the "acting out" child, responding in a way that promotes emotional safety may be experienced as paradoxical and unfamiliar.

I was once asked to evaluate a 16 year-old young man who had been in considerable trouble at school and was likely going to be placed in a juvenile detention facility. He had a long history of fighting with other students and had been suspended from school on many occasions. His behaviors had recently increased in severity and frequency. In the latest incident, he pushed a teacher in the hallway between classes who had confronted him on his loud and disruptive behavior. After being pushed, the teacher he took two steps back and tripped. He fell to the ground and sustained a slight head injury. The 16 year-old was charged with assault. My first interview with the young man was at his school. After reading his school record and hearing of his most recent actions, I was expecting to see an intimidating, *tough guy*. I entered the interview prepared to recommend placement in a restrictive treatment program. I was very surprised upon meeting the young man.

The 16 year-old was relatively large and physically intimidating, yet he presented himself as very polite and well mannered young man. How could this person be responsible for so much mayhem at school? He answered all of my questions in a very truthful manner – admitting to and taking full responsibility for each offense. There was no blaming of others. At first I thought I was getting manipulated: *"If I'm honest about everything, they will go easy on me."* However, for some reason this explanation just did not seem to fit. He was able to identify and communicate his emotions very well. He was able to empathize with the injured teacher and the students he previously assaulted. He did an excellent job telling me how he was feeling and how being placed in a detention center might impact his family and his future. This was not characteristic of the typical bully.

We had a week before my evaluation was due, so later that day I called the young man's mother and arranged an in-home family assessment. The father's whereabouts were unknown. I wanted to see the 16 year-old and his family interact. Something did not add up. This "something" became apparent as soon as I entered the home and met the family. It was a dark and dank home. The window shades were drawn, and there was a musty, smoky odor throughout the house. The furniture was unusual. For some reason the legs on the sofa and chairs had been cut off and were a good 6 to 8 inches lower than what I was accustomed to. There were three dogs in the house – two Chihuahuas and one toy poodle who, for some unknown reason, was loosing most of his fur. There were two babies in the household. These belonged to the 16 year-old's two sisters. When I arrived, one baby was sleeping on a large stack of laundry piled in a corner of the living room. The other baby was placed in some kind of rolling walker that allowed the toddler to move about the house like a pinball. I use a pinball description as the toddler would move from person to person seeking attention. The baby would park himself in front of a family member with his arms outstretched and would merely stare at the adult before him waiting for a response of attention. After a few moments he would silently move to the next person, arms outstretched. He seemed to be invisible to the family.

Besides the 16 year-old boy, his mother, the two sisters and their babies, there were two other adults residing in the house – the mother's older brother and her uncle. As far as I could tell, both had lived in the house for several months. Nobody in the home was employed. In summary, there were five adults, my 16 year-old client, two babies and three dogs living in a relatively small three-bedroom house. All lived on some sort of governmental assistance, and they rarely left the house. The puzzle was starting to take shape.

I sat down on one of the amputated sofas as introductions were made by the 16 year-old boy. I was immediately joined by the three little dogs. The balding poodle snuggled between my legs and the sofa. The Chihuahuas immediately jumped on the sofa and became glued to me. It seemed as if these animals were clinging to me for dear life. I did not shoo the dogs away when they approached me. I'm by no means an animal behavior expert; however, I believe they immediately interpreted my acceptance as a safe and welcoming gesture and decided to move in. The dogs' behavior offered a good subject to get the interview going. It seemed as if the dogs were viewed as an inconvenience by family. They were fed, watered, and let outside to do their business from time to time; however, they were described as always getting in the way and being a general nuisance. There was simply no room in this home for the dogs. It struck me that the dogs' behavior offered a pretty good metaphor for the 16 year-old. The dogs' world did not appear to be very safe or secure. They were not openly accepted or welcomed in the crowded house. Their world was unpredictable and without sound structure. There was little space, little privacy, and little capacity for down time or growth. The dogs clung to anything that offered any bit of security.

The family interacted in a rather peculiar way. I observed that all members constantly insulted each other. Strangely, the insults would quickly switch to various members defending each other just as passionately at the blink of an eye. One minute somebody was throwing an insult or criticism toward somebody else, then almost immediately, he or she defended the same person against the insults of a third family member. This characteristic dominated every discussion and interaction. There was no structure to this family. Nobody was in charge. Nobody had a clearly defined role in the house or family. There was no parental hierarchy. It was survival of the fittest. And yet everybody was very polite to me, well spoken and seemed concerned that the 16 year-old might be removed from the home and placed in a locked detention facility.

The cramped quarters, lack of any parental leadership in the family, and dreary conditions left this place anything but an emotionally safe and secure place to call home. It was very difficult to question the 16 year-old about his understanding of these conditions as this was all he had. He was powerless to improve the situation to any great degree. Yet, I believed there were tremendous resources here that, if identified and exploited, might prove to be very helpful to the situation. These resources were to be found in the mother's natural desire to protect her son. I believed the 16 year-old's behavior at school was directly related to the conditions at home. He had neither the skills nor life experience to communicate frustrations he had about his family and home in an appropriate manner. These frustrations were later identified and processed. They included things such as not having a place to sleep in the home, having to compete with family members for food, and living in a house where arguments and insults were normative ways to interact. He was conflicted. On one hand, he was **not** afraid of being placed in the detention center. In fact, when I asked him about the prospects of being locked up, he appeared to speak of the idea with enthusiasm. As strange as it might sound, such a facility offered much needed structure, direction, and a level of predictability that was absent in the family and household. On the other hand, he was conflicted. Being placed in the detention center would also mean leaving or abandoning his family, to whom he was loyal. There were problems at home, and he felt as if his family needed him. As strange as it might sound, the structure and *comforts* associated with a locked detention center were in conflict with the desire to make things better at home. This is a tough place for a 16 year-old to find himself.

I asked the mother how she attempted to address her son's violent behaviors at school. She said there were punishments, primarily attempts to ground him (keeping him in the home); but these were entirely unsuccessful. He would merely ignore her directives when he found them inconvenient. The 16 year-old never got violent at home yet the mother stated that she did not want to push him too far.

We had little time as the authorities were awaiting my report and recommendations. If the 16 year-old was to avoid being placed in the detention center, drastic measures were in order. The mother suggested additional punishment as a solution to the problem and an alternative to his being incarcerated. She stated that the other family members – including the two house guests – would join in to help enforce grounding the young man. The mother was surprised when I suggested the exact opposite. Punishment was not in order nor appropriate in this situation. I suggested a drastic and paradoxical approach. Create a safe home for the young man. This meant she had to make immediate and significant changes in the household. The focus should be taken off the son's behaviors and placed on the underlying – *systemic* – causes for the behavior (*The child who **acts out** is often seeking safety and security. When the parent encounters the "acting out" child, responding in a way that promotes emotional safety may be experienced as paradoxical and unfamiliar.*). This meant taking steps such as:

1. Getting the mother's uncle and brother out of the home immediately.

2. Placing the 16 year-old's sisters and their babies in a single room.

3. Giving the 16 year-old his own room.

4. Ensuring the above changes came directly from the mother. No family discussion on the matter was to be made. No alternatives were to be considered.

The mother was to assume charge of the household. These actions would be anything but comfortable for the mother. In fact, she initially stated that I was crazy. The mother believed these suggestions were the last thing that would be helpful. She believed that by giving the boy his own room he would be rewarded for his acting out at school.

Yes, turning the focus away from the 16 year-old's behaviors seemed paradoxical and strange to the mother. It was too easy to focus on and find fault in his more obvious problems at school. I was encouraging the mother to consider an alternative perspective, *that problematic behaviors have a purpose in most families.* They are usually a symptom of systemic problems within the family rather than just a behavioral problem with a single individual. In this case, the 16 year-old's behaviors were bringing attention to the unbearable conditions at home such as having to sleep on the floor most nights while his uncle or great uncle slept on the sofa. Was ensuring the boy had a safe place to sleep really rewarding his disruptive behavior in school?

The mother did not want her son removed from the home and locked up. Yet, I could not recommend he be allowed to remain in a home that was instrumental in stimulating the young man's behaviors. I reviewed this Parenting Assumption with the mother and asked her to make the choice. She was in charge of the outcome. Her choices were to confront the conditions in the household and family and thereby keep her son home or, ignore the topic of safety and security and have him placed in the detention center. It was her choice. If she did not want the role of head of household I could not force her to assume the position. I was merely an observer or coach in this decision process. In the end, she made a very healthy and helpful decision. Above the objections of everybody in the family she took charge and implemented the few steps previously mentioned.

It was tense in the home for a day or so. The mother's house guests begrudgingly found other places to live. The single mothers soon thereafter entered into a job training program in an effort to gain employment. Apparently, their new cramped quarters were a significant motivator to find jobs and new places to live. The young man's behavior and performance at school improved dramatically. My report recommended that he be placed on a final probation while the family attended family therapy. The judge accepted the recommendation. The young man's probation officer gave the mother a lot of support by ensuring that there was authority in the limits, boundaries and consequences she established for her son. If the 16 year-old stepped out of line at school or at home, he would be picked up by the probation officer and immediately transported to the juvenile detention facility. I was quite certain this would not occur as the young man's motivation to see this happen had been eliminated. After several weeks of family therapy, improvements were made throughout the household and the family system. The window shades were lifted, smoking was no longer allowed in the house, the poodle's fur began to grow back, and the mother was making decisions that left her in charge of the household. This was now a safe and secure place for the 16 year-old to call home.

Now, this is a rather drastic example of how emotional safety and security impacts behavior. Most parents will not encounter such situations. Yet, most parents will encounter a child whose *acting out* behaviors are directly related to their desire to find safety and security. The 16 year-old did not know what the answers to his dilemma were. Nor did he have the skills or life experiences to identify or communicate his true frustrations. Yet, once the mother shifted focus off the problematic behaviors and onto creating emotional safety and security, we saw immediate changes. The same will be true on smaller matters of parenting. The child who is disruptive in class is often struggling to grasp the material. Feeling behind and unable to do well is very frustrating. The parent who shifts focus from the child's disruptive behavior to empathizing with his or her classroom frustrations may find the process of identifying and implementing effective ways to be helpful relatively easy.

41. Communications are essential and should never be cut off. The angry parent can still communicate in an effective manner. The angry child still has open ears.

The essence of this Assumption is that open communications are necessary for the development of healthy parent-child relationships. This should not comes as a great surprise to most parents. Yet, in some families surprisingly little attention is given to keeping the parent-child communication channels open and healthy. When little attention is devoted to developing and maintaining healthy communications, or when parent-child communications are taken for granted, children are left vulnerable. That is, if communications falter or become weak, children are unlikely to receive the full benefit of the parent's input, guidance, direction, and perspective. This is especially true during times of parent-child disagreement and conflict. I believe this particular Parenting Assumption highlights one of the most important absolutes regarding parent-child communications, *angry parents can still communicate in an effective manner and angry children have open ears.* This statement may seem to contradict some everyday experiences encountered by parents. However, as parents improve their understanding of systemic thought, the underlying premise and utility of this Assumption will become strikingly clear.

This Assumption uses the phrase *cut off*. It might be helpful to explain how this phrase is being used and to differentiate it from merely *taking a break* or *a time out*. *Cut off* has very specific implications here. When disagreements between parents and their children are avoided or cast aside, without open processing, we can say that a portion of their communications has been *cut off*. In extreme circumstances, *cut off* can also pertain to relationships that are completely severed so as to prevent the exploration of differences that result in parent-child conflict. On the other hand, *taking a break* or a *time out* is merely a calming period or a time in which to regroup or organize one's thoughts and perspective. A *break* or a *time out* implies that persons will return to the subject of the disagreement in order to process differences and to consider each other's perspective. I think it is important to mention here that differences between persons, especially parents and their children, do not necessarily have to be resolved in order to enjoy healthy communications. Healthy communication only requires that differences are openly processed and opposing perspectives are considered by the disagreeing parties. Many disagreements between parents and children will take some time to resolve. Some differences may never be completely ironed out. Even though parents and children may not always find themselves in total agreement healthy communications can be realized.

My experience as a family therapist leads me to believe that parent-child communications are often *cut off* even when healthier options are still available to them. The parent or child casts aside or avoids the disagreement, and sometimes the entire relationship, without openly discussing differences. This may be attempted in any one of a number of ways. For example, a child may explode in an angry outburst or may completely shut down and refuse to cooperate with the parent. A parent may punish a child in a particularly harsh manner or may simply refuse to interact with the child. I have worked with many families where a child will adjourn to his or her bedroom following a disagreement with the parent. The child will emerge some time later, after emotions have calmed, but the disagreement is not revisited or processed. The disagreement is ignored or put aside and life continues. Essentially, communications regarding the issue of disagreement have been cut off by mutual consent between the parent and child.

This may alleviate a certain amount of short term discomfort but will eventually lead to a strained parent-child relationship. Healthier and more helpful opportunities are missed by cutting off these particular communications.

The act of exploring opposing perspectives is often as important, if not more so, than finding actual resolution to differences. Many parents are quick to jump to the conclusion that a child or adolescent is simply not listening or that a particular issue or subject is inapproachable. Rarely have I ever found this to be the case. These conclusions are usually a reaction to the uncomfortable emotions that may be briefly encountered when a parent and child face each other with differing perspectives. Rather than exploring these differences and experiencing brief moments of emotional discomfort, a parent will succumb to anger. Many parent-child relationships are needlessly cut off or experience lesser degrees of intimacy as a result of *allowing* communication pathways to deteriorate and by accepting a communications cut off as the only option. Many parents approach me with problems relating to communications. For example, I hear comments all the time from parents such as, *"My adolescent just won't listen to me. We seem to get so angry with each other."* Or, *"My five year-old will simply not do as he is told."* And, *"I haven't spoken to my daughter for years, she's unapproachable."* There are no magical solutions to maintaining open communication pathways. It takes a certain amount of skill, practice, and desire to keep them open. Parent-child communications and relationships tend to be cut off when the parent has difficulty looking beyond the immediate disagreement. This responsibility falls predominately on the shoulders of the parent. In most instances, the child should not be expected to have the maturity and life experiences necessary to engage the parent in a process of exploring each other's perspective, especially during times of conflict or disagreement. The child has a certain degree of responsibility for participating, but parenting requires the child to take a secondary role in assuring healthy communications are maintained.

A systemic approach to parent-child communications is usually necessary to avoid cut offs or to mend fences when they do occur. That is, several interacting variables must be considered if the parent is to keep the communication channels open and healthy. Again, there is no single method or response that will work every time for every parent and child struggling to communicate. However, I have yet to see a combination of systemically focused considerations, skills and

tools to be unsuccessful in keeping channels open regardless of the
conflict, situation, or variables influencing the relationship.[23]   These
particular skills and tools are found throughout *Systemic Parenting*.
As you read the Parenting Assumptions found throughout these
pages, and the examples presented in each, consider how the parents
use a *combination* of skills to promote healthier and more helpful
communications – even during times of conflict and disagreement.
Pay particular attention to how the following skill interacted to keep
communications open between parent and child.

- Differentiating Process from Content, Parenting Assumption number
  56

- Use of Empathy and Promoting Intimacy, Parenting Assumptions
  23 and 56

- Thinking Errors, Parenting Assumption 78

Most importantly, remember that communications are essential to
a healthy parent-child relationship and that *the angry parent can still
communicate in an effective manner. The Angry child still has open
ears.*

**42. Enhancing development of the child's uniqueness is
more helpful than implanting your own. The former leads
to individuality, strength, and trusting relationships. Both
the child and parent will be rewarded. The latter promotes
confusion, dependence and indecision. Initially, the parent may
be rewarded yet both child and parent will eventually suffer.**

After reviewing this Parenting Assumption over and over, I have
come to the conclusion that it speaks of self-esteem. Self-esteem is
a complicated and broad subject – one that seems to be misused by
both parents and professionals. Parents frequently come to my office
stating their son or daughter has a problem with *self-esteem*. Parents
also frequently bring reports from their child's teacher stating the
student has a poor sense of *self-esteem*. Furthermore, mental health
professionals throw this term around like plastic beads at Mardi Gras.
Professionals, parents, and teachers will point to self-esteem as being
a problem without knowing exactly what it is or how it impacts the
individual and family. When I hear parents, teachers, and fellow mental

health professionals using this phrase, I make it a point to ask them: *"Help me understand exactly what you mean by self-esteem? What is it and how does it apply to this specific issue, incident, or problem?"* These questions do not help me make very many friends. They usually anger my fellow mental health professionals. The teachers tend to get very nervous and defensive, and parents will usually clear their throat a lot and just shut down. I'm not trying to offend anybody. I merely want to uncover specifics about the subject matter or problems being presented.   If these questions are left unanswered the discussion to follow should have particular relevance.

There are literally hundreds of definitions for self-esteem to be found in the academic, pop–psychology, and self-help literature. Few of these definitions take into consideration the family's role in self-esteem nor the influence of one's self-esteem on family functioning. So, let's complicate matters a bit by adding another definition of self-esteem to the literature.   I believe this definition will embrace a broader systemic understanding of the subject while moving discussion of this particular Parenting Assumption forward.   This is a relatively complicated definition. It may be helpful to read it a few times.

Self-Esteem: The level of *confidence* and *satisfaction* one has in him/herself. That is, and broadly speaking, confidence in *who* he or she is, confidence in *where* he or she is going, confidence in *how* he or she is getting there, and the level of confidence one has in *those* with whom he or she interacts.

As this *confidence* fluctuates so does the level of *satisfaction* (proportionately).   That is, satisfaction in *whom* he or she is, satisfaction in *where* he or she is going, satisfaction in *how* he or she is getting there, and finally, the level of satisfaction one has in *those* with whom he or she interacts.

Confidence refers to that level of regard (high regard ↔ low regard) one holds in each of the areas identified (*who he or she is, where he or she is going, how he or she is getting there, and those with whom he or she interacts with*).

Satisfaction refers to the level of emotional benefit, reinforcement, and support received from each of the areas identified.

Confidence and satisfaction in *who he or she is* refers to one's understanding and belief that he or she is a valued member of and able to contribute to the family, the social arena, the workplace, and the community.

Confidence and satisfaction in *where he or she is going* refers to the individual's goals, ambitions, desires, abilities, activities, and general life direction. That is, with what regard does the individual hold and what emotional benefits are realized from his or her goals, ambitions, desires, abilities, activities, and general direction?

Confidence and satisfaction in *how he or she is getting there* refers to one's understanding of and regard for values, ethics, and spitituality.[24]

Finally, confidence and satisfaction in *those with whom he or she interacts* refers to the level of relative security, safety and trust found in one's family, social arena, workplace, and community.

Again, this is a pretty complex definition of self-esteem. It covers a lot of territory. However, if you refer to and review this definition while exploring the Parenting Assumptions throughout this book, its importance, utility and meaning will become very clear.

I cannot tell you how often adults come to my office seeking therapy because they are unhappy with the direction their life is taking. Many of these adults have been prescribed antidepressant medications by their physician or psychiatrist to help alleviate their uncomfortable feelings. These medications typically offer some relief from the symptoms. Unfortunately, the underlying issues causing the unhappiness and depression tend to go untreated. This general sense of unhappiness, even when treated with medications, can eventually manifest itself in what many people term "a midlife crisis." When somebody in their late 30s and early 40s abruptly purchases an expensive or exotic sports car, those close to this individual tend to think, "Oh, he's just having a midlife crisis." When a spouse or partner abruptly announces that he or she "needs space" and leaves the relationship, many therapists will attribute this to "a midlife crisis." I believe these seemingly impulsive actions are much more complex than a mere "midlife crisis." The origins of these behaviors can be traced back to one's childhood and how they were parented. Chances are, their parents gave little attention to developing the child's sense of uniqueness and self-esteem.

Let's clarify this by taking a look at some adults presenting themselves in my office seeking relief from feelings of unhappiness and mild depression. In nearly every incident, the person sitting before me will have dreams, ideas, and beliefs that have either failed to materialize or are somehow in opposition to how he or she is living his or her life. These adults tend to believe their dreams, ideas, and beliefs are a central part to *who they are* as individuals, yet somehow feel prohibited from making them a "reality." They believe any attempt to pursue or even discuss their dreams, ideas or beliefs might set them up to be chastised or viewed as irresponsible and would result in unhealthy consequences or leave them feeling disloyal to their family, parents and upbringing. I hear many statements in my office that seem to be an indication that the individual's core beliefs, dreams, and ideas about living differ from how he or she is actually living. For example, I often hear: *"I feel like a slave to my house and mortgage. Do I really need the space? Why do I spend my weekends doing yard work? Is this how I want to spend my time with my family and children?"* And, *"I always thought I had a book or novel in me. It seems like everything gets in the way of working on it."* And, *"I don't seem to get it anymore. I disagree with almost everything I hear in church, and I have a hard time watching the news on TV. It seems like there is so much hypocrisy in the world. . . . in my own life."* And, *"I used to be involved in so may activities. I had so many dreams and ambitions. What happened to them?"*

Great discrepancies are created when our internal beliefs, dreams, and ideas differ from how we choose to live our lives. This discrepancy will most certainly lead to internal emotional conflict. This conflict will often manifest itself as depression, generalized feelings of unhappiness, or impulsive "midlife crisis" behaviors. Adults who struggle with this conflict can find tremendous relief through therapy. In my office, I encourage the unhappy or mildly depressed adult to identify their internal dreams, ideas, and beliefs. We will safely explore these dreams, ideas, and beliefs in great detail and eventually formulate a plan to responsibly integrate them into his or her living and relationships. More often than not, this process will greatly alleviate the generalized feelings of unhappiness, depression, and impulsive actions. I find it unfortunate that so many adults live their life incorporating or relying upon beliefs, dreams, and ideas that greatly differ from those that are internally and secretly maintained.

Parents can give a great gift to their children by ensuring this situation is avoided by promoting a healthy sense of self-esteem early in life. This entails continually looking at the four areas defined in our understanding of self esteem: **1) who he or she is; 2) where he or she is going; 3) how he or she is getting there; 4) the level of confidence and satisfaction he or she has in those with whom he or she interacts.** It is helpful to have ongoing discussions surrounding these four subject areas to help ensure that one's core beliefs, ideas, and dreams closely parallel how one chooses to live.

This Parenting Assumption presents one way to support development of a healthy sense of self-esteem, by enhancing development of the child's uniqueness rather than implanting your own. This means exposing your children to a variety of life situations and activities, then paying particular attention to and encouraging the child's emerging interests, skills, and personality. For example, suppose a parent loves to hunt and fish. This parent may be determined to encourage like interests in his or her children. If this parent limits his or her children's primary exposure to hunting and fishing activities, the child's uniqueness may be stifled. This child may very well have the potential and desire to become an exceptional soccer player, rock climber, or musician. Unfortunately, these opportunities may be lost while the parent attempts to implant his hunting and fishing interests. The Parenting Assumption to follow will provide a more detailed example to help clarify this point. However, if a parent allows a child's uniqueness to develop and emerge, the youngster's confidence and satisfactions are sure to rise. If the child of the hunter fails to develop an interest in, or skill for, these activities, his or her confidence and satisfaction will likely be impacted in less than healthy ways. This child is heading for an eventual mid life crisis.

I placed this Parenting Assumption under Paradox because many parents feel obligated to pass along their interests, hobbies, beliefs, and dreams to their children. This is unfortunate, as the parent will miss an opportunity to support the child's development in a very healthy way. As the saying goes, "the apple does not fall far from the tree." The child will develop many of the same beliefs, interests, dreams, and goals held dear to the parents without much input or encouragement from the parents. This occurs out of a natural and biological loyalty all children have for their parents. If a parent is an avid hunter, chances are the child will absorb similar interests or at least an understanding of the activity. If, in addition to hunting, this parent supports and encourages involvement in a variety of other activities and intellectual interests, everybody will benefit. The child's uniqueness will be supported. Quite often this belief feels paradoxical to many parents.

43.   Seek to find the child's strengths and interests. Explore and encourage those that may differ from your own. Both parent and child will grow together in this process.

When I discuss this Assumption with parents, I am often met with two distinct reactions representing vastly different parenting styles and beliefs. Some people believe it is the parents' responsibility to mold their children in their own form. That is, the parents will primarily promote ideas, beliefs, behaviors, and activities that are familiar, known and traditional to their family. Those that fall outside of the family's accepted belief structure or tradition are frowned upon or discouraged. Other parents will explore ideas, beliefs, and activities that differ from or fall outside of their family traditions and beliefs without discomfort. To these parents, raising children who follow in their exact footsteps is not a paramount goal. Both groups of parents seem to vigorously defend their respective approach.

I do not want to offend any parent by asserting one approach is in any way superior or healthier than the other. As we will see, an argument can be made for promoting one's family traditions as well as exploring avenues outside the bounds of family traditions. The two are by no means mutually exclusive. Problems seem to occur when parents become *concretely* attached to one belief or the other – animatedly sticking to, or blindly casting away, traditional beliefs, affiliations, and activities. This subject tends to come to my attention when a child develops ideas or interests that deviate from concretely held family traditions. I'm usually asked to help support the parents resolve family conflict by convincing the child to see the world as the parents see it. I also seem to come across this issue when asked to work with children who are failing to thrive or have been diagnosed with depression.[25] These conditions are often intimately connected to this subject as well. Let's explore how and why children confront family traditions and why this process can actually be healthy for the family and future generations.

It is not uncommon for children to develop interests or values that differ from those held by their parents. This seems to be a developmental inevitability. All-to-often these differences become a source of stress between parent and child. Problems typically arise when children begin exploring dress, music, religious beliefs, political views, recreational interests, social networks, educational paths, and career choices that are foreign to the parents' own beliefs, understanding, or comfort level. I have had many parents in my office who were struggling with thoughts that they had somehow failed because their child's beliefs or actions differed from those which were desired or expected. For example, I worked with several people who questioned their competency as parents because their children dyed their hair blue or got their nipples pierced. Other parents were struggling because they believed their child's religious convictions were not as strong as or differed from their own, or that their child failed to develop interests held dear by other family members, such as a family with a long tradition of hunting with a child who views these activities as cruel and inhumane. Should these be considered failures in parenting? I don't think so. However, these situations may be somewhat more complicated than initially meets the eye. Let's consider some of the variables important to understanding the breadth of these situations.

On several occasions throughout this book I state that parents are *the primary educators of their children.* In other words, the parents will have a far greater impact on their children's overall character, whether their children experience future successes or failures, and the relative health of their children's future relationships, than any other influence outside of the family. This is not to say that children are blind to discovery or that they are immune to information and ideas that fall outside of the parents' range of influence. It is important to realize that children have *a natural drive to discover,* to learn, and to expand their understanding of the world around them. This natural drive toward discovery is a powerful force in children and young adults and will at some point expose them to ideas, beliefs, and activities that differ from those held in high regard by their parents. These newly discovered ideas, when introduced to the family system, will not always be welcomed and are likely to create a certain amount of tension. If parents attempt to limit discovery to only their understanding of the world, by discouraging outside or alternative ideas, the child is left at a great disadvantage. The child may feel compelled to discover and explore but experience tells the child this might not be well received by the parents and other family members. This forces a child into a bind. The child must choose between being loyal to his or her parents or to go with the natural drive to discover.

Children have a natural loyalty to their parents and, for the most part, will subscribe to and support the basic values, beliefs, and activities exhibited and advanced by the parents. Deviating too far from the parent's belief structure and family tradition is often uncomfortable for the child. Yet, the natural drive to discover and to expand one's understanding of ideas, beliefs, and activities that exist outside the realm of family tradition can exert considerable influence on the child. This drive does not exist merely to make parenting difficult or to destroy traditional beliefs and expectations. It actually serves a very important purpose. A child exploring alternative ideas and beliefs may actually be helping to prevent stagnation within the family by forcing it to look inward and to evaluate the validity of its belief structures and traditions. This is where things get tricky and may seem a bit paradoxical. When the child explores, considers, or reaches out to ideas, beliefs, or activities new to the family system the status quo within the family may be disturbed. These actions may be seen as a threat to stability within the family or an assault on tradition. In fact, the child's seemingly wayward actions can actually promote growth within the family system.

If a child's sense of discovery is suppressed or discouraged, as a means of supporting the existing status quo within the family, the traditions and expectations the parents are attempting to protect will actually be *less* likely acquired and perpetuated by one's children. If parents discourage children from taking traditional family beliefs and placing their own mark or signature on them, the child's personal investment in continuing these traditions will be greatly reduced. If a child is pressured to perpetuate a traditional belief merely because he or she is expected to, and without the option of critiquing or adding to that tradition, it will lack any real relevance to the child. This greatly reduces the chances that this tradition will be passed along to future generations.

Racism is an excellent example of how a family tradition, belief, and behavior is passed from generation to generation and how the child's drive to discover may be responsible for simulating healthy change within the family system. The ideas and values associated with racism are passed from parent to child when the discovery process is discouraged. Without *discovery* fueling evaluation of family traditions and beliefs, future generations would be handicapped by stagnated beliefs that lack relevance to the society around it. Racism is a stagnant belief that only serves to create distance between cultures and races without any justification or relevance to everyday life. A family that assists and supports the discovery process by exposing the child to a broad spectrum of ideas and stimulating experiences, while simultaneously exploring alternative beliefs and ideas raised by the child, will find less helpful and healthy traditions, such as racism, confronted, evaluated and eventually phased out rather than being mindlessly perpetuated. This process begins with the child's drive to discover, which will bring him or her in contact with different cultures or races. When these experiences differ from that which the family tradition of racism has prepared the child, questions will be asked and traditional family beliefs challenged. This will either stimulate exploration and growth, or conflict and stagnation within the family system. The direction it takes rests primarily upon the shoulders of the parents.

When differences between a parent's belief structure and a child's emerging interests arise, the parent can choose to view these differences as a parenting opportunity rather than responding to them with hostility or indifference. Viewing differences as parenting opportunities by no means implies that the parent must compromise his or her personal beliefs to accommodate the child. By parenting opportunity I mean the parent can open the door to greater parent-child exploration. For example, say a child asks a parent about a religious belief that differs from those held dear by other family members. Say a teenager expresses favor for a political party different than that favored by the parents. What if a child, coming from a family of avid hunters, believes killing for sport or game is cruel and inhumane? Is there anything unhealthy or inappropriate with the following:

- *That's different from what I believe. Help me understand where you're coming from.*

- *I don't know about that. Let's find out more!*

- *It's hard for me to agree with that belief. Help me understand what it means to you.*

These, or similarly worded responses, may be very uncomfortable for some parents. However, they tend to be very engaging when parent and child are faced with differences of opinion. These responses tend to open the door to emotionally safe interactions while simultaneously stimulating healthy cognitive and emotional development. If the parent chooses to respond to differences in a more concrete and less open manner – *"You're wrong, end of discussion"*; *"I don't want to hear you talk that way in this home"*; *"That's stupid."* the child will merely explore these alternative thoughts, beliefs and interests on his or her own and without input, support, or commentary from the parents. The differences in perspective generated by the natural discovery process will not magically disappear from the child's mind just because it creates discomfort for the parent and conflict within the family.

Some parents find themselves intimidated or threatened when they explore beliefs and ideas that differ from their own. That is, there is a feeling that if the parent actually engages a child in the exploration of a belief, an idea, or an interest that differs from what the parent believes, that he or she is actually encouraging them. Recall the adage *an apple does not fall far from the tree.* A child's natural loyalty to his or her parents will usually keep the child in the general area of the family's shared beliefs and in line with acceptable behaviors. So, what happens in those situations where children rebel in dramatic ways? What about examples of those who have gone to great lengths to remove or cut themselves off from their family? I have worked with hundreds of such families and, at first glance, these individuals seem to no longer subscribe to the shared belief structure that binds the family together. However, after exploring these situations in great detail, I have come to the conclusion that these *apples* did not merely fall far from the tree, but were *driven* from its limbs. In nearly every instance the differences that emerged from the process of natural discovery were met with concrete responses from parents and/or other family members. Over time these differences grow and solidify – eventually resulting in one taking dramatic actions such as obvious rebellion or completely cutting themselves off from, or being cut-off by, the family.

Discord among family members surrounding family belief structures also seems to be at play in many instances of child/adolescent depression and when a child fails to thrive. *Unprocessed* differences between a family's traditional belief structures and a child's emerging strengths, interests, ideas, and beliefs, if not expressed through overtly rebellious acts, tend to be internalized. A child will remain loyal to the parents and family by suppressing these emerging feelings, thoughts and beliefs. Over time, the process of suppression will likely manifest itself as depression, apathy, or a myriad of other self-destructive behaviors. Treatment for the depression or self-destructive acts often entails nothing more than opening the door to safer exploration of these different perspectives and reassuring the parents that "*the apple*" will not likely fall too far from the tree during this process.

Let's conclude by looking at this Parenting Assumption from a slightly different perspective. Below are two hypothetical statements made by a young child – 6 or 7 years-old – to one of his or her friends. These are simple statements, yet they provide great insight to the quality of the parent-child relationship. Which statement do you think is indicative of a healthier, more intimate and open parent-child relationship?

1. *"My dad knows everything!"*

2. *"My dad and I figure things out together."*

The first hypothetical statement may leave a parent feeling proud. *"My child looks up to me, trusts me, learns from me, sees the world as I do. He's a chip off the old block."* The second statement may be less complimentary to the parent's ego, yet, it hints of a very intimate relationship where exploration, problem solving, individuation, and parent-child interactions are important. If the child expressing the second statement were to come across ideas, interests, or beliefs that differed from family tradition – say he objected to racially derogatory remarks uttered by his parents. I would think that these differences are more likely to be processed and explored in the second example.

Blending new ideas with traditional belief structures can be uncomfortable from time to time. However, this process is likely to impact the parent-child relationship in very rewarding, healthy, and helpful ways. Discovery is a wonderful human characteristic that can enrich the lives of both parent and child. Parents may support this process by seeking to find the child's strengths and interests. Explore and encourage those that may differ from your own. The child will absorb family traditions and expectations through a process of natural loyalty. That is given. The parent may assist the child in claiming ownership of these traditions by encouraging him or her to contribute to and advance the ideas, beliefs, and activities that make up these traditions. Both the parent and child will grow together in this process.

44. Growth can be promoted in the midst of personal and family tragedy. This should always be remembered as a paradoxical part of living.

I whole heartedly believe that growth can be promoted in the midst of personal and family tragedy. I believe families can come together after the death of a member. Parents can find new levels of intimacy and strength after a child is diagnosed with a terminal or chronic medical condition. As a family therapist, I have been placed in the position to work with dozens of such situations. These experiences have led me to believe that growth within an individual and the family during these periods of stress and trauma may even be a crucial component to a healthy bereavement and the family's ability to move forward. I certainly do not want to minimize the impact tragedy has on the family and its individual members. I only make this assertion after having worked with many families that seemed to disintegrate after the death of a beloved member. I make this assertion after having worked with several parents who divorced or separated shortly after the death of a child. Although many factors contributed to these reactions, one component was missing from each family and each couple, *the paradox of growth emerging from tragedy.*

This Assumption actually came to me as I was touring Yellowstone National Park in Wyoming shortly after a catastrophic forest fire. The landscape was barren as far as I could see. Wildlife had either fled or perished. I hiked for mile after mile among trees stripped of their life, some fallen, some remaining mere skeletons of their previous vigor and beauty. Then, out of the corner of my eye, I notice a color that seemed odd in the blackened and grey landscape. In the middle of this seeming wasteland was a patch of beautiful wild flowers. These flowers were emerging in areas previously shielded from the sun's rays by thick forest. The colors were stunning and the contrast left me awestruck. There was growth in the midst of this tragedy. I returned to Yellowstone several years later. Wild flowers were everywhere and interspersed in the burned out forests were young saplings just a few feet tall. Life for the forest continued despite great tragedy.

This metaphor may at first seem contrived and inappropriate to families who have experienced the loss of a loved one, or parents who outlived a child. Maybe it is. However, when I think back to the families and couples that I worked with who were unable to rebound from their own tragedy, one thing seemed strikingly absent from each. Families and couples who survive seemed to connect to this idea of the paradox of growth emerging from tragedy. The families who seemed to disintegrate and couples who separated after a tragedy missed this connection.

A warning might be in order here. Families who respond to tragedy in a healthier manner do not minimize their loss. They do not lose sight of the burned out forest surrounding the patches of wildflowers. They merely provide an environment that allows the flowers to emerge and recognize them as being present and contributing to the entire landscape.

I worked with a family whose oldest son, 6 years-old, was diagnosed with a terminal medical condition. His life was expected to end in less than six months from the initial diagnosis. This was a heart breaking situation that was tearing the family apart. Members of this family were working away from having greater intimacy rather than toward greater intimacy. The family was Catholic and were referred to my office by their parish's priest. The priest was concerned that the family was falling apart and wold not survive. When the family arrived in my office, we simply explored the paradox of growth that could emerge from the tragedy. My role was relatively minor. During the child's remaining months I merely encouraged the parents to process the rapidly approaching loss and to make every conceivable effort to increase and encourage greater levels of intimacy between all family members. We defined and explored intimacy and empathy and how each played an important role in creating safety and security during such difficult times.

I met with the family a week after the child's death. We processed the entire tragedy. One important thing stood out to me, the parents arrived at a point where they could look at both the wild flowers and the devastated forest. They recalled the memories of great times spent with their now deceased son. They described the feelings of joy and love that filled their heart when they thought of him. And, they described the feelings of pain, sorrow and unfairness that accompanied their loss. Finally, they were able to acknowledge the support and comfort that had come from each member of their family. New relationships emerged from this tragedy; relationships that enjoyed much greater levels of intimacy. This intimacy did not exist as the family was falling apart immediately following the boy's diagnosis. This was the paradox of growth that emerged from their tragedy. Had these parents, this family, failed to make this connection, I fear they might not have survived their painful and tragic loss intact. *Growth can be promoted in the midst of personal and family tragedy. This should always be remembered as a paradoxical part of living.*

45. Care for the child by caring for yourself – paradoxical thoughts are often necessary in artful parenting.

I was on an airliner some time ago. As the jet left the terminal, the flight attendant began the standard presentation. We heard about how to buckle up, our attention was directed to the emergency exits; we were informed that the seat cushions double as flotation devices, and how to properly place oxygen masks over our faces. Normally, I use this time to organize my in-flight reading material, but this day I listened. The attendant stated that if the cabin should lose air pressure, oxygen masks will drop from above. Adults or parents who were traveling with small children were instructed to first place a mask on themselves, *then* place a mask on the child. *Parent first, then the child.* The reasoning behind this is relatively straight forward. If the parent places the mask on the child first, he or she may slip into unconsciousness prior to getting their own mask on. A young child will likely be unable to assist the unconscious parent and thus risks losing the parent in this scenario. The parent who initially cares for him/herself will be in a much better position to give to and assist the child. This thought has far reaching applications – care for the child by caring for yourself.

When I discuss this topic with parents many respond, "my child always comes first," or "I would sacrifice anything for my child." These are noble thoughts. Unfortunately, they are neither realistic nor necessarily conducive to helpful or healthy parenting. The parent who places the oxygen mask on the child first may very well save that child (a noble act). However, the potential long-term consequences to the child are less optimistic. Caring for the child by caring for yourself is a paradoxical thought that is helpful to long-term and healthy parenting.

I can think of many realistic examples that highlight the importance of this Assumption. In my practice I frequently came across parents who were considering separation or divorce. These couples told me their relationship was great for the first couple of years. Then, "something happened." They became increasingly distant from each other. In more cases than not, these parents did a wonderful job parenting. In fact, I often found that the focus of their relationship was parenting their children. The children came first (a noble thought). Yet, over time these parents lost focus on caring for themselves and their relationship. The couple lost touch with the collective interests that brought them together during the early months and years of their relationship.

Many parents have informed me that they felt guilty taking time away from their children to pursue personal or common marital interests. Other parents have informed me that peer, family, or religious/church pressure to focus solely on the child and away from personal or relational interests were formidable. *Care for the child by caring for yourself.* Ask yourself this, which child will likely have a greater number of comfortable experiences while growing up: one whose parents are always working toward greater intimacy in their relationship and are involved in activities that bring joy and esteem to the relationship or parents who sacrifice intimacy in their relationship and the special activities that were at one time an important part of living for the couple? Frankly, I would prefer happy and healthy parents over dedicated parents willing to martyr themselves and their relationship for the children. *Paradoxical thoughts are often necessary in artful parenting.*

I lived in Colorado for several years. While there, I met a young married couple. Both were very active, athletic, and involved in outdoor activities such as hiking, rock climbing, and camping. When the couple had their first child, many members of their peer group thought they would fall off the face of the earth. The camping, rock climbing, and hiking activities would most certainly cease or would be greatly reduced. Well, they didn't. In fact, I ran across the couple and their 8 month-old daughter hiking and camping in Rocky Mountain National Park. The couple had forged a balance between parenting, caring for themselves, and real world responsibilities (e.g. going to work, paying rent, etc.). The couple would frequently find a responsible baby-sitter and go rock climbing for a morning or afternoon. The child would be included in activities if at all possible and when a sitter could not be found or afforded. The couple made it a point to remain focused on their relationship and their emotional well being. This was by no means selfish nor was the child in anyway ever neglected. In fact, the exact opposite was realized. The level of intimacy between parent and child seemed to grow exponentially. Years later I visited the couple. They had a second child. They were experiencing great success in their marriage and their respective careers. Their first child was probably one of the most outgoing, self confidant, and mature children I have ever encountered. She had an open, intimate, and very trusting relationship with her parents. The parents still prioritized their time together and made it a point to care for themselves.

I have a second example that may be worth noting when speaking of this particular Parenting Assumption. I was filling my car with gasoline one day. I was alone and minding my own business when a woman, who was parked nearby, asked if I wanted "a couple of teenagers." I just smiled in response and went about filling my car up with gas – assuming she was just making a joke. She had several children of various ages in her vehicle. Her next comment surprised me a bit. She stated, "I ask everybody if they want them." That was a bit strange. Why was she telling a complete stranger such things? The children were sitting silently in the vehicle. Their faces showed little emotion. If this woman were in my office and I had time to ask her a few questions, I'm quite certain I would find that she was lacking the tools to care, nor was she focused on caring for herself. She was likely overwhelmed and unable to find a way to a healthy balance between parenting and self-care. I wonder what social/familial support structures were in place for this woman. I wonder what non-parenting activities this woman held dear in her life. I wonder about emotional intimacy in this woman's life. Is she working toward or away from having greater intimacy with other persons in her life? I believe these to be important questions for this woman to consider. Unfortunately, from my brief encounter with this family, I doubt these questions would be explored or addressed. The future consequences will be great, as the children in the vehicle were learning lessons about many topics. These lessons will play themselves out in less helpful/healthy ways in their later lives and relationships – especially lessons about caring for themselves.

46. When the child is in a constant state of distress the parent should look inward.

This Assumption came to my mind after working with dozens of parents who wanted their children placed on medications to help curb undesirable or problematic behaviors. This is a relatively common parental reaction to a child demonstrating signs of attention deficit, impulse control, or anxiety disorders. In most instances, these children had been evaluated by a psychiatrist or their family physician. They were placed on medications then referred to my office for follow-up and family therapy. Perhaps this Assumption was on the physicians' minds as well.

I do not want to minimize the important role medications have in the treatment of childhood emotional disorders. Nor would I ever recommend that parents refrain from exploring the appropriateness of pharmaceutical interventions for symptoms of severe emotional and behavioral problems. However, I do recommend that before children are medicated, that parents first consider what I see as a common misconception widely held by mental health treatment professionals - that the *first* course of treatment for childhood emotional disorders and behavioral problems is medication. This approach may treat the symptoms but often neglects the many interdependent family and relational issues contributing to the symptoms. When a child is given a mental health diagnosis then treated individually, as is often the case with pharmaceutical interventions, he or she may be destructively stigmatized, while the underlying conditions that likely helped precipitate the problematic behaviors go untreated. There are many long-term and less healthy consequences associated with only treating the symptoms. For example, imagine that you have a toothache. If the symptoms of this problem, pain and discomfort, are treated with pain medications, the underlying conditions, decay and abscess, may be masked. Many of the troubling symptoms may be alleviated, but the tooth's future health will likely be less promising.

The misconception that medications alone are the most effective treatment for many childhood mental health and behavioral disorders is accepted with open arms in a society eager to define behavioral problems in terms of diseases, chemical imbalances, and genetics. These medical explanations, and the corresponding pharmaceutical interventions, gain almost instant acceptance because they help alleviate complex systemic and societal pressures. For example, medical explanations relieve busy and often overwhelmed parents of a certain degree of parental responsibility - *If my child's behaviors are the result of a chemical imbalance, treatable with medications, I am relieved of some of the pressures associated with parenting well.* A school struggling with the challenges associated with increased class size, budgetary cutbacks, poor parental and community involvement, will eagerly jump on the disease bandwagon by advocating pharmaceutical solutions for their *problem students*. Many of the families that I have evaluated over the years were referred to my office from school counselors recommending a child be placed on medications for his or her attention deficit. Also standing in the background are many therapist, psychiatrists, physicians, and the ever present and powerful pharmaceutical industry pushing a potpourri of medications as a necessary solution to what woes our children. Finally, we mustn't leave out the medical insurance industry who saves a substantial sum of money each year by discouraging family therapy in lieu of pharmaceutical interventions for child behavioral and emotional problems.

From a clinician's perspective, it is much easier and financially lucrative to diagnose and medicate a struggling child than it is to work with the family to uncover the systemic variables influencing the undesirable behaviors. Unfortunately, taking the easy route may alleviate the immediate symptoms but will likely leave the child's future less promising. I refer many children to psychiatrists for medication consultations, however, these referrals are almost always accompanied with family therapy. The medications can offer a great deal of relief for the child while the family and I explore the underlying systemic issues resulting in the problems.

I believe this Parenting Assumption asks parents to consider a larger perspective before assuming a child's undesirable or troubling behaviors are disease states treatable with medications alone. In some cases they are. In most cases, *when a child is in a constant state of distress the parent should look inward.* The underlying variables leading to the problematic behavior will likely be found in the family system rather than a disease, a chemical imbalance or a genetic predisposition for such behavior. This is often experienced as a paradoxical thought to parents.

47. A loving parent who finds difficulty establishing and enforcing limits, boundaries, and consequences may have a narrow view of love.

Early in my career I worked with many adolescents. Most of these young adults were being treated for drug and alcohol abuse and were inpatients in a rehabilitation hospital. As part of their treatment, they would attend weekly individual sessions with a therapist. They would also sit through daily educational classes on drug and alcohol related issues and have an occasional family therapy session. Yet, by far one of the most helpful treatment activities was the daily group therapy session. These groups were 90 minutes in length and typically involved one therapist and 6 to 10 participants. I enjoyed this particular treatment activity as it gave me the opportunity to see many adolescents successfully confront and process a variety of severe personal and family problems. I witnessed adolescents who were labeled as "troubled" demonstrate amazing thoughts and insight. When these young men and women worked together as a group, they consistently arrived at conclusions that probably would have surprised their parents. The insights and thoughts frequently verbalized by these adolescents were instrumental in my understanding of this particular Parenting Assumption.

Parents will frequently describe their adolescent children *as always wanting to push the limits of the parent's patience.* Topics that are commonly cited by parents as hotspots for tense interactions include children pressing for later curfews, more privacy, more allowance, and less family/household responsibilities. Many parents also describe their children as radically deviating from beliefs and values traditionally held by the family. It's not uncommon for parents to also report that their adolescents favor clothing styles that leave the parent feeling very uncomfortable. These behaviors are not uncommon and in some instances represent a healthy aspect of human development. Parents choose to react to their children's desire to push the limits in a variety of ways. Some parents are relaxed in their approach to parenting an adolescent while others attempt to maintain very stringent rules.

A casual poll of adolescents would likely show they prefer a parent that is relaxed in their enforcement of limits and boundaries – letting them stay out later and later, letting them wear whatever they want, and letting them pursue beliefs and ideas without parental involvement. That is what an informal poll might demonstrate. However, my experience with those "troubled" adolescents participating in group therapy exposed me to a much different perspective. These adolescents would initially state that parental limits, boundaries, and consequences were "*a pain in the butt,*" that they were "*an embarrassment,*" and that they felt "*suffocating.*" With time, reflection, and input from the group, however, these same adolescents tended to migrate to a much different conclusion. These adolescents would time and time again come to a similar conclusion – that they felt loved and supported when and if their parents enforced limits, boundaries, and consequences. Most of these adolescents were not in treatment voluntarily – they came to treatment kicking and screaming. Yet, within a relatively short period of time, these same adolescents were stating that treatment had been a long time in coming, that it was tremendously helpful, and that they were glad their parents – or a parental surrogate – took the drastic steps necessary to get them hospitalized.

Many of the adolescents who described their parents as relaxed – essentially allowing them free reign to do whatever they wanted – expressed envy toward their peers who described their parents as *"over involved."* The adolescents who described their parents as *"suffocating"* and *"over involved"* in their life, freely admitted this level of involvement felt comforting. They admitted to feeling loved and cared for. It seems these adolescents craved enforcement of limits, boundaries, and consequences.

Let's look at a brief excerpt from a conversation with a 15 year-old who described his parents as "allowing him free reign." This conversation took place during a group therapy session.

Therapist: *Jonathan, you look sad today.*

Jonathan: *I am sad.*

Therapist: *What's going on?*

Jonathan: *Last night I was thinking that I've really fucked up.*

Therapist: *Oh?*

Jonathan: *Yeah. It seems like I've been fighting my parents for as long as I can remember. The sad part about it is that I've been really good at it. I win most of the time.*

Other Group Member: *What do you mean by that? That you "win most of the time."*

Jonathan: *Well. . . . I think my parents must be afraid of me because I always seem to get my way. Like, I would come home two hours late and all drunk. They would yell and stuff. They would even try to ground me. What a joke. I would yell back, maybe punch a wall or throw stuff around and continue doing what I always do. It was like they had no power and I knew it.*

Therapist: *What would you have them do differently?*

Jonathan: *That's a good one. <pause> About a year ago my dad threatened to send me to some kind of military academy. I'd have to wear a uniform, march around a lot, and act like I was in boot* *camp. He went to the trouble of sending for their brochure and entrance packet. He was waving them in my face one night as some kind of threat. I know he didn't have the balls to send me away, but I played the game.*

Other Group Member: *You played the game?*

Jonathan: *Yeah. I told my father "go ahead, send me. You'll see how fast I'm out of there. It will be a big waste of your money" I told him that things would get real ugly around the house if they attempted to send me anywhere where I had to cut my hair. And it worked. He never brought it up after that.*

Therapist: *Again, what would you have him do?*

Jonathan: (Tearing up) *It seemed like I was being guided by remote control. I mean it. Inside I knew things were not good. My friends and I were fucking off in school. We were drinking all the time and for some reason we believed all that was somehow cool. Deep down inside I hated it. I was bored. I wanted other options but didn't think I had any.*

What would I have him do? Send me away. I deserved it. Thinking back, I actually wanted him to. I took a look at the brochure the school sent him when my father wasn't around. Having them cut my hair would have sucked, but there was a lot going on there – more than sitting around and getting high. I wish I would have said "OK Dad, you're right. I think this is a good idea. When do I go?" I didn't have the balls.

He would have flipped.

Other Group Member: *If he sent you away how would you have felt?*

Jonathan: *After looking at my behavior leading to it. . . . loved and cared for. It would have been tough for a while but I don't think there would have been a permanent wedge between us, that is if he sent me away. It must have been tough for them. That's why I'm not pissed they* [his parents] *had the police bring me here. Maybe I'll get a haircut tomorrow!*

Group: <laughter>

Earlier I stated these adolescents, those in group therapy, craved enforcement of limits boundaries and consequences. I believe Jonathan, in the above conversation, was expressing just this point. My experience with adolescents leads me to believe this is not an aberration or merely an isolated occurrence but rather a common component to the parent-child relationship. Limits, boundaries and consequences established by the parent and *justly enforced* are experienced by the child as loving. This statement may seem paradoxical to parents who experience their children as being extremely resistant to the limits, boundaries, and consequences they establish and attempt to enforced. My explanation for this resistance is simple. The adolescent's reaction to parental limits, boundaries and consequences can be attributed to growth.

Children and adolescents develop valuable cognitive skills by processing and questioning information and experiences. From a developmental perspective, little benefit comes from merely accepting what one is told. Taking what one is told, such as parental limits and boundaries, and processing them, looking at them from many perspectives, and questioning the validity of the information requires a significant amount of effort. It also fosters development of valuable cognitive skills. When the child and adolescent arrive at conclusions that are somehow out of line with the parents' expectations (e.g. *"There's no problem being 2 hours late for my curfew."*), just consequences will stimulate additional assessment of the information. Parental limits, boundaries, and consequences are vital for the child/adolescents growth and development. This is a loving way a parent can give to his or her child.

48. One who only uses favor to show love ultimately finds respect waning.

I was standing in line at a convenience store one day. Behind me was a young woman and her son. The boy was probably 8 or 9 years-old. As the mother stood in line to purchase her groceries, the boy left her side and traversed the store's aisles. He hurriedly picked up a grocery item, would examine it, then return it to the shelf and move on. Within a period of less than two minutes the boy had nearly canvassed the entire store. In the process, he checked out at least 10 different items. Eventually, he reached the store's refrigerated section and found a snack package containing lunch meat, cheese, and

crackers. This seemed to spark his interest. The boy ran to his mother
with the snack pack in hand, demanding she purchase it. I heard no
mention of '*please*' or any respectful questions from the boy such as,
"*Hey mom, this looks good. Can we get it?*" I heard, "*Buy this, I want
it!*" repeated over and over. The mother initially ignored the boy's
demands. In response, he merely raised his voice and added an angry
tone. Eventually, the mother turned to her son and snapped "*No!*" The
boy abruptly turned away from his mother, returned to the refrigerated
section, and threw the snack pack onto the shelf – knocking several
other items over in the process. This got the attention of almost
everybody in the store. There was no reaction from the mother. She
paid for her groceries and the two went on their way.

Some might describe this boy as spoiled. I'm not sure I would
necessarily disagree. The behavior I observed may have been a one-
time occurrence, but I sincerely doubt it. The boy was determined
to find and convince his mother to buy the *special item*. The mother
appeared to be very skilled at ignoring her son's demands. I believe
this was a regular occurrence between mother and son. He had done
this many times in the past. The mother had learned to ignore the boy's
irritating demands.

What are the origins and implications of such behavior? *One who
only uses favor to show love ultimately finds respect waning.* This
child learned this behavior from his parents. Somewhere in his life he
learned that his parents are the ones who give "things" – "things" that
bring some kind of comfort or pleasure. Over time, this understanding
became a primary component of the child-parent relationship. That
is, the importance of material giving or showing verbal favor far
outweighed the importance of emotional process. The boy learned that
parental love and affection is equated with the successful solicitation
of "things" rather than emotional interactions. This is a losing
proposition for both parent and child. I have yet to encounter a parent
who is capable of meeting the insatiable appetite of a child's desire for
"things" and favor when emotional process is weak. When the child
reaches the parent's limit to provide things on demand, he or she will be
conflicted and confused. "*What's going on here? Does my parent not
love me? No, that couldn't be. I must try harder to get this thing, their
favor, their love.*" I suspect the young boy was experiencing something
other than hunger pains when he threw the snack pack back into the
store's refrigerator. His response was out of line and incongruent to

the situation. That snack pack should not have been so important to the child and had value that went beyond its nutritional content.

By far the healthiest way to avoid the trap of showing love with favor is to enhance one's understanding of emotional process (see Parenting Assumption 56 and 30) and through well–defined and communicated limits, boundaries, and consequences (see Parenting Assumption 47). All parents must assume their child will have a larger appetite for "things" and verbal favor than what can be realistically satisfied. The earlier the parent recognizes this fact and concludes that understanding *emotional process* and enforcing *limits, boundaries and consequences* are appropriate and healthy ways to show love, the sooner healthy respect in the parent-child relationship will be realized. Rarely will you be confronted with *"Buy this. I want it!"*

How would I respond to the boy in the convenience store if he were my son? I would like to think the whole situation might be avoided in the first place. However, if faced with *"Buy this, I want it!"* I would probably try to respond in a manner similar to the following:

Son: *Buy this. I want it! Buy this. I want it!*

Parent*: Sounds like that's pretty important to you. Why is that?*

Son*: It looks good.*

Parent*: Yes it does. . . . but when you make demands like that, it feels rude and very impolite to me.*

Son*: Oh?*

Parent*: I really don't want to reward that behavior by buying you that snack. If you're hungry we will get something at home. Now, help me understand why you demanded I buy it for you?*

Son*: I don't know. I just want it!*

Parent*: Well, I don't feel comfortable buying that for you right now. Especially after how you approached me on the matter. Please put it back. We have to go.*

In this instance, the child will still be disappointed yet these feelings will likely be accompanied with a certain amount of respect for the final decision and a slightly greater insight to how his behavior can affect others and the outcome of an interaction between people. If he

responded to his disappointment by throwing the snack pack back into
the refrigerator, we would do a lot more processing of the event in the
car on the way home. I would start the conversation by letting him know
how I was impacted emotionally by his behavior, then I would ask him to
describe his perspective on the matter – his thoughts and emotions. Some
parents might feel I was taking this matter much too far. Some parents
might feel that a simple "No" or threat of punishment would suffice. I
disagree. This relatively small incident represents a tremendous parenting
opportunity. If this matter is processed between parent and child – to the
point of excess – similar behavior will be less likely to occur in the future.
More importantly, crucial lessons can be learned from this very simple
interaction. The parent who processes these matters more often than
not is helping the child make healthy and helpful connections between
thoughts, emotions, and consequences. The child is also learning about
empathy, all from a simple parent-child interaction that is almost as simple
for the parent as merely saying *"No"* or making threats to punish the child.
When a child experiences several similar parent-child interactions, his or
her understanding of healthy relationships will grow. From the parent's
perspective, it can also be a tremendous relief simply telling a child how he
or she feels about a particular behavior?

This point may seem paradoxical to parents who rely heavily on
showing favor as opposed to the use of emotional process and limits,
boundaries and consequences to show love. Why? When I work
with parents on how to improve emotional process and to formulate,
communicate, and enforce limits boundaries, and consequences, it may
not feel very "loving" at first. Many parents state their efforts feel
like punishments. With time, practice, and reflection, most parents
committed to evaluating their parenting come to the conclusion that
using favor is only one part of showing love. Interactions such as the
alternative above are in themselves very loving. This parent is helping
the child make connections between thoughts, emotions, behaviors, and
consequences. What a great gift.

*49. The concept of wealth, to children, often varies from the
parents' understanding of the same. Often parents can learn
from their childhood and children about wealth.*

Parents have a natural desire to give to their children. Quite often
this natural desire to give manifests itself as a focus on material
possessions, gift giving and status acquisition – toys, snacks, money,

and clothing. This manifestation is understandable, as the experience of giving a child a toy, a desired snack, or keeping them in the most current fashions is usually pleasurable for both parent and child. Giving a teenager money to purchase clothes can be a pleasurable experience even when the parent detests the clothing selected by the teen. The concept of wealth is often limited to the possessions we have, the gifts we are able to provide, and the status we achieve and represent. This belief is constantly being reinforced by peer pressure, standards established and communicated by television programs and advertisements, and other media such as magazines, radio, and movies. Yet, if we take a few moments to look at wealth and giving, some surprising ideas will emerge.

Many adults are often hard-pressed to recall the gifts and possessions they received during their childhood and youth. Rather, the memories typically recalled from childhood are of activities and relationships. For example, an adult may have a hard time recalling birthday gifts received from a favorite uncle. However, this same adult can easily recall the activities that occurred while spending time with that same uncle. I personally recall fishing, picking beets, playing basketball, and eating ice–cream with one such "favorite uncle." Wealth in this relationship was not represented by the possessions or gifts that might have existed but rather by the experiences that were shared. When I think back to my childhood, I am able to recall with ease hundreds, if not thousands of experiences I had with the various members of my family. Many of these are comfortable and pleasurable experiences while others are uncomfortable and less pleasurable. All of these experiences have one thing in common: they were and are memorable and have become a valuable part of who I am as an individual and an adult. When I try to recall the material goods of my childhood, I am less successful.

I can recall times when there was scarcity and times of plenty, but these memories lack significant detail about specific "things" that might represent wealth. These memories suffer by comparison to memories of interactions with family. The few material possessions I can recall from my childhood are memorable because they are associated with memories of experiences. For instance, I can recall receiving snorkeling equipment as a gift. This was a nice gift; however, my memories of the gift would not be as vivid had the equipment not been accompanied with the experience of enjoying it while snorkeling with my family. Memories of equally thoughtful gifts fall to the wayside when not accompanied by interactive experiences.

When parents come to my office and complain about how hard it is to *keep up with the Joneses*, or how hard it is to ensure the kids have the most recent computer game, or the most recent fashions, I visit this Parenting Assumption. Sure, there is some value to the material gifts, the status items, and the possessions one has, but I like to reinforce the importance of providing rich parent-child experiences. These are usually free or come at a very low cost. One couple I worked with had few financial resources, in fact, they were very poor. Yet, their children were wealthy beyond belief. Rarely did a weekend pass where parents and children were not off on some adventure. Some weekends they would go fossil hunting. Others they would have a picnic and pick wild berries. Other weekends and evenings they would make homemade frozen yogurt pops. The family would go on hiking and camping trips and maintained a garden in their small yard. The children were constantly involved in the composting of the household trash to help enrich the soil and in the planting, weeding, and harvesting of the garden. The children's apparent social status – as evidenced by their possessions and fashions – was low. Yet the wealth of these children was worthy of envy. I asked these parents if their children ever complained about the family's lack of material wealth or if there were problems with peer acceptance, especially since the oldest children were in their teens. The parents stated the issue would come up from time to time. When this occurred, the family would have an open and frank discussion about different life styles and the difference between "wants" and "needs." The family's needs were never in question. They were clothed, housed, and well fed. The parents were also actively involved in the kids' education and extracurricular activities. The family's *wants* were not always met; however, the experiences they encountered more than compensated for any deficit that would arise.

If a parent takes time to differentiate between *wants* and *needs*, most will find the needs have a way of being met. If resources for the wants – that new computer game, the new and best sneakers, and so on – are not available, take a few moments to revisit your childhood. What memories do you have? Then find ways of creating experiences, even simple ones, that will last a lifetime. At times, this may feel like a paradoxical thought. Especially, when facing the powerful influence of peer and family pressures. *The concept of wealth, to children, often varies from the parents' understanding of the same. Often parents can learn from their childhood and children about wealth.*

|| Chapter 6 Fear

A feeling of uneasiness or apprehension; concern.
To be uneasy, anxious, or doubtful.

Imagine if you will, two rafts drifting down a river. Each rafts is occupied by one person. The rafters are enjoying a pleasant day. The sun is shining and the gentle rocking motion produced as the rafts meander down the river is soothing and relaxing. All of the sudden both rafters notice a faint sound that appears in the distant and seems out of the ordinary. At first little notice is given to this noise. Yet, as the rafts progress farther down the river, the noise becomes noticeably louder – until such time that both rafters cannot deny that they are approaching a substantial waterfall. One of the rafters pulls out the oars and begins to make way toward shore. The second rafter, although aware of the approaching waterfall, does nothing to avoid it. This rafter sits back and continues enjoying the day. The first rafter pulls the vessel to shore, picks it up, and walks around the waterfall. While on the path around the falls, this individual thinks, *"Next time I'm going to get a river map. That was too close!"* The other rafter, after plunging over the falls, questions *"Why am I in so much pain?"* This person looks to shore in an attempt to find somebody who might have offered a warning. This person thinks *"Somebody should have told me about this!"*

This chapter only presents 6 Parenting Assumptions. Each is intimately connected to the simple definition of fear presented above and the rafting metaphor. Each Assumption explores a different aspect of fear as it relates to parenting. The first Assumption directs us to an aspect of fear that few give much consideration.

50. In parenting there are no constant conditions. The parent who finds comfort in maintaining the status quo is promoting emotional stagnation. The parent who finds comfort with fluidity is promoting maturation and growth.

Parenting demands fluidity. That is, children grow, develop, and make ever changing demands upon their parents. As stated in this Parenting Assumption, there are no constant conditions in parenting. Quite often parents feel uneasy and ill-prepared when faced with the constantly changing playing field resulting from the child's growth and development. I believe this particular Assumption directs us to evaluate the emotional fluidity associated with this growth and development. What parent has not sent their child off to the first day of school without experiencing a feeling of uneasiness, apprehension, concern, or doubt? What parent did not feel somewhat uneasy, anxious or experience a feeling of self-doubt when holding their baby for the first time? These emotions, although uncomfortable, are healthy and helpful to the parenting process. They are a crucial component to what may be termed *the parenting lifecycle.* They should not be ignored or suppressed. In fact, many of the more uncomfortable emotions every parent experiences serve as important guides as we pass through this parenting life-cycle.

Both rafters in the river metaphor likely experienced similar emotions when faced with the waterfall threat. Yet, each reacted much differently. I imagine both rafters experienced feelings of uneasiness and apprehension as the noise emanating from the waterfall became too loud to ignore. One rafter processed these emotions and reacted in a manner that was beneficial. The other rafter suppressed these emotions – maintaining the status quo – and was blindsided by the painful consequences.

The parent who embraces the fluid and progressive nature of parenting will be in a better position to process and benefit from the often uncomfortable emotions encountered throughout the parenting lifecycle. As the rafter who walked around the waterfall showed us, there is nothing wrong with feeling uneasy, concerned, apprehensive, or doubtful. It's how we respond to these emotions that is of critical importance.

Consider the first-time-father who is handed his baby in the delivery room. Every father I've spoken to about this moment reports experiencing a rush of emotions. This cascade of emotions obviously included many that were joyous and exciting. Yet, mixed in with this rush was a certain amount of anxiety, uneasiness, and perhaps self-doubt. When I asked these first-time-fathers if these uncomfortable emotions were first encountered in the delivery room, rarely do I receive a "yes" response. In fact, most fathers state these emotions surfaced several time throughout the pregnancy – typically surfacing during each pregnancy milestone. They were encountered when they first discovered they were to be a father, when they first heard the baby's heartbeat, when they saw the ultrasound results, and when they felt the baby's first kicks. Many fathers freely spoke of the more comfortable emotions encountered during each of pregnancy milestone, such as joy, happiness, excitement, and anticipation. Yet, they tended to suppress, minimize, or keep secret less comfortable emotions, such as doubt, apprehension, and uneasiness. These fathers were responding in a way similar to the rafter who chose to lie back in his raft and enjoy the day – putting aside the emotions associated with the waterfall ahead.

I asked many of these fathers what they thought would happen if the less comfortable emotions were explored with the mother to be, with other fathers, with their parents, siblings, and friends. For instance, while talking about the joy associated with learning that one is to be a father, what harm would come from mentioning that this is an intimidating experience? What harm would come from letting others know that, although the news of the pregnancy is joyous, he is experiencing a certain amount of self-doubt and apprehension? Rarely will mothers to be, other fathers, and family members interpret these statements, these emotions, as a weakness. No, in fact, most are able to relate to these feelings and will freely offer supportive input – further enhancing the parenting experience for the father to be. The rafter who removed his vessel from the river and walked around the falls stated he might want to get a river map next time. He was not bashful about asking for input in the face of these uncomfortable emotions.

The fluid nature of parenting will keep you on your toes. If you, more often than not, sit back and enjoy the day as the second rafter did, and in so doing choose to ignore the emotional signals every parent receives, trouble will most certainly lie ahead. Embracing the fluid nature of the parenting process will benefit both parent and child. The child will benefit from a parent who understands and is willing to process the fear often accompanying the parenting process. This is a great gift and lesson for any child. The parent will benefit, as many painful consequences will certainly be avoided. *In parenting there are no constant conditions. The parent who finds comfort in maintaining the status quo is promoting emotional stagnation. The parent who finds comfort with fluidity is promoting maturation and growth.*

51. If problems are left un–addressed parental fatigue sets in – greatly hindering the ability to nurture.

There is a behavior that family therapists commonly observe in their practice. A couple or family will arrive for an appointment. Time passes and the session nears its conclusion without anything too dramatic occurring. Then, with just a few minutes remaining, a parent or family member will reveal something significant. For example, on one occasion I had parents inform me, while reaching for the door knob on their way out of my office, that their 12 year-old daughter was pregnant. The previous hour was filled with discussion of relatively minor family and parenting issues, then in a casual *oh-by-the-way* manner, the child's father stated, *"did we tell you that Megan is pregnant?"*[26] I had other patients in my waiting room and was unable to do anything but acknowledge that we had a lot to talk about the next week. When the parents arrived the following week I asked them about the previous session. I was not as interested in the facts surrounding the daughter's pregnancy as I was in why they waited until the last minute to bring it up. I believed this to be a telling sign of problems in their family system.

In the field of family therapy it is generally thought that these situations – families waiting until the last moment to bring up important issues – are the result of general anxiety surrounding the problem. That is, when facing the discomfort associated with a significant problem, some family members may compartmentalize uncomfortable emotions and procrastinate taking action.[27] In other words, they put off dealing with the problem as long as they can in an attempt to avoid or delay experiencing the uncomfortable emotions associated with the problem. Procrastination, as we will see, comes with a cost. The family described above agreed among themselves to bring the matter of the pregnancy to my attention during our first appointment yet waited until the last moment to do so. The second time I met with the family I asked each member to recall what they were feeling during the first session, but prior to point at which the father mentioned the pregnancy. Everybody stated they were feeling tense and on edge. I then asked each family member if they were able to recall what we discussed in the first session, prior to the father mentioning the pregnancy. Nobody in the family could accurately recall what was discussed. The family was physically present in the same room I was, yet the emotional weight of the family crisis left them distracted and emotionally detached. Understandably, their attention was somewhere else. They reported feeling tense, on edge and having difficulty focusing on the session. It was not until the father felt that he had to mention the problem that it surfaced. Then, it only surfaced at a time when there was no opportunity to process the information in any detail whatsoever. Unfortunately, this resulted in a missed opportunity for the family. Their procrastination permitted them to put off dealing with the problem for at least another week. Perhaps mentioning the problem brought some sense of relief – *"Now the cat's out of the bag. The therapist has been informed."* But, how did the delay impact the family?

During our second session, the family stated that the week between the first and second session was full of tension. Conversations between family members were brief. Everybody in the family stated that it felt as if they were walking on egg shells all week long. The parents reported that between sessions one and two they frequently yelled at and punished their pregnant 12 year-old daughter. The parents also stated that no one mentioned the pregnancy between our first two sessions. It was as if this issue did not exist. The problem had been exposed to the therapist yet it remained un-processed, un-addressed and appeared to be profoundly impacting the family's ability to function.

During our second session we began to process the daughter's pregnancy. Every family member's perspective was solicited and discussed. No questions were off limits. No subjects were too sensitive to explore. No resolutions were made and no decisions were finalized during this session. The second session was devoted to merely opening the door to the subject of the pregnancy. We attempted to bring a sense of emotional safety to a very uncomfortable family problem.

At the start of our third session, I again asked each family member how they were feeling. Everybody agreed that they were experiencing a tremendous sense of relief. Their relief did not stem from resolution of the problem. The 12 year-old girl was still pregnant and no decision on how they were going to proceed had been made. The relief experienced by the family was a direct result of opening the subject matter and beginning the process of exploring the problem in detail. The family members stated that between sessions 2 and 3, conversations in the household were much different than the previous week. Communications were more intimate, more supportive and were lacking the tension that was experienced between the first two sessions. Unlike the previous week, the topic of the daughter's pregnancy frequently came up in the family's conversations. The family was no longer walking on egg shells and the parents were in a better position to nurture.

Earlier I stated that perhaps there was a relationship between what I observed in my office – a pattern of procrastination – and a family condition that might have left the daughter vulnerable to getting pregnant at such a young age. In this family, problems, sensitive subjects, and disagreements were usually left un-processed and un-addressed. There was an unwritten belief that problems or uncomfortable situations would eventually resolve themselves or simply disappear if they were ignored long enough. The parents knew this would not be the case with the pregnancy and sought professional input from a family therapist. Yet, even in my office they attempted to delay processing the issue by waiting until the last moments of our first session to raise the topic. As we saw between sessions one and two, leaving problems un–processed and lingering resulted in a further decrease in intimacy and an increase in tension and hostility within the family. The parents were distracted and emotionally incapacitated by the lingering problem. Leaving the matter open appeared to be fatiguing both the parents and family.

The problem presented by this particular family was significant. It was about as big as they come. Most families will rarely encounter issues as large as this. However, we should not underestimate the significance of the smaller problems every family is likely to encounter. Leaving even less severe problems un-addressed will have a similar emotional impact on the parents and the family system. There are numerous examples of less severe problems that are often overlooked or left un-addressed in family systems – that if ignored will eventually leave parents emotionally fatigued. For example, a child's temper tantrum or an adolescent's verbal outburst represent problems requiring attention but which are frequently overlooked by parents. Another example of a seemingly minor issue that, when ignored by parents, can lead to fatigue would be when a child fails to complete family chores or household responsibilities. Some parents may conclude that it is just easier to overlook these minor issues than it is to address them when they occur.

Often it may feel as if the consequences of addressing relatively minor issues or problems are more uncomfortable than the fatigue experienced if the matter is left alone.[28] Unfortunately, there is a cumulative affect of leaving matters (large and small) un-addressed. For example, it is infinitely more difficult to have a child whose room has been a mess for six months to change his or her behavior than it is to address the problem when it initially occurs. An adolescent who verbally lashes out at his or her parents did not merely stumble upon this method of parent-child interaction. It developed over a lengthy period of time. Many less healthy parent-child interactions likely occurred prior to the outburst without being addressed. I suspect that a cumulative effect of many un-addressed issues, in part, left the 12 year-old vulnerable to getting pregnant.

52. Parents who prepare for life-cycle shifts in advance will be at ease and competent.

At times, feelings of fear, *a feeling of uneasiness or apprehension; concern; to be uneasy, anxious, or doubtful,* will be experienced while parenting. These are important feelings and should not be ignored. They are usually an indication that the parent is presented with a parenting opportunity. If the matter that stimulates these feelings is ignored or overlooked, thus giving the parent a brief reprieve from the uncomfortable emotions, nobody benefits. However, if the parent becomes better skilled at addressing these opportunities when they occur, every family member will benefit. The previous Parenting Assumption speaks of the unhealthy consequences that might be experienced if problems are left un-addressed in a family system. Parenting Assumption 52 takes the concept a bit further by asserting that many issues can be addressed prior to them becoming problematic.

The 12 year-old girl getting pregnant is an excellent example of the potential consequences of parental procrastination. This particular family exhibited a characteristic that is very common. The parents provided their children with very little input and direction regarding natural life-cycle shifts.[29] The children were left to their own devices to cope with many of these shifts. In the previous example, the young girl received little to no parental input regarding subjects such as body development, sexual urges, peer pressure, and so on. The parents merely scratched the surface regarding these subjects, and then only when they felt forced into dealing with them. For example, the daughter's first menstrual period came to her as a complete surprise. There was no previous discussion of menstruation between the parents and their daughter. The parents responded by having a very brief discussion with the girl and then they left her with some reading material.

The subject definitely stimulated feelings of uneasiness, apprehension, anxiety, and doubt – *fear* – within the parents. They delayed processing the subject as long as they could, then, guided by fear, only provided a minimal amount of information and direction. Subjects such as how to understand and manage sexual feelings and urges were just too sensitive for the parents to breech and went completely un-addressed. When the young girl began experiencing sexual feelings and urges – a completely natural aspect of maturation and adolescent development – she was unprepared and became vulnerable to external manipulation – such as, by a 14 year-old male neighbor. Approaching her parents with questions or concerns about her feelings, the urges she was experiencing, or the pressures she was encountering from outside of the family system was completely out of the question. This option was simply not in the girl's immediate consciousness. She was not parented to see this as a viable or emotionally safe option. Figuring things out for herself was how problems such as these were addressed. Becoming sexually active with the neighbor boy, although an unhealthy option, was an attempt to figure out or place meaning to this most recent life-cycle shift.

For contrast, let me describe another family's approach to this particular life-cycle shift. I was at a wedding reception awhile back and saw some friends who had moved away several years earlier. When they moved their daughter was 6 or 7 years-old. She was 13 when I saw her parents again. I asked how the girl was doing and was informed that she was well. The parents told me that they were a bit surprised that she had had her first menstrual period just before her 12th birthday. They felt this particular life-cycle shift started a bit early. I asked my friends how they reacted to this event. Their response indicated that in spite of being surprised they had been prepared for this life-cycle shift well in advance. Discussion of body development and sexuality occurred in a relaxed and age-appropriate manner from year one. Conversations about the differences between boys and girls were common among members of this family. There were plenty of age-appropriate books and videos about sex and body development introduced into the household throughout the child's life. These books and videos were frequently read and viewed in a very relaxed and intimate manner. Questions that children naturally have (e.g. about the differences between male and female bodies, where babies come from, etc.), were always immediately explored in a very forthright and honest manner. When this girl experienced her first menstrual period there was no shame or embarrassment within the family. It was understood as a completely natural and exciting aspect of life and maturation. It was a developmental milestone equally as important as a child's first steps, a child's first words, or graduation from high school.

The manner in which this family reacted was in direct contrast to the family with the pregnant 12 year-old. I believe the chances of my friend's daughter becoming sexually active at such a young age were very remote. I would also predict that if she were pressured to have sex, such as, by a boy in their neighborhood or a friend from school, her parents would probably be informed almost immediately. I am confident the parents would probably use this situation to reinforce the previous conversations they had had with their daughter about how to handle issues surrounding one's sexuality. As a result, this girl would be significantly less vulnerable to sexual manipulation and very unlikely to experience an unplanned pregnancy so early and under such unhealthy circumstances.

My work with the family with the pregnant 12 year-old did not focus specifically on the pregnancy. They were aware of the numerous options available to them, such as adoption, abortion, and raising the child. How they were going to proceed was a collective decision for the family to make. I am of the belief that a therapist should support the family in making the healthiest decision for their circumstances and beliefs, without swaying the decision in any particular direction. My work with this particular family focused on Parenting Assumptions 51, 52, and 53 rather than helping them decide how they were going to deal with the pregnancy. *The pregnancy was merely a symptom of an underlying problem within the family system.* Focusing on the pregnancy might alleviate some of the immediate stress, but would leave the family unaware of the underlying issues that led to this problem in the first place.

In this family, problems were routinely left un-addressed leaving the parents' ability to nurture greatly impaired. As a result, emotional safety and intimacy within the parent-child relationship was poorly developed. The 12 year-old daughter was left further vulnerable by the fact that she was not prepared in advance for natural life-cycle shifts.

These shifts were handled in an awkward and reactionary manner by the parents. My job as a family therapist was to help the parents recognize this unhealthy pattern of family functioning and how it left the 12 year-old vulnerable to getting pregnant. It was my job to help the parents explore the origins of this less helpful and unhealthy family characteristic while simultaneously helping them develop healthier alternatives. It was too late to prevent the pregnancy; however, these parents were presented with a great opportunity to make healthy and helpful changes in their family system by learning how to comfortably prepare for future life-cycle shifts well in advance.

53. Those who are encouraged to grow during life-cycle shifts will excel. Those encouraged to support or maintain status quo will stagnate and regress.

In the previous two Parenting Assumptions we saw one family who dealt with life-cycle shifts in an open and forthright manner. We also looked at one family where life-cycle shifts were a source of discomfort, fear, and anxiety. The former family seemed to excel while the latter family struggled and experienced very troubling consequences. From birth to death, we experience a series of developmental and experiential milestones. I refer to these milestone as life-cycle shifts. Birthdays, one's first steps and first words, religious milestones (e.g. baptism, first communion, bar mitzvah, bat mitzvah), learning to ride a bicycle, graduation from various educational levels, entering puberty, getting a driver's license, marriage, the birth of a first child, and retirement are all milestones that are commonly celebrated within family systems. Sometimes these milestones are achieved without a corresponding shift in the family system. That is, we celebrate one's maturation, accomplishments, and experiences, yet may resist advancing our own views of, and expectations for, that person. We resist seeing change, maturation, and growth of the individual even when a milestone is celebrated.

The numerous life-cycle shifts that occur during adolescence are when the most obvious examples of parents supporting stagnation and regression rather than growth can be found. Let me explain this observation. Adolescence is the life-cycle shift in which one matures from a child to a young adult. There are physical changes such as musculoskeletal growth, maturation of the sexual organs, and well defined cognitive developments. One's thoughts progress from being childlike and dependant to demonstrating more independent, creative, and complex characteristics. One's thoughts become more adult-like. These changes are often the source of conflict within the parent-child relationship. This conflict will often stem from the adolescent's inexperience applying these newly acquired cognitive skills. Although their thoughts are significantly more complex, their skills in applying them are immature and not very well practiced. The adolescent makes mistakes as he or she figures out the most helpful and healthy way to use these emerging cognitive skills. At times this can be frustrating to a parent unaware of this developmental process.

Conflict between a parent and adolescent can also occur when the natural growth process goes unrecognized and is not honored. That is, the parent fails to recognize the adolescent's emerging cognitive skills as growth but rather continues to see the emerging adult as a child, still dependent upon the parent and prone to making mistakes. The emerging skills are not celebrated and encouraged but rather suppressed through criticism and/or punishment. In other words, as the child develops, the parent attempts to maintain the status quo – growth is not promoted. This leads to a condition of emotional stagnation and regression in both the child's life as well as the parent-child relationship. Physically, the child will continue to mature, yet many unhealthy behaviors will emerge when the physical maturation is met with family/systemic resistance to the emotional and cognitive growth.

The example of the pregnant 12 year-old previously presented is an excellent case in point. The 12 year-old's maturation was met with a parental desire to maintain the status quo. Her maturation was not recognized or appreciated by the family system. This left the girl unprepared and vulnerable. Fortunately, most families will not have to face such dramatic consequences. Many families will, on the other hand, experience less obvious and dramatic consequences of maintaining the status quo during adolescent life-cycle shifts. These consequences will often be observed as an adolescent failing to thrive or failing to reach his or her full potential. Significant conflict in the parent-child relationship, drug and alcohol experimentation, and getting into trouble outside of the household are also good indicators that parenting in the family supports the status quo rather than promoting growth.

This Parenting Assumption states that *those who are encouraged to grow during life-cycle shifts will excel. Those encouraged to support/ maintain the status quo will stagnate and regress.* To this point, we have primarily focused on the shifts that occur during the adolescent period of development. What about the other life-cycle shifts? For example, when a child takes his or her first steps or utters his or her first words, how exactly does a parent encourage growth or promote stagnation and regression? Let's explore this question by taking a brief look at some of the more familiar life-cycle shifts.

A Child's First Steps: I enjoy watching the joy and glee parents express upon witnessing their child's first steps. It is truly a wonderful event. However, after the novelty of seeing their child take those early steps wears off, many parents are quick to restrain the child. Millions of dollars are spent each year on walkers, strollers, and other devices intended to limit the child's mobility – for the convenience of the parent.[30] I never gave much thought to this subject until I observed a group of parents and their children in a park one July afternoon. There were probably 20 to 25 parents and at least 15 two year-olds. The kids were running around completely unrestrained in the middle of a large field. There were various toys such as large beach balls and balloons but nothing too sophisticated. From a distance, the whole sight seemed a bit carnival-like and somewhat surreal. I had to find out what was going on. I was informed by one of the adults that the group was part of a cooperative parent-child tumbling & physical activities group that met several times a week. The sole purpose of the group was to support increased physical activity among their children. As one parent stated, *"These kids just learned to walk. Why not encourage it?"* What a novel thought in a nation with skyrocketing levels of childhood obesity and type II diabetes. The group would meet at a local park when the weather permitted and at a community center during inclement weather. The group's mission was simple: *to promote growth through physical activity*. Every child participating in the group appeared enthusiastically engaged in the activities and seemed to be having a great time. These parents were encouraging growth rather than stagnation during this particular life-cycle shift. They were keeping the novelty of their children's early steps alive while simultaneously enriching the kids lives through activity and stimulation.

As I walked away from the tumbling & physical activity group, I passed two mothers walking their children. The kids were probably two years-old. Both were in strollers and both were either struggling or crying. The contrast between the two scenarios was striking. I am by no means implying that children who have just learned to walk should be required to do so at the grocery store, when accompanying a parent while shopping, or when traveling from one location to another. This would be impractical and inappropriate. The point I'm attempting to make is that during and after this particular life-cycle shift, most parents can create opportunities to promote growth by increasing the child's physical activity. As that one father stated, *"The kid just learned to walk. Why not encourage it?"* Consider turning off the video or DVD. Find a large beach ball and go to a park.

A Child's First Words: A child's first words are just as monumental as the first steps. They signal the beginning of a very important developmental life-cycle shift. More precise verbal communication is emerging. Parents look forward to hearing, and tend to cherish, their child's first words. Yet, after the first words have been recognized and celebrated, the novelty may wear off; especially when the child loudly and repeatedly experiments with new words and sounds. I have had the opportunity to work with many families with children who are just learning to speak. Some of these families seem to tolerate, or even encourage, a young child's verbal experimentation while others wish they could put cotton in their ears to lessen the noise. The latter families tend not to encourage or promote verbal experimentation. The differences between children whose parents promote verbal interactions and experimentation from those who do not is obvious. Children who are encouraged to grow during this life-cycle shift tend to excel in other aspects of their cognitive development and seem to have stronger and healthier interpersonal relationships with others. Growth during this developmental life-cycle shift can be encouraged in many ways. A regular routine of reading to a child and engaging in playful verbal games and interactions are probably two of the best ways I know to promote growth.[31] The child benefits from the exposure to various speech patterns and new vocabulary. In addition, and perhaps more importantly, the child benefits from the intimate verbal interaction between parent and child.

I have worked with many families in which the parents do not regularly read to their children or partake in playful verbal games and interactions. These children are left to their own developmental devices, and must pick up verbal stimulation and exposure to interactions wherever and whenever they can. As a result, their understanding of the complexities of verbal interaction must be pieced together and will likely be incomplete. Unfortunately, these children are beginning life with a slight developmental disadvantage. Intimacy that results from reading to and with a child, and the intimacy that emerges from playful verbal games and interactions, will not materialize if the parent promotes the status quo and leaves the child to his or her own devices. My recommendation is that parents read to and with their pre- and post-verbal children daily. Both the parent and child will benefit immensely.

An Adolescent's Emerging Cognitive Skills: Many of the Parenting Assumptions found throughout this book contain examples of parent-adolescent interactions. The life-cycle shifts that occur during this period of development are certainly exciting and probably worthy of such attention. One of the most important developments that occurs during this life-cycle shift would be the emergence of sophisticated and independent cognitive processes. The adolescent's brain starts processing information and experiences in new and distinct ways. The emerging cognitive skills allow the adolescent to make connections and understand things independently of parental explanation. That is, the adolescent attempts to *connect the dots* for him or herself rather than relying upon the parents to connect these dots. Rather than taking the parent's word that *something is so*, the adolescent attempts to determine this for him or herself.

From a parent's perspective, this developmental process can be very frustrating. The adolescent's skills at connecting the dots are not fully developed, sometimes resulting in poor decisions and actions. Any input offered by the parent regarding these decisions and actions is often rejected or completely disregarded. The parent may choose to respond by encouraging the adolescent to use his or her developing cognitive and decision–making skills. This tends to normalize the developmental process. One of the most helpful ways I know to support or encourage this process is to ask many open-ended and engaging questions. These questions provide the adolescent with valuable guidance and experience in figuring things out for him or herself. Some examples include:

"What do you think about. . . . ?"

"How do you think this might . . . .?"

"I'm wondering what might happen if. . . .

These leading questions can be considered exercise for the adolescent's emerging cognitive processes. Arriving at a *"right"* answer is not nearly as important as the adolescent gaining experience in exploring many questions from different directions. Parents can play an instrumental role in providing their adolescent children with these opportunities.

Parents may also choose to support the status quo during the adolescent developmental period. These are the families that usually end up in my office seeking therapy or assistance resolving significant problems. The status quo is supported when the adolescent's emerging cognitive and decision making skills are discouraged through punishment or harsh criticism. The status quo is supported when the adolescent is discouraged from exercising his or her emerging cognitive skills and when the parent focuses on the answers and behaviors rather than on the decision making processes that resulted in the answers or behaviors. As I have already suggested, arriving at a *"right"* answer is not as important as the adolescent gaining experience in exploring problems from many different directions.

Graduations: When I was growing up, high school and college graduations seem to be the only graduations that were seriously celebrated. Yet, during the last several decades I have noticed a trend emerging in some parts of the country. Graduation ceremonies seemed to be occurring as a child progresses from elementary school to middle school and from middle school to high school. I have also noticed an increase in formality and ceremony at the completion of non-school related programs, such as sports camps, music programs, and religious programs. My first thoughts were that this particular trend was a bit odd and that the importance of these accomplishments was being blown out of proportion. It was not until I considered the perspectives of those partaking in these celebrations that I gained insight to, and greater understanding of, this trend.

This topic reminds me of a socio-economically devastated area of North Philadelphia. Statistically, only one third of all children growing up in this neighborhood would graduate from high school. An amazing two thirds of children would drop out before or during high school. The statistics would seem to indicate that education, along with the opportunities and responsibilities it provides, were not valued by many residents of this particular community. Yet, a great deal of energy went into these elementary and middle school graduations. Why? I was initially under the impression that these graduation ceremonies were given to children as a substitute for a high school graduation that, in all probability, was unlikely to occur. I felt that perhaps the parents in this community had given up and fully expected the pressures from the street to pull their children away from school.

I asked one particular family, while the mother proudly showed me pictures of her eldest daughter's middle school graduation, what motivated such an elaborate ceremony. The mother was very direct and forthright with me, bringing insight to the importance of Parenting Assumption 53. This mother stated the ceremony was essentially irrelevant. It was the expectations that accompanied and followed the ceremony that were meaningful. She went on to explain that most of the children in her community did not complete high school. She believed the high dropout rate was the result of many families failing to promote growth and success throughout their children's early lives. She believed growth simply was not reinforced and encouraged in many families within their community. Over the course of several generations, this became the normative behavior for the community; a characteristic that was accepted and expected. This mother believed many of the children were left without significant parental input, guidance, and encouragement. In her mind, the graduation ceremonies were becoming an institutionalized means, through ceremony, to highlight a child's growth and advancement.

This particular mother felt the ceremonies were basically a nice effort, but believed they would only be beneficial if they were accompanied by increased expectations at home and from the family. For example, she told me that with each passing school year, she would sit down with each of her children and process the growth she had seen during the previous year. She would also communicate expectations she had for each child for the upcoming school year. The mother stated that she made it a point to address and interact with her children in accordance with the expectations that she communicated to them. She was essentially promoting growth by altering the manner in which *she* interacted with her young children. This mother stated the graduation ceremonies were *"icing on the developmental cake."*

The mother in North Philadelphia was facing pressures absent from the lives of many families. Chances are her children would not complete school had she chosen to take a more passive approach to raising her kids. She believed that if her children were not provided such strong input, or that if she relied heavily upon the school, the community, or her church to keep her children focused on their education, they would not succeed. The status quo in her particular community was to approach education from a passive perspective, merely *hoping* one's children would complete school. This particular mother rejected the status quo. She celebrated her children's accomplishments and encouraged them to grow by making it a point to alter her view of them. I do not think it was coincidental that the children in this family were excelling in school while residing in a community that did not seem to value these accomplishments. For this family, the elaborate graduation ceremonies were a symbol of defiance; a reminder that the status quo in the community could be rejected and growth promoted.

Marriage: Growth does not cease when a child reaches the age of 18. A parent is provided with many opportunities to give to their children as they pass through adult life-cycle shifts. For example, when one's adult child decides to marry, the parent can choose to view their son or daughter as an adult, capable of establishing a meaningful relationship with the spouse independently of the parents. The parent may also choose to view the newly married son or daughter as needing to be enmeshed with the parents in order to succeed. The former promotes growth while the latter is likely to lead to stagnation and regression in the newly formed marriage.

As a family therapist, I have had to assist many parents learn how to be supportive of their newly married son or daughter by backing away and providing them an opportunity to form a working relationship independently of the parents. Perhaps the most common example of parental enmeshment I come across occurs when a parent intervenes or takes sides in a disagreement unfolding in their adult child's marriage. A parent's loyalties tend to fall on the side of the son or daughter. Refusing to act on this loyalty, by not siding with the son or daughter, can be difficult and uncomfortable at times. However, it is often more helpful if the parent supports the marriage rather than the son or daughter. In instances of marital conflict it may be helpful for a parent to listen to his or her son or daughter's perspective. A response such as *"Perhaps it is important for the two of you to process these differences"* can be very helpful. Jumping into an adult child's marital disagreements or conflicts is rarely helpful in supporting a successful marriage.

The previous pages have provided a few examples of life-cycle shifts experienced by individuals and families. It is important for parents to look for life-cycle shifts and developmental milestones. They occur frequently. Celebrate them when possible and use the opportunity to adjust your understanding of the child. Encourage growth and the responsibilities that accompany these shifts and milestones. From time to time this may produce a certain amount of parental discomfort. However, the benefits experienced by a child whose parents encourage growth rather than the status quo far outweigh any brief moments of discomfort.

54. War is based upon deception – not parenting. Children recognize deception even when parents do not. Children can handle honesty even when parents cannot.

This Assumption reminds me of a husband and wife I had the opportunity to work with several years ago. I was employed as a staff family therapist in an inpatient drug and alcohol rehabilitation facility. The husband was receiving treatment for drug and alcohol abuse and had been hospitalized for nearly two weeks. The couple had two children – an infant and a five year-old son. I asked the couple how the father's abrupt absence from the family was explained to the eldest child. The parents informed me the boy was told that, "*Daddy was out of town on business*" and would be gone for several weeks. I asked them why the truth was withheld from their son. Both parents looked at each other and appeared to be very uncomfortable with the subject. The mother eventually stated that they did not believe the boy would understand the complexities of the problem and that it was "*just better if he didn't know.*" The father agreed with his wife and added that he did not want his son to see him as a "*druggie and a drunk.*"

I asked the parents what life was like in the home prior to the father's admission into the rehabilitation program. Both agreed that life was a bit out of control. There were frequent arguments between the parents. The father was either inebriated or high most evenings and almost every weekend. There were few, if any, healthy family activities and emotional intimacy was practically nonexistent. To the couple's credit, they recognized the marriage was not going to last unless the alcohol and drug abuse was addressed. I believed the parents' deception assumed the son was somehow unaware of, or oblivious, to the tension and problems in the household. They wanted to believe the boy was immune to the problems in the family and his father's drug-related activities merely because he was 5 years-old. The parents and I explored this issue in great depth.

We were able to identify many indicators that led the couple to believe that the boy *was*, in fact, enmeshed in and aware of the family crisis and his father's drug and alcohol abuse. For instance, their son would often physically place himself between his parents when they were arguing or fighting. On other occasions when the parents fought, the boy would start to cry and retreat to his bedroom or the bathroom. Their son would also make occasional reference to *"the stuff that makes dad act different."* The boy was also having a difficult time concentrating and interacting with other children at his preschool. The preschool director even informed the parents that their son was exhibiting behaviors indicative of attention deficit disorder. She recommended that he be evaluated by a physician for an accurate diagnosis and possible medication therapy. The parents gradually began to connect the general lack of emotional safety and stability in their son's life to these behaviors and the problems he was having in preschool. Could the parents expect their son to relax and be at ease for the 4 to 5 hours he was at preschool when his home life was unpredictable, full of tension, and lacking emotional safety? After much consideration, the parents came to the conclusion that their son was very aware of the family problems and that he was able to connect the drinking and drug use to these problems. His reactions – the less desirable behaviors described by the parents – matched his age and developmental stage. That is, a 5 year-old had neither the developmental skills nor the life experiences to verbally process the uncomfortable emotions he might have been feeling. These emotions were therefore expressed through his behaviors. Wouldn't it be nice if the 5 year-old child could verbalize the following:

> *Daddy, I get really scared when you drink or get high. I'm not sure what's going to happen. I don't know if you're going to be nice or if you're going to become impulsive, unpredictable, and angry. I want to make everything better, but I don't know how. Sometimes I feel really confused, overwhelmed, and unsafe.*

Unfortunately, young children are unable to verbalize themselves in this way. It is up to the parents to interpret and understand their children's behaviors and conversations in order to arrive at these conclusions. With this in mind, I asked again why the parents were attempting to deceive their son. Did they think the child was unable to handle the truth – explained in an age appropriate manner? We explored the possible long-term consequences of deception and the benefits of being forthright. With my assistance the parents were able to identify the following possible consequences of deception and benefits of being forthright with their son:

Possible Consequences of Deception	Likely Benefits of Being Forthright
• Decreased parent-child intimacy • Possibility of decreased parent-child trust • Potential to compromise the parents' ability to be healthy role models • Compromised sense of morality or ethics • Burdened conscience • Increased emotional burden (baggage) • More skeletons in the parents' closet • Conflicted and incongruent emotions (this situation/ story does not match the emotions being experienced)	• Increased parent-child intimacy • Increased parent-child trust • Parents' position as a healthy role model strengthened • Strengthened sense of morality and ethics • A conscience that is free from burden • Less emotional baggage to maintain • Fewer skeletons in the family closet • Incongruent emotions will be lessened (the situation/ story matches the emotions experienced)

Both parents agreed that what had been happening in their marriage and household had been painful for everybody. They wanted it to simply go away. Yet, when they stopped to look at the potential long-term consequences of further deception, they agreed the issue should be addressed in a more helpful manner. The parents eventually concluded their deception was based on their own anxiety and embarrassment rather than their son's perceived ability to handle the truth. We role-played several ways the parents could tell their son the truth.

Several days later the mother brought the boy to visit his father. Their conversation went something like this:

Father: *Your mom and I have been fighting a lot lately. I think this fighting has probably been hard for everybody – including you. Your mom and I are working hard to make things better.*

Mother: *This place is a hospital where daddy is getting help for some problems.*

Son: *A hospital! Are you going to be OK?*

Father: *I'm working hard to be OK.*

Son: *What kind of problem?*

Father: *Well, when I drink alcohol, I make poor decisions, and I have a hard time being a good father and husband to your mom. I really want to change that.*

Son: *I'm glad.*

Father: *If you ever have any questions about this I want you to feel OK to ask me or your mom.*

Son: *When will you be home? I miss you.*

War is based upon deception – not parenting. Children recognize deception even when parents do not. Children can handle honesty even when parents cannot. The son in the example above was probably aware of the deception on a very basic level. There were a lot of problems at home. His father had never traveled on business before. Now he was gone for weeks and his mother was crying all the time. Things did not add up emotionally. If family life were to magically improve after the father returned home, the child would wonder what was going on. The parent's story, in addition to the incongruent emotions he experienced, would not make sense to the child. Rather than questioning his parents, he would, out of a natural loyalty to his parents, question his own emotions and understanding of the circumstances.

The parents received support for the embarrassment they were experiencing and practiced several ways they might explain the situation, in an age appropriate manner, to their son. They experienced a great sense of relief after having this heart-to-heart conversation with their son. The boy did not reject his parents nor did he seem too surprised by the situation. In fact, the parent's input seemed to help the child solve a very complex puzzle that was bouncing around in his mind. The parent's explanation helped the boy put several crucial pieces of this puzzle together. Their son was able to handle honesty even when the parents were having difficulty doing so.

In the practice of marriage and family therapy, I encounter similar situations quite often. Never have I come across a situation where being forthright – on an age appropriate level – did not result in healthier outcomes than what results from deception. Several years ago I was confronted on this topic by a parent during a parenting workshop. Her marriage had been marred by several instances of infidelity. She insisted her children must be protected from the reality of the infidelity. In front of about 150 workshop participants we role-played this scenario. She took the role of her young children and I took the role of parent. It went something like this:

Parent: *Things have been really tough around here lately. Your father and I are having some problems in our marriage. These problems are pretty serious. However, it's important to let you know that we both love you very much and that these problems have nothing to do with anything you have done.*

Child(ren): *I'm scared.*

Parent: *It's OK to feel scared right now. Your Dad and I are also scared. I think if we keep talking about how we are feeling it might help us be less scared.*

Child(ren): *How come daddy doesn't come home very often? Who's that other person I hear you yelling about when he's here?*

Parent: *Sometimes when moms and dads are having a hard time getting along, they will separate for a while. This is what your dad and I have done. We're going to use this time to think about what would be best for our marriage and the family. It's going to be tough for a while, but I'm sure we will be able to get through this OK.*

Child(ren): *What about the other person you yelled at daddy about?*

Parent: *Sometimes when married people have problems, they will try to fix them in ways that can harm the marriage. That other woman* *you heard me talk about is one part of the problem your father and I are having. This is a problem that will take us a while to figure out. But I want you to know that your father and I will be honest with you about everything that is going on and that we both love you very much.*

This is obviously a very difficult situation. The parents will have to be very careful in order to avoid causing significant and long-term distress in their children's lives. Yet, this type of conversation can occur between parent and child(ren). The important and emotionally charged issues were not circumvented. The parent that confronted me on the issue and who participated in this role play stated that she experienced considerable discomfort but left the conversation feeling secure, safe, and welcome to approach the issue again as needed. This parent stated the discomfort she experienced was probably unavoidable as separation and divorce come with many uncomfortable emotions. I would agree.

55. When you suspect deceit, allow the child an opportunity to experience consequences that are equitable and fair. In this manner you will not likely fold when there are challenges and you experience anxiety.

When I was in graduate school, one of my professors related a story from his own life that I believe to be relevant to this Parenting Assumption. I held this professor in very high regard. He was an excellent and insightful instructor and appeared to have a thriving marriage and family therapy practice. His professional skills and experience placed him in high demand. He and his wife were scheduled to attend an out of town conference for five days. While out of town they chose to entrust their house and automobile to their 17 year-old son. Their only instructions to the young man were to use the automobile for emergencies and to make good decisions. Upon returning from the conference, the father was relieved to see that everything appeared to be in order. Almost everything. When the father inspected the automobile, he noticed that a small coat of road salt covered the finish. The father wondered if it had snowed while he was out of town and checked the recent newspapers stacked in the recycle bin. The weather had been clear and unseasonably mild the previous week. The son's girlfriend graduated from high school a year early and was attending her freshmen year of college approximately 200 miles north of their house. The father suspected his son paid a visit to his girlfriend while they were away. I believe he handled the situation in a very admirable way. He approached the young man and stated something similar to the following:

Father: *Son, is there anything you would like to tell me about this past week? Anything I need to know about?*

Son: *No. Nothing I can think of. Why?*

Father: *Are you sure?*

Son: *Yeah. Why?*

Father: *I would hope that if there was something you thought I should know about, you would feel safe approaching your mother and me about it.*

Son: *Sure.*

The father thought he might check the regional weather reports later that day to see what was going on 200 miles to the north.

Early the next day the son approached his father and asked if they could talk. The son admitted to visiting his girlfriend and to putting nearly 500 miles on the automobile. He told his father that the separation was difficult and that he wanted to do whatever he could to try to make the relationship work out. The son apologized for his deception and expected it to end there. The father stated that he was glad his son had come forward and that they, the parents, would come up with a punishment that was fair and equitable to the situation. The son was apparently disappointed that the father was considering punishment but appeared remorseful and understanding that there would be further consequences.

Later that evening the parents met with their son and communicated their feelings about the whole incident. They told him both were disappointed by the decision he made and that they were hurt that he chose to further the deceit by initially failing to be forthright. The parents also reiterated that they were glad he chose to come forward rather than continue the lie. The father told his son that his employer reimburses him for mileage at a rate of 35¢ per mile. The parent's punishment was that the son would reimburse them at this rate (35¢

x 500 miles = $175.00). In addition, he would not have use of the car until the debt was paid in full. Furthermore, he would be required to pay for all the long distant calls to his girlfriend until the debt was paid off. The son had a part time job, but this was a significant amount of money to the young man and would take some time to work off. He was obviously disappointed yet appeared to feel the parents' decision was just. A month later the debt was paid – including the cost of the long distant calls he made – and the son regained use of the family automobile. The father stated he believed the incident – including the punishment – had actually brought the parents and son closer together. The father stated that had he been in his son's shoes, he probably would have done the same thing. The boundaries the son chose to challenge could have been significantly more destructive. The father never told his son about noticing the road salt nor that he confirmed there was a winter storm in the area where the son's girlfriend attended college.

I believe that when a child attempts to deceive his or her parents, the family is presented with an opportunity for growth. If the parents approach the child with emotional process – communicating how they were affected by the deception and attempting to understand the child's position – and the consequences enforced are equitable and fair, everyone will benefit. This appeared to be the case in the example above. If the parents chose to ban their son from using the family vehicle for an excessive period of time, say a year, or if they chose to prohibit the young man from communicating with his girlfriend, increased emotional distance between parents and child would have resulted. When this occurs, the parents will likely have a difficult time enforcing these consequences.

In my practice of marriage and family therapy, I find many parents very uncomfortable with or fearful of interactions such as those found in the example above. Many parents feel that if the deceit is not confronted immediately, the opportunity to do so is lost. Other parents tend to believe that it is best to put all of one's chips on the table at once and to confront the child immediately with all the evidence. I would like to think that if the child is encouraged and feels safe to come forward and admit to the deception rather then to be openly confronted with the facts, everyone will be more likely to benefit. I asked the professor what he would have done if his son had not come forward. He stated he would have eventually confronted his son with more of the facts without directly telling his son what he (the father) thought had happened – giving him additional opportunities to come forward with the truth. The professor also stated he would have spent considerably more time with his son exploring the topic of trust after the truth was disclosed.

| Chapter 7 Skill

A great ability or proficiency; expertness that comes from training and practice.

56. *To understand process without being distracted by content is the acme of parental skill.*

People arrive in my office presenting a broad spectrum of family, parenting, and personal problems. Over the years I have come to the conclusion that, by far, the most important skill I can bequeath my clients is the ability to differentiate *process* from *content*. All who acquire and utilize this skill find it to be most helpful when dealing with the diverse problems and parenting challenges encountered in our living. Differentiating *process* from *content* is most important! What are *process* and *content*? To help you better understand these concepts I will do three things. First, I will present very brief definitions of both. Secondly, I will present several vignettes that will help clarify these definitions.[32] Finally, I will present a very complex family problem that was raised by one of my clients in therapy. This example will highlight how this Parenting Assumption helped one family deal with a very difficult situation.

Let's begin with some simple definitions:

Process: *Process* is the *underlying meaning* of what we say and do when interacting with others.

Content: *Content* is what one **actually says, hears, or otherwise experiences** during interactions with others.

These definitions may seem closely related, yet, when people interact (e.g. a parent and a child, a husband and a wife, co-workers, and so on), *content* will often differ from *process* in very significant ways. These differences often lead to problems in our family, parenting, personal, and work relationships. As the distance between *process* and *content* increases, so will the severity of problems found in these relationships. When I evaluate the origins of an argument or conflict, I consistently find that a significant gap exists between process and content.

The best way I know to help clarify the difference between *process* and *content* is to present several brief vignettes. These vignettes consist of comments between children and their parents. As you read these comments, try to remember that *process* is the underlying meaning of what we say and do when interacting with others. The underlying meaning will often differ from what is actually said (content). These differences are highlighted in something I call a *process interpretation*. Each vignette is followed by a *process interpretation*. The *process interpretations* presented do not necessarily represent the actual thoughts of the person in the vignette. Rather, they are intended to be close approximations of what the child or parent might be experiencing or thinking. *Process interpretations* should identify variables that may be influential to the underlying meaning (process) and influencing the *content*. Quite often we are unaware of the many variables that impact *process*. However, by attempting to identify a few of the variables and bringing the emotions associated with them to the surface, we are able to greatly reduce the gap that sometimes exists between *process* and *content*. After reviewing each vignette, ask yourself this question: If I were to read the *process interpretation* to the parent or child in the vignette, would they be more likely to say, *"Yes, that hits the nail on the head. That's what I'm feeling right now"* or would they be more inclined to say *"You have it all wrong!"*

First Vignette:

A young child blurts out the following to his parents after being disciplined: *"I hate you!"*

Process Interpretation: Does this child really hate his or her parents? Not likely. The **content** is *"I hate you."* The **process** interpretation – from the child's perspective – might be something similar to:

> *I'm really frustrated right now. I don't understand your limits, boundaries and consequences. I feel like things are*

not going my way and this leaves me feeling vulnerable, disappointed, powerless, and miserable. I don't know how to work through these feelings or communicate how confused I am right now. It seems like the only way I can communicate the gravity of my feelings is by lashing out – telling you "I hate you." This will get your attention. This is uncomfortable and painful for me. I feel like I hurt you by saying this, yet I'm willing to take the consequences. I wish I had other options. I'm frustrated.*

*(Note: Keep in mind that a young child is unable to verbalize that which is stated above. This *process* statement is far beyond the child's developmental capabilities. However, the child **is** capable of experiencing, and is likely to understand the emotions and concepts presented in this paragraph. Therefore, it is not inappropriate to use language, concepts, or descriptions that are beyond the child's capability to verbalize when formulating your *process interpretation*. The *process interpretation* is intended to help you understand the underlying meaning of the child's statement.)

Second Vignette:

A young teenage girl sits silently through dinner. This is uncharacteristic of the teenager. She is playing with her food. She responds to her parent's repeated inquiries about *what's wrong with her* by stating: *"There's nothing wrong. OK! Just leave me alone."*

Process Interpretation: Is there something going on here? Probably so. The **content** is *"There's nothing wrong."* The **process** interpretation might be something similar to:

I'm feeling really down right now. There's a number of things bothering me. The list seems so long. I know you guys are concerned, but right now I'm just trying to put it all together for myself. I'm struggling with problems at school, I'm having problems fitting in with my friends. My relationship with you guys seems to be changing in all kind of ways. How does one get through this? I wish I had the answers. I wish I could come up with the right questions to ask you. Yes, there's something wrong. These problems feel very real to me but they also seem silly. I'm embarrassed to bring them up. I should be able to figure these things out for myself. I hope.

Third Vignette:

A very young boy begins to place a stone in his mouth. The concerned mother instructs the child not to do this, that it may be dangerous and not good for him: *The boy initially hesitates then ignores his mother's directive by placing the stone defiantly in his mouth.*

Process Interpretation: Is this just a case of a "bad" child? Of course not. The **content** is the child's defiant behavior. The **process** interpretation would be something similar to:
You've got this all wrong Mom. Why can't you see that? This stone needs to go into my mouth. Why else would it be this size and why else would I feel this way? It seems natural to put things in my mouth. Somehow, I get some satisfaction from it. I don't understand where Mom's coming from right now. It doesn't make sense. I'll show her how big I am and that I know what's right. She'll be proud. I want to please her. Everything will work out.

Fourth Vignette:

A middle school student responds to his parent's inquiry about his performance in a particular class – specifically about his attention to the homework. The child responds with the following: *"I don't do homework in that class because the teacher is such a jerk."*

Process Interpretation: Is the teacher a "jerk"? Hopefully not. There are probably other factors at work here. The **content** is – *I'm not doing the homework, and it's the teacher's fault.* The **process** interpretation would be something similar to:
I'm so lost in that class. I sit there scared out of my gourd. Every time I'm called to the chalkboard, I know everybody's laughing at me. I feel like the teacher must be doing this on

purpose. He's a sadist. This stuff seems to come easily to the other kids. There must be something wrong with me. How do I get out of this mess? I don't want to let mom and dad in on the fact that their son is a failure. If the teacher was any good he would help me out. It's his fault. I wish somebody would help me. I'm confused.

Fifth Vignette:

Parents repeatedly ask their daughter to clean her room. The young teenager appears completely unconcerned with the disarray and mess that is her room. The parents respond by yelling at their daughter: *"What's wrong with you? Do you want people to think you're a slob? Get in there right now and don't come out until the room is cleaned up!"*

Process Interpretation: Why is the daughter's room chronically a mess? How is this affecting the parents? Are parents and child coming closer together here? The **content** is – *there's something wrong with you.* The **process** interpretation would be something similar to:

We love her very much. However, the condition of her room actually scares us. We don't understand how she could live that way. We are concerned where this might lead. We are also beginning to question ourselves as parents. Why can't we get our young teenage daughter to do something that seems so simple? Why does this whole situation have such powerful control over us? We are adults. She is a teenager. We should be in charge here. We hate to yell, but what else is there for us to do? We are confused and would give anything to know what is motivating her right now.

Sixth Vignette:

Parents ask their son why he is staying home on Friday night when they understood he had a date with a new girlfriend. The son responds with the following to his parent's inquiry: *"I stood her up because she's been ignoring me lately."*

Process Interpretation: Does the girlfriend deserve to be stood up? No. Is the son's explanation accurately describing the entire situation? No. The **content** is – *I have no responsibilities in this matter. She brought this on herself.* The **process** interpretation differs greatly from this content:

> *It feels like she's ignoring me. Maybe she wants to break up. That would hurt so much. We've only been dating a few weeks, but I really like her. I would like to ask her straight-up what's going on, but the thought of that makes me nervous. I don't think I can do it. What if she dumps me? No way am I going to put myself through that. I need to be in control here. She's going to have to call me. If she doesn't – oh well. Everything works out this way. I should stand her up. It's best all around.*

There are an infinite number of possible *process interpretations* for the vignettes presented above. Many parents will point this fact out to me as we explore the subject of *process* and *content*. It seems as if they want to disprove *process* exists or that a parent's attempt to formulate a *process interpretation* is too difficult or somehow impossible. Sometimes I think parents would rather remain focused on the content (e.g. *"I hate you"* – as presented in the first vignette) rather than explore *process* (the *underlying meaning*) of what is said. Unfortunately, failing to explore process leaves the parent with only the content to work with. This is unfortunate because the parent only has a limited amount of information, which is often misleading. If the parent chooses to ignore process, he or she will likely be making less helpful and healthy parenting decisions and interventions.

Let's take a closer look at the first vignette. The child responds to his parent's attempt to discipline him by stating *"I hate you."* If the parent chooses to focus on the *content,* he or she might have a difficult time guiding this interaction in a healthier or more helpful direction. The parent might respond to the child's remark by increasing his punishment, placing him in timeout, yelling at him, getting angry, and so on. These actions might feel like a natural reaction or perhaps somewhat easier than pursuing *process.* However, the parent and child will likely find themselves feeling more distant rather than closer to each other when all is said and done. Neither will know exactly why or how this emotional distance occurred. Let's look at a parent responding to *"I hate you,"* with an understanding of *process.* This parent is able to avoid being distracted by the *content*. The parent might respond in a manner similar to the following:

Child (after being disciplined by his parents): *"I hate you."*

Parent: Hmmm. . . . *If I were you I might feel really frustrated right now. It's probably pretty hard to understand why your father and I do some of the things we do -- like when we punish you. Sometimes you might feel pretty frustrated or confused when this happens. When you tell me that you hate me...... well, that really hurts. However, I think it probably means that you might be having a hard time telling me how you really feel. What do you think?*

Child: *????*

Try to put yourself in the child's shoes for one moment. Is this child likely to respond to the above input with another *"I hate you"* or is he more likely to respond in a less confrontational and more productive manner? My experience leads me to believe the latter is more likely. For example, can you picture the child responding to the parent with *"I don't understand why I have to be punished?"* This response would not be uncommon and leaves the parent in a position to turn this interaction into a healthier educational experience for both. What if the parent's *process interpretation* is way off? Will this result in greater emotional distance between parent and child? Probably not. In fact, the child will probably be more inclined to correct the parents by attempting to tell them how he really feels. This should come as a relief to the parent – and serve to draw the parent and child together in healthy and helpful dialogue.

How does a parent arrive at an accurate *process interpretation*? This requires the parent to utilize empathy skills. That is, the parent must attempt to place him/herself in the child's shoes and see the world/situation from his or her perspective. The parent must strive to understand the child's emotions, thoughts, views, limitations, and strengths – even if it differs from his or her own. Once the child's perspective is considered, the parent can use an intuitive approach to help determine if the *process interpretation* is close to being accurate. For example, the parent would ask him/herself if the emotions identified in the *process interpretation* lead back to the content. The child in the first vignette might be feeling frustrated, confused, disappointed, powerless and miserable. He might be feeling hindered in his ability to better express himself and unable to affect change and get what he wants. If you experienced similar feelings and were unable to verbalize these emotions, might the chances of lashing out in a hurtful and inappropriate manner (e.g. *"I hate you"*) be increased? If you answered "yes," you are understanding the intuitive approach and have found yourself getting close to the underlying *process*. A parent who arrives at an intuitive connection between their *process interpretation* and the *content* will find him/herself in a position to greatly increase intimacy between parent and child.

The parents in the first vignette are faced with an opportunity to promote significant emotional growth. The *"I hate you"* can actually be a tremendous parenting opportunity if they choose to focus their attention on *process*. The *content* is merely an indicator, a flag so to speak, of an area that might benefit from parental attention. In this case, the attention would involve assisting the child deal with frustration, disappointment, and confusion in a more productive manner rather than lashing out. Focusing on the underlying *process* will help guide the parent in a direction that will benefit child and parent alike.

Let's take a look at a more complex situation. I was facilitating a group therapy session consisting of 7 or 8 men. These men were referred to therapy by the criminal justice system after being convicted of non-violent crimes. Therapy was an alternative to incarceration for these individuals. One of the group members presented a family/ parenting problem that was causing him great distress. In fact, he informed the group that he was completely overwhelmed by the problem and was at his wits end. This group member, Phil, arrived home from work to find his house in a complete state of chaos. Apparently his 13 year-old stepson had thrown an ashtray at his mother nearly hitting her in the face. The ashtray broke a kitchen window. Phil's wife was bordering on hysteria and the 13 year-old had run away. The other children in the house were agitated and fighting with each other. Phil's efforts to restore calm were unsuccessful. He stated there seemed to be no right answers or actions. Phil was asked to give the group a detailed description of the whole situation as he understood it. Below is a summary of Phil's account:

Background:

Phil married his current wife approximately one year prior to this incident. His wife had four children from a previous marriage (ages

8, 13, 14, 15). The family resided in a three bedroom, double-wide mobile home. The conditions were described as cramped. The children had a relatively good relationship with their biological father as well as their step father (Phil). Phil was court ordered to complete a counseling program after he was arrested for, and convicted of, a non-violent crime. This counseling required a considerable investment of time and financial resources. The family was experiencing severe financial hardships as a result of the counseling, yet, this expenditure was a far better alternative than incarceration. Several weeks prior to the ashtray incident a 21 year-old relative (the wife's cousin) temporarily moved into the household after his fiancé broke off the engagement. He was sleeping on the couch in the living room.

The Incident (content):

The 13 year-old stepson arrived home from school and proceeded to get something to eat. The 21 year-old cousin instructed the 13 year-old to get started on his chores. The 13 year-old stated he would get to the chores but that he was hungry and was going to make a sandwich. The 21 year-old attempted to physically restrain the teenager from making the sandwich and a fight immediately broke out. The mother heard the commotion and separated the two. She apparently asked each what was going on. Unfortunately, neither could verbalize themselves very well at that moment. The mother dismissed the 21 year-old cousin and was going to send the 13 year-old to his room to calm down but never had the opportunity. As soon as she directed her attention to the teenager, he became agitated, backed away from his mother, picked up an ashtray and threw it at her head. He immediately exited the house and ran away. The mother became completely overwhelmed with a rush of uncomfortable emotions and just began to cry. The cousin attempted to take control of the other children in the house which resulted in additional verbal conflicts, exacerbating an already difficult situation. This is when Phil arrived home. He made an initial attempt to locate the 13 year-old but was unsuccessful. Eventually the condition in the household calmed, yet tension around the home was described as unbearable. The 13 year-old was found two days later. He had been staying at a friend's house. Phil asked his stepson what had happened. His description was very limited and focused on the content described above.

I was very concerned about the situation described by Phil. The other group members were concerned as well and attempted to help him by contributing many suggestions. Unfortunately, Phil's solutions, as well as the group's input, lacked something – a very critical factor. They were solely focused on the *content* and did not incorporate any consideration of *process*. For example, one group member suggested that the 21 year-old cousin be asked to leave the house. This group member felt the cousin's presence was an obvious disruption to the family. Other group members suggested alternative disciplinary actions and parenting suggestions, such as better ways to initiate time-outs and reducing household tension by scheduling access to the VCR, TV & computer games. The group's suggestions were not necessarily wrong; however, were they the most helpful course of action? I interrupted and said that I was going to provide a *process interpretation* of the whole event. I was going to attempt to put myself in each person's shoes and was going to try to understand and verbalize each person's perspective. The *process interpretation* went something like this:

Process Interpretation:
13 Year-old Boy:
I miss having my father around. I love him very much. However, my stepfather is an alright guy. Are the positive feelings I'm having for my stepfather an indication I don't need my father anymore? How can I be loyal to Dad when I'm loyal to my step dad? Who do I listen to? Both? This is confusing. Things are pretty cramped around here, and now my mom's cousin is living on our couch. What right does he have to be here? Things are tough enough. This sucks. My mom's cousin is telling me what to do. Now I have three fathers as if two weren't enough. I feel powerless. I've been here longer than him. I am determined not to yield to him. No way. Things are already too cramped around here. He must go at all costs!

21 Year-old Cousin:
This is so humiliating. I really love my ex-fiancé. I thought this was it. Then she just kicks me out. I'm devastated. I had to beg my cousin to stay at her house, on her couch, until I can find a cheap apartment. Twenty one year-olds should not be living this way. I feel completely powerless. At least I can help out with things around here. Maybe I'm not worthless. I will help keep these kids in line. Perhaps I'm good for something!

Stepfather/Husband (Phil):

I used to live here alone. This was my house. I fell in love, got married, and now we are a family. I'm conflicted. I love them all, but I feel crowded, uncertain, insecure. Did I make the right decision? Things are so cramped here. The fact that I did something stupid and now have to go to counseling doesn't help either. I never got into trouble before all this started. Perhaps we could sell the truck and move into a larger house. I wish I did not have to pay these court fees and counseling bills. This hurts. I don't think I've ever been this frustrated and overwhelmed. I've got to hold everything together. I'm determined to make this work out. But it's hard. It's like I'm never home anymore. I feel powerless. I've just got to work harder. I've got to make things work.

Wife/Mother:

Boy am I stressed. I just need to put my feet up and fade away for a while. My husband must complete counseling and move on. The counseling seems hard on him. When he comes home he looks so exhausted. I'll bet he would like to fade away for a while as well. I'm too exhausted to really be there for him. All we seem to do is fight. I don't want that. I'm beat from the increased parenting and household responsibilities. I'm amazed that I haven't lost my job yet. Everything feels like a burden right now. Money's short; I hardly see my husband; we're cramped in this trailer. I'm confused but also hopeful. How can that be? I know I'm resilient. I hope things get better soon, . . . before this frustration gets the better of me.

With this *process interpretation* in mind, let's put the 21 year-old cousin in the kitchen with the 13 year-old and watch a destructive chain of events unfold before our eyes.

The Event – process interpretation continued:

The cousin feels powerless, humiliated, devastated by his love loss, and worthless. He is feeling low and does not want to be the lowest one on the food chain. He sees an opportunity to gain power (inappropriately) by attempting to parent the 13 year-old and other children in the household. There is no way this 13 year-old is going to go for it. Two fathers are enough for him. The cousin was intruding into a household that was already stretched to its capacity emotionally, physically, and financially. When the cousin inappropriately asserted himself the balloon popped. The 13 year-old lost control. The 21 year-old could not bear losing any more power and refused to back down when challenged by the teenager. When the 13 year-old's mother broke up the fight, nobody could explain what actually happened. The process was elusive. Both person's explanation was confusing and without merit. She dismissed the cousin and was going to have her 13 year-old son cool off in his room. However, he again lost control before his mother spoke her first word – he was certain that he was going to be unjustly punished. Any punishment would be perceived as unjust at that particular moment in time. He wanted Mom to know what was really going on inside of him, but his explanation kept coming back to his just wanting a sandwich before starting his chores. The 13 year-old knew there was more to the problem yet could not adequately express his feelings. This further frustrated an already frustrated teenager. His emotions were boiling over and ready to explode. The ashtray was the closest thing he could find. It missed his mother's head by inches and broke a window. That was enough for the mother. She felt as if she was going to faint and just began to cry. The 13 year-old probably did not know why he threw the ashtray and was terrified at what he had done. The cousin, now feeling even more powerless and useless, attempted to compensate by taking control of the situation by shouting orders at the other children. They would have nothing to do with it and were more concerned with their mother. Phil enters the scene. His wife is unable to express herself coherently; the 13 year-old is gone; there is a broken kitchen window; the cousin and children are yelling at each other. Phil felt as if he was losing his mind. He needed to take control of this situation and started telling people what to do, including the 13 year-old when he was located 2 days later. This had little positive effect. Tension remained in the house for days without relief in sight.

My suggestion to Phil was to spend some time considering each family member's perspective. For example, what emotions were each family member experiencing? What underlying factors might be influencing each family member? What frustrations were each family member facing? What topics might each family member wish to explore with the family, and why were they feeling prohibited from doing so? Phil was encouraged to formulate and communicate to the family – in his own words – his *process interpretations*. This action might not answer the question of why emotions were not being openly processed; however, it would likely move the family in a direction of being better able to work with the emotionally charged subjects and situations they were facing.

The next week Phil arrived with great news. He assembled the family and presented his thoughts and feelings. These were based upon his increased understanding of the underlying *process*. Phil said the family reacted well and that they had a long, in–depth, and intimate conversation. He reported the tension that previously filled the home immediately dissipated. Phil also stated the conversation between family members felt as if it *"was somehow controlled without anybody taking control of it."* The conversation between family members took on a healthy life of its own. Finally, Phil stated he was experiencing a great sense of relief. The positive benefits he experienced from just this single family interaction were obvious and very reassuring. He informed the group that he had every intention of continuing to incorporate use of *process* in his personal, family, and work relationships.

Weeks later Phil reported that his stepchildren and wife were beginning to use some of the same tools he had been incorporating when interacting with them. He did not instruct or encourage them to begin using these tools, but merely incorporated them into his interactions. When the family was faced with the option of continuing to interact with Phil in ways that were less healthy and less likely to be helpful versus interacting in ways that might be momentarily uncomfortable but healthier and more likely to be helpful, they opted for the latter. Again, Phil did not encourage them to interact in any particular way. He simply focused on his own actions and reactions, which incorporated the use of *process*. The family was becoming more comfortable expressing their emotions and considering each other's perspective. When perspectives differed from person to person, they were explored without significant conflict.

Phil's family was rapidly becoming better able to deal with the numerous stressors that were facing them. This is not to say the family "was cured" of all that ailed them. In fact, the family struggled for some time. However, in the midst of this struggle the family found themselves moving in healthier directions. This was accomplished without me or the other group members telling the family "what to do" or "what not to do" (e.g. kick the 21 year-old cousin out of the house). The family was capable of arriving at solutions that best met their unique needs and circumstances once they were assisted in developing helpful tools such as differentiating between process and content. They were acquiring a systemic understanding of family interactions.

Many parents report they get so wrapped up in or distracted by the *content* that they find it difficult to consider the underlying *process*. My experience leads me to believe this is likely the result of two problems: **1) Conversations and interactions move too quickly for the parent to explore** *process* – the parent is distracted by the pace at which the situation escalates to an argument or disengagement; **2) The parent struggles with the use of empathy**. Let's explore these two problems.

I find that many parents believe they must have an answer, *the right answer*, immediately available when interacting with their children. This belief may be a by-product of the parent's instinctual desire to provide the best possible parenting they can. Having *the right answer* may be thought of as being synonymous with providing good parenting.[33] I believe this instinctual reaction might benefit from some refinement. I have interacted with hundreds of parents and have yet to find one who had all the *right answers* available to them on demand. I do not think such a parent exists. On the other hand, I have worked with many parents who seem to have skills that allow them to arrive at answers that are more helpful – as opposed to less helpful – to the situation more often than not. Focusing on *process* without being distracted by *content* is probably the single most effective method of consistently arriving at these *more helpful* answers.

Simply *slowing the parent-child interaction down* can be tremendously helpful in achieving a greater understanding of the underlying process. Conversations or interactions that move too fast really do not allow the parent an opportunity to consider, explore or extract the underlying process. It is the parent who is in the position to set the pace of all parent-child interactions. If a child is upset, anxious, or disappointed, he or she may act or react in a manner that is inflammatory to the parents. In these situations the parent is faced with a choice – to immediately respond to the child with an emotionally charged reaction, quickening the pace of the interaction, or to step back and slow things down a bit.

From time to time I will intentionally pause when interacting with a family in therapy. I usually do this when things seem a bit out of control (if the family is arguing, yelling at each other, or making emotionally charged accusations). These pauses may range from 5 to 30 seconds – longer if emotions are extremely heated and the tension overwhelming. My pause usually leaves the family feeling a little uncomfortable. This discomfort may be an indication that the family is accustomed to impulsive conversations that escalate in undesirable ways. When I get around to responding following the pause, I will likely have their attention. The interaction will have been slowed down and the family will be more inclined to feel as if I invested considerable thought into my response. If this is not successful, I will assertively inform the family or individual with whom I am interacting that I wish to slow things down a bit. I will usually say something similar to: *"I'm not too comfortable with how this conversation is going. I would appreciate it if we could slow things down a bit. It's difficult for me to process all of this information, your perspective, and my thoughts, when things start moving this fast. I'd like to think both of our perspectives can be considered. How about it?"* This is an excellent method of preventing conversations from escalating into an argument where one's perspective is not considered. Parents who practice slowing down interactions with their children will find this to be most beneficial – especially when combined with the second recommendation: learn to better utilize your empathy skills.

How can the parent best utilize a momentary pause? He or she may silently search for that single *most helpful* or best response or the parent may choose to *use his or her empathy skills*. Most parents tend to prefer the former; whereas, I usually recommend the latter. Let's explore empathy. There are numerous definitions of empathy. I have arrived at the following definition after studying dozens:

> *Empathy is a heightened emotional state which evolves as one's understanding of another's perspective grows. This entails, but is not necessarily limited to, considering another's emotions, thoughts, motivations, stressors, inhibitions, strengths, weaknesses, experiences, interests, and situation.*

One of the best ways I know to develop empathy in my relationships is to initially look inward prior to making assumptions about those with whom I am interacting. That is, I take a few moments to clarify or identify my emotions and personal perspective. The above definition basically asks us to place ourselves in the shoes of those with whom we interact. How might looking inward help us understand the other's perspective?

Let's return to our previous vignettes to explore this concept. In the second vignette, the parents notice uncharacteristic behavior from their teenage daughter – she sits silently through dinner, playing with

her food. She rebuffs their initial inquiry as to what is bothering her.
Rather than have the parents immediately make assumptions regarding
the teenager's emotions and thoughts, let's have them focus *inward*
and see where this takes us. What emotions do you suppose a parent
might experience in this situation?[34] When I try to place myself in the
parent's shoes, several emotions come to mind. For example:

Concerned: The parent may experience concern – something appears to
be bothering his or her daughter.

Discouraged: The parent may feel discouraged after finding the topic
difficult to approach.

Hopeful: The parent might feel hopeful that the topic can be opened up
and that he or she may be helpful.

Disconnected: The parent may feel disconnected from the daughter
when she refuses his or her support.

Compassionate: The parent may feel compassion for the loved one who
is struggling.

Confused: The parent might feel confused by the daughter's opposition
to his or her desire to help. The parent wants what the best for
her.

Understanding: The parent might experience understanding when he or
she considers that the daughter is now a teenager and compelled
to figure things out for herself.

Committed: The parent may feel committed to assisting the daughter in
the best way possible.

Helpless: The parent may feel helpless as he or she knows it would be
futile to attempt to pry thoughts from the daughter – unless she is
willing and prepared to share them.

Ill-at-Ease: The parent may very well feel ill-at-ease by the whole
situation.

Insecure: The parent may feel insecure and may question if he or she is
doing everything possible to help.

Pressured: The parent may feel pressured to make everything better.

Reassured: The parent may feel reassured by his or her daughter's
previous decisions – most have been pretty good and resulted in
relatively few unhealthy consequences.

Thwarted: The parent may feel thwarted by the daughter's terse
response.

Uncertain: The parent may feel uncertain as to how to proceed.

Warm: The parent may have a warm love for his or her daughter. Seeing the daughter struggle reminds the parent of this love.

Identified above are sixteen emotions a parent in this situation might easily experience. When the teenage daughter responds to her parents with *"There's nothing wrong. OK! Just leave me alone,"* the parent will likely be hit with these or similar emotions all at once. This may result in a brief emotional *rush* or *log jam*. When a person experiences an emotional rush or log jam these feelings tend to merge into a single secondary emotion – such as anger. A secondary emotion is an emotional reaction that can emerge when multiple emotions are experienced and blended. For example, anger, jealously, rage, and fear are all examples of common secondary emotions. Each can be broken down into multiple emotions (e.g. anger may be a response to an onslaught of several emotions such as surprise, frustration, anxiety, and inconvenience).[35] If the parent pauses before responding and attempts to sort out the emotions being experienced, both parent and daughter will likely benefit. This requires discipline on the parent's part as the impulse to immediately respond to this rush is powerful. Many parents I work with tend to succumb to this impulse and respond with a secondary emotion, primarily anger. The secondary emotion is not necessarily incongruent to the situation, but will usually result in consequences that are less helpful to the situation. When the parent takes a moment to identify the emotional components of this rush – the primary emotions that make up the secondary emotion – he or she will be less likely to react impulsively or in a way that may later be regretted.

There are many responses that tend to indicate that a parent is responding to the rush of unsorted and unidentified emotions. For example, parents in the second vignette may impulsively respond with:

- You don't look OK!
- Hey, don't get snippy with me. I'm just trying to help!
- What's wrong with you!?

This parent is neither empathetic to the daughter's situation nor responding in a manner that will likely be helpful. Emotional distance between parent and child has been increased. If the parent takes a moment to look inward – sorting out the emotions stimulated by the daughter's input – he or she will find the interaction slowed down. More importantly, the parent will have gained valuable information regarding the daughter's emotions. Remember, one of the key components of empathy is working to understand another's emotions. When we interact with others, our emotional responses are usually closely tied to those around us. The parent in the second vignette may experience emotions similar to the 16 previously cited. The daughter is probably, **and not coincidentally**, experiencing similar emotions. For example, the daughter might be experiencing the following emotions:

Concerned: *How am I going to deal with all of these feelings?*.

Discouraged: *There are so many things going on. So many problems. There's no way I can handle this. I keep running into walls.*

Hopeful: *I think that with some time, I should be able to figure out these feelings.*

Disconnected: *I don't feel comfortable explaining this to my parents. Somehow I feel disconnected from them.*

Compassionate: *I know they are concerned and want to help out. They may be hurt by my attitude. This is probably very hard for them.*

Confused: *Will time heal this wound? This confusion?*

Understanding: *They're my parents. I guess it's their job to pry into my feelings and problems.*

Committed: *I'm not going to give in to them. This is my issue. It's none of their business. I don't know why but I'm committed to this position.*

Helpless: *I wish I had answers. I wish I could come up with the right questions to ask my parents. I feel so helpless.*

Ill-at-Ease: *This whole situation is difficult. I don't know the best way through this. I feel so uncomfortable and ill-at-ease by the whole thing.*

Insecure: *I don't want help from Mom and Dad, yet can I deal with this by myself? I feel so insecure right now.*

Pressured: *I wish they would get off my back. Why are they pressuring me?*

Reassured: *It's nice to know they are there. That they are interested in what's going on in my life. They haven't led me astray before.*

Thwarted: *They (parents) are not making this comfortable.*

Uncertain: *I don't know how to proceed here. This is new territory for me.*

Warm: *I love my parents.*

Both parent and child are on very similar emotional ground, yet the *content* of their conversation is miles apart. The parents have little information regarding what might be bothering their daughter. Yet, they have options other than responding impulsively or walking away from the matter and letting her figure it out. How do you think the daughter might respond to the following parental response?

A young teenage girl sits silently through dinner. This is uncharacteristic for the teenager. She is playing with her food. She responds to her parent's repeated inquiries about *what's wrong with her* by stating: *"There's nothing wrong. OK! Just leave me alone."*

Parent to Daughter: *Ok. I hear what you're saying and I'll respect that. It's just that I'm seeing you act a bit differently. I don't know why. I can't make you tell me what's up, but not knowing leaves me feeling concerned, disconnected, a little confused, and a bit uncertain. It's important for me to let you know how I feel. I'm confident you will find the best way through whatever may be on your mind. You've got a history of making healthy decisions. Let us know if there is anything we can do to be supportive.*

This parent's response contained just a few of the 16 emotions identified. This response, even though it was primarily based on the parent's emotions, was quite empathetic to the situation of the child. Consider how you might react if you were that teenager and your parents responded as above. Would your reaction be different than if you experienced: *"Don't get snippy with me"* or *"You don't look Ok!"* My experience as a family therapist has demonstrated over and over again that responses that slow the conversation or interaction down and incorporate empathy are infinitely more likely to result in more healthy and helpful conclusions. The example just presented may seem a bit unfamiliar and uncomfortable to some parents, however, with just a little practice, these skills will emerge. *To understand process without being distracted by content is the acme of parental skill.*

57. When being engaged with hostility, block the attempt by addressing process.

In the previous Parenting Assumption I stated that, *"One of the key components of empathy is working to understand another's emotions. When we interact with others, our emotional responses are usually closely tied to those around us.*" I have an example that demonstrates this point fairly well. Years ago, I worked in the intake office of a locked psychiatric hospital. This facility evaluated and hospitalized people who were in extreme emotional or psychiatric crisis. This included people who were feeling suicidal, people who were psychotic and representing a threat to themselves or others, and people who, for reasons attributable to a psychiatric condition, were unable to care for themselves. Many people were brought to this hospital involuntarily and were potentially dangerous. It was my job to perform the initial interview and evaluation. After I completed my evaluation, a psychiatrist would evaluate the client and a decision was made as to how the hospital's treatment team might be helpful.

One evening the police arrived with a man in his mid 30s that appeared very agitated. He had verbally threatened several complete strangers at a nearby shopping mall. This man was placed in one of our locked interview rooms until I could get my paperwork together. His wait was about 15 minutes. In my haste to get to the interview, I entered the room without visually checking the interviewee's status. I should have taken a moment to glance through the window. When I entered the interview room, I wished I had had several orderlies with me as the man was quite agitated. He was pacing rapidly back and forth in the 10 foot by 10 foot room. He was clenching his fists as if wanting to punch somebody, and he was talking to himself incoherently. This was not a great situation to find myself in. This man was clearly agitated and potentially explosive. My job was to make the initial assessment. I could have reported that he appeared agitated, explosive, and psychotic. However, this would not have been very helpful for the hospital's treatment team. I sat down and quickly searched the broad spectrum of emotions I was experiencing. It was easy for me to arrive at the following list:

Concerned – I did not know what was going on in the man's head.

Uncertain – I did not know how this situation was going to pan out.

Threatened – This man was clearly quite disturbed and very unpredictable.

Even before introducing myself, I attempted to contain the situation by addressing the underlying process. I did this through use of self-reflection and empathy. I stated the following: "*You know, right now I'm feeling a bit **concerned** by this situation. I'm also little **uncertain** now and feeling a bit **threatened**. If I'm feeling this way, I can only imagine what you might be experiencing.*" With this said, the man abruptly stopped his pacing. He turned toward me and shouted at the top of his lungs "*you're damned right!*" Then he took a deep breath and sat down for a lengthy and detailed evaluation.

Evidently, I made a connection with this threatening and agitated man through the use of empathy and by addressing process. He had a difficult time expressing himself; however, he was able to tell me that he had been experiencing severe auditory hallucinations for weeks. He was hearing voices telling him that other people – including complete strangers – were evil and out to get him. These hallucinations were terrifying to the man. He was *confused, disoriented*, and *uncertain*. He was also feeling very *threatened* by the police that picked him up and the process that brought him to this particular hospital. Even though our situations were significantly different, we found ourselves experiencing similar emotions. Addressing the underlying process was as simple as identifying and verbalizing my emotions as they related to the situation, and asking him if he could help me understand what he was experiencing.

My interview lasted about 30 minutes and proceeded without incident. I communicated my findings to the psychiatrist, who took little note of my comments. This was unfortunate. She entered the room staring at her clipboard and stated the following: "*Hello, Mr. Jones, my name is doctor Smith. How are you today?*" The patient immediately drew his arm back and punched the psychiatrist – successfully breaking her nose in the process. The patient did a fairly good job of communicating how he was doing that day.

This is an extreme example of "***when being engaged with hostility, block the attempt by addressing process.***" The psychiatrist avoided process and experienced an unfortunate consequence. Parents reacting to their children's occasional hostility by addressing process will find this to be a valuable skill. It takes practice and a lot of trial and error. Chances are, however, your child will not break your nose as your sharpen your skills.

58. If emotionally depleted, do not engage in hostilities. Withdraw, reflect and recompose.

This Parenting Assumption came to me while I was working as a consultant for a manufacturing firm. This was a family owned business and had well over 100 employees. They had been in business for 30 years. The company's President and founder had attempted to retire on three separate occasions. Yet, each time the date for the President's retirement neared, some kind of company crisis would occur, resulting in the retirement date being pushed back. The President's intentions were to pass leadership of the business to his eldest daughter who was a very competent engineer and leader. She had been involved with the company's day-to-day operations for more than 5 years and was well suited for the new role as President and CEO. After the third retirement date came and went, I was hired to help the family and firm move forward. It seemed as if the President and his wife hade made a great many plans for their retirement. The wife was becoming frustrated by the pattern of postponements.

The problems facing the company and family were very complex. No single bit of advice or single recommendation would completely solve the problems they seemed to be having in transitioning the leadership from father to daughter. If the transition was to be accomplished in a healthy and helpful manner, many perspectives would have to be taken into consideration. This would include the perspectives of the current President, his wife's, his eldest daughter's, the younger siblings', the company's senior managers, the company's workforce, and the perspective of the company's long established customer base. All were going to be potentially affected by the transition and all had some responsibility in the three delays that had already occurred.

I met with the company's President and found him to be a very dynamic individual. He was an energetic and engaging leader. I could understand why this company had experienced such success during its 30 years of existence. This man loved his work and it showed. However, he seemed particularly distressed about the difficulties being encountered during this period of transition. The President also appeared to be preoccupied with many very complex emotions. This is not uncommon as one approaches a significant life-cycle shift, such as retirement. However, the company, its President, and all of the other persons potentially affected by this transition did not seem to be heading in a direction whereby the matter was going to be resolved in a healthy manner.

The President was being pulled in many directions by many people at the same time. His senior managers had worked hand-in-hand with their boss and mentor for years. The managers had unquestioning loyalty for their boss. There was no guarantee that the President's daughter would continue managing with the same skill in which they had become accustomed. This left them feeling apprehensive and somewhat vulnerable. These emotions surfaced in subtle and sometimes passive-aggressive ways. For example, rather than embracing the daughter as the chief executive, or simply talking to the President about their concerns, many of the senior managers withheld important information from her and depended upon her father to identify and correct the problems which this created. This type of behavior, and the pressures they created, were not isolated to the senior managers. The problems seemed to come from all directions. For example, several of the company's larger customers knew the President to be a man of integrity and unparalleled honesty. They also had an unusually high degree of personal access to the President. Many of these customers made it clear that they would not hesitate to find alternative suppliers for their products should the daughter fail to rise to the standards established by her father.

Many of the President's younger children lived in other states and one resided overseas. All had children of their own. The company had historically consumed a considerable amount of the President's time. The President's children were now exerting pressure on their father to take the time to visit with their families and the grandchildren.

The eldest daughter was typically a very confident and capable manager and engineer. She had numerous accomplishments to her name and seemed to inherit her father's ability to manage people and organizations very well. Yet, with each successive delay, she appeared to be becoming increasingly less assured of her abilities. She was beginning to reconsider her decision of taking over the leadership role in the family's business. She was obviously concerned about the potential flight of customers and the actions of the senior managers.

The President's wife was also becoming increasingly steadfast in her desire to enjoy their retirement together. There were almost daily reminders from the wife that it was time to move away from the workplace.

These were considerable pressures for a man who had looked forward to beginning his retirement. The President was a man who did his best to address the needs of those around him. Yet, at this particular time, the persons around him seemed to be in direct opposition with each other. Too many people were demanding the President's time and attention. By the time I was employed to assist with this situation, the President was *emotionally depleted*. The pressures he was facing were immense, even for a man with his leadership and business skills.

I first met with the President for breakfast. We spent an hour or so reviewing the scope of the problem then drove to his office. As soon as the President entered the front door of his building he was immediately accosted by four different people demanding his immediate attention and input. His response was predictable. He became very tense and short tempered, however, he did his best to address the various concerns that were thrust his way. I spent the next several hours trying to keep up with the President as he moved form the company's administrative spaces to the factory and assembly floor. I tried to listen in on the many conversations he had with his managers, people within his workforce, and the telephone calls he answered from the company's customers. Eventually, I had the undivided attention of the President and made three observations. The first was that he had been working at a near frantic pace for several hours. The second observation was that he had responded to nearly everybody he interacted with in a very short tempered manner. And finally, I noted that his daughter was nowhere to be found. I asked the President to consider one question. I did not want an answer; I only wanted him to consider the question: *Who's in charge here?*

The President and I agreed to meet the following morning and parted ways for the day. The next morning I asked, that upon entering the company building, he not address or respond to the employees that were sure to confront him with the problems or crises that required *his immediate attention.* The President was to refuse to engage in any conversation with these employees and was to go directly to his office. We entered the building and, as predicted, several people were waiting in anticipation of his arrival. The President assertively waived them off and firmly stated "*not now.*" When we got safely to his office I asked him how he was feeling. Stressed, exhausted, anxious, and tense were the words that immediately came from his mouth. At this point I repeated my question from the previous day, "*Who's in charge here?*" After several moments of consideration, the President stated "*I don't know, surly not me. I'm running around here like I don't know what I'm doing. My daughter's not in charge, either. It seems as if everybody but me is calling the shots these days.*"

The President and I spent the next hour or so exploring the level of stress that had been placed on his shoulders during the previous months. We explored how he had responded to this stress. We discussed the uncharacteristic short-tempered manner in which he responded to his employees and customers. We explored the possible perspectives held by his customers, his senior managers, the company's workforce, his daughter and her siblings, and his wife's perspective. The President seemed momentarily bewildered. He stated that somehow he had completely missed or overlooked numerous variables that were influencing the behaviors and emotions of the persons that might be potentially impacted by the transition of leadership in this company.

The President then did something quite unexpected. He dictated a memo that was to be copied to every employee in the company, to their larger customers, and to his eldest daughter. The memo stated that effective as of that day he was retired. The memo stated that his daughter was the new President and Chief Executive Officer. The memo concluded by stating that he had worked with his daughter closely during the previous five years and that he had the utmost confidence in her ability to lead the company in the years to come. Within ten minutes the memos were printed and being distributed. The President removed the memo addressed to his daughter's attention and wrote personal note on it. The note reaffirmed his confidence in her and opened the door for her to contact him for any advice or input that she may want in the future. The note concluded by stating "*the company is yours.*" The President then made two phone calls. The first was to his lawyer to ensure the transition was formalized and that his daughter had full authority over the company's affairs. The second phone call was to his wife. He essentially asked her to pack their bags. It was time to hit the road and play with the grandkids.

As the pressures surrounding the transition of authority and leadership within this company mounted, the President became emotionally depleted. This was evident in his uncharacteristic short temperedness, his inability to delegate authority to his senior employees, and the postponement of his retirement. In the process of becoming emotionally depleted, he lost the objectivity that helped him manage the business so well for so many years. The President's wife and eldest daughter initially interpreted his behaviors as a sign that he did not want to retire. The daughter was frustrated by the prospects of working indefinitely in a state of purgatory. She was prepared to take over the company but was prohibited from doing so, as long as her father remained on board. The wife was disappointed by the idea that her husband seemed to love his work more than his wife and family. Both the daughter's and the wife's interpretations were far from the truth. The President was eager to spend time with his wife and was wanting to see his daughter succeed as President and CEO. He just found himself in a strange bind. He was engaging all the opposing perspective while in a vulnerable state. He was emotionally depleted and struggling to remain objective. It took little effort on my part to help the President stand back and to recognize the process that was occurring around him. He merely had to withdraw from this process, reflect upon his priorities, and recompose himself. He needed a brief timeout. Following this brief timeout he again had access to the leadership skills that made him and the company such a success.

The above example explores a family business problem. However, the concepts are nearly identical to parenting. When parents find themselves emotionally depleted, any attempt to engage their children on difficult matters will be less healthy, less helpful and less effective than when not emotionally depleted. This statement may seem obvious and a bit transparent, however, many parents will resist the idea of withdrawing, reflecting , and recomposing. They continue to engage their children in an emotionally depleted state and lose a great deal of parental objectivity and efficacy. At one point, the President in the previous example simply waived off several of his employees and adjourned to his office. While in his office the President explored his emotions and the perspectives of those around him. He also evaluated the situation that had left him feeling depleted. This is a process that is too rarely exercised by parents when feeling emotionally depleted, short tempered, or ineffective. This is a parental version of a timeout. However, it is up to the parent to recognize the feelings of emotional depletion and then to withdraw. *If emotionally depleted, do not engage in hostilities. Withdraw, reflect, and recompose.* There is no shame in this process for Presidents of companies or parents.

59. To recognize the obvious is not the acme of parenting. Rather, it is recognition of the hidden which determines skill.

You may have noticed that in the previous pages I have frequently used phrases such as *helpful, healthy, less helpful* and *less healthy* when describing and exploring parent-child interactions. My particular use of this verbiage may have seemed unusual or novel to some readers. However, the selection of these phrases was intentional. In fact, their use, when exploring matters relating to parenting, is a very important language skill that is rarely provided much attention. This particular Parenting Assumption will explore and support my choice of verbiage.

The Parenting Assumptions presented to this point have focused a significant amount of attention on the concept of emotional process. That is, understanding the intimate connections between *thoughts, emotions, behaviors,* and *consequences.* The breadth of these connections may be elusive to or *hidden* from many parents. As such, further discussion of emotional process could easily monopolize this Parenting Assumption as well. I would like to explore this Parenting Assumption from a much different perspective, a more technical perspective. Let's explore how very subtle changes in our language – a *behavior* that has an intimate connection to our *thoughts* – can have a significant impact on the emotions, thoughts, and consequences we experience when interacting with others. The changes I suggest are relatively few and straight forward. Yet, they will have a significant impact on your parenting, family, social, and professional relationships when implemented more often than not. I'm going to suggest that you greatly reduce, or give thoughtful consideration to your use of, six words from your *commonly used* vocabulary. I'm also going to suggest several alternatives for the words I recommend you give thoughtful consideration. The six words I suggest you greatly reduce are: *good, bad, right, wrong, positive* and *negative.* Many parents gasp when I make this suggestion, as these words are used often – especially when interacting with children. Unfortunately, these words set us up to lose focus on emotional process and greater systemic understanding. They often lead us into concrete beliefs, a limited understanding of our relationships with others, and can greatly hinder our ability to learn

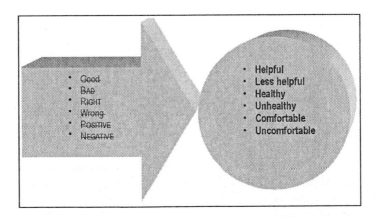

from the numerous situations we encounter daily. As we will see, the frequent use of these words hinders emotional process between individuals. In their place I suggest the following words: *helpful*, *less helpful*, *healthy*, *unhealthy*, *comfortable*, and *uncomfortable*.

What I'm suggesting here may feel difficult or uncomfortable at first. Therefore, I believe an explanation and few examples supporting my suggestions are in order. Below is a simple figure that represents 100% our decisions, actions, and reactions. These vary greatly and range from relatively insignificant decisions and actions, such as what shirt to wear to work, to more complicated decisions and actions, such as how we choose to interact with our children, friends, and colleagues.

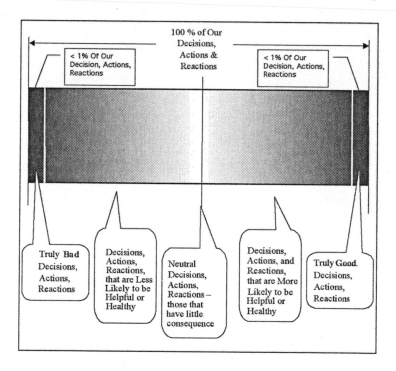

Over the course of any day we make literally thousands of decisions. We provide input to others, and we react to the input from others throughout our day. Many of these decisions, actions, and reactions are relatively small and insignificant. Individually, they have little impact on our overall lives. Most of these decisions, actions, and reactions are unconscious to us as we go about our daily business. They simply occur and, individually, do not have a great impact on our lives.

There are, from time to time, decisions, actions, reactions that have great importance in our lives. When we examine the ratio of minor decisions, actions, and reactions to those that have critical importance in our lives, it becomes clear that we make relatively few major decisions. I would approximate that less than 1% of our decisions, actions, and reactions would fall into the *critical importance* category. It is these that fall into this "critical importance" category that words such as *good, bad, right, wrong, positive* and *negative* might be appropriately used. For example, the decision to donate a kidney to help save the life of an ailing sibling might be appropriately described as a "good" decision, the "right" choice, or simply a "positive" thing to do. On the other hand, the decision to rob a bank or to physically harm or sexually abuse your child or spouse would be a "bad" decision, the "wrong" choice, or simply a "negative" thing to do.[36] Again, decisions, actions, or reactions of this magnitude represent a very small percentage of the total. We are more likely to be faced with decisions such as what clothes should we wear to work, how to respond when a child misbehaves, or how to react to a rude comment made by a co-worker. Unless you place of employment has a strict dress code, the decision of what to wear will have little consequence on your life and relationships. This would probably be considered a neutral decision in most instances.

If a parent chooses to yell at his or her child when the little one misbehaves rather than processing the event with the child, the parent is making a decision then acting in a manner that is *less likely to be helpful* and *healthy*. Yelling at the child does not necessarily represent a *bad* decision or reaction. It is simply *less likely to be as helpful* or *healthy* in comparison to other alternatives. Cutting off communications with a co-worker who makes a rude comment to you or responding by talking behind that person's back is not a *bad* decision, action, or reaction. It is simply *less healthy* or *helpful* than taking a moment to let that person know how their comment impacted you and how uncomfortable the workplace may become if the matter is not processed.

Earlier I stated the use of *good, bad, right, wrong, positive,* and *negative* will set us up to lose focus on emotional process and that these words may lead us into concrete stances and beliefs. What do I mean by this? Well, imagine the following interaction between parent and child:

Parent to Young Son: *Please don't place that stone in your mouth.*

Son: *Why not?*

Parent: *It's bad for you. Just don't.*

Son: *OK* (Removes and discards the stone)

This seems pretty straight forward, and the parent met the objective of having the boy remove the stone from his mouth. Now consider the following:

Parent to Young Son: *Please don't place that stone in your mouth.*

Son: *Why not?*

Parent: *Well it's not a 'healthy' thing to do. You could get hurt. When I see you do that, it leave me feeling very uncomfortable.*

Son: *What?*

Parent: *That stone could get stuck in your throat, and you could choke. That thought scares me. What do you think?*

Son: *I don't want that.*

In this example, the process between parent and child went much further when *bad* was replaced with *not healthy* and *uncomfortable* – both in the parent's thoughts and speech. The child asked *"What?"* in response to his parent's comments. In this instance, the boy was not necessarily confused by his parent's comment, but rather soliciting additional information. You will find that when a parent tells a child that something is *right* or *wrong*, *bad* or *good*, *positive* or *negative*, the child will merely accept this fact and is unlikely to pursue the matter further. There is little depth behind the child's acceptance and understanding. These are concrete phrases that we learn very early in life not to question. In this example, the child removed the stone from his mouth. This met the parent's objectives. Other than avoiding being harmed by the stone, how is the child better off? What exactly did he learn? How did he benefit from his parent's input? By changing a few thoughts and words, the parent sets the stage for further *intimate* interaction between parent and child. In a small way, this may have helped the child gain a greater understanding of his world and the relationship between thoughts, emotions, behaviors, and consequences. This is a valuable skill.

The parent/son example above is very simple and contrived. However, if you learn to recognize how often *good, bad, right, wrong, positive,* and *negative* are used throughout your day, and make a conscious effort to switch *to helpful, less helpful, healthy, unhealthy, comfortable,* and *uncomfortable,* interactions with others will likely move to greater depths and have much healthier conclusions. When I present this concept at parenting workshops and seminars, I receive many pessimistic looks and cynical reactions. Some parents will openly mock my suggestion – refusing to even consider the recommendation to evaluate the impact of and greatly reduce the use of these words. This is one reason I chose to place this discussion under this particular Parenting Assumption. The importance of this suggestion is *hidden* until such time that a parent experiences firsthand the healthy and helpful consequences after giving it a try. I have yet to find a parent who, after making a serious attempt to implement this suggestion in their interactions with others, did not find it to be a tremendous benefit.

Below are a couple of examples of various interactions demonstrating how this process works. Again, these may seem a bit scripted, yet when this practice is implemented, more often than not the benefits will soon be realized – especially in the parent-child relationship.

Dog Training Incident

I once saw two small children attempting to train their pet dog, a golden retriever, in front of their house. Both children were violently yanking on the dog's leash and screaming various commands at the poor animal (e.g. *No, Bad, Come, Sit, Stay,* etc.). These commands were coming in rapid succession and were even difficult for me to discern. The family pet looked terrified, tortured, and confused. I believe the children might have been attempting to imitate training they had seen their parents do in the past. They were not intentionally torturing their pet but were rather emulating their parents in an effort to help out. Unfortunately for the family pet, the children lacked the maturity, skill, and life experience to train the dog in a more compassionate and healthy manner. If the children's parents were to witness the kids' actions, they might intervene in any number of ways.

For example, one can easily imagine a parent yelling the following at the children:

"Stop that! What are you doing? That's wrong. You're hurting him!"

The children were making a genuine attempt to train the dog. Their efforts were likely an attempt to help, to give to the family, and were probably behaviors that somehow emulated their parents. These are examples of wonderful thoughts that were unfortunately acted upon in a manner that was not too healthy for the dog. This whole situation represents a great opportunity for a parent to give to the children. If the parent intervenes as above: *"Stop that! What are you doing? That's wrong, you're hurting him!"*, what is really accomplished? The dog will most certainly be relieved, but what ideas or thoughts might the kids walk away with? *I shouldn't emulate my parents? It's a bad idea to try to help? I'm incompetent? My behaviors and attempt to help were wrong.* This incident in itself will not seriously traumatize or harm the children. The parent's response is not "bad". The response is merely *"less helpful"* or *"less healthy"* than a reaction that incorporates additional emotional process and a few vocabulary changes. Consider the alternative reaction:

Parent: *Hey, Boys?!*

Parent: [Gently taking the leash from the sons]

Parent: *What's going on here?*

Sons: *We're training [name of pet]*

Parent: *Wow, that's great! You want some input from me?*

Sons: *Okay!*

Parent: *Well, [pet's name] will really benefit from your training, but I'm not sure he understands you.*

Sons: *What do you mean?*

Parent: *Well, it takes time for him to translate your language into dog language. I heard you shout at him then discipline him immediately by yanking on his leash. He seems kind of scared and confused. I suspect he was trying to figure out what you were saying to him but couldn't. What do you think?*

Sons: *Oh?!*

Parent: *It might be more helpful to slow things down a bit. Want to give it a try?*

Sons: *Yeah!!*

This interaction reinforces the wonderful things these children were attempting to accomplish – to emulate their parents and attempting to help out. The children would likely walk away from this interaction slightly more knowledgeable about dogs and with healthier beliefs about themselves. They would also see the intervening parent as a resource rather than just a disciplinarian. By changing a few words in his or her thoughts and actions, this parent's understanding of the whole situation changed. The children were not doing something **bad** or **wrong** – requiring severe and drastic interaction. Their efforts to train the pet were just not as helpful and healthy as an alternative that was unfamiliar to them. The example of the first parental reaction wasn't **bad** – it met the parent's objective of stopping the ineffective training and protecting the dog. The first reaction was simply not as helpful in the overall parenting process as the latter.

Playing with Matches

On several occasions parents have entered my office seeking support and guidance after discovering their child was playing with matches and fire. I like to use this example to explore an action that, for all practical purposes, approaches or falls toward the truly bad decision, action, or reaction end of the spectrum (see the previous figure). In one instance the father of a young boy smelled gasoline and smoke in his house. He investigated and discovered his son lighting small fires in the dusty crawl space under the house. The father reacted immediately by yelling several expletives at the boy, spanking him on the spot and sending him to his room. The parents were terrified by their son's decision to play with fire. He could have easily destroyed their house or been seriously injured. The parents were not satisfied that the father's immediate reaction and subsequent punishment of grounding the boy sufficiently addressed the issue. They believed their son was likely to continue playing with fire.

Where on the spectrum do the child's actions fall? Where on the spectrum does the father's reaction fall? Where on the spectrum does the decision to seek outside or professional input fall? I believe the child's actions approached the far left side of this spectrum. That is, the potential for harm to the boy and his family was so great that his decision to play with fire can be viewed as a *bad* one. I do not believe the boy had any intention of harming himself, his family, or his family's home. In fact, no harm was done. There were no injuries and no property damage. Yet, this was still a *bad* decision. Let me explain. In all likelihood, the thought of asking his mom and dad, *"Hey, Dad, Mom, can I use some of the lawn mower gas to build a fire in the crawl space? I think it would be fun, and I'm confident I can handle it"* never entered the boy's head. No, at some point in the boy's life he received the message that this would not be well received by his parents.

The boy secreted the fuel and matches to a location he believed safe from parental discovery and intervention. He made a deliberate decision to experiment with fire and followed through without his parent's knowledge. It's important to realize this boy was probably too young developmentally and experientially to fully comprehend the potential consequences of his decision and subsequent actions. This is where parenting comes into play.[37]

From time to time, children do things that are terrifying to parents. Any parent that has seen their young child run toward a hot stove or seen their child walk toward a busy street probably understands the emotional response to which I am referring. More often than not, these actions are simply examples of children acting without the benefit of age, experience, and developmental maturity. The parent must protect their children from such dangers while simultaneously educating them about the hazards and risks that exist in our world. I'm not going to assert that the father's initial reaction was in any way wrong or harmful. I'm sure the boy received the father's message loud and clear that fire play was not acceptable behavior. Yet, the parents were still concerned that the subject was not or should not be closed. How could they be certain the boy would not repeat the behavior?

The parents initially investigated a program offered by the local Fire Marshall's office. This program was specifically designed for children who were discovered playing with matches or fire. This program was essentially designed to scare the children in an attempt to discourage further fire play. They would view videos of homes that burned down, listen to interviews of both parents and children involved with such tragedies, and would sit through lectures from uniformed fire fighters speaking to them in a loud and harsh manner about the potential hazards associated with fire play.

The parents were uncomfortable with the Fire Marshall's program and chose to solicit the input of a therapist prior to enrolling their son. Would the fire department's fire play program have been a *bad* choice? No. Would it have been the most helpful reaction to the boy's decision and actions? I don't think so. The question of *why* the child secreted the fuel and matches into the crawl space beneath the house is not addressed in the fire play program. Fire represents a very mysterious subject for children. It has a powerful draw. Why did the child not explore his curiosity and questions with his parents prior to acting upon them? Again, the boy received the message somewhere in his life that fire play was *bad*. The parents did an effective job of imbedding this very direct and concrete message in the boy. Yet, he decided to ignore this message. Why? I believe the message – that fire play is *bad* – essentially shut the door for additional process. When the boy was confronted with his natural curiosity surrounding fire, he had nowhere to go. Remember, children will merely accept the message that something is *bad* without further consideration. If he were to approach his parents regarding his curiosity, their message would likely be the same – fire play is bad, end of discussion! Without the developmental maturity or experience to fully comprehend the impact or consequences of his decisions or actions, the boy was left in a bind – *"What do I do with these curiosities, feelings, and questions? Mom and Dad will tell me that my curiosity, feelings and questions are bad, that playing with fire is bad. But my desire, my feelings and questions are real and legitimate to me. I'll just keep Mom & Dad out of the loop."* In a small way, the fire department's fire play program for children reinforced a less helpful process – driving natural feelings, questions, and curiosities underground. This is not *bad*, as the fear created in the child's mind will more often than not keep the child from further fire play and thus meet the objective of the program. It was simply not as helpful to the child's overall development and the parent-child relationship as another alternative.

The parents and I considered the following:

- Why was the child secreting the fuel, matches, and his actions?
- Why did the child not explore the subject of fire with the parents?

My work with the parents focused on shifting the messages associated with fire play from *"it's bad"* to *"well, let's talk about it."*

Over the period of several weeks the parents and child had many conversations about fire. They talked about how curious one can be about fire and that these are natural feelings. There's nothing *wrong* with the feelings themselves. Through these conversations, it was becoming safe for the boy to approach his parents on the subject.

Eventually, the question I was waiting for came. The boy asked his parents if they, parents and son, could experiment or play with fire? These parents had prepared for this question in advance. The gut told them to respond with a firm and deliberate *"NO!"* This response probably would not have been too helpful. But what about a *"yes"* response? This might be considered irresponsible. What were they to do? Rather than giving their son a "yes" or "no" answer, they made an appointment with their local fire chief and allowed their son to ask this person the same question – *"is it ok to play with fire?"*

The fire chief gave the boy a tour of the fire station. He allowed the boy to watch those *intimidating* fire fighters in their uniforms and bulky equipment put out a fire intentionally set in a bucket. The fire chief then talked to the boy about the dangers of fire play. He spoke of the extensive training real fire fighters must have to safely work with fire. The fire chief allowed the family to borrow some of the same videos used in the children's fire play program. The parents and child watched these videos in the emotionally safe environment of their home and spent considerable time discussing them in an open and honest manner. The parents stated their son had a couple of nightmares the week after viewing these videos. The content of these dreams was openly discussed by the family. The parents and their son came to the conclusion that these nightmares were okay, as the subject of fire play was serious and can be scary. This helped reinforce the point that before acting on one's curiosity, it might be helpful to slow down and consider potential consequences.

This whole process helped the youngster acquire valuable life experience and knowledge about his world. It was nice to know that this boy now had the benefit of parents who were skilled in moving subjects out of the realm of **bad, good, positive, negative, right**, and **wrong** and into that of open process in a supportive family. I believe this boy will more likely approach his parents on important issues in the future.

During our final meeting, these parents made an interesting comment to me. They stated the small changes they made regarding simple interactions with their son had resulted in great benefit. In retrospect they had a hard time believing these small changes had eluded them prior to the fire play incident. *To recognize the obvious is not the acme of parenting. Rather, it is recognition of the hidden which determines skill.*

60. The skillful parent rarely misses an opportunity to enrich the child's living.

Parenting is probably one of the few activities that I can think of that, if done well, is both selfish and selfless.[38] Examples of the selfless aspects of parenting abound. One need only see the physical sacrifices that are made during pregnancy and the birth process to understand the depth of selflessness associated with parenting. After birth of the child, the selfless acts of parental giving continue. The demands of caring for an infant are relentless and seemingly without end. Yet, these duties and responsibilities are usually met without question. Why do parents subject themselves to such a demanding and prolonged process of selfless giving? The explanation is quite simple, parents are selfish. That's right, selfish. The emotional rewards of producing life, nurturing growth, and witnessing a child's maturation and developmental milestones are almost indescribable. If we did not have this selfish component to our human nature, that is, if we did not yearn for the emotional payoffs that accompany parenting, I doubt the human species would be long for this planet. The parent-child relationship is, in its purest form, quid pro quo. Both parent and child benefit and the human species continues to propagate.

How does this idea of selfishness and selflessness relate to *Systemic Parenting* and this particular Assumption? I find myself constantly reminding parents that it is perfectly acceptable to be selfish in their parenting. That is, it is okay to parent in a manner that maximizes the emotional return for the parent. It just so happens that one of the most effective ways I know of getting more from the parenting process – selfishness – is to give of yourself – selflessness. This is where the *Systemic Parenting* concept of *skill* comes into the picture. Remember, skill is *a great ability or proficiency*. It is *an expertise that comes from training and practice*. With practice, a parent can become quite proficient at maximizing his or her emotional return by constantly seeking opportunities to enrich the child's living. From a child's perspective, there is no activity more enriching than healthy parent-child interactions.

One particular example that demonstrates the ability of healthy and engaging parent-child interactions to enrich a child's living comes to my mind. Years ago I was asked to consult with a colleague. She was a social worker tasked with helping a family whose son was failing to thrive. The boy was 12 years-old and doing very poorly in school. His academic performance was so poor that he was being considered for placement in a special education program. In most instances, such poor performance would justify this placement. If this were merely an academic deficit, the additional support and attention provided by the specialized program would have been appropriate and helpful. However, in this case, tests of the boy's abilities indicated that he was above average by every measure except his actual grades. He should have had little or no difficulty succeeding in school. He was simply underachieving.

The school counselor was aware of this child's abilities and wanted to avoid having him placed in a program that was inappropriate for his specific needs. Why label the child as having a learning disability if other factors were adversely impacting his performance? She assigned a social worker to identify and treat, if possible, the conditions contributing to the child's underachievement. The social worker worked passionately with the boy. She helped him develop better study habits, she arranged tutors and ensured that his teachers gave him additional time to take quizzes and examinations. Yet, after several months, little change in the boy's performance was observed. As a final measure I was consulted. The social worker and I met with the family at their home for two sessions. The underlying issues impacting the child's ability to succeed were immediately apparent.

The immediate family consisted of the parents and their son. Both parents had physical disabilities which seemed to limit their mobility. This was not necessarily the problem. The problem impacting the boy's academic performance was how the parents responded to their disabilities.[39] The parents led a sedentary lifestyle. They rarely left the house unless attending a medical appointment or shopping for groceries. The parents' days were spent in their living room experiencing life through their television set. The parents and their son seemed to enjoy a very close relationship. This was evident by the eagerness exhibited by the 12 year-old to get home from school in order to spend time with his parents. Unfortunately, this time was not what you would consider very enriching. Interaction between family members was limited as everybody's attention was centered on the television. The boy would arrive home from school and immediately do his homework. He would then hurry to watch the afternoon programs with his parents. Dinner would be prepared and eaten while watching television, after which the family would settle in for the evening programs. The boy's only physical activity was demonstrating professional wrestling moves – as seen on TV – for his parents. When the boy's social worker and I arrived for our scheduled appointment with the family, the television was left on. It remained on for the first few minutes of our meeting. The parents' attention shifted back and forth, from the TV program to our discussion. This continued until I requested it be turned off.

I met with the social worker the very next day and made several recommendations. The boy's poor performance in school was not related in any way to his skills or abilities. The boy's poor performance was directly related to the quality of parenting he was receiving. I believe this was why the social worker's efforts to promote better study skills, provide tutors, and ensure the boy had additional time to take tests were of little value. These efforts did not address the systemic variables that were adversely impacting the boy's performance. The problems within this family system were complex. I felt the boy's poor academic performance was a symptom of these problems. It would take considerable time and effort to address them. However, I believed that merely *beginning* the process of enriching the boy's life through healthier parenting would result in significant improvements in his school performance. My recommendations to the social worker were as follows:

1. Forget about the boy's performance at school for the time being. His failure to excel was merely a symptom not the primary problem. Focus attention on the underlying/systemic issues that were causing those symptoms. Work with the parents.

2. The boy was a source of stimulation for the parent's otherwise sedentary life. They seemed to benefit more from the boy's presence than the 12 year-old did by interacting with the parents. This process had to be reversed. The boy would fervently rush home everyday after school. He was involved in no extracurricular activities and had very limited social networks both in and out of school. The parents benefited by having the boy around; they seemed to discourage activities outside of the home. Unfortunately, the sedentary lifestyle promoted by the parents was not very healthy

for the child. Supporting the parents in breaking this cycle was of paramount importance. The parents could gain the same, if not more, emotional benefit by learning to enrich the child's life.

3. For the parents to be able to enrich their son's life, and thus receive greater emotional benefits, they would require support and additional resources. The parents' current lifestyle was anything but healthy. Their complicated medical conditions were evidence of, secondary to, and exacerbated by their sedentary habits. I provided the social worker with several community resources that would likely be helpful for these parents. These resources included the name of an exercise physiologist that specialized in helping the morbidly obese become more active, a physical therapist, several support groups, and the name of a dietician that was willing to work with these parents. The social worker could provide valuable assistance by encouraging the parents to utilized these resources.

4. Finally, I suggested the social worker help the parents identify activities other than watching TV that parents and son could partake in together. These activities would require a great deal of parent-child interaction and did not involve sitting in front of the TV. Examples would include attending school sponsored sporting and theatrical events, feeding the ducks and geese at a nearby park, making yogurt pops together, playing chess, and so on. I also suggested that the social worker encourage the parents to suggest that their son involve himself in school based, extracurricular activities.

The social worker took my recommendations and went to work. I had a follow-up appointment with the family and social worker one month later. The situation looked remarkably different at this follow-up meeting. The parents accepted support from the social worker. They attended weekly support groups, they were working with the exercise physiologist and physical therapist and both had individualized treatment plans that promoted physical activities within their ability level. The family greatly reduced the amount of TV they watched. They would review the TV schedule and only watch programs that were of particular interest. Constantly turning the TV channel in search of an interesting show was an activity that no longer existed in their household. The 12 year-old boy joined the chess club and a computer gaming club at school. Also, to the surprise of everybody, the boy got a part time job caddying at a local golf course. He even came across a discarded set of golf clubs and was hitting balls at the club's driving range. Most importantly, the boy's grades went from Ds and Fs to As and a few Bs. The parents stated that the quality of their interactions with the boy also improved. They were talking more and truly enjoyed the time they spent together. The parents were gaining emotional benefit by attempting to enrich the child's life. The boy grew in many ways as a result.

I understand that the family in this example is by no means representative of the majority of families. This situation and the results of the intervention were quite remarkable. However, I believe this example demonstrates the impact of enriching a child's life and how important the parents are in this process. When I see a parent make an effort to enrich a child's life by doing things such as pointing out a strange looking insect, singing a song with the child, when I see a parent playing with a child on all fours, reading a book with a child, or just walking with a child and listening to what he or she has to say, the family in the previous example comes to mind. The situations may be dramatically different but the outcome will be similar. Surely, these children are benefiting by enriching interactions. The skillful parent rarely misses an opportunity to enrich the child's living. This is a *quid pro quo* relationship from which both parent and child will certainly benefit.

61. A skill of parenting lies in the identification of the unlimited family resource.

A key component to understanding the bigger picture associated with family systems lies in identification of *the unlimited family resource*. What exactly is meant by *the unlimited family resource*? Well, let's put on our anthropologist hat for a moment and look at the function of a family. Why do families exist and what purpose do they serve? This is a pretty big question but let's see if we can come up with a reasonable explanation. Families, in various forms, would not exist nor would they have survived for so long had they not served a beneficial purpose. As it turns out, the list of benefits is pretty long. It is beyond the scope of this book to go into great detail but let's briefly explore a few of the more important benefits that emerge from family.

Perhaps the most important purpose of family, one that is usually given little thought but influences much of our behavior, is the protection of our genes. The family system and all of its benefits pretty much exists to help ensure one's genes are protected and propagated. This is not usually in the forefront of our daily thoughts, however, if we keep this idea in mind as we touch upon a few of the other benefits of family, the influence of protecting and passing on our genes will become apparent.

Let's briefly look at eight benefits of family groups or systems.

1. The first benefit of family has already been mentioned, the *protection and propagation of our genes*. Family systems assist in the process of propagation by providing close proximity to a mate and by reducing threats, struggles, and discomforts encountered by the present and future generations of family. Why invest in the next generation? Why should we prepare our children to handle life's challenges and threats? Again, with our anthropologist hat on, perhaps it is the innate drive to successfully pass on our genes and to ensure the diversity of our species. The remaining benefits of family, at least indirectly, support this purpose and design.

2. The second benefit of family is the *transference of wisdom*. Many of our family interactions either directly or indirectly pass wisdom and knowledge between and within the generations. Obviously, there is a great deal of information exchanged between people outside of the family system – for example an employer teaching a new skill to an employee. However, the motivation behind the transfer of knowledge and wisdom differ significantly within the family. Rarely does a father ask for payment or servitude from his son for instruction on how to ride a bicycle. A parent rarely expects money spent for music or dance lessons to pay future financial dividends. The motives behind a parent helping a child with homework or teaching a child how to cook are unique to family. When one's adult child starts his or her own family, the grandparents or other extended family members, will often provide important knowledge, information and wisdom that has been gained from their personal or family experiences. Again, the motivation for transferring this knowledge is to benefit the new family, to help ensure successful continuation of the family.

3. The third benefit of family is *companionship*. There are definite
emotional benefits from having access to others. The dynamics
of companionship within family systems often differ from
companionship found outside of the family. For example, one can
find a certain level of companionship by joining an organization, a
club, or through close friendships. But the bonds that bind one to
these organizations or people are relatively easily broken. One can
usually disassociate from non-familial relationships or organizations
without too many repercussions. From time to time a family
member will be cut off by or will disassociate from the remaining
family. If we objectively evaluate these incidents we see they have
significant emotional consequences and repercussions to both the
individual and the family. The benefits of familial companionship
are lost. This brings us to the fourth benefit of family, *loyalty*.

4. *Loyalty* is extended to family unlike that seen in any other
relationship or organization. We do not have to look very far to find
examples of remarkable loyalty outside of family groups. However,
nowhere else do we find such a deep rooted and broad spectrum
sense of loyalty. As a therapist I see instances of family loyalty all
the time. For example, a child who defends a parent who has been
incredibly abusive and cruel is demonstrating the depth of loyalty
that exists within the family system. This may be an example of
an unhealthy side of family loyalty, however, when we examine the
overall benefits of familial loyalty we find that healthy aspects far
outweigh the less healthy instances. The natural loyalty that exists
within family systems allows us to make mistakes and still have the
opportunity to recover. This by no means is intended to imply that
family loyalty justifies abusive or harmful behaviors. No, natural
loyalty only provides us with an opportunity, that usually does not
exist outside of the family system, to recoup and make amends.
This loyalty provides stability and a sort of adhesiveness for
families.

One particular example of family loyalty from my practice of
family therapy stands out in my mind. I was working with a family
whose adult daughter was receiving treatment for drug addiction.
The parents reported that over a period of several years their
daughter broke into their house and took thousands of dollars worth
of the parent's possessions – including a total of 5 television sets.
The parents knew who was breaking into their house. They knew

their daughter was stealing their possessions and selling them for drugs. Yet, after treatment and a significant period of time during which the daughter remained abstinent, her parents willfully and enthusiastically embraced her and engaged her in family activities. This level of loyalty would probably be less likely between friends or business associates. This sense of familial loyalty is closely tied to our next benefit of family.

5. *Acceptance* is our fifth benefit of family. A great degree of acceptance for undesirable behaviors, conflicting ideas, or difficult conditions exists within family systems. That is, families tend to have a higher threshold than non-familial relationships. For example, a father whose political beliefs might fall on the conservative side of the spectrum might very well end a friendship with an individual who expresses more liberal beliefs. However, the reaction will likely be much different if the father's adult child expresses the same liberal beliefs. The father might demonstrate a greater degree of acceptance for his son's opinions and beliefs than he would for a friend, coworker, or acquaintance.

It is not too hard to identify many deeds of acceptance within family systems. For example, parents are able to accept their child's crying without discomfort while non-family bystanders are irritated by the same. This level of acceptance serves a valuable purpose, to protect the family system from *bumps in the road*. This level of protection helps maintain a certain stability so as to ensure the family will remain intact despite differences, inconveniences, and challenges. Acceptance helps ensure the family remains together long enough to experience the other benefits of family.

6. *Shared responsibility, collective resources, and transference of wealth* is the sixth benefit of family. Every culture known has some means of transferring wealth and resources from one generation to the next. Some of the more obvious examples are the transfer of possessions, money, property, and resources. In other less obvious instances, the transfer of wealth from one generation to the next will take the form of status, privilege, tradition, or knowledge. For example, a nomadic family with few material possessions may transfer a rich verbal history of the family or knowledge of favorable routes and natural resources from one generation to the next. This transfer helps ensure success for the generations to

follow. It, in part, helps guarantee one's genes will prosper in future generations.

A sharing of responsibility within family helps the family achieve more than might be possible by an individual. I remember a celebratory dinner I attended years ago with a large Italian-American family. This dinner was a real joy for me. The whole family joined together to prepare a marvelous meal – a feat that would be difficult without a great sharing of responsibilities. One thing I noticed during the meal's preparation was that the family embraced the services of its more elderly members to make the dinner a success. The more senior members of the family prepared the salads, set the table, and cared for the infants that were present. They were not asked to retreat to some removed area until the meal was ready to be served, but shared in the responsibilities. The elders of the family lessened the burden for the other family members, freeing them to give more attention to creating this marvelous feast. This may be a relatively simple example of shared responsibilities. Childcare, housework, transportation, financial support are all other examples where shared responsibility contribute to family functioning – allowing members to achieve a greater degree of success than would be expected without this benefit.

7. The seventh benefit of family is *security*. On a very basic level there is security in numbers. This applies to family systems as well. There is security in family. The concept of security is pretty broad when applied to family. There is the physical security one may experience when surrounded by family. For example, a person whose house has been devastated by a flood is usually welcome into the home of a family member or parent. There is also emotional security that comes from acceptance, loyalty, and the eighth benefit of family, *history and familiarity of experiences*.

8. A shared *history and familiarity of experiences* is an important element to the basic structure of a family. In fact, I believe this is one of the most important bonding agents of family. A shared sense of history and knowledge provides what I phrase *a privileged information set* for a family. This privileged information helps define the family from all others. It helps define who's in and who's not. This knowledge and intimate level of familiarity is an important boundary that defines and differentiates the family from

other groups. It is a boundary worthy of important consideration for both parents and therapists. By striving to understand ones family history and then replacing less helpful and healthy patterns with healthier patterns, considerable change is possible.

There are many other perspectives and explanations of the benefits of family. My list may differ from others, however, the benefits listed above seem to surface over an over again in my practice of family therapy. These particular benefits have been influential in nearly every family that I have had the opportunity to work with. When a parent or fellow therapists confront me with benefits I might have missed or neglected to mention, I find myself feeling satisfied that perhaps they have given thought to a subject that is rarely visited. I usually embrace these alternative perspectives, even when they differ from my own.

Let's shift gears back to our present Parenting Assumption. *A skill of parenting lies in the identification of the unlimited family resource.* The previous paragraphs were intended to highlight the importance of family. Not just the day-to-day aspects of family life, but the importance of the family system. Many of the resources and benefits associated with the family system are given little consideration or go completely unnoticed. Yet, many of the conflicts and problems that I see on a daily basis seem to emerge when members of a family become disconnected or removed from these benefits and the unlimited family resource they represent. I believe it is a great parenting skill to be able to recognize and embrace these benefits. However, many parents will resist developing this skill. These parents tend to focus on the complex family and parenting challenges that seem to be insurmountable barriers to identifying the unlimited family resources. In my years of working with fairly complex family problems, I have yet to encounter an individual or a family who could not find benefit in identifying the unlimited family resource, even if it was not present in his, her, or their family. I believe this point is illustrated in the following example.

An adult woman was in therapy with me several years ago. Her life was a mess. She was depressed and had twice attempted suicide. She had a history of very destructive and abusive relationships with men. She had a daughter who had been removed from her custody and placed in foster care. She was unemployed and facing homelessness. I was probably the fourth or fifth therapist she had been to in as many months. She had also been in counseling with a leader from her church.

All seemed to be unsuccessful in addressing what ailed her. This woman's family history was not very encouraging. Both of her parents had been alcoholics. Her father had been both physically and sexually abusive throughout her childhood and into her adolescence. This abuse continued until the father's eventual death from complications directly related to his alcoholism. The daughter was 15 years-old at the time. After the father died, the girl's mother remarried and simply left town with her new husband, abandoning the then 15 year-old girl. Five years later the daughter of these parents finds herself in my office. Now, one might ask, *how can anybody identify the unlimited family resource in this situation?* Is it even realistic to make an attempt?

The previous therapists and the church counselor were all aware of this woman's history of victimization, her family history, and her current struggles. It also seemed as if these therapists and the counselor approached the problem from a common direction, that is, *to forgive, learn coping skills, and move on.* I believe these therapists were doing a great disservice to this woman by taking this particular approach. This woman had been harmed, injured, and tortured in ways most people cannot even begin to comprehend. I'm not sure I could muster the courage to ask this woman to *forgive* the persons who had committed such unethical, harmful, and unjust acts upon her. I could not ask her to simply *develop coping skills* and *move on.* Her continued struggles with depression, her destructive relationships, her inability to provide basic parental care for her own child, and her failure to thrive were indicators that perhaps she was not ready, wanting, or prepared to *forgive and move on.* I feel strongly that from a therapist's perspective such a request would offer little relief nor would it be very healthy for this woman.

The idea of forgiveness, the mere suggestion that she forgive her parents and family for the experiences and mistreatment they provided, was a huge barrier for this particular woman. It is a huge barrier for many people who have been harmed in one way or the other. And rightly so. In many instances of abuse, the act of forgiveness can be a continuation of the power inequity that resulted in the mistreatment or abuse in the first place. Forgiveness tends to minimize the victim's experiences, emotions, and perspective. The idea or concept of forgiveness is often a means of *just putting the matter behind you and moving on* without acknowledging the impact the abuse or mistreatment had on one's life. From a victim's perspective, forgiveness can feel as if the perpetrator of the mistreatment or abuse is being let off the hook.

It would seem that an important step is missing; a step that must occur long before forgiveness even becomes a consideration.

To this point, the woman seated before me had been encouraged to select between two options. First, she could ignore the abuse she experienced for most of her life and continue to make decisions that were resulting in very unhealthy consequences. Or, this woman could *forgive* her parents and attempt to develop the coping skills necessary to make healthier decisions. Of these two options the second was obviously preferred to the first. It was better than doing nothing. Unfortunately, the second option did not seem to be offering the woman much relief. She was still struggling. I proposed a third option, to **exonerate** those who had harmed her. In so doing, the topic of the unlimited family resource might be opened.

Exoneration is a process through which a person who has been harmed, mistreated or abused explores *why* and *how* the perpetrator could inflict such pain upon another human being. To exonerate requires one to consider a bigger picture, to explore the perpetrator's motives, deficits, and to consider the perpetrator's familial and relational experiences. The process of exoneration provides the victim with a degree of insight that is very empowering as the victim attempts to move forward in a healthy manner. Through the process of exoneration, the victim will find him or herself in a better position to justly hold the perpetrators accountable rather than perpetuating one's status as a victim. To exonerate means to relieve the perpetrator of his or her or their emotional grasp on the victim by gaining greater insight and understanding. Sometimes forgiveness can follow exoneration, however, this is by no means required. The victim has every ethical right to use the insight and understanding gained through the exoneration process to simply move on. The important point here is that the person who has been harmed or mistreated makes the decision regarding forgiveness. The victim is in charge, thus establishing a more equitable emotional balance. The harmful effects associated with forgiveness lie in the sense of guilt that can be experienced if there is any external expectation or pressure exerted to forgive the perpetrator. If the victim is not wanting or prepared to forgive, any attempt to encourage the victim to do so only perpetuates his or her victimization. The great misnomer is that one must forgive in order to move on. This belief has been demonstrated to be incorrect in almost every case of abuse I have worked with in my career as a therapist.

Let's apply this idea of exoneration to the woman in our example. Her life was a mess. It seemed as if almost every decision she made would result in further deterioration. Most of her choices, her actions, and reactions were less than healthy. We used none of our first sessions together to develop coping skills. We spent no time whatsoever looking to the future. Nor did we spend any time trying to identify additional social service agencies that might offer her support. We did nothing that might reinforce or perpetuate her role as a victim. We spent our first sessions exploring as much family history as we could. We explored the possible perspectives of as many family members as she could remember. We explored family secrets, how various members of her family related with each other, how power, authority, and control were defined within the family and who exerted it. We looked at who seemed to succeed in the family and who struggled. This in depth exploration of the family yielded information and a perspective the woman never gave much consideration. She continued to view her parents as perpetrators of horrible acts of violence, abuse, and abandonment. She deeply resented these acts and the parents' apparent lack of concern for her well being. Yet, by gaining a greater understanding of the *whys* that influenced the behaviors within her family, the total lack of parental concern that she experienced began to make sense. She learned about the long history of abusive behaviors in her family and the impact it had on everybody it touched. She saw how unhealthy patterns repeated themselves from generation to generation and how these patterns were now being repeated with her daughter. She learned that her parents, perpetrators of horrible acts of mistreatment and abuse, had nobody in their lives with whom to explore *the unlimited family resource.*

Through the process of exploring the family's relational history, this woman realized that few people in her entire family ever realized or experienced many of the benefits of family (transference of wisdom, companionship, loyalty, acceptance, shared responsibility, collective resources and transfer of wealth, security, and history and familiarity of experience). It would be difficult to imagine that this was not, at least partially, responsible for the several generations of family dysfunction that preceded these current events.

What did this woman do with this information and insight? She did not forgive her parents and family. This ceased to be important, or even an issue worthy of much discussion. She was able to exonerate her parents and family. That is, she was able to understand and place meaning to the events and emotions that had been so destructive to her present-day decisions, actions, and reactions. This mother had gained a greater understanding of and control over her family history rather than being victimized by it. She was now in a position to forgive those who had harmed her, *if she so desired*. Any acts of forgiveness would now be *just* and with meaning, rather than a ploy designed for a quick and easy resolution to a very complicated and multigenerational problem. If this woman's victimization and pain left her in a place where she was unable to offer forgiveness, that was okay as well. She now had a greater understanding of how such abuse could and did occur and was in a better position to interrupt these destructive family patterns. She had exonerated those who harmed her and was no longer a victim to these destructive family patterns.

After several months this woman was able to regain custody of her daughter. She found gainful employment and eventually returned to school. In one of our last sessions I asked the woman what she would say if she were to encounter her mother at some time in the future. She said, *"I would introduce her to her beautiful granddaughter."* A skill of parenting lies in the identification of the unlimited family resource. This particular mother was well on her way to understanding and benefiting from this most important resource.

62. A child is safest when he or she is not required to assume a defensive position more often than not. A skilled parent is able to recognize and shatter the need for defense when it is encountered.

Imagine for a moment that you have a 15 year-old daughter. Now imagine this daughter approaching you and freely stating, without pressure or prompting from you, that she recently and for the first time experimented with drugs. This example is not fictitious. Similar scenarios have presented themselves in my office several times over the years. This scenario always seems to raise many questions from parents while simultaneously stimulating many conflicting emotions. Should the parent be happy with the daughter's honesty or should the parent be enraged with her actions?

As a family therapist, I like to promote parent-child relationships that are emotionally safe and secure. In a safe and secure relationship, a child will more likely seek parental consultation and input on really big issues – such as drug and alcohol experimentation and sexual activity. Promoting a safe and secure relationship, whereby the child is able to freely solicit and benefit from non-judgmental parental input, is probably one of the most challenging tasks any parent will face. The child who has a safe and secure relationship with his or her parents is better able to fully benefit from the parents' life experiences and resources. This task requires the parent to constantly work toward greater intimacy in the parent-child relationship (see Parenting Assumption 23). It also requires the parent to utilize his or her empathy skills while simultaneously balancing ever important limits, boundaries, and consequences (see Parenting Assumptions 47).

When I present this example (a 15 year-old telling her parents that she experimented with drugs) at parenting workshops, participants usually ask two questions:

1. How do you respond to a child or adolescent who has freely admitted partaking in behaviors that are alarming to the parents (e.g. sexual activity, drug and alcohol use, etc.)?

2. How can parents foster a parent-child relationship whereby the child will feel safe enough to approach them on issues typically kept from them?

This particular Parenting Assumption contains a crucial component for answering these questions. A defensive child is less likely to see his or her parents as a resource. Rather, the defensive child will essentially view parents as obstacles. This is most often recognized by the child lying and/or withholding information from the parents. For example, let's say a parent notices that a drinking glass has been broken and discarded in the garbage. The parent asks the child if he or she knows anything about it. The child lies to the parent by denying having any knowledge of it when in fact he or she actually broke the glass. This child lied about his or her actions thereby assuming a defensive position. Why has this child felt it necessary to take such actions? Why are truth and openness so threatening? This child's defensive position can be directly attributed to the parenting he or she has received.

Understanding how a parent can move from being an obstacle to be avoided to a resource that is approached is relatively simple. Parents are presented with *parenting opportunities* daily. That is, their children will naturally create situations whereby the parent is required to respond or provide some kind of input. For example, any time a child misbehaves, the parent is presented with an opportunity. When a child makes a mistake, the parent is presented with an opportunity. And, when a child approaches a developmental milestone, the parent is presented with an opportunity. I call these *parenting opportunities,* as the parent is able to respond in ways that are either *more likely to be helpful* or *less likely to be helpful* to the child's living and development (see Parenting Assumption 59). Again, these *opportunities* occur daily in the parent-child relationship. It takes a certain amount of *skill* to recognize these situations as opportunities to enrich your child's life, living, and future. Any single opportunity has relatively little impact on the child's overall development; however, the cumulative affect of many opportunities will greatly impact how the child learns to interact with others and his or her environment.

Let's look at another example to help clarify *parenting opportunities*. When a child makes a mistake or misbehaves, a parent's actions and reactions will influence how the child: 1) views the parent and, 2) how the child views him or herself. Consider the following:

A family has a pet dog who is scheduled for a surgical procedure. The dog's veterinarian instructed the owners not to feed him for 24 hours prior to the surgery as it might create complications when the animal is anesthetized. The family also has a young son who is about 7 years-old. The boy was instructed by his parents not to feed the dog. Unfortunately, when the young boy was faced with the begging face of his beloved pet, he gave in and gave the dog several handfuls of kibble the morning of the surgery. During the operation the dog vomited and aspirated the recently eaten food. The dog narrowly survived the ordeal; however, this complication resulted in a veterinary hospital stay of nearly two weeks. This mistake also cost the family over $3,000. When confronted by his parents, the child reluctantly admitted to feeding the dog the morning of the operation.

Here are two different ways the parents might react to this scenario. One response uses this unfortunate incident as a *parenting opportunity* while the other misses the *opportunity*.

Response 1:

Parent: *Did you feed the dog this morning?*

Son: [Reluctantly and with tears] *Yes.*

Parent: *Did you know that you almost killed him? It would have been your fault if he had died. Entirely your fault because we told you not to feed him. Not only that, but it's going to cost us over $3,000 to fix the whole mess. That's a lot of money. Do you know how much that is? Probably not! What do you have to say for yourself?*

Son: [No Response]

Response 2:

Parent: *The vet told us that somebody fed the dog this morning. Did you give him any food?*

Son: [Reluctantly and with tears] *Yes.*

Parent: *Your father and I told you not to feed him. Help me understand why you went ahead and fed him after we asked you not to. This is important to us.*

Son: *He seemed really hungry this morning. I don't know why I didn't listen to you. I didn't mean to hurt him!*

Parent: *It must have been hard to see him hungry. It doesn't feel good to be hungry does it?*

Son: ...... *No.*

Parent: *So, in some way you kind of knew how he felt this morning.*

Son: *Yeah, I think so.*

Parent: *So, it felt good or comforting to make sure he didn't go hungry.*

Son: *Yes. He was happy when I fed him.*

Parent: *How did you feel?*

Son: *Happy... too.*

Parent: *Well I'm glad you were trying to take care of him. That's very helpful. However, sometimes we have to do things that leave us feeling uncomfortable or sad – like not feeding the dog for a whole day before he has an operation. I think the vet knew that not feeding him for the day would be uncomfortable for all of us,*

*but he also knew that feeding him might cause problems. I'm
disappointed that you didn't ask us first – especially after we
asked you not to give him any food or treats. It's caused a lot of
problems. He almost died today.*

Son: [Starts to cry]

Parent: *This was a close call, but I think he's going to be okay. How
do you think we might avoid this from happening again in the
future?*

Son: *I should ask you first?*

Parent: *That would be great! Do you want to go visit him in the
hospital?*

Son: *Yeah!*

These two parental responses are worlds apart. Unfortunately,
the first response is all-too-common while the second is more likely
to elude parents. I believe the second response is more likely to be
helpful to the child's overall development as well as the parent-child
relationship. Let me explain why I believe this to be true. The child
in both examples knew that he should not feed the dog yet succumbed
to the animal's begging. The child's life experiences and cognitive
development were not sufficient to see through the uncomfortable
emotions associated with seeing a loved pet beg with discomfort. The
potential consequences were not in this child's realm of understanding.
This proved to be disastrous for the dog and the parents' checking
account. However, the child's actions were understandable. The
child, after nearly losing his dog, likely felt terrible. Parental scolding
similar to the first response will do little to promote insight to why
feeding the dog was a harmful act or why listening to his parents'
directions was important. Chances are this type of response left the
child feeling **defensive** and unsafe. After experiencing many parent-
child interactions similar to this one, the child will be less likely to
think of his parents as a valuable resource. Rather, this child will
seek alternative sources of information, input, and support. This child
will be significantly less likely to ask his parents about important
issues such as sex, drugs, alcohol, relationships and how to handle
disagreements.

The child in the second response is much better off. Again, he is likely to punish himself to a much greater degree than his parents can after realizing his beloved pet might have died as a direct result of his actions. This parent, by no means, let the child off the hook. Rather, she responded by entering into helpful and engaging dialogue. The matter was processed in a manner that brought the parent and child closer together. This child has little reason to be defensive. He learned from the unfortunate incident and became closer with his parents in the process.

Let's revisit the example of the 15 year-old girl informing her parents that she recently experimented with drugs. These parents are faced with a tremendous *parenting opportunity*. They are presented with this opportunity because prior to this event, they were able to eliminate the need for the daughter to be defensive. Her comments would seem to indicate that she has a trusting, safe, and secure relationship with her parents. This 15 year-old is likely seeking what she understands to be competent input from her most valued resource – her parents. This type of relationship will only emerge after many interactions similar to the one presented in the second parental response above.

Now, what do you (as a parent) say if presented with news that your 15 year-old daughter experimented with drugs? This is up to you. You know your child better than any therapist. However, keep this Parenting Assumption in mind. She is presenting you with an *opportunity*. Let her know how you feel. For example, *"Wow, I'm a bit shocked, a bit frightened, and a little disappointed by this."* There is nothing wrong with the parent letting a child/adolescent know how her (the child's) actions impact others around her – especially the parents. Then, I would recommend you solicit her perspective. For example, *"Tell me what happened?"* And *"Help me understand why it was important for you to experiment with drugs?"* Remember, children who approach their parents in important matters such as this want something. They are probably struggling in some manner and are looking for advice, input, or support during a difficult time. Parents who do not eliminate the need for defense will find they have missed a valuable opportunity to give to their child in a very helpful way. If the parents respond to the child's news by yelling, scolding, or becoming judgmental of her decision to experiment with drugs, what are the chances that this child will return to them for input in the future? She opened a door for the parents. It's up to them to keep it open.

63. Parents who avoid entrenchment in emotional reactivity will be wiser when confronted with challenge and more apt to facilitate trust.

A 15 year-old boy was kicked out of his house after a heated argument with his mother. The boy's parents were divorced. He moved in to his father's house which was only a few blocks away. The father immediately ran into trouble with the boy. Apparently, the boy had great difficulty telling the truth and always appeared to be scheming. He was a skilled manipulator and liar. After a few weeks, the father was at his wit's end and came to me for some much needed help. The boy and his mother were invited to my office as well but refused to attend. The father offered to hogtie the boy and drag him to our session against his will. Although this was an interesting proposition, I did not think it would be necessary nor likely to be very helpful. So, my efforts with this family initially began with the father alone.

I spent several hours with the father preparing a genogram.[40] We looked at four generations of the family, starting with the 15 year-old's generation, his parents' generation, the grandparents' on both sides, and the great grandparents' generation. I'm not going to review all the details that emerged from this family assessment. However, one particular family characteristic seemed to surface over and over again within each generation; this family characteristic, extreme emotional reactivity, seemed pertinent to the boy's current behaviors. Everybody reacts with emotions. This is an important human characteristic. As far as I know, it's pretty much impossible to interact with other human beings, go to work, and to manage the affairs of one's life without reacting emotionally. So, why was emotional reactivity a problem for this particular family? Emotional reactivity becomes a problem when it prohibits one from considering another's perspective. When one is quick to judge, react, or respond to an interaction with another person in a manner that is simply incongruent to the situation, we may say this person is responding with *extreme emotional reactivity*. Let's look at a few examples uncovered from the boy's family.

The mother apparently reacted with great exaggeration to many of the boy's behaviors and actions. The father merely believed this to be a quirky aspect of her personality and of little consequence. However, review of the genogram showed that this particular characteristic has been present in the family for several generations. It now appeared to be repeating itself in the boy's generation as well. Almost every interaction the boy had with the mother would result in an overly dramatized response. For example, if the boy were to spill a glass of milk on the kitchen table during a meal, the mother would react as if this were a catastrophic event. She would raise her voice at the boy and would likely use a few expletives. The mother's mood for the remainder of the meal would change dramatically. The significance of the mishap – spilled milk – was exaggerated and blown out of proportion. She would have a difficult time moving beyond the incident. This small event would continue to irritate her for some time. This same process would occur if the boy arrived home late from school or if any of his household chores were not completed to the mother's satisfaction.

The father and I discussed this topic – extreme emotional reactivity – in detail. He admitted that extreme emotional reactivity in their marital relationship had played a significant role in their decision to divorce. This particular characteristic had greatly impeded ongoing development of intimacy in their marriage. The father was able to divorce himself of his wife; however, this was not an option for the boy. From day one, and by nature of birth, he was loyal to both parents. With time he naturally discovered that it was best to "give mom what she wanted." That is, tell her what she wanted to hear and act in a manner that left her less likely to react in such extreme ways. Essentially, the boy was conditioned throughout his life to provide the exact behaviors that were currently problematic. The father was by no means a casual observer to this process. He provided his son with an example of a more painful way to co-exist with the situation. The father would often confront his wife with reactions that were equally exaggerated. For example, if the boy spilled a glass of milk during a meal, the mother would react with extreme emotional reactivity. The father would attempt to match his wife's reaction by defending the boy just as animatedly – further feeding the emotional fire. The father's response might be something like, "Hey, give the boy a break! He just spilled a glass of milk. What's your problem?!" The boy learned early on that it was best to give his family what they wanted to hear and see in order to avoid these uncomfortable situations. Over time, the line between truth and fiction became blurred for the boy. He eventually came to the belief that this method of interaction, by lying, manipulating, and scheming, was "just how one gets along." When the boy was caught in a lie, he would then fall back to the second method of interaction – by responding with extreme emotional reactivity.

This whole situation developed slowly over time. The father knew something in the family was just not working well, yet he could not place his finger on this particular process nor did he have any idea how to intervene. Again, he viewed his best option as divorcing himself of the problems. It was not until the boy came to live with the father that a more appropriate and helpful solution was deemed necessary.

When the father was presented with the idea that the family might be entrenched in extreme emotional reactivity, he was greatly relieved. It made sense to the father and gave him something to work on with respect the his son's current behaviors. The father and I worked on ways he could begin to lessen the need for his son to lie and manipulate. This process began with the father having a simple talk with his son. The father placed no blame on the boy, the boy's mother, nor himself. The father told his son that he hoped to eliminate the need for lying and manipulation in their relationship. The father told his son that he was going to take a greater interest in his son's life. Rather than being quick to react or being judgmental of the son's behavior, he was going to show a greater interest in the boy's perspective.

According to the father, the boy seemed surprised by this turn of events. He seemed uncomfortable with the father's newfound interested in his (the boy's) perspective. My work with the father primarily focused on helping him implement this new style of interacting with his son. For example, when the father caught the boy in a lie, he would not yell at him, punish him, nor express disappointment. The father stated he initially believed walking away from these very familiar responses (yelling and punishing) would be difficult for him. However, gaining some understanding as to why his son might have been lying in the first place made this transition easier than expected. The father was asked to find ways to explore his son's lies and manipulations. He would ask probing questions such as, *"Help me understand why it's important for you to make me believe* [the lie]?" And, *"I'm really confused about this situation* [surrounding the manipulative behaviors]. *I'd appreciate if you would help me understand what's going on here?"* This exposed the boy to a radically different method of parenting – one that was sure to be uncomfortable for him. Lying and manipulating was familiar, known, and comfortable to the boy – even when it resulted in uncomfortable consequences such as punishment. This was how he responded to authority figures in his world.

The father's emerging skills were a threat to the boy's comfort zone. The father initially stated his attempts to probe the lies and manipulations would be brushed off or minimized by his son. Yet, in less than four weeks, the boy started to respond in a much healthier manner. He began to open up to his father. He began to answer the father's probing questions rather than brushing them off. For example, the father would ask the boy something similar to:

Father: *"I believe what you just said to me is a lie. Help me understand why it's important to you that I believe that?"*

Son: *"I don't know. I really don't. It just seems easier to lie than give it to you straight. That's strange isn't it?"*

This type of response would not be possible if the boy believed there was punishment or scorn to follow. As this type of interaction became more common place and comfortable for father and son, many doors between the two were opened. The need and motivation to lie was very effectively eliminated between them.

I never had the opportunity to meet with the boy's mother; however, eight weeks after I first met with the father, his son arrived at my office. The boy said that he was going to take his father's place that day. We had a long talk about the recent changes in the family. He expressed great enthusiasm about the trustful relationship emerging with his father. However, this enthusiasm was bittersweet for the boy. As the father-son relationship improved, the emotional distance between mother and son was increasing. This reinforced a belief that the boy's mother was at fault for many family problems – the parent's divorce, the boy's reliance upon lies and manipulation, and the long history of family conflict. I was surprised by the boy's maturity and insight. He recognized this process and wanted to stop it before it got worse. He did not want to harbour ill feelings for his mother but was struggling to keep them away. Unfortunately, he wanted me to do all of the work for him. The father's original offer to "hog tie" his son and bring him to my office came to mind. I asked the boy if forcing him against his will to come to therapy or attempting to force him to make changes in his life would have been helpful. He responded with an insightful "No". Hogtying his mother and forcing her to my office – although an interesting proposition – would unlikely result in any benefit.

The boy and I reviewed the topic of extreme emotional reactivity and its origins in his family. We also began exploring ways he could maintain a relationship with his mother without feeling compelled to respond to her with lies and manipulation. This would take some time as the boy's skills were deeply engrained. However, he left my office that day with an understanding that alternative options were available to him. He did not have to be a passive player in the course of the mother-son relationship. The boy was invited to return, which he did on numerous occasions. He was not able to change his mother's reliance upon extreme emotional reactivity, nor did he try. However, he was able to accomplish something very worthy. He was able to halt this particular family characteristic in his generation and probably many to follow.

Parents who avoid entrenchment in emotional reactivity will be wiser when confronted with challenge and more apt to facilitate trust. The father faced a challenge when his son moved in. He initially confronted his son's lies, manipulation, and deceit with emotional reactivity – leading to punishment, arguments, greater emotional distance, and reinforcement of the son's disruptive and unhealthy behaviors. When this father took a step back and avoided further entrenchment, trust was almost immediately realized in their relationship.

Many families face very similar circumstances. I have seen this many times in my practice of family therapy. The circumstances surrounding extreme emotional reactivity are vastly different; however, the consequences to the family system and the parent-child relationship are consistent. It is a skill to recognize reactivity that prohibits one from considering another's perspective. This is a skill worthy of practice.

64. There is no disgrace in modifying parenting tactics that are ineffective.

This Parenting Assumption often comes to mind when I'm struggling to help a family move through difficult times or address challenging problems. The job of a family therapist is often a difficult one. Sometimes it seems as if what I ask of parents is just too difficult for them. Usually, my requests center around evaluating and modifying a particular aspect of their parenting that, from my experience, is neither healthy or helpful. This tends to be difficult because the manner in which one approaches parenting is heavily influenced by family tradition. That is, the parenting methods, beliefs, and attitudes one embraces have, for the most part, been passed from generation to generation. From where I sit, it feels as if these attitudes, beliefs, and methods are often set in concrete. Families tend to resist change. When I ask parents why they act or react in a particular manner, I'm often met with a response similar to, *"I don't know. My parents did it that way, and I turned out okay."* Finding ways to encourage parents to evaluate and modify certain aspects of their parenting is a central tenant to my job. Yet, self-evaluation and even minor modifications can stimulate a number of uncomfortable emotions and result in a great deal of resistance. Let's take a moment to look at why evaluating and modifying parenting tactics may, **1) feel uncomfortable** and, **2) be a helpful and healthy process.**

By *modifying parenting tactics*, I simply mean modifying how parents parent. How does the parent communicates with his or her children? What limits, boundaries, and consequences does a parent embrace and enforce? What stimuli and experiences does the parent expose the child to? As I previously stated, the majority of our parenting skills and knowledge comes directly from our own experience of being parented. When I mention this to people who feel dissatisfied with how they were parented, I am often met with comments such as *"I'm nothing like my parents."* Or, *"I learned **what not to do** from my parents."* I hear this all the time in my office, yet, rarely do I have to look very far to find more similarities than differences between the generations.

Those who are determined to raise their children differently than how they were parented typically find this to be a monumental challenge. It takes a lot of work and tends to be very difficult to fully comprehend the depth of family traditions and patterns, and how they impact the manner in which we relate to our children and the world around us. My job as a family therapist is not to totally disrupt these traditions and patterns or attempt to significantly modify how one chooses to parent his or her children. I'm not sure any therapist has the skill or power to accomplish anything that dramatic. A skilled family therapist is able to help parents recognize and understand the family traditions and patterns that influence how one parents. Then the therapist helps the parent eliminate the less helpful and less healthy aspects, traditions, patterns, or tactics while supporting the more helpful & healthy. I find that when parents are asked to evaluate their parenting tactics and then modify the less helpful and less healthy aspects, they will frequently struggle with three issues.

First and foremost, there is the issue of **familiarity**. We are creatures of habit and often resist change. We gravitate toward routine and known behaviors and conditions. A familiar environment, familiar actions, and familiar reactions are usually preferred over the unfamiliar. This holds true even when the familiar is less helpful or less healthy. For example, some couples will respond to disagreements by arguing and yelling at each other. During the course of these arguments, insults, hurtful or inflammatory comments may be passed back and forth. This reaction to a disagreement is often **familiar and known** to these couples. Yet, it is by no means as helpful or healthy as processing the disagreement in an open, direct, and honest manner – where one's primary emotions are identified and communicated; where differences are identified and explored, and where each person's perspective is taken into consideration. Arguing is familiar and known to these couples. Processing this disagreement is not. It is very likely that disagreements were handled in a similar manner in their families of origin. If I encourage a couple to process disagreements rather than to argue and insult each other, they are likely to experience this as very uncomfortable.

Discomfort is the second struggle for parents evaluating and modifying how they parent. How we act and react are traits that develop over a lifetime. They are molded by generations of family tradition. Our friends and family come to expect us to act and react in a certain way. Deviations from this status quo are rarely encouraged by those around us. Take the couple who finds comfort in arguing rather than processing their disagreements. If one person in this relationship were to suddenly change how he or she responds to a disagreement, the relationship would be shaken up a bit. For example, rather than yelling and insulting each other, what would happen if one person were to calmly respond with something similar to the following? *"Listen, it feels as if we are on different sides of the fence on this issue. This is frustrating and very uncomfortable for me. I'm not sure I completely understand what you're thinking or saying here. Help me understand where you're coming from and why this is important to you?"* If arguing is familiar and known to the couple, this statement might be met with an aggressive response. For example, *"Don't give me any of that psycho babble bullshit. You're wrong! Period. End of discussion!"* A more healthy and helpful response will likely be experienced as uncomfortable, unfamiliar, and thus discouraged. Altering how one chooses to parent will be met with equal discomfort. Many of the Parenting Assumptions and suggestions found throughout this book will likely stimulate discomfort for the parent. Part of this discomfort is the result of deviating from the familiar and known. The discomfort is also the result of a subject that is rarely discussed – family loyalty and disloyalty.

Loyalty/Disloyalty is the third struggle for parents evaluating and modifying how they parent. Quite often one's religion, political affiliation, recreational activities, diet and level of physical activity are closely tied to his or her parents' beliefs, practices, and traditions. One rarely selects a particular political affiliation because *it has all the right answers*. Rather, said affiliation is more often aligned to how the family has traditionally thought and acted. The religion one chooses is less likely to represent *an ultimate truth* but rather more likely to be associated with family traditions and peer/community influences. One's recreational activities and understanding of things such as diet and exercise are, again, closely tied to family traditions. The mere thought that family tradition has such a powerful impact on who we are as individuals and what beliefs we hold dear can be very uncomfortable for some people. Very few people want to hear this. This idea often threatens one's belief that his or her thoughts and beliefs are completely autonomous.

There is great pressure within family and social arenas to remain loyal to traditional beliefs and practices. This is where statements such as the following come from: *"My parents spanked me when I was a kid and I turned out okay. It's worked for me and it will work for my children"* and, *"Why am I Catholic? I was raised Catholic."* Loyalty to family beliefs and traditions and the discomfort that is commonly experienced as one deviates from them are strong motivators. For example, I was invited to a good friend's house for Thanksgiving dinner several years ago. This friend had a young child, and both parents were extremely intimate with the youngster. Hugs, kisses, and emotional processing were frequent in this household. Yet, these behaviors immediately ceased after the in-laws arrived. There were no parent-child hugs, kisses, or open discussion before, during or after dinner. I privately asked my friend what was going on? He said that neither he nor his wife were raised in a family where people hugged or kissed each other very often. Open and honest discussion and conversations that included statements about one's feelings were virtually non-existent in their families of origin. My friend stated that when the grandparents were around, displays of parent-child intimacy were *"just uncomfortable."* These parents were demonstrating loyalty to their families of origin. They obviously have taken great steps to change some family traditions by increasing the level of intimacy in their household but were still loyal to how previous generations interacted.

So, modifying parenting tactics can be difficult. Is it worth it? I think so. I previously stated that my job as a family therapist is not to totally disrupt how one chooses to parent their children but rather to help the parent identify and eliminate less healthy and less helpful aspects of their parenting while simultaneously supporting the more helpful and more healthy aspects. Why is this effort necessary? Family traditions regarding parenting are valuable. They are imperative to the passing of knowledge and wisdom from generation to generation. It is only when this process becomes static – when we lose the ability to self-evaluate and make modifications – that families will experience less healthy consequences. Why is having the flexibility to modify parenting tactics important? Let's look at two concepts to help us understand: Macro- and Micro-Parenting Influences.

Macro-Parenting Influences refers to external or societal variables that stimulate changes in the parenting traditions passed from generation to generation. These societal or Macro-Parenting Influences are beyond the individual family's ability to alter or influence. For example, research has demonstrated that children are entering puberty at an earlier age today than they were several decades ago. This trend will have an impact on how issues relating to sexuality and body image are processed within the family. Discussions about sexual development that were at one time appropriate for our grandparents may not meet our children's needs. Family traditions must be altered to respond to larger macro issues external to the family.

The recent explosion in media and communication technologies (e.g. the Internet and cellular technologies) is another example of a Macro-Parenting Influence. These technologies are enmeshed in virtually every aspect of our children's lives and are capable of influencing them in profound ways. It would be virtually impossible to shield our children from this influence while hoping to produce healthy individuals. The parenting a child receives must consider and account for these Macro influences. Traditional parenting – that passes from generation to generation – must be flexible enough to adjust to Macro

Parenting influences so as to better prepare our children to function within the society they will inherit.

Micro-Parenting Influences are variables influencing an individual family that can prompt changes in the parenting traditions passed from generation to generation. For example, a family with a member that has been afflicted with a chronic illness or who has a child with a learning disability are facing Micro-Parenting Influences. Family traditions relating to education, recreation, social relations and certain developmental milestones may not necessarily be followed as a result of these variables. The parents are placed in a position where they must modify or adjust their ideas relating to parenting in response to the unexpected variables. In some instances, family tradition may leave parents well-prepared to deal with the issues facing the family. In other instances, deficits in family tradition will exist that leave the family vulnerable to responding to Micro-Parenting Influences in less than healthy and helpful ways.

Micro- and Macro-Parenting Influences are a part of everyday family life. They require flexibility in parenting to help ensure future generations excel in all matters of life and living. The family with whom I shared Thanksgiving dinner with is an example of a family responding to a Micro-Parenting influence – a tradition of constricted communications within their families of origin. The couple viewed this particular tradition as a potential deficit, that if perpetuated might hinder their children's development. The couple responded by learning about intimacy and by promoting it within their parent-child relationship. These young parents modified traditional parenting tactics they believed to be ineffective. The flexibility this couple demonstrated is a crucial parenting skill. Unfortunately, the discomfort they experienced when in the presence of their senior family members would indicate that some family and systemic traditions continue to impact the couple and their parenting. There is no disgrace in modifying parenting tactics that are ineffective. This process will be accompanied by certain discomfort, yet understanding the origin of this discomfort and the importance of altering tradition from time to time is a most valuable *skill* for any parent.

65. Clearly communicate consequences that are to be enforced by the parental hierarchy.

Friends of mine have a daughter who does well in school, excels athletically, and has several very close friends. However, when she was about 12 years-old, she started to show signs of impulsivity and having a quick temper. These are not unusual characteristics for children entering the adolescent years. However, in this particular case, the youngster's reactions to stressful situations were often violent and destructive. The girl would respond to arguments with her parents by breaking drinking glasses and dinner plates. If things were not going her way, she was prone to punching holes in walls and doors throughout the household. These behaviors are not characteristic of early adolescence. They went way beyond behaviors that are common in homes with an adolescent – such as slamming doors, stomping one's feet, and yelling.

The girl's parents were concerned and asked for suggestions that might be helpful in curbing these troubling behaviors. After hearing the parents description, I thought the girl's behaviors might be an attempt to gain control over situations where she perceived that she had none. If a situation or interaction with a parent was not going her way – representing a loss of control to the girl – she would attempt to change the focus and direction by becoming violent. For example, the parents told me their daughter recently broke a window in their dining room. This was an intentional act after she found herself unable to open the window on a hot day. The girl's thought process might have been something similar to, *"Boy it's hot in here, I can't seem to get this window open. It's painted shut and will never open. I'm really hot right now. The window never should have been painted shut. Stupid window."* The girl's focus was probably not on finding an alternative solution to the problem (e.g. stepping to a cooler part of the house for a few minutes or asking her parents for help getting the window open), but rather on blaming a window for her discomfort. The focus was off her (e.g. *"What options do I have here?"*) and on a window perceived to be defective and causing her discomfort and harm. In response, the girl picked up a heavy object and broke the window. In her mind, she gained a feeling of control over a situation in which she perceived herself as powerless. In the girl's mind the window's flaw *entitled* her to break it in order to gain relief. An emergency was created in her mind and then dealt with. Other options simply did not exist at that particular moment in time.

Various degrees of this particular thought process and pattern of behavior are not uncommon for adolescents who are developing more sophisticated thought processes and reasoning skills, such as how to process frustration and disappointment. Parents will often be frustrated and challenged as their children pass through these developmental periods. Parents are by no means passive observers to this process. They can and should play an important role in assisting the youngster grow and acquire valuable skills during these developmental periods.

I asked the parents of the 12 year-old girl how these outbursts and violent behaviors had been handled. They primarily relied upon timeouts – sending her to her room. Yet, in addition to the timeouts there was a lot of yelling and lecturing. They were beginning to use grounding their daughter as a punishment following a destructive episode. However, this was not proving to be very helpful. The parents' reactions to their daughter's behaviors all had one thing in common: they occurred *after the fact*. That is, the daughter would act out and then be punished for her actions. I proposed the parents take an alternative approach. The girl's behavior occurred frequently enough to be considered a less healthy or undesirable pattern. When she became frustrated, she physically lashed out without consideration of the potential consequences. I suggested both parents consider Parenting Assumptions 65 through 67. First and foremost, I suggested the parents discuss their daughter's pattern of reacting to stressful situations with each other. This was to ensure they were both noticing the same problem and pattern. I then suggested both parents discuss their concerns with the 12 year-old, letting her know what they were noticing and how they felt about it. This was *not* to occur after she committed an impulsive, violent, or destructive episode, but rather at a time when everybody was relaxed and at ease. I suggested the parents be open and frank with their daughter, telling her exactly what they have been observing and how concerned they were about the behavior. It was recommended that the parents communicate consequences that would be enforced should the daughter choose to react in such a destructive and impulsive manner in the future (e.g. paying for damage she caused, losing privileges, etc.). Most importantly, it was suggested that the parents provide their daughter with an alternative to the troubling behavior, such as taking a self-imposed timeout, walking away from the stressor or talking to the parents about it.

The parents agreed to consider my suggestions and went on their way. They spoke to their daughter the very next day. Sure enough, several days after their conversation she hit the kitchen sink faucet – breaking it – after having a relatively minor disagreement with her father. Rather than responding by yelling at the girl or grounding her, the parents asked her to take a walk to cool off. When the daughter returned from her walk the three processed the event.

66. If children are punished without open process there will be further disobedience and greater distance.

The parents started off by soliciting their daughter's perspective. They asked her what was going through her mind – what was she thinking and feeling before lashing out? They did not begin by lecturing, yelling, punishing, or passing judgment. They merely solicited her perspective. With a little encouragement, the daughter was able to communicate her thoughts and emotions quite well. The parents did not attempt to correct any flaws in their daughter's thoughts nor did they criticize her actions. The daughter knew she had acted inappropriately. Having the parents remind her would not likely be very helpful. The parents acknowledged their daughter's input (e.g. *"I'm glad you were able to let us know what was going on inside you. This is really important to us, thank you."*).

The parents then told their daughter how her actions had impacted them. In this case the parents told their daughter that they get *scared* when she loses control and starts breaking things. They told her that they are *concerned* about how this behavior will impact her in the future if she fails to identify and use healthier options when feeling frustrated. Finally, the parents stated that they feel *disappointed* and *angry* and do not want to continue making repairs to, or replacing, the things she breaks. The parents informed their daughter that she will be paying for the replacement faucet from her savings and will assist in making repairs. The next day the mother and daughter purchased a replacement – costing nearly $200. The daughter sadly counted the cash from her savings and paid the bill. Later that day she learned a little bit about plumbing.

67. If threats of punishment are not enforced when called for, later attempts to effectively discipline will grow exponentially more difficult.

I spoke to the parents several months later and was informed that the faucet incident was the last time the daughter impulsively destroyed anything in the house. They said she still showed her temper from time to time but that these episodes never progressed to violent or destructive behaviors and were always processed between daughter and parents. At first the parents believed shouldering their daughter with the cost of the faucet was too severe. This nearly depleted her savings account. However, in retrospect they were glad they followed through. Their previous punishments were *never communicated in advance* nor did the parents *always and completely follow through with them.* For example, they would ground their daughter for a week and then enter into a week of negotiations in which the daughter would beg for compromises and exceptions. There would be a seemingly endless dialogue about the importance of attending "this event" or "that function." More often than not the parents would eventually be worn down by the daughter's relentless demands to reevaluate the punishment. The punishment levied by the parents would always seem to lose its impact after being renegotiated over and over. Yet, in this case the undesirable behaviors and consequences were clearly communicated in advance. When the daughter acted out, the event was processed. Both the daughter's and the parents' perspectives were communicated and considered. Somehow, this made following through much easier and significantly more effective.

68. When little attention is devoted to communicating a moral foundation other aspects of parenting will be severely hampered and without enlightenment.

How often have you heard that it's the parents' job to teach their children the difference between right and wrong? I agree with this statement. This is a responsibility that falls squarely on the shoulders of the parents. However, I wish the line between right and wrong was clearly marked. It is not.

In Parenting Assumption 59 we broadened our understanding of *good and bad* and *right and wrong* by differentiating these concepts from various degrees of *helpfulness and health.* If you will recall, most of our decisions, actions and reactions can be understood by evaluating how helpful and healthy they are to our living and relationships. Our discussion in Parenting Assumption 59 also suggested that relatively few decisions, actions, and reactions fall into the categories of *good, bad, right* or *wrong.* Yet, where the line falls between **less helpful/less healthy** and **bad** and between **healthy/helpful** and **good** has yet to be adequately defined. What exactly makes something *bad* vs. *less* *helpful/healthy*? What exactly makes something *good* vs. *more likely to be healthy/helpful*? This is where one's moral foundation comes into play as these distinctions vary between individuals and families. Where one places the line is influenced by a number of variables. These variables include the laws of the society in which one resides, community mores that outline acceptable behavior, and the morals to which an individual and family subscribe. Of these three factors, individual and family morals have by far the most influence over where these lines will be found.

When I bring up the subject of morality, many people immediately jump to the conclusion that I want to speak of religion or one's religious convictions. In my way of thinking, nothing could be farther from the truth. In fact, I'm going to go out on a limb and assert that religion has very little to do with morals or morality. One's sense of morality is solely determined by how they define *good*, *healthy/helpful*, *less healthy/helpful*, and *bad*. Religion may serve as a supportive adjunct to the development of morality, that is, helping to differentiate between right and wrong. However, establishing a healthy sense of morality is by no means dependent upon having and maintaining a religious foundation.

The lines between good and bad are ambiguous and flexible. The rigid and concrete beliefs and dogma found in many religions will often hinder the emergence and objective evaluation of morality. With this said, parents often ask me how they can instill a healthy sense of morality in their children. The most helpful thing I can do is to provide parents with a greater understanding of *empathy*, *intimacy*, and *emotional process* (see Parenting Assumptions 23 and 56). If one strives to understand these concepts and incorporates them into their living, relating, and parenting, the line between *good* and *bad* becomes remarkably clear – regardless of one's religious beliefs.

I came to this conclusion while working as a therapist in a psychological practice that primarily treated sexual offenders.[41] This practice was located in a geographic area most would consider to be a very conservative part of the country. There is a high degree of religiosity among those living in this area. Approximately two thirds of the sexual offenders I worked with were members of the area's dominant religion. These perpetrators considered themselves to be spiritual individuals and were very religious. They came from very religious families with long histories of participation in religious activities. Despite this, their sense of morality was anything but healthy. Many of these individuals performed heinous sexual offenses. During the course of treatment I noticed several variables were consistently absent among this population. These individuals lacked the ability to be *empathetic*. These individuals lacked a firm understanding of *intimacy*. These individuals also lacked the ability to *process emotions* in an open and safe manner. The absence of the above factors left these individuals emotionally empty and capable of partaking in activities that were extremely destructive to others. The lack of these important skills left these sexual offenders without a sense of morality. They were unable to differentiate *good* from *bad*, *healthy* from *unhealthy*, and *helpful* from *unhelpful*.

A person who lacks empathy, an understanding of intimacy, and the ability to process emotions will find achieving and maintaining healthy connections with others difficult if not impossible. Hence, the sexual offender is able to harm others without guilt, remorse or an understanding of how the abuse impacted their victims. Treatment of the sexual offender entailed a long process of defining these skills – empathy, intimacy, emotional process – and determining what prohibited their development in the first place. I then set out to repair the damage through a variety of clinical and therapeutic means. It was only after the sexual offender was able to incorporate a basic understanding of empathy, intimacy, and emotional process into his or her living that anything resembling a healthy relationship could be established with others. Without these skills, no treatment would be helpful. The offender would be at high risk of committing additional sexual offenses and creating additional victims. Over and over again I witnessed people who embraced religion – yet failed to embrace these core skills or concepts – partake in very unhealthy and destructive behaviors. One will find that morality cannot exist without these skills.

My understanding of morality emerged from the work I did with sexual offenders. This is not to say that all persons lacking morality will sexually offend. When I work with others struggling with a variety of problems significantly less severe than sexual offending, I find certain similarities. For example, a young man identified as a school bully and his family were referred to my office for an evaluation. The adolescent identified as a bully by his school had limited ability to empathize with his victims. His ability to relate to others in an intimate manner was severely hindered as were his abilities to process emotions. Unfortunately, the young man's ability to inflict pain and harm on others without remorse or insight was quite proficient. The boy's parents arrived in my office only after their son's school threatened to expel him. They were loving and caring parents yet were limited in their ability to promote development of these crucial skills through their parenting. This family was lacking a strong moral foundation. My work with the family consisted of helping them develop the skills necessary to make healthy emotional connections with others. We spent considerable time exploring this problem from a historical perspective. We explored how past generations of family members processed emotions and how they incorporated intimacy and empathy into their relating. As I suspected, these skills were not very well defined in previous generations within this family system. The bullying behaviors were merely a manifestation of this particular family history and trait. The clash between community mores, the rules governing behavior in school, and the adolescent's behavior forced the parents and son to evaluate their understanding of morality. The son's predicament – possible expulsion from school – served as strong motivation for the parents.

When I asked the father how he interpreted his son's behavior in school he responded that *"It's a dog eat dog world"* and, *"If you are not strong, you will be devoured."* The adolescent's lack of empathy and his inability to relate to others in an intimate and emotional manner seemed to be viewed as strengths within his family system. This represented a challenging situation. The young man was behaving precisely as he had been instructed to behave by his parents. His actions appeared to be reinforced and supported by his father's beliefs and comments. The young man's behavior was rewarded by his father's approval. The family's sense of morality – where the lines are drawn between *bad/less likely to be healthy and helpful* and *good/More likely to be healthy and helpful* – was contrary to the rules governing behavior in school. He was using intimidation, threats, aggression, and violence against other students to get his way.

The school received numerous complaints regarding the young man's behavior from parents of other children. It would appear his behaviors were also conflicting with the community's mores regarding appropriate behavior. My efforts to address problems within the moral structure of this family began with having the parents explore the concept of **strength** and **success**. From the parent's perspective, it appeared as if their son was acting appropriately. They believed the skills he demonstrated in school would contribute to his later success in the workplace and living. The parents were asked to identify factors they believed to be indicators of their son's *strength* and *success*. I was looking for those indicators that would – in their mind – justify his behaviors. They arrived at seven.

1. Their son's grades were better than average.

2. Their son was excelling in school athletics.

3. The young man demonstrated respect for his parents.

4. The parents believed their son to be faithful to his Christian upbringing.

5. The parents' believed their son was respected by his peers.

6. The parents believed their son was developing and maintaining a strong sense of masculinity.

7. The parent's believed their son was strong in body.

These indicators of success differed somewhat from my own. However, I felt we could work with them as we evaluated the family's sense of morality.

The young man was, for all practical purposes, successful if we limited our discussion to the factors identified by the parents. One might question how respectful his peers truly were or might question the parents' understanding of Christianity and how they defined masculinity. But let's set these issues aside for the moment. I asked the family to help me understand their understanding of empathy, intimacy, and emotional process. This is where we ran into a brick wall. They did not have any idea as to how to work with these concepts. They had a very difficult time even talking about the topics of intimacy, empathy, or emotional process. These topics left the family very uncomfortable. So we began to talk about them. In fact, we had to discuss these subject at length, almost to the point of ad nauseam. The family had a deficit that existed for many generations. I was of the belief that the parents' understanding of success (1 to 7 on their list) could embrace these concepts. So, every week for many weeks we looked at empathy, intimacy, and emotional process from every possible direction. We did not speak of the young man's behavior in school. That was not necessary. We were going after the underlying causes of the troubling behaviors.

After approximately three months, the parents stated that they had had enough. They told me they were tired of rehashing the same thing week in and week out. The parents stated they felt there was more to their son's behaviors than an understanding of intimacy, empathy, and emotional process. Surprisingly, the son was also able to tell me how uncomfortable it was for him to come to therapy each week. He stated it felt as if there was something wrong with him and that it wasn't fair to impose any additional burden on his parents. Finally, the parents stated they could no longer understand why it was necessary to continue in therapy as the young man's behavior in school was no longer a problem. Recent reports from school were problem free. There were no complaints from other parents, and the intimidation and aggression had ceased. Bingo! I had the parents and son re-visit the seven indicators of strength and success they provided months earlier. I asked them how, if at all, their understanding of these indicators had changed. We were all surprised by the discussion that followed.

1. The son's grades moved from *"better than average"* to being in the top quarter of the class.

2. The son stated he was enjoying sports more than ever. His own words were, *"I don't feel like I'm the lone player on the field with a bunch of other people. I feel like I'm contributing to the team effort. My performance is important to me, but it feels better if the entire team does well and wins."*

3. The parents stated the number of fights – between the parents and their son – had decreased significantly. They could not remember the last time they yelled at their son and vice versa.

4. The parents stated they were now understanding how empathy is an important component of Christianity. They stated they had been merely going through the motions of going to church and partaking of the dogma. Their belief now had a deeper, more personal meaning to them.

5. The young man stated he believed *"his friends were his friends now."* When asked to explain this statement, the young man said that he believed his peers used to hang around him because they feared him and that they wanted to be on his good side or else experience his wrath. The young man stated it was a lot easier just being *"a friend."*

6&7. The parents stated their understanding of masculinity now resided in the mind rather than in the muscle. They no longer believed or encouraged their son to solve problems through violence. They encouraged him to think his way through a problem and only use his brawn as a defensive measure.

The parents thanked me for "*beating this horse to death.*" That is, continuing to address the topic of intimacy, empathy, and emotional process at considerable length. Their understanding of morality had improved. This was their final session with me.

So far, I have mentioned sex offenders and a school bully while discussing morality. These are pretty significant problems. This Parenting Assumption states: "*When little attention is devoted to communicating a moral foundation, other aspects of parenting will be severely hampered and without enlightenment.*" We do not have to use such dramatic examples of problems to see the benefits of devoting attention to communicating a moral foundation to children. When one understands intimacy, empathy, and emotional process and integrates them into their living and parenting, every parent-child experience will be greatly enhanced. Many problems, both minor and significant, will be avoided.

69. *The parent who is confident in his or her ability to relate unhindered with the child will be a pillar to the child's ascension to adulthood.*

This Parenting Assumption is best approached by first considering the parent's ability to relate with other adults. I like to use the following example when discussing this topic. Imagine that I am in a committed relationship. Let's say that I'm married. My wife has a very dear friendship with another woman. They've been friends for at least 15 years. While at a crowded party, this friend secretly gives me her business card. This is done in a way that might be interpreted as flirtatious. Written on this card is the woman's home and cell phone numbers. She says, "*let's have lunch some time, just you and I.*" What are my options? I am faced with many decisions. Do I accept the card? Then what? Do I throw it away, put it in my wallet, secretly have lunch with my wife's friend? Do I tell my wife about the situation? How would this be interpreted by her? Will she think I was flirting with her dearest friend? If my wife confronts her friend, what response might be expected? This situation can get very complicated very quickly. If not careful, I might find myself in a difficult position without knowing exactly how I got there.

These situations are relatively easy to deal with when one becomes skilled at relating to others unhindered. What exactly do I mean by relating to others unhindered? Let's return to our example. When I am first presented with the business card, I will be confronted with many questions and emotions. More often than not, these questions and emotions will be given little consideration. We tend to act on impulse when confronted with awkward situations. When I try to put myself in this position, I think I might be a bit *surprised* and *confused*. I would be wondering about this woman's intentions and how my wife might interpret and be affected by this situation. I think I might also be a bit *nervous* and feeling as though I've been *put on the spot*. When I say *relating to others unhindered*, I am referring to one's ability to recognize and freely verbalize emotions and thoughts. For example, let's call my wife's friend Joan. Where do you think the conversation would go if I responded in the following manner when presented with Joan's invitation and business card?

> *Joan, thanks for the invitation. However, I'm a bit uncomfortable, surprised, and confused right now. I'm wondering what your intentions are and how [my wife] might interpret this. To be perfectly frank, I'm feeling a little put on the spot right now. Help me understand what's going on here.*

Many people have told me that this response is too direct, too forward, and a bit too aggressive. Some people might find this response uncomfortable. Some people might find my words impolite. I prefer *unhindered*. Yet, when I explore other responses (e.g. I take the card then throw it away and forget the incident; just say no, I'm not interested; have lunch with Joan; accept the card and hold on to it) I easily find myself facing increasingly stressful situations. *I also find myself moving away from having greater intimacy with my wife.*

I believe people who accuse me of being too direct, too forward or too aggressive find the uncomfortable emotions experienced with situations such as this difficult to stomach. They believe that uncomfortable emotions are something to avoid rather than to process and understand. The uncomfortable emotions I am experiencing in this situation – confusion, surprise, discomfort, put on the spot – are actually very healthy and helpful. They are letting me know that I am approaching potentially hazardous territory. If I choose not to process these emotions, that is, neither identify nor verbalize them, I am more likely to enter this hazardous territory. I will likely have a difficult time getting myself out of this mess after I enter if I choose to ignore these emotional signals.

I imagine Joan will try to take back the invitation to meet for lunch after she experiences the above response. She will likely minimize the intentions of her invitation and go away – never to make a similar invitation again. If I am skilled at relating to others unhindered, I will also approach my wife later that evening and let her know what had happened. I would let her know how uncomfortable I was with the situation and how I responded. I would solicit and be open to considering my wife's perspective, even if she accused me of flirting or bringing on the invitation. This situation would eventually become an issue between my wife and her long-time friend – after we had processed it unhindered. They may be able to straighten it out or this may be the catalyst that will end their friendship. The outcome would depend upon their ability to process disagreements and conflicts.

What does this have to do with parenting? Everything! Over and over again I find that being forthright and honest when confronted with uncomfortable situations will result in helpful and healthier conclusions. Yet, many people will opt for less helpful/healthy options. They will avoid uncomfortable confrontation and emotions. This is evident in their adult-to-adult interactions as well as in their parent-child interactions. They do so to avoid the uncomfortable emotions that are certainly associated with these situations. This is a less helpful skill we learn directly from our parents and family of origin. We are taught *not* to relate with others unhindered. As a result, we waste way too much energy getting out of difficult situations that could have been easily avoided from the start.

If you believed my response was too direct, too forward, or too aggressive, I suggest you put yourself in Joan's shoes for a moment. If Joan's intentions were *to get something started with me* – her friend's husband – how might she interpret my response? I believe she would clearly understand that I was not interested and that I was going to remain boundaried. She would likely go fishing for companionship elsewhere and not likely revisit this fishing hole again anytime soon. Now, what if her intentions were completely innocent, that she wanted to meet with me to plan a surprise birthday party for my wife. My response would certainly not prevent Joan from clarifying her intentions. She would likely apologize for any misunderstanding and probably let me in on the secret – that she was planning a surprise party and was soliciting my input and cooperation. In either situation, my unhindered response promotes a healthier and more helpful conclusion.

If this is difficult to understand, I would bet uncomfortable emotions are rarely openly processed – identified and verbalized – in your family. If this is the case, you are in a position to present your children with a great gift – interrupting a less helpful and less healthy pattern of relating that has probably been in your family for generations. If your child experiences you as having the ability to identify your thoughts and emotions, especially those uncomfortable emotions, and being able to verbalized them, he or she will absorb this skill almost immediately. Years later situations such as that described above will present no problem for your child. These situations are controlled by the person skilled in relating unhindered rather than being controlled by the situation. Potential emotional traps will be identified and easily avoided. This is indeed a great and very empowering skill. A parent who works to improve his or her ability to relate unhindered with the child will be a pillar to the child's ascension to adulthood.

70. Parents intervene when it is advantageous. However, it is often advantageous to do nothing. The latter is the most difficult to do wisely.

Children learn by *doing*, *participating*, and *processing*. This is a reality that many parents tend to forget. For example, if I were tasked with repairing an old wooden chair by tightening a few screws, I could use this opportunity to enrich a child's life. I could, have him sit on a stool and watch as I tightened the screws or, I could hand the boy a screw driver and offer him direction and guidance as *he* attempts to complete the job.

I believe the second choice to be the more helpful option. He is doing and participating. If the boy accidentally scratched the chair with the screw driver or stripped a screw, so be it. The opportunity to provide a learning experience would be well worth any damage the boy could do while under close supervision. The child will learn by doing. After completing the project, we would most certainly *process* it, talk about it, boast about the child's abilities, and assign credit for the boy's contribution. Again, this will only serve to enhance the child's experience, cognitive skills, and sense of self-esteem. Let's take this *learn by doing* example a bit further.

I watched two young boys fight over who was going to sit in the front seat of their parents' automobile while their mother loaded groceries into the car's trunk. The two seemed as if they were about to figure it out when the mother, apparently tired of the boys' bickering, randomly assigned one to the front seat and the other to the back seat. Her intervention stopped the bickering, but was it the most helpful response? What if the mother finished loading the groceries without intervening? How far would the children have carried their argument? Would they have figured out a solution that might work for both of them? Who knows? The answer to these questions depends upon many variables such as their age, their maturity, and past successes in working through similar problems. Children learn by doing. It can be tremendously helpful to do nothing but observe, intervene only if absolutely necessary (e.g. if the children start to throw punches and physically fight), and most importantly, process the event after some solution has been reached. This can be true even when the child is working toward an incorrect or less helpful solution. For example, let's say one of the children pushes the other aside and jumps into the front seat. The second child complains then reluctantly gets into the back seat. There are several helpful and healthy ways the mother might process this event and the solution arrived at by the children. For example,

Mother: *I noticed that you both wanted to sit in the front seat. You had quite a little argument back there. How did you guys resolve the issue?*

Son – Back Seat: *He pushed me out of the way, then jumped in. What a rat!*

Son – Front Seat: *You were just slower than me!*

Mother to Son in the Front Seat: *Do you think that was the best way to deal with the problem?*

Son – Front Seat: *I don't know.*

Mother: *Would you like it if I pushed you out of the way every time I wanted something? Would that be the healthiest way for me to get what I wanted?*

Son – Front Seat: *Probably not.*

Mother: *Probably not, hmmm?*

Mother to Son in the Back Seat: *What do you think? Do you think pushing you aside to get into the front seat was the most helpful way of dealing with the problem back there.*

Son – Back Seat: *Probably not.*

Mother: *We will be home in about 10 minutes. Why don't you two figure out a better solution to who gets the front seat next time this becomes a problem....*

When faced with two bickering youngsters, assigning seats is probably one's first impulse to have the matter over and done. I believe the skillful parent can react in a manner that will prove more helpful to the child's overall development. In the above example, a fair and equitable solution might have been reached by the mother. For example, the child who had the front seat on the way to the store would be assigned the back seat on the way home. This parental intervention would have been fair, but would it have been as helpful as assisting the children figure this out for themselves? Valuable cognitive and coping skills are developed when one works through problems. *Parents intervene when it is advantageous. However, it is often advantageous to do nothing. The latter is the most difficult to do wisely.*

Chapter 8 Art

A creative application of skill. A way of making or doing of things that displays form, beauty, and unusual perception.

71. The parent who understands that small interactions are as important as the larger ones will be more effective in all matters of parenting.

By the time parents find their way to a family therapist's office, they usually have some *big* issues to discuss – *My child always disobeys me. My son is using drugs. Our daughter is promiscuous. Our children are not doing well in school. Our daughter is school phobic. Our son was arrested for shoplifting. Our son's school believes he is hyperactive and recommends he be placed on medications. Our daughter does not socialize well with children her own age.* Indeed, these are important issues that can usually be successfully addressed with support from a professional family therapist. I find that parents presenting these or similar issues often seek a direct cause and effect explanation for the issues causing the family distress. I often encounter questions such as *"Why is he or she doing this?"* and *"Where did we go wrong?"* or *"How could this have been prevented?"* and *"How do we fix it?"* These are completely understandable and natural responses to the problems facing the family.

When I'm working with a family facing a *big* problem, I must constantly remind myself and the family that small interactions are as important as the larger ones. That is, try as we may, it is unlikely that we will find a single *cause* to the problem facing the family. A single interaction or a single event did not likely result in or cause the *big* problems being presented. More often than not, the presenting problem or problems emerged over time and after a number of seemingly insignificant and small parent-child interactions. So, for the parents to seek a simple answer to a complex problem or for a therapist to prescribe a simple solution or offer a simple explanation for the problem, is naïve and unlikely to be very helpful. It is my job to remember that small interactions are as important as larger ones. It is also my job to help guide parents to the same conclusion. Every interaction a parent has with his or her child represents an opportunity to give in a healthy and helpful way. The *artful* parent will learn to recognize this to be true.

The previous chapters and Parenting Assumptions have presented examples and ideas that are likely to help parents recognize the importance of the daily opportunities that present themselves as seemingly minor interactions. For example, below are two parental responses to a child's request for another cookie after having had three already. One response is more likely to promote emotional safety while stimulating cognitive processes. The child in both responses will be disappointed that he or she did not get the cookie. But, why not use this relatively small interaction to promote growth? This is an example of artful parenting.

Child: *I want another cookie.*

Parent: *No*

Child: *Why not?*

Parent: *You already had three and because I said so.*

Child: [starts to cry]

Child: *I want another cookie.*

Parent: *You've already had three. That seems like a lot to me. What do you think?*

Child: *I want another.*

Parent: *They're pretty good, aren't they?*

Child: *Uh Huh.*

Parent: *I would really like to give you another. It feels good to do things that make you happy but that wouldn't leave many cookies for later. Also, it's easy to eat too many cookies... because they're so good. Sometimes that's hard to understand, isn't it?*

Child: *I think so?*

I anticipate the cookie example above may catch many parent's attention. Some parents might be skeptical of the ease in which the parent interacts with the child in the second example. Some parents might also question a child's capacity to respond as he or she did in the second example, "*I think so?*" versus just starting to cry. Interactions similar to the second example will become commonplace in parent-child relations with just a little parental persistence. Initially, the child's response will be nearly identical for the first and second parental responses, the child will start to cry. Yet, as the child becomes accustomed to the more sophisticated and engaging parent-child style of interaction important cognitive processes will be stimulated. The child's behaviors will become less resistive and increasingly engaging.

Taking small interactions and expanding them a bit, by talking them through, seeking input from the child, and presenting your own feelings, can be very helpful and healthy. This may seem like an insignificant point and a small issue not worthy of much attention. However, after many such interactions, the child's outlook, cognitive skills, understanding of his or her parents, and abilities to interact with others will develop in very healthy ways. If this process is started early in the child's life, large problems such as those described earlier will be significantly less likely to occur. Fortunately, it is rarely too late to begin focusing on the small interactions. I often work with people in their 30's and 40's who are having some kind of conflict with their parents. My focus will not be on the conflict itself but the **small interactions** that occur daily and whose impact help create an environment where conflict will emerge. It is typically easier to alter the way one acts and reacts within the parent-child relationship when the child is young. However, these small changes are just as helpful at any stage of one's life or relationship.

72. Parenting requires one to follow the "situation of the child."

I once heard a proverb that stated "*A fish can never know its home as it is unable to view it from the outside.*" I believe this has particular relevance to parenting. It is difficult to *know the child* unless from time to time the parent views life from the *situation of the child*. This means leaving the realm of adulthood and placing yourself on the child's developmental level and in his or her situation. What exactly does this mean? I believe parents will benefit by becoming keen observers. That is, observing where the child is in his or her developmental stage as well as attempting to see what the child sees. Let's take a look at a simple example to help clarify this point.

I was walking my dog at a park one day. After completing the walk, my dog and I got in my truck and were about to pull out of the parking lot when, what appeared to be a father and son, caught my eye. The father and son were preparing to launch a model rocket. The boy was probably 6 or 7 years-old. As a child I spent many hours building, launching, and chasing many such rockets so naturally I was interested in their activities. I took a few moments to watch the two. The father set up what looked like a launch platform. He then placed the model rocket on the platform. The boy was an enthusiastic observer to this process. The father fiddled with the rocket a bit, then unwound a wire that stretched about 30 feet. This appeared to be a battery powered igniter that would fire the rocket's engine from a safe distance. The boy watched as his father pressed the button that was supposed to fire the engine. Nothing happened. The father said something to the boy then disconnected the battery from the wires and walked toward the launch platform.

The boy watched for a few moments while his father again fiddled with the rocket. The boy appeared to be bored and began looking around. He noticed a couple of trees nearby and immediately ran to them. He began climbing and swinging upside-down from the lower limbs. The father continued to fiddle with the rocket unaware that his son had apparently lost interest. After several minutes the repairs appeared to be complete and the father, after locating his son, called him over to watch the launch. This time the rocket fired on command and raced skyward. After a few moments the rocket's engine ran out of fuel and a parachute was deployed. The boy and his father ran after the slowly descending rocket. Both arrived at the rocket at nearly the same time. The father snatched the rocket out of the air before it hit the ground and handed it to his son.

Was this father following *the situation of the child*? Probably not. It appeared to me as if the father was enriching his own life and leaving his son behind. Children have very active minds and imaginations. Children also have a natural desire to be involved and to be active participants. This is how they learn. When shut out of activities, they will act out in frustration or move onto something else. This father appeared well-intentioned, yet was not artful in placing himself in the boy's shoes. The father missed several cues. He did not see his son move onto a more interesting and engaging activity – it's more fun to swing from a tree limb than to watch Dad fiddle. I would bet the father's enjoyment would have been tremendously enhanced if he had observed and guided his son in setting up the launch pad, if the boy – under the father's supervision – had set the rocket engines, if the father had allowed the boy to press the launch button, and if the father had allowed the boy to catch the descending rocket. I bet that if this father followed *the situation of the child* a bit more closely, his son would have had a very exciting story to tell his mother and siblings later that day. As it turned out, it was the father who probably told the story of the day. The artful parent will make it a point to follow *the situation of the child*.

73. The momentum of growth is with the child – this is his or her responsibility. Timing of the experiences he or she encounters is with the parent – this is his or her/their responsibility. Parents need to constantly remind themselves of this.

I believe this Parenting Assumption asks parents to consider a simple but very important question. This is one of those *big picture* questions, on the order of *"what is the meaning of life?"* However, with this Assumption I believe we are encouraged to begin exploring the question *"what is the meaning of parenting?"* This question can be refined a bit. How about if we ask, *"what is the parent's job?"* This is still a *big picture* question, but at least it is a question that we have a chance of being able to formulate a reasonable answer. *What is the parent's job?* I do not think that merely producing a child necessarily makes one a parent. Parenting is significantly more challenging that that. I would say that it is the parent's job to: *Prepare the child for living. To prepare the child to handle the responsibilities and challenges that he or she will certainly face. And, to prepare the child to embrace the experience of life while simultaneously leaving future generations and the community in a healthier state when the child's life-cycle eventually ends.*

After birth there are few certainties other than eventual death. Yet, as long as we are alive and relatively healthy, we usually continue to grow and develop. Our growth and development includes our physical being, our intellectual experience, and our spiritual awareness. During early life the momentum of this growth and development in these areas is rapid. Our physical being rapidly grows and develops, our intellect expands exponentially, and our spiritual awareness emerges. How well the child is prepared for living will be almost completely dependant upon how the parents time the experiences the child encounters.

There are four concepts interwoven into the remaining Parenting Assumptions that speak specifically to *the timing of experiences.* These concepts are referred to as *proactive parenting, reactive parenting, infantilization,* and *parentification.*[42] As you explore the remaining Assumptions keep in mind that timing is crucial to preparing *a child for living.* Timing is essential for *preparing the child to handle the responsibilities and challenges that he or she will certainly face.* Timing is certainly critical for *preparing the child to embrace the experience of life while simultaneously leaving future generations and the community in a healthier state when the child's life-cycle eventually ends.* The remaining Assumptions, especially those relating to timing, pertain to the artful aspects of parenting. They ask the parent to apply a great deal of skill. These Assumptions require parents to take their responsibility seriously and to assure that they are the most important and influential person in their child's life. Art advances one from the act of merely producing a child to being highly skilled at parenting a child. Keep this in mind as you explore the remaining Assumptions.

74. *The parent who prepares in advance (proactively) will be at ease. The parent who approaches parenting during or after the fact (reactively) will be rushed and weary – making less helpful moves.*

The concept of *preparing in advance* has been explored in several Assumptions throughout this text (see Assumptions 51 to 53). The discussions that follow these Assumptions primarily focus on the importance of preparing in advance for various life-cycle shifts (e.g., preparing a child for the physical changes that occur during puberty). For this particular Assumption we will move away from shifts that occur as part of our natural life-cycle and begin to look at events common to everyday family life.

Let's start our exploration of this Assumption by differentiating proactive from reactive. Proactive simply means that one prepares in advance for anticipated events or problems. For example, a parent may proactively prepare a child for kindergarten, several months in advance of the first day, by discussing the various activities in which he or she may be asked to participate. The parent may take the child on a tour of the school well in advance of the first day and may explore the emotions the child might encounter when he or she leaves home on that first day. Reactive simply means *letting the chips fall where they may.* That is, let events occur or problems surface without preparation or forethought then responding to any consequences that may result. A parent who puts off preparing the child for kindergarten until the day before class is scheduled to begin is taking a reactive approach. Needless to say, this child's reaction to the first day of class will likely be different than the child who was prepared well in advance.

The kindergarten example may seem too obvious to some parents. The thought of not preparing a child for school may be incomprehensible. Unfortunately, I have encountered this exact situation on numerous occasions in my practice of family therapy.

Parents have waited until the day before their young son or daughter was to begin kindergarten to start the preparation process. This usually results in a variety of unhealthy behaviors, school phobias, and unnecessary stress. Fortunately, this is the exception rather than the rule. Most parents do a wonderful job of preparing their children for the first days of school. Not every parent-child interaction will be as significant as getting one's children ready for the transition from home life to school life.

Parents are faced with lesser, but still important, opportunities to interact with their children in either proactive or reactive ways. As a general rule, I think that taking a more proactive approach to parenting yields healthier results. Unfortunately, many parents tend to interact in ways that seem reactive when it comes to these less dramatic issues of parenting. Some examples of other situations where parents will either interact proactively or reactively include discussions about drug and alcohol abuse, exploring the influence of peer pressures, and educating one's children about sex. Let's take a look at an example that might help us understand what motivates some parents to take a proactive or reactive approach to parenting. Like the kindergarten example, this example centers around a pretty significant family issue. I use this example because it provides some insight as to why many parents choose to parent reactively. I think important inferences can be made between this example and many of the smaller, everyday challenges facing parents.

The situation from which I draw this example began when a young mother arrived at my office with her 5 year-old daughter. The child was refusing to go to her kindergarten class and was having several severe temper tantrums each day. The mother informed me that these were not common behaviors for the child. She stated her daughter always enjoyed kindergarten activities and rarely fussed about anything. Apparently the child had never had a full blown temper tantrum prior to these recent events. These behaviors coincided with the recent departure of the child's father. He was a career Marine Corps officer who had just deployed to a location overseas and was expected to be gone for nearly a year. The family was unable to accompany the father on this assignment as it was to an area of the world with significant political instability and where conflict was highly probable. There were no family accommodations on this assignment.

The mother knew that the daughter's behaviors were likely connected to the father's deployment since they began the day he left, yet she did not know exactly why they were occurring nor how to address them. Everything she tried just seemed to make the situation worse. I asked the mother how she and her husband prepared the child for the father's departure and prolonged absence. She told me they had given this a lot of thought and decided it was not necessary to "needlessly" upset their daughter. They chose to wait until just before the father's departure to give her the news. In fact, they waited until after dinner, the night before he was to leave, to break the news to the child. The mother stated that trying to smile through dinner was one of the hardest things she had ever done in her life.

These parents took a reactive approach to dealing with the father's deployment. It was pretty obvious that the child's reactions were not merely coincidental but were intimately connected to how they chose to handle the situation. Rather than focusing on the child's reaction, let's take a moment to explore the motives behind the parent's actions. When I asked the mother why they delayed informing their daughter about the deployment, I was told they did not want to "needlessly" upset the child. The mother stated that all was well in the child's world and asked "why rock the boat?" This typifies common reasoning of parents who choose reactive, as opposed to proactive, actions. I find that parents, including the parents in this example, will choose to parent reactively rather than proactively for three primary reasons. These reasons are as follows:

1. Parents believe they are protecting their children by withholding information. They want the child to be "happy as long as possible before breaking uncomfortable news to them" or they don't believe the child will be able to handle the news or information.[43]

2. The situation is simply too uncomfortable for the parents. The matter is avoided with the hope that the future consequences will somehow be less severe or non-existent.

3. Parents are simply unaware of the concepts of parenting proactively or reactively, or they lack the skill base to interact with their children proactively.

All three reasons seemed to be involved in this particular example. These parents made a conscious effort to protect their daughter from the certain discomfort that processing the father's impending deployment would stimulate. Their actions were certainly motivated, in part, by love for the child. However, I'm sure the decision to delay discussing the deployment until the last moment was also motivated by the discomfort the subject would likely cause the parents. This was certain to be a painful separation for the entire family – including the parents. Putting off breaking the news to the 5 year-old probably brought the parents temporary relief. This brief reprieve from the uncomfortable emotions associated with the father's deployment was probably a powerful motivator to avoid proactively dealing with the situation. These parents were not inept, rather, they were merely doing the best they could with the tools they had at the time. They had little experience dealing with such issues proactively. They were unaware that the uncomfortable emotions they might encounter by preparing the child for the father's deployment in advance would be accompanied by feelings of confidence, security, and preparedness. They were also unaware that the reactive approach they chose, waiting until the last moment to break the news to the child, would likely result in less desirable consequences – such as the daughter's acute temper tantrums and resistance to going to school.

With time the daughter would certainly adjust to the father's absence. The temper tantrums would eventually disappear and her interest in kindergarten class would probably return. This should not mask one very important point; the daughter's behaviors were unlikely the result of the father's actual deployment but were probably a reaction to how the parents approached the deployment. I would bet that the 5 year-old felt as if her parents had deceived her. Trust in the parent-child relationship had been compromised. The young girl, even at 5 years of age, knew her parents had withheld important information from her. She was probably struggling to make sense of this deception. Her temper tantrums and resistance to going to school were merely symptoms of this struggle.

The father was communicating with his wife and daughter via e-mail almost daily. My recommendation to the parents was to simply acknowledge the deception and to spend some time processing their feelings about the separation. The parents took my advice. They admitted to withholding information from their daughter and explored with her the emotions they were experiencing. They made no attempt to defend or justify their actions. This was not necessary. The parent's sincerity and openness would resonate with the daughter. This was a pretty courageous act for these parents. Their actions had an immediate affect on the child. The behaviors that brought the mother and her daughter to my office ceased immediately. There were no more temper tantrums and her enthusiasm for school returned. I do not think this was coincidental. I believe the parent's actions helped the daughter regain trust that had been lost.

There are many less dramatic examples of everyday situations where a proactive approach to parenting will yield healthy consequences. Parents can approach issues such as reading, homework, conversations about drug abuse, getting adequate physical activity on most days of the week, and striving for a healthy diet in a proactive manner. Should parents assume their children will naturally develop strong reading skills or that they will consistently do their homework to the best of their ability? Might routinely reading with one's children or reviewing homework *daily* be a *proactive* approach to parenting? How might a child be affected if a parent just assumes that the school will sufficiently educate the child? What type of approach would this be? Having regular and ongoing discussions about drug and alcohol use and abuse is a proactive approach to parenting whereas assuming one's child will avoid these pitfalls is reactive. Will each approach have similar outcomes? Ensuring one's children are getting adequate physical activity by taking walks with them and encouraging physically active play is a proactive approach. Discussing the nutritional content of food in an age appropriate manner while preparing meals is taking a proactive approach to helping children make healthy dietary choices.

I have had many opportunities to work with children and parents who were struggling with very real and troubling situations such as addictions, failing grades, and obesity. In nearly every case, the parenting these children received was predominately reactive in nature. When the conditions afflicting these families became a crisis, the parents found themselves struggling to respond in ways that were helpful to the crisis. They were rushed and pressured. These parents seemed to take a reactive approach to parenting because, 1) They believed withholding information would somehow protect their children (e.g. "If I make drugs or alcohol a topic of discussion in this family they will become curious and actually be more inclined to experiment."); 2) They were avoiding the emotional discomfort often associated with interacting proactively with one's children; 3) They were simply unaware that dealing with these or similar subjects in advance is tremendously healthy and helpful (e.g. it is easier to review homework daily than to coordinate summer school or to support a child financially who dropped out of school). *Parents who prepare in advance (proactively) will be at ease. Parents who approach parenting during or after the fact (reactively) will be rushed and weary – making less helpful moves.*

75. The reactive parent likely finds proactivity foreign and uncomfortable.

Many of the Parenting Assumptions found throughout this book require parents to interact with their children in a proactive manner. In fact, parenting systemically is by nature a very proactive endeavor. Parenting Assumptions 51, 52, and 53 took a rather detailed look at proactivity. Even if a parent agreed with everything presented on the subject of parenting proactively, there is little guarantee these concepts will be embraced in one's actions. Many well informed parents will continue to respond to their children in a reactive manner. There is a relatively simple explanation for the discontinuity between one's knowledge and one's actions, **there is comfort in familiarity**, and **change takes practice**. Let's take a look at a brief example to help us understand these explanations.

I was once asked by a President and Chief Executive Officer (CEO) of a sizable company to help him resolve a rather significant problem. It seemed as if there was considerable disagreement and conflict among the senior executives within this company. This translated into poor performance and declining morale on every level of the company. The senior executives were very talented and simply replacing them was not considered a viable option. I interviewed the CEO and all the senior staff. The problems within the company were easily recognized by an objective outsider and should have been relatively easy to correct. I developed a plan of action for the CEO that should have corrected the problem and then went on my way. Three days later I received a phone call from the CEO. He seemed a bit angry. After less than three days he determined that the plan of action I designed for the company was ineffective. This is where I made an error. My plan failed to mention that, 1) **There is comfort in familiarity**, and 2) **Change takes practice.** My plan failed to consider the emotional elements associated with change.

When the CEO and I initially reviewed the corrective plan of action, I was certain that he was clear to its concepts and principles. However, he was not clear to the emotional elements involved with change. The corrective plan was based largely on the senior executives experiencing the CEO in a much different way. He was the company's leader and authority. The corrective plan tasked the CEO with interacting with the senior executives in a healthier manner and to expect them to respond in kind. Unfortunately, the CEO made only a few attempts to incorporate the ideas outlined in the corrective plan into his interactions. His first efforts were largely met with skepticism and little immediate success. The senior staff did not seem to respond in kind. Furthermore, the CEO experienced a great deal of discomfort with this *new method of managing* the senior executives. He quickly resumed a management style that was familiar, known, and comfortable to him, even though it was this style that had demonstrated itself to be highly ineffective. The CEO and I amended my contract and we began meeting weekly for several months. During these meetings the CEO would cite examples of communications between the senior executives and himself that were problematic. I would offer suggestions of responses that would likely result in healthier and more helpful outcomes.

During the first several weeks the CEO would immediately respond to my input with one of several comments. For example, he would assert *"I wish I thought of that,"* or *"I thought of that, but three hours after the interaction took place. That's three hours too late."* Finally, the CEO would respond with *"I can't say that to these people."* These responses are very typical of business leaders wanting to improve how their company functions as well as parents who are looking for ways to improve their parent-child relationship. Both of these circumstances usually require some degree of identifying reactive elements of our interactions, whether they be with senior management staff or with our children, and replacing them with more proactive strategies and approaches. Again, the underlying reasons to the CEO's discomfort with healthy and helpful change are nearly identical for the parent, **there is comfort in familiarity,** and **change nearly always takes practice.**

I probably met with the CEO a dozen times before unfamiliar, but proactive, interactions with his senior managers became more familiar to him. It took many interactions with these managers for the CEO to feel practiced in confidently implementing the healthier interactions outlined in the corrective action plan. The gap closed from the CEO being completely unable to arrive at a healthier and proactive response, and having the response come three hours too late, to having such a response available to him almost instantaneously. The CEO moved from believing he could not interact in a proactive and healthier manner to becoming quite practiced at it. After several months, the senior managers began incorporating these skills into their interactions with others. Productivity within the company improved as did overall morale.

Many parents present the same dilemma. They are aware of a means of improving the parent-child relationship, yet when the parent's plan or ideas are actually attempted, the initial lack of success is very discouraging. The parent is quick to return to interactions and methods that are familiar and comfortable. The parent's plan or ideas for improving the parent-child relationship are given little practice and thus fall to the wayside. It is important to keep this in mind as the concepts associated with *Systemic Parenting* are incorporated into one's parenting. Keep in mind that *the reactive parent likely finds proactivity foreign and uncomfortable*. The Assumptions in this book will become familiar and comfortable with practice.

76. Those skilled in the art of parenting engage their children on difficult matters rather than being engaged on said matters by the child's actions/inaction.

Some time ago I heard an elderly man make a comment that went something like this: *"Until the truck runs you over, you don't care. As you watch the truck drive away, you realize it would have been healthier to step aside."* I don't recall what this man was referring to but I found the comment catchy and remarkably applicable to this particular Parenting Assumption.

There are few certainties in parenting. This is especially true when we consider issues surrounding child and adolescent drug and alcohol abuse, sexual activity, and peer relationships. Most parents that I know wish the best for their children. They do not want to see their children make mistakes that might be unhealthy or harmful to them in any way. Yet, many of these same parents *"wait until the truck runs them over"* to explore important issues with their children. That is, issues such as drug and alcohol abuse, sex, and peer pressures are only discussed when and if it becomes absolutely necessary. Unfortunately, for many of these parents this is too late, their children have already involved themselves in activities that might prove to be unhealthy and harmful. The truck has hit the family and is driving away.

Parents who **consistently** and **repeatedly** explore topics such as drug and alcohol abuse, sex and reproductive health, peer pressure, physical activity and diet, issues relating to ethics, spirituality and morality, empathy, and integrity are unlikely to be engaged on these matters by their child's behaviors. The artful parent will weave discussion and examples of these very important topics into their parent-child interactions on a regular basis. In so doing, the parent greatly reduces the chances of having to struggle with these subjects after the fact and in a reactive manner.

77. Children are programmed to grow and challenge. When stagnant, it is the parents' position to promote movement.

A young boy was referred to my office by his pediatrician. Apparently the twelve year-old had been experiencing chronic headaches. The headaches occurred daily and were apparently pretty severe. The pediatrician and several neurologists ruled out every possible medical explanation. Physically he was a very healthy adolescent. The pediatrician believed a family therapist might be able to provide a non medical explanation for the symptoms. This was perhaps one of the easiest cases I have ever encountered and is a perfect example for this Parenting Assumption.

It seems the adolescent's headaches began early into the summer break from school. Both parents worked and the family lived in a sparsely populated area. The parents assumed their son was very active throughout the day while they were at work. The opposite was quite true. After the parents departed for work, the boy would watch a couple of situation comedies on TV, then would spend several hours playing with a set of dominoes. He would use these as building blocks to construct relatively complex structures. Once satisfied he would tear each creation down and begin again until his parents returned home from work. This continued for weeks. He was bored. I believe this boredom manifested itself in the form of headaches.

Children are programmed to grow and challenge. When stagnant, it is the parents position to promote movement. Apparently the child was becoming quite skilled at the use of dominoes as building blocks. For a 12 year-old this activity alone was an inadequate way to spend the summer. The child was definitely stagnant, and it was the parents' job to get things moving along. In some way, I think the parents would have preferred a medical diagnosis – a problem that could simply be treated with medications. The treatment I proposed had nothing to do with medication but rather parental involvement and some sacrifice. The child had a very active mind and growing body. It was time to challenge both. Unfortunately, he had neither the resources nor the life experiences to breakout of his stagnation by himself. As previously stated, the family lived in a fairly secluded area. It was by no means rural, but the few neighbors that were in close proximity had no children the boy's age. Furthermore, there were no community centers or recreational facilities nearby.

The parents were instructed to make arrangements that would get the boy out of the house and leave him challenged physically and intellectually. The parents asked their son what he wanted to do for the remainder of the summer. He had no idea and asserted that things were okay just the way they were. The parents appeared frustrated but were again instructed to **take charge** of the situation and make arrangements, any arrangements, that would break the child's routine and get him out of the house. It took a couple of days, but eventually the parents found and enrolled their son in a day camp that specialized in computer skills development, including access to some pretty sophisticated computer games. This camp also provided access to many recreational and athletic activities.

The camp was a considerable distance from the home and the parents' workplace. The parents' commute to work was increased by an hour in the morning and afternoon. The boy was initially resistant to the idea of attending the camp and remained silent during the drive – leaving the parents feeling somewhat irritated. However, after just a few days, the atmosphere in the car changed during the afternoon commute. The boy enthusiastically described his day. It was no coincidence that the headaches ceased immediately after the boy was in a position to interact with others and when given something challenging to do. The pediatrician was satisfied, the boy seemed satisfied, and the parents – after seeing the remarkable changes in their son's attitude and health – appeared to be satisfied.

Several weeks later, the parents made a follow-up appointment with me. They were concerned that they had been placing too much emphasis on their careers and had been negligent in their parenting. These parents were really struggling and had some serious issues to work through. The mother reported that they received the bill for the two diagnostic procedures their son was subjected to in an attempt to rule out a medical cause for the headaches. These procedures were expensive. Luckily, they were covered under the family's health plan; however, it gave the parents something to think about. They were more than willing to have their son subjected to several very invasive and frightening medical tests, yet felt irritated when inconvenienced by the lengthy but temporary commute to the day camp. Indeed, we had a lot to talk about and the parents were motivated and open to discussing systemic parenting.

When parents bring misbehaving children to my office, I often discuss this Parenting Assumption. The child in the above example was stagnant. Again, this manifested itself in a somatic complaint – the headaches. This is not uncommon. Behavioral problems secondary to stagnant and unchallenging situations are just as likely. The artful parent will look inward to their parenting when facing behavioral problems. Quite often these problems can be addressed by confronting stagnation and promoting movement.

78. Recognize your child's style of action and reaction. Rather than attempting to change the child, change the methods of acting and reacting in yourself. The child will naturally follow. This is tremendously difficult as it is more comfortable but less effective to look outward for antagonists.

Many parents seem to know when their children are lying to them, are trying to manipulate them, or are involved in some kind of mischief. Recognizing these aspects of our children's behavior is largely an instinctive and intuitive aspect of parenting. However, intuitive recognition of less healthy or manipulative behavior does not necessarily guarantee the parent will know how to intervene in the most helpful or healthy manner. This seems to be a skill that is learned rather than reliant upon intuition or instinct. There are innumerable ways to work with a child who is demonstrating less healthy behavior. For example, Parenting Assumption 13 explores the concept of looking inward, at our internal antagonists, rather than attempting to place responsibility for problems on external antagonists. This was presented as one means of addressing emotional rifts that might develop between parent and child – resulting in a lie or other manipulative behavior – while simultaneously enhancing the level of intimacy within the family system. Parenting Assumption 78 builds upon the concept of *looking inward* to advance one's parenting skills to the level of *art.*

It seems as if the most effective and healthy methods for responding to a child's undesirable behaviors tend to be less obvious or apparent. The suggestions made under this Assumption probably fall into this "less obvious or apparent" category. Yet, time and time again, parents who explore this Assumption and choose to utilize this *less apparent* approach to addressing a child's undesirable behavior report tremendous success.

Years ago, the term *thinking error* was coined to describe an inherently unhealthy thought process that, when acted upon, results in manipulative and unhealthy behavior.[44] For example, a child who chooses to lie to his or her parents is relying upon a thinking error. *"If I* [the child] *tell Mom or Dad something they want to hear, but is completely untrue, I can get what I want."* Over the years, many common thinking errors have been defined and categorized for easy reference. This has been a tremendous help for therapists working with people having difficulties interacting with others in healthy ways. That is, after thinking errors were defined, it became much easier to help others make connections between their specific actions and reactions (e.g. I lie to my parents) and the resulting consequences (their level of trust in me decreases). Many therapists will point out their patient's thinking errors and then encourage methods of interacting with others that are less manipulative and more likely to result in healthy outcomes. This has been a great deal of help in a variety of treatment settings – such as programs treating persons with drug and alcohol addictions and perpetrators of domestic violence. Unfortunately, little work has been devoted to exploring the role of thinking errors in the family system. Specifically, what purpose do they serve and how do they develop? I hope Parenting Assumption 78 will open the door to this subject.

Following are some of the most common types of thinking errors.

Excuse Making, Blaming, and Justifying: Excuse making, blaming, and justifying are thinking errors used when somebody wants to absolve themselves of responsibility for their own behavior. That is, one attempts to manipulate another by presenting a situation or a problem (an excuse), that is either out of the individual's control or likely to elicit feelings of guilt or emotional discomfort in the other. For example:

"I'm late because the damned alarm clock didn't go off again." As apposed to, *"I seem to be having a difficult time getting going in the morning. Perhaps I should make it a point to turn off the TV and go to bed earlier."*

"I'm dumb. That's why I failed the class." As opposed to, *"This is a really hard class for me. I feel like I fell behind early in the year and was embarrassed to ask for help."*

"My friends were writing on the wall at school. I didn't want them making fun of me so I joined in and did it too."

"It's ok to steal from him. His family has plenty of money anyway, they'll just buy him another one."

Excuse making, blaming, and justifying is a thought process that allows an individual to externalize responsibility for his or her actions or lack of action.

Redefining: Redefining is very similar to excuse making, blaming, and justifying. It differs in that an attempt is made to shift the focus of attention from one issue to a completely different and often unrelated issue or problem. A person attempts to redefine an issue or problem so as to avoid taking responsibility for his or her behaviors. For example,

Parent to Son: *"Why is your room so dirty?"*
Son's Response: *"Your office seemed awfully messy the last time I was there."*

After being caught stealing money from a parent, the child responds: *"If my allowance was fair I wouldn't be forced to take the money from your wallet."*

Teacher to Student: *"Your performance does not justify a passing grade."*
Student: *"I've worked harder in this class than my other classes and I passed those."*

Parent to Daughter: *"Why didn't you do your homework?"*
Daughter's Response: *"The teacher only collects it half the time. Do you believe that?"*

Parent to Son: *"Did you pressure her into having sex with you?"*
Son's Response: *"She has a reputation of sleeping around."*

Mark Gaskill

Superoptomism: I've heard this thinking error described as the "*I think, therefore it is*" thinking error. I prefer to think of it as *learned naiveté*. Superoptomism occurs when somebody wants something to be a certain way and makes it so in their mind. This thinking error may emerge when exploring a subject, situation, or a problem objectively would result in emotional discomfort. For example,

"*My daughter will surely come to me if she has any problems.*" (e.g. If her boyfriend pressures her to have sex; If she needs information on body development; If she is depressed and feeling suicidal.)

"*They* [my children] *won't experiment with drugs or alcohol.*"

"*I spent 4 years in college and paid my tuition. I'm guaranteed success.*"

Exploring subjects such as these openly and objectively might be uncomfortable for some people. Superoptomism allows one to function in a way he or she wants rather than in response to the objective facts (e.g. chances are one's children will experiment with drugs and alcohol, especially if the issue is not repeatedly discussed with them; children will unlikely come to a parent seeking input on significant problems unless to do so has been made emotionally safe by the parent; a college degree does not in itself guarantee success).

Lying: Lying is perhaps the most commonly utilized thinking error. Essentially, there are three categories of lies. Each category differs in its approach to deception. All lies, regardless of which category they may fall into, are intended to manipulate others or to avoid responsibility for one's actions or inaction. Knowing the three categories of lies is very helpful in recognizing them when they are encountered or attempted.

Commission: A lie of commission is telling something that is simply not true or is a complete fabrication.

Omission: A lie of omission is commonly referred to as a *half-truth*. This type of lie occurs when somebody conveniently and knowingly leaves out important facts in order to mislead or manipulate others.

Assent: A lie of assent usually entails telling somebody what they want to hear in order to manipulate them or to avoid responsibility for one's behaviors or thoughts. An example of a lie of assent would be when one's husband, wife, or partner asks if he or she likes a new outfit or hairstyle. If the husband wife or partner really dislikes the outfit or haircut but responds favorably this, is a lie of assent. Also, if a teenager befriends a classmate that he or she really does not like just because the classmate has an automobile, this would be a lie of assent.

Making Fools Of and Build-up: This particular thinking error usually entails putting others down in an attempt to help build yourself up. This thinking error may also take the form of creating havoc in other people's lives by agreeing to do something but not following through; intentionally talking about somebody behind their back in order to stimulate conflict; creating false rumors; and so on. This thinking error leaves one feeling important or more powerful without actually taking the steps required to achieve or promote healthy self-development.

Assuming: This thinking error is commonly referred to as *mind-reading* or *magical thinking.* It is impossible to know exactly what somebody else is thinking or feeling. Yet, many people assume they know what is going on in another person's head. That is, they make assumptions about another person's emotions, motivations, and thoughts. This information is somehow used to justify one's own behavior, beliefs, or to avoid personal responsibility. No attempt is made to get more accurate information or input directly from the person whom assumptions are made. For example,

That teacher is out to get me, so I cut class.

I'm not going to tell her the truth, she'll be really angry.

He doesn't like me.

She's just on some kind of power trip.

The person in each of these examples is making an assumption about the person who is the subject of the comment. The persons verbalizing these assumptions have the capability of, and option to, clarify their concerns with the person whom they are speaking; however, they choose not to do so in order to avoid the brief discomfort that might be experienced had they chosen to be forthright. For example,

Student Commenting to a Friend (utilizing a thinking error): *"That teacher is out to get me, so I cut class."* This assumes the student knows exactly what is motivating the teacher (the teacher is out to get the student). This assumption is unlikely to be accurate. The student is unable to read the teacher's mind. The student uses this inaccurate information to justify cutting the class. Any problems that might exist between the student and teacher are unlikely to be addressed in a healthy and helpful manner. Let's look at an option that may be momentarily uncomfortable for the student but more likely to be helpful to the situation.

Student Commenting Directly to His or her Teacher (no thinking error): *"I'm really uncomfortable in this class. Sometimes I feel as if you are out to get me, or that you are coming down especially hard on me. What are your thoughts on this?"*

I'm Unique: A person utilizing this thinking error believes, acts and reacts in a manner that would indicate that rules applying to others do not apply to him or her. A person utilizing this thinking error believes he or she is different, special or somehow exempt from rules that apply to others. For example,

"It's ok for me to cheat on this exam because I'm smart. I'm not like those other cheaters. I could pass without cheating if I wanted to."

"I can experiment with drugs. People who cannot control their drug use are stupid and weak."

This thinking error allows people to avoid taking responsibility for their actions. It is a means of compartmentalizing uncomfortable thoughts or situations or a means of justifying hypocrisy that exists in their actions, inactions, or beliefs. For example, *"It's okay for me to lie to Mom and Dad; however, it's wrong for parents to lie to their children. That hurts."*

Ingratiating: This is also commonly known as *kissing up*. Ingratiating is a thinking error whereby one overdoes being nice, is too complementary, goes overboard acting interested in another person, or falsely aligns oneself with the beliefs held by another person. These behaviors are usually motivated by a desire to avoid the discomfort or consequences associated with forthright communications. Being forthright, honest, and direct may be difficult for some people. This thinking error usually is an attempt to avoid these uncomfortable situations. For example,

> **Child to Parent:** *"I would really like to wash the dishes tonight if that's okay with you?"* This child probably wants something from his or her parent yet approaching the subject directly is thought to be unsafe. The child feels as if he or she must prepare or manipulate the parent prior to dealing with the problem or request.

Parent to Child: *"What do you want from me?"*

Versus

> **Child to Parent:** *"I would like to stay out an hour later this Friday night. Can we talk about it?"* This is a more direct approach. The child does not feel the need to ingratiate the parent before presenting the problem or request. There is no need to butter up the parent.

Parent to Child: *"Well, let's talk about it."*

Association: This thinking error occurs when an individual avoids taking responsibility or ownership for his or her beliefs, thoughts, or feelings by inappropriately associating with a larger group. A person utilizing this thinking error will attempt to find anonymity with a larger whole or group in order to protect oneself or to build up one's position. A subtle claim that one represents a larger group is made to bolster one's beliefs or position when in fact, no agreement or connection exists with any larger entity. For example,

A Student to His or Her Teacher: *"We believe you should give us a multiple choice exam final exam rather than an essay exam."*

An Adolescent to His or Her Parents: *"My friends and I think you should let me go to the party this Friday."*

Grandiosity: This thinking error entails blowing a relatively minor event out of proportion so as to avoid responsibility for one's actions or inactions. For example,

> *"There was a fire drill at school today. It was so chaotic, people were everywhere. It was the worst one they ever had and I couldn't even get back to my class in time for roll. It was horrible."*

Minimizing: Minimization is pretty much the opposite of grandiosity. A person utilizing this thinking error will downplay the importance of an action, inaction, belief, or event in order to avoid responsibility or consequences. For example,

> *"I only cut three classes. Come one, I was there for the rest of them."*

> *"So I ate a few of your cookies. It's not like your can't get more."*

> *"I was only a half hour late for the dinner party. What's 30 minutes?"*

Minimization is an attempt to avoid exploring the impact an event, belief, action, or inaction may have on another. It is an attempt to block intimacy, empathy, or personal responsibility.

Vagueness: Vagueness is a thinking error whereby one speaks in broad terms, dances around important issues or evades detail in order to avoid being pinned down, committing oneself, or processing uncomfortable emotions or subjects. This thinking error is often experienced when somebody responds to a question with a question. This thinking error may also be recognized when a person responds to a question that was not asked. For example,

Parent to Child: *"When's your final exam?"*

Child's Response: *"I've got plenty of time to prepare for that.*

Girlfriend to Boyfriend: *" How do you feel about me?"*

Boyfriend's Response: *"We've been dating for a year haven't we?"*

The child in the first example appeared to dance around the exact day of his or her final exam by answering a question that was not asked (*"Do you have time to prepare for your final exam?"*). The boyfriend in the second example attempts to avoid an uncomfortable subject by responding to the girlfriend's question with a question.

Power Plays: Many parents are familiar with a relatively common power play, the *temper tantrum*. This thinking error is termed power play as a person attempts to force another to see things his or her way. A child having a tantrum creates discomfort in order to get his or her way. The parent is forced into succumbing to the child's demands in order to gain relief. A husband or wife who refuses to communicate after having a disagreement is entering into a power play. Refusing to process the disagreement creates further emotional discomfort until the spouse gives in and makes a compromise.

Power plays are considered thinking errors because they result in manipulation of others in unhealthy ways. They are a means of circumventing healthy processing of perspective and differences. One attempts to force the other to compromise. The compromise is by no means collectively achieved.

Victimization or Victim Stance: Victimization usually occurs when somebody either does not possess the skills to problem-solve well or to view problems objectively. Victimization fills this void by projecting blame to others. A person steeped in victimization believes he or she is unable to succeed as a result of external variables. If he or she does not get what is wanted or desired it is somebody else's fault. That is, he or she is a victim and success is out of their control. A person relying upon victim stancing often invites others to rescue or to make things better for them, thus avoiding the real consequences of his or her actions or inaction. For example,

"What was I supposed to do? He placed the cocaine on the table in front of me. It's not my fault I got high."

"I was pulled over by the police because they don't like me. I only had a couple of beers. They're making up that stuff about my car swerving just to get me."

"You guys punish me too much. Can't you just leave me alone!?"

"These bill collectors are sharks. If they would just leave me alone my life would not be so miserable."

"I'm overweight because fast food is just too good."

"I'm overweight because I just don't have the time to exercise." (In this example the person is playing victim of the 24 hour day rather than evaluating difficulties he or she may have with personal motivation or prioritization and organizational skills.)

These are pretty obvious examples of victim stancing. Most people will encounter less dramatic examples of this thinking error on a daily basis. The key element of victimization is that a person attempts to place blame on others for the consequences or potential consequence of their own actions, inactions, or beliefs.

Drama & Excitement: Drama & excitement is also commonly known as *attention seeking*. This thinking error involves getting attention through exaggerated or overly dramatized behaviors. This thinking error will usually occur when one either does not have the skills to get emotional needs met in a more healthy manner or when one perceives that their environment does not provide the opportunity to get needs met in a more appropriate manner. In either case, an individual draws attention to him or herself without significant regard for its impact on others. For example, at a formal dinner a young child intentionally knocks over a full glass of water. The child might have been bored or feeling out of place, yet he either did not have the skills nor felt safe asking to be excused from the table.

Ownership: Ownership is a thinking error utilized when empathy skills are poorly developed. Essentially, one subscribes to a belief that if *"I want it, it's mine."* This belief can be acted upon in many ways – ranging from a minor theft of property to behaviors as serious as physical abuse of others or sexual assaults.

These are just sixteen types of common thinking errors. There are many others defined throughout the academic literature and within popular psychology books. However, the sixteen types presented above seem to be those that I most frequently encounter in my practice of family therapy. I find that after one becomes familiar with these thinking errors, they tend to leap out at you when interacting with others. Many people, after learning to recognize thinking errors, are surprised at how often their friends, family, and co-workers rely upon these errors to *manipulate others* or to *avoid taking personal responsibility*. Many people also report that familiarizing themselves with thinking errors has helped them understand how often they attempt to manipulate others in a similar fashion. How do children come about these thinking errors? Parents need only look inward to answer this question.

Children will not *lie* when it is emotionally safe to be forthright. *Excuses* and *blaming* will not be relied upon when emotional process is strong within the parent-child relationship. There is no need to *redefine* when one is comfortable working toward greater intimacy rather than away from greater intimacy. One is unlikely to rely upon *assuming* when he or she has a healthy sense of self-esteem. A more direct route, such as simply asking somebody what they might be thinking or feeling, represent no problem when one has a healthy sense of confidence and satisfaction. There's no need to assume. A child will not steal or inappropriately claim *ownership* if he or she grasps the concept of empathy.

The thinking errors that stimulate unhealthy and less desirable behaviors in children are learned directly from interaction with the parents. Sometimes the less desirable behaviors are learned from direct observation. For example, a child might reason "*I see Mom and Dad engaging in power plays to get their way all the time. This must be the best way of getting what one wants.*" However, direct correlations such as this are not as influential in the development of thinking errors as one might think. Let's consider for a moment the evolution of a lie. A *young* child's language, cognitive, and relational skills are probably not sophisticate enough to recognize when a parent has lied to the child. The child's natural loyalty to his or her parents also makes recognition of parental deception unlikely. Rarely will you see a 4 year-old confront his or her parents about the deception surrounding Santa Clause. How then does a young child learn to lie? How does this less desirable skill emerge? It would be fair to assume that the child's thinking error, his or her lie, is unlikely the result of direct observation. Again, the answer is to be found in the quality of the parent-child interactions.

If parents continually promote healthy *emotional process, intimacy, empathy,* and *self-esteem* development in the family system, thinking errors will not be necessary to get one's need met. These are the systemic variables that guard against most thinking errors and many behaviors that are considered by parents to be undesirable. When there is little emotional processing in the family, when there is little intimacy between family members, when empathy is not explored, and when self-esteem is not fostered, thinking errors and the corresponding undesirable behaviors are sure to emerge. Therefore, when a parent observes an undesirable behavior and addresses it without exploring the underlying motives and systemic variables, little is being done to prevent the behavior from reemerging in the future.

Looking inward at our internal antagonists – our own methods of acting and reacting – is infinitely more helpful than focusing on the external antagonists – the child's specific behaviors. Rather than attempting to change the child by focusing solely on his or her behaviors, attempt to change the methods of acting and reacting within yourself. Additional attention fostering intimacy, healthy emotional process, empathy, and greater self-esteem will not be wasted effort. This seems to be a less obvious approach to addressing a child's undesirable behavior. However, it is an approach that is infinitely more likely to be helpful.

79. The artful parent reduces shame associated with weakness while simultaneously reinforcing strengths. This is the essence of character and self-esteem development.

Fostering a child's sense of self-esteem is certainly an important aspect of parenting and worthy of considerable attention. In Parenting Assumption number 42 we began exploring this topic by presenting a comprehensive definition of self-esteem. In the above Assumption we shall return to the topic of self-esteem by exploring other variables influential to its healthy development.[45] Specifically, we will explore the importance of promoting a child's strengths while reducing shame associated with weakness.

I have had the opportunity to work with many children struggling with low self-esteem. Unfortunately, by the time these children and their families find their way to my office, behaviors that indicate the child has poor self-esteem are pretty obvious. Examples of some of these behaviors include temper tantrums, difficulty interacting with peers and/or bullying, thievery, lying, promiscuity, drug and alcohol abuse, eating disorders, gang activity, poor school attendance and performance, and self-mutilation. Fortunately, parents do not have to wait until these symptomatic behaviors present themselves to recognize that a child's self-esteem is low. There are earlier and more subtle signs. I frequently come across four such signs. They are:

- A child finds it difficult or uncomfortable to take a compliment

- A child has a hard time maintaining eye contact

- A child has a difficult time dealing with failure

- A child is reluctant to voice his or her perspective.

When I encounter these subtle signs, I make it a point to cautiously explore the topic of self-esteem with the entire family. I use the word *cautiously* because some parents may try to change these specific behaviors, the symptoms, rather than address the underlying issues that result in the low self-esteem and these behaviors. For example, a parent may insist his or her child look into the eyes of the person with whom he or she is interacting rather than explore the underlying variables that leave the child uncomfortable with direct eye contact. The former is less helpful and healthy than the latter. A parent may *demand* a child, uncomfortable with compliments, respond favorably or politely when complimented rather than focusing on the underlying variables that stimulate the child's discomfort. Again, the former is less likely to be helpful and healthy than the latter. Thus far in my career I have yet to come across any parent who was able to promote healthy self-esteem through insistence and demands. The process of self-esteem development is significantly more complex than that. Let's take a look at an example from my practice of family therapy to help explore this very complex subject.

Parents will often seek input from a therapist after a child has been diagnosed with an eating disorder, such as overeating, binging, anorexia, and bulimia. In every case that I have worked with, problems with low self-esteem contributed to the disorder. This particular Parenting Assumption seems relevant as the children with the eating disorder had low self-esteem and the parents tended to focus on the child's weaknesses while ignoring or minimizing the child's strengths. Let's take a moment to look at one particular example of a 14 year-old girl who was obese. The girl appeared to have little self-control over the quantities of food she consumed and often binged out of control. Her physician ruled out medical conditions that might cause such behaviors and referred the family to me after the daughter threatened to commit suicide. During our first session it was obvious the girl had a very low sense of self-esteem. It was also obvious that the parents were oblivious to helpful ways of supporting healthy self-esteem development. The parents tended to focus on the symptoms of poor self-esteem rather than the underlying systemic variables that were, in part, responsible for the problem. Let's look at how the parents and daughter responded to my questions during our first session.

Therapist to Family: *How might I be helpful?*

Parents: *Our daughter has been threatening to kill herself. Our family physician thought we should talk to somebody.*

Therapist: *Tell me more about it, the problems in the family that is.*

Parent: *Well our daughter, as you can see, has a weight problem. This is obviously hard for her. We're pretty sure this is why she wants to kill herself. She won't listen to us at all. Her eating is completely out of control.*

Therapist to the Daughter: *What are your thoughts about problems in the family?*

Daughter (looks away, making no eye contact with anybody): *I don't know.*

The parents continued to focus on the child's weight issues throughout the entire session. The young girl became increasingly elusive and disengaged as the session progressed. The parents seemed oblivious to this fact and became angry with their daughter as she withdrew emotionally. I learned a lot about interactions within this family during our first session. First, the daughter was uncomfortable

making eye contact with me and her parents. Secondly, it appeared
that presenting her perspective was an uncomfortable process for the
14 year-old. And finally, the parents did not seem to be very skilled at
working with their daughter's weaknesses or strengths. They seemed
to approach the problems in their family in an emotionally sterile
and callous manner. They focused on symptoms rather than factors
stimulating the problematic behaviors. This family certainly had a lot
of work to do in order to move forward.

My goals for the second session were much different than the first.
I wanted to learn more about the 14 year-old. There was certainly
more to her than the symptoms that brought the family to therapy.
My goal was to begin a process where focus was removed from the
troubling symptoms so that we could explore the underlying issues
causing these symptoms. The girl's eating disorder and suicidal
threats were overshadowing other important aspects of this child's
character, such as the young lady's strengths. It appeared to me that,
as the parents became increasingly focused on the girl's vulnerabilities
and weaknesses, the unhealthy and destructive behaviors became
increasingly pervasive and pronounced. Her threats of suicide were
merely a continuation, a worsening, of this process. I believed it was
important to disrupt this cycle if the family was to move in healthier
directions.

The second session began in the following manner:

Therapist to Family: *Last week we met and I heard a lot
about* [the daughter's] *weight problem and the recent suicidal
threats. This is important, however, I'd like to get away from
that for a bit. I think it would be helpful if I knew more about
each of you. You know, things like your interests, your dreams,
goals, frustrations, accomplishments. Things like that. I don't
want to hear you guys describe each other. I would prefer
hearing it from you directly, your perspective. So please don't
help each other out here. I would like to hear from everybody.
Now last week the parents did most of the talking so why don't
we start with* [the daughter].

Daughter [making immediate eye contact with the therapist]: *What
do you mean?*

Therapist: *Seems like there are some significant issues in this family.
It's hard for me to offer input if I don't know you guys very well. I*

heard some of the troubling stuff last week. Let's fill in the spaces with the everyday stuff, like your interests, strengths, goals, likes, dislikes, frustrations. Stuff like that.

Daughter [maintaining eye contact]: *Well, I really like to sing and I have a really good English teacher.*

This session progressed in a much different manner than the previous one. The daughter was a bit shy at first, but with some encouragement, she had little difficulty opening up with her dreams, her goals, her frustrations, and accomplishments. As it turned out, she was an accomplished vocalist and her grades were well above average. She was also forthcoming with some of her frustrations and weaknesses, which included the difficulties she had finding fashionable clothing and her love of pizza. The parents made several attempt to re-direct this session back to the daughter's eating disorder, her weight problems, and her talk of suicide. However, I ensured these efforts were not successful. The parents were reminded of the goals for this session and encouraged to remain on task. I was not minimizing the importance of the eating disorder nor the daughter's references to suicide. These were important symptoms.

However, as was demonstrated in the first session, the daughter would likely became elusive and emotionally shut-off if the focus narrowed to merely these behaviors, these symptoms. Continuing on such a course would not be very productive.

A very unhealthy cycle had established itself in this family. The cycle looked something like this:

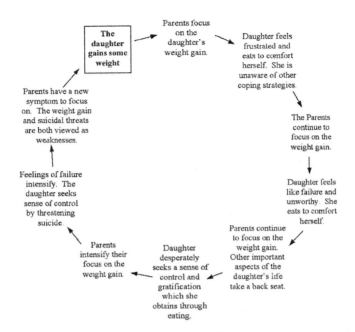

The daughter gains some weight

Parents focus on the daughter's weight gain.

Daughter feels frustrated and eats to comfort herself. She is unaware of other coping strategies.

Parents have a new symptom to focus on. The weight gain and suicidal threats are both viewed as weaknesses.

The Parents continue to focus on the weight gain.

Feelings of failure intensify. The daughter seeks sense of control by threatening suicide.

Daughter feels like failure and unworthy. She eats to comfort herself.

Parents intensify their focus on the weight gain.

Daughter desperately seeks a sense of control and gratification which she obtains through eating.

Parents continue to focus on the weight gain. Other important aspects of the daughter's life take a back seat.

This cycle would likely continue until there is some intervention (e.g. a therapist helps the family break the cycle), the daughter acts upon her threats to harm herself, or the parents and child eventually sever their relationship several years down the road. The parents were unaware of this particular cycle nor were they aware of the many subtle ways they drew attention to their child's weight. The parents were proud of their daughter's accomplishments. However, these accomplishments were always overshadowed by her weight problems. For example, the daughter was given an award at school for her vocal accomplishments. The parents responded with joy and satisfaction but then added one annotation. They remarked that if she would just lose some weight she might be selected for a role in a school musical where everybody might hear her beautiful voice.

These parents were doing the best they could with the parenting tools they had. Their actions were motivated by love and concern and were well intentioned. Unfortunately, their actions were not very helpful or healthy. I believe the callous nature in which the parents responded during our first session was just a symptom of their frustration and feeling of impotence. They were doing the best they could and seemed to be getting nowhere. In fact, matters seemed to be getting worse with the emergence of the suicidal threats.

I have no idea how this cycle began in this particular family. Many factors contribute to eating disorders. In some instances, the underlying causes are obvious (e.g. childhood abuse and neglect.) In other families the contributing factors are less clear and take considerable work to identify. However, in every instance of an eating disorder, and the vast majority of other major parenting problems, self-esteem development will always be part of a helpful and healthy solution.

This brings us to my 90/10 rule. This rule was first introduced in Parenting Assumption number 36 and can be applied to our current discussion. This rule, as I stated in Parenting Assumption 36, is by no means scientifically based or a proven fact. It is merely something that makes sense to me and, more often than not, has demonstrated itself to be pretty accurate. In this case the 90/10 rule would assert that children who struggle with issues relating to poor self-esteem experience their parents as primarily focused on perceived weaknesses and undesirable behaviors, about 90% of the time. The remaining 10% of a parent's energies focus on highlighting and reinforcing the child's strengths. Time and time again this has demonstrated itself to be true in my interactions with families whose children struggle with a variety of behavioral problems. My goal is to assist parents reverse these percentages. That is, I encourage parents to devote a mere 10% of their energies to the less desirable behaviors and 90% to highlighting and reinforcing the child's strengths. Let's take this rule and apply it to the family in the above example.

The second session began a process whereby important aspects of self-esteem were identified – the young woman's strengths. In this family, these were neither well defined nor were they frequently the focus of attention. In just the second session alone we were able to identify a long list of strengths. Again, these strengths are the building blocks for self-esteem (see Parenting Assumption 42 for details on self-esteem). With the emergence of the weight gain and eating disorder, these strengths were overlooked and all but forgotten. For this family to move forward in a healthy manner, a change in mindset was necessary. A majority of parental energy would have to be shifted from the perceived weaknesses, the eating disorder, the weight gain, and threats of suicide, to the daughter's strengths, her musical talents, her success in school, her honesty, her sense of humor, etc. This was an uncomfortable process for the parents. They were heavily invested in changing their daughter's less desired behaviors through direct intervention. This less direct approach of addressing the underlying factors causing the eating disorder, was foreign and left them feeling vulnerable. The parents stated that if they left the eating disorder alone it would only become worse. This is the change in mindset I referred to earlier. The parents would not be leaving the eating disorder alone, nor would they be neglecting their daughter's well being. They would be addressing the systemic variables affecting the 14 year-old's behavior.

The next several sessions with this family served as a model for the 90/10 rule. Most of my energies were directed to identifying, exploring, and reinforcing what I thought were strengths in the family, both within the individuals and the family system. Very little effort was focused on the perceived weaknesses of the daughter's weight problem and bingeing activities. After several weeks of progressing in this manner, these problems seemed as if they were more approachable. They had been demoted to a role of lesser significance. The shame that had once been associated with these weaknesses had been lessened. The manner in which these weaknesses were addressed had also shifted (with some assistance and encouragement). Rather than only focusing on the child's weight and appearance, the whole family began exploring healthier lifestyles. The solution was not to be found in counting the number of calories consumed or purchasing scales, but rather in promoting increased physical activity and maintaining a balanced diet. After several weeks, the family's energies and focus shifted from what they perceived as a weaknesses to collectively working to promote healthier living. The family explored ways they could increase their physical activity and meet with a dietician to learn how they could incorporate a healthier diet into their daily lives. This healthier diet was not a crash diet intended to induce dramatic weight loss, but rather ways the family could support increased health through a balanced and realistic nutritional plan.

Over the course of several weeks this family learned to reduce the shame associated with a perceived weakness. Through this process they actually opened the door to a healthier and realistic solution. The daughter's binging ceased and after several months her weight dropped significantly. This occurred without crash diets or fad nutritional supplements. More importantly, the daughter began excelling in many other areas of her life. Her grades went from good to great, her self-confidence increased, she started participating in some sporting activities, and she involved herself in the school theater. These were fairly dramatic results. The success seen with this family is not merely limited to eating disorders. As I mentioned earlier, some symptoms of poor self-esteem are pretty obvious and include temper tantrums, difficulty interacting with peers and/or bullying, thievery, lying, promiscuity, drug and alcohol abuse, eating disorders, gang activity, poor school attendance and performance, and self-mutilation. Families struggling with these problems can find similar success by reducing the shame associated with weakness while simultaneously reinforcing strengths. The outcomes, if parents can change their mindset, are usually very healthy.

80. Always be reflective and cognizant of your impact.

This Parenting Assumption is relatively straight forward but is too often cast aside. This is unfortunate as there are few things we can do other than self-reflection that will have a healthier impact on our parenting. This is stated in many ways and approached from many different angles throughout this book. Every time we interact with another human being, we have some kind of impact on that person. Most of the time this impact is relatively small and insignificant. Other times, what we say and do to others can have a tremendous impact on them and our relationship with them. I have an example of a personal experience that occurred many years ago – while I was in high school. My example does not involve an interaction between parent and child. However, I believe it demonstrates the point of this Parenting Assumption. This experience had quite an impact on me and to this day remains clearly embedded in my mind.

I was by no means a stellar student during my high school days. I was motivated in many areas – but not in academics. Late into my junior year I made an appointment with my high school counselor. Let's call her Mrs. P. I came from a family that expected everybody to go to college. My older brother set the example by getting accepted to and attending a fine university. It was time for me to begin planning my future. I asked Mrs. P what I needed to do to get into college. After a quick review of my academic record, she looked at me and stated, *"Mark, I don't think college would be in your better interests. I'm not sure you're college material. Perhaps you should consider a trade."*

I was shocked and devastated. It felt as if somebody dropped a piano on me. Not only was I disinterested in working a trade, but I had either failed or done poorly in every shop class I had ever taken. What was this woman saying to me, and why was she saying it? Could it be true? Here was a professional guidance counselor telling her charge that his future would not or should not include collegiate involvement. What was I going to do? My family had expectations. I had expectations. The circles I traveled in at the time all had college expectations. It took a long time for me to rebound from Mrs. P's comments. My confidence in myself was rocked as well as my sense of self-worth and self-esteem.

I had many fine qualities and a lot of potential. Yes, I was an underachiever, but should this fact serve to extinguish my goals, hopes, and ambitions? In retrospect, I believe many important decisions made in the months following this appointment were influenced by this brief encounter. As it turned out, I was accepted by several state universities but chose to enter military services. I'm certain this decision was one of many influenced in part by my guidance counselor's input. I wonder why Mrs. P did not take our conversation a bit further. Why did she not ask me about my interests? Why did she not seem more concerned about my poor academic performance? Why did she fail to probe into the factors that were contributing to my poor performance? I wonder why she did not assist me in establishing a plan to guide me in a direction more aligned with my interests rather than recommending I write them off altogether? She was a *guidance counselor,* wasn't she? Was she aware of the impact she had on those whom she counseled? Perhaps she was having an unusually busy day. Maybe she was struggling with her own personal problems and was distracted. Perhaps she was just poorly suited for the position.

It is probably impossible to know exactly how we impact those with whom we interact; however, it is important to be open to and reflective of our influence on others. I wonder how things might have been different if Mrs. P had taken a minute before our appointment to reflect. For example, what if she said to herself, *"Hmmm, my next appointment is with Mark. A classic underachiever. I wonder what he wants? Why did he make this appointment with me? This seems like an opportunity to have a helpful impact on the young man."* – or – *"I'm having a terrible day. All I see are the problem kids. Is there any hope for this world? I need to take a minute or two to clear my head so these feelings do not get in the way of my next appointment."*

No other interaction is as important as the parent-child interaction. Even small and seemingly insignificant comments and actions can have a tremendous and lasting impact. I see this in every family I have had the pleasure to work with. In those unfortunate instances where a child has been abused, I constantly find a parent who somehow lost, or never had the ability to, reflect upon their impact. They were not skilled in the use of empathy. In instances where both parent and child excelled or where the family was well adjusted and healthy, there were always clear examples of the parents reflecting upon their actions, reactions, and impact. Again, this book is filled with examples of how parents may impact their children. Many of these examples depict healthy and helpful interactions while other less so. Artful parents will keep this thought in mind as they interact with their child or children. It's okay to slow down and be reflective of our impact on others – especially our impact on children.

81. Always turn misfortune to advantage. Not to do so promotes cynicism. To do so promotes optimism.

Many of the Parenting Assumptions presented thus far have explored some of the major components of parent-child communications. The primary focus of this exploration has been understanding and enhancing intimacy, safety, and emotional process. This particular Assumption opens the door to yet another aspect of parent-child communications, an area infrequently discussed in very much detail. This Assumption encourages parents to consider how their parent-child interactions influence a child's global outlook and perspective. Are they promoting a global outlook within their children that is based upon *optimism* or one that is based upon *cynicism*. Let's take a brief look at these two global perspectives, optimism and cynicism.

We can learn a lot about a person's global outlook by observing how he or she interprets and responds to problems, inconveniences, and challenges. For example, a person whose global outlook is based upon a more cynical foundation might be prone to respond in the following manner:

Everyday problems, inconveniences and challenges are seen as true burdens. Small problems, inconveniences and challenges are often blown out of proportion and seen as catastrophic events or issues. They are often made unnecessarily worse. Problems, inconveniences, and challenges are understood to be aspects of life that are best avoided. A person whose global outlook is based upon a cynical foundation rarely focuses on resolution and action, but rather on drawing attention to the burden created by the problem, inconvenience or challenge. Large problems, inconveniences, and challenges are often consuming, overwhelming and immobilizing.

A person whose global outlook is based upon a more optimistic foundation is likely to interpret and respond to problematic events, inconveniences, and challenges in the following manner:

Everyday problems, inconveniences, and challenges are addressed as they are encountered. They are understood as a part of everyday living. They are identified, confronted, and embraced. They are frequently seen as creating opportunities for growth and advancement. The focus remains on resolution and action rather than avoidance and procrastination. Small problems are just that, small. Large problems, inconveniences, or challenges are evaluated, dissected, and resolved when and if possible. They are used as springboards for growth and advancement whenever possible.

Examples of one's global outlook can be observed in nearly every aspect of his or her living. For example, a person who accidentally breaks a drinking glass then responds by shouting expletives and slamming a closet door subscribes to a more cynical global outlook. A person who shuns away from an unfamiliar activity, an unfamiliar food, or who refuses to consider a perspective that differs from his or her own, may be approaching life with a more cynical global outlook. A person whose first response to a challenging situation is to focus on why it *cannot be done* rather than attempting to identify *what is necessary to address the challenge* is embracing a more cynical outlook.

A child's global outlook develops slowly and over a great length of time. A child's outlook is most profoundly impacted by the manner in which he or she experiences the parent. That is, the manner in which the parent communicates with the child will largely determine how that child interprets and responds to life's problems, inconveniences, and challenges. This is where the present Parenting Assumption becomes relevant.

Each time a parent responds to a problem, inconvenience, or a challenge with a secondary emotional response such as anger, by blowing the situation out of proportion, or by taking a chronic naysayer stance (*this cannot be done* or *the situation is hopeless* versus *this is a difficult situation* and *what is necessary for us to deal with this situation*), the child's global outlook slowly moves in a more cynical direction. If a parent attempts to turn *misfortune to advantage,* more often than not, the child's global outlook is likely to move in a more optimistic direction. When a drinking glass is broken, a carton of eggs is dropped to the floor, an appointment is missed, or the automobile has a flat tire, seek to discover the advantages associated with that situation and communicate them. If you are unable to find advantage then process the thoughts and emotions being experienced. Fewer responses will promote optimism in the face of hardship and challenge. Remember, the child's global outlook is dependant upon how he or she experiences the parents: cynically or optimistically.

82. Allow space and time to consider and reflect. The impulsive parent seeking immediate gratification will hear what he wishes and experience what he fears.

This Parenting Assumption makes a great prediction. That is, if a child experiences his or her parents as impulsive, more often than not, the child will quickly learn to give the parents what they want to hear and see rather than what is probably most honest and forthright. Perhaps the healthiest and most helpful safeguard against this outcome is to vigilantly seek the child's perspective on nearly all matters of living. This process can be complimented by making time to explore important aspects of development, relationships, and life's many challenges. The parent may not hear what he or she wishes, but the parent-child experiences will certainly be rewarding.

83. There are times when children should not obey their parents – this may be indicative of growth and should be recognized as such. The artful parent recognizes growth from deceit.

In Parenting Assumption 24 we explored the topic of trial and error learning. If you will recall, the discussion that followed Assumption 24 asserted that some mistakes made by children can be attributed to the maturation process. A child will try something that is beyond his or her developmental skill level and will not succeed or will make a mistake. It was suggested that parents might benefit by recognizing these trial and error mistakes and responding in a manner that promotes healthy growth and increased parent child intimacy. The above Assumption is very similar to 24 but rather than focusing on mistakes, this Assumption explores the motives behind disobedience.

In every family a time will come when a child disobeys his or her parents. This is not always an unhealthy event or a malicious act. In fact, it may be a signal to the parents that they should evaluate the quality of their parent-child interactions. Children possess a naturally loyalty to their parents. This loyalty can be expressed in many ways but almost always includes a high level of obedience to the parents. A child will usually remain loyal to, and will obey, parents unless motivated to do otherwise. Sometimes motivation to disobey is purely an attempt to self-gratify (e.g. *"I see the cookie; I want the cookie. Mom says 'no' but the value of that cookie is greater to me than the punishment I am likely to receive if she catches me taking it."*).

In other instances, a child's disobedience can be attributed to trial and error learning. The child must learn through the enforcement of parental limits, boundaries and consequences that disobeying the parent is undesirable (see Parenting Assumption 24). From time to time disobedience can be a reaction to *incongruent, unjust,* or *confusing* parenting. This Assumption is placed in the Art chapter as deception or disobedience motivated by incongruent, unjust, or confusing parenting can be tricky to distinguish. The parent must be willing to look inward rather than immediately placing blame on the child when deception or disobedience is encountered. This requires considerable patience and effort on the parents' behalf. Let's take a look at some very simple examples that might help clarify this point.

If a parent fails to recognize a maturing child's emerging skills and capabilities by infantilizing the child, treating the child as an infant or less capable, disobedience might be an expected and appropriate reaction. The child is placed into a position where he or she must force his or her emerging developmental capabilities into the parenting mix by way of disobedience. Parenting would be a lot simpler if children were capable of communicating with their parents in the following manner rather than through disobedience:

"Mom, Dad, I'm maturing, growing, and developing new skills and cognitive processes every day. I feel as if you are

lagging behind in recognizing my growth. Your parenting seems
***incongruent** to my development. Perhaps it would be helpful if
you took some time to evaluate and adjust your perception of me
so that we could all be on the same page.*"

Now, this statement may seem a bit absurd. I cannot imagine a
child making such a statement. However, when a child disobeys his or
her parents, this may be exactly what the child is attempting to say but
lacks the developmental skills to accomplish. When parenting is *unjust*
or when parent-child communications are *confusing* I can imagine a
child's thoughts might be similar to the following:

*"Mom, Dad, I'm troubled by your response to this situation.
I know I have a perspective and feelings, yet these have not
been considered by you. In fact, it feels as if my perspective, my
emotions, have been completely disregarded and ignored. This
somehow feels **unjust** and is very frustrating.*
And,
*"You're telling me that I should not smoke cigarettes because
it's bad for me. Then I see you smoke. That's **confusing** to me.
This "do as I say not as I do" approach doesn't make a lot of
sense to me. Is there something going on that you're not telling
me?"*

Again, these statements are beyond the capabilities of any child I
have ever encountered. Yet, most children are capable of acting on
these or similar situations. If parents choose to view rebelliousness
or disobedience as merely poor behavior on the child's behalf, a
significant parenting opportunity has been lost. I suggest that parents
become accustomed to processing a child's disobedience by evaluating
their role in the behavior. Both parent and child will surely benefit
from this artful approach to parenting.

**84. Weak is the parent who intimidates the child – this wearies
the child by keeping him constantly anxious and mistrusting
his own emotions. This stifles growth and exploration. This
parent is powerless in the grand picture of parenting and will
eventually lose any hope of receiving the long-term benefits of
an intimate relationship with his or her children.**

For this Parenting Assumption I'm going to look inward to my own family experience. I'm going to briefly look at the relationship I had with my father. Unfortunately, this Assumption is profoundly appropriate to our relationship. Some of my earliest memories of my father surround his fraternity paddle. For those who are not aware of what a fraternity paddle is, let me explain. This is a wooden paddle used to administer punishment by beating. My father's paddle was approximately two feet long and four or five inches wide. These paddles are typically decoratively engraved with the Greek letters of a particular college fraternity. I never joined a fraternity but assume these paddles might have been awarded to newly initiated or hazed members. I would not be surprised if the paddle was somehow instrumental to the initiation process.

The earliest memories of my father are of him using this paddle to hit me after I misbehaved. This seemed like a regular occurrence during my childhood – my misbehaving and the paddling. When I look back to these experiences, I find myself concluding that this method of parental discipline left me in a constant state of anxiety and weariness. I doubt my focus was ever directed toward evaluating the thought processes and behaviors that resulted in the punishment but rather how to avoid my father and the paddle. Some proponents of paddling and spanking might say these are one and the same. By avoiding the behavior that might elicit a paddling, the youngster learns the intended or desired lesson. I strongly disagree with that supposition. The lesson learned from paddling and spanking are much different than what many proponents would have you believe. Paddling and spankings are used as a means of manipulating behavior without process and are inherently intimidating to the child. Any in-depth exploration of the motives, emotions, thoughts, and beliefs surrounding one's behavior is all but impossible when one is intimidated and anxious. This is true with adults and children alike. Rather, one's understanding of the situation that resulted in the paddling is at best superficial. The child learns 'what' not to do but gains little insight into 'why' the behavior is inappropriate or undesirable. This makes it difficult for the child to apply the lesson learned to other situations he or she might encounter. Furthermore, emotional distance between the parent and child widens following any action that serves to intimidate – especially spanking and paddling.

When parents enter my office seeking input on disciplining their children, I do not stand on my soapbox professing the evils of spanking. This is not the role of a family therapist. The method one selects to discipline their children ultimately rests with the parents. My role is to present parents with additional options and to explore the long and short-term benefits and consequences of each. It is also my job to assist parents identify and dismantle barriers that interfere with them being able to successfully implement healthier and more helpful methods of disciplining. Let's look at an example of parents who asked me for assistance identifying alternatives to spanking.

Therapist *So, how do you discipline your son now?*
Father *We give him one warning, then we usually spank him. Not too hard, just enough to get his attention.*
Therapist: *Help me understand why you do that - spank him.*
Mother: *We've always done that. We've never really discussed it.*
Father: *It was good enough for me. I was spanked when I was a kid. I turned out okay.*
Mother: *[jokingly] That's questionable.*
Therapist: *Were you both spanked as children?*
Mother & Father: *Yes.*
Therapist: *Why are you coming to me right now?*
Mother: *We read an article in a parenting magazine stating that spanking is bad. So we wanted to stop.*
Father: *But, everything we tried, besides spanking, doesn't seem to get his attention.*
Therapist: *What do you mean by "get his attention?"*
Father: *Well, if he's misbehaving or acting out, a spanking - after we warn him - will stop the behavior.*
Therapist: *Is that what you want? To stop the troubling behavior?*
Mother: *Yes..... What do mean?*
Therapist: *When you discipline or punish your son, what do you want to accomplish?*
Father: *Yes, we want the behavior to stop.*
Mother: *Well, we want him to learn from the experience. I don't want to keep spanking him for the same things over and over again.*
Therapist: *Does that ever happen?*
Mother: *Sometimes. He's a pretty spirited boy.*
Therapist: *Oh.*
Father: *Where's this going?*

Therapist: *Can you give me an example of an instance when you spanked your son?*

Father: *He came home from school last week using the "N" word, you know, "nigger". We warned him not to use that word, but he kept going with it. I gave him a spanking. Now he doesn't use it.*

Therapist: *Sounds like your intervention worked.*

Father: *Now you're scaring me. Are you saying that was the right thing to do?*

Therapist: *Let's work with this example a bit.*
You said your son was using an offensive word and after a spanking he stopped using it. Right?

Mother: *Right.*

Therapist: *The spanking got his attention.*

Father: *Right away.*

Therapist: *Help me understand what he might have learned by this experience.*

Father: *Not to use the "N" word.*

Therapist: *What else?*

Mother: *That it's bad to use the "N" word.*

Therapist: *How do you know that's what he learned?*

Mother: *He's not using the word any more.*

Therapist: *How do you think your son felt while he was being spanked?*

Father: *Not too happy. He was crying.*

Therapist: *Do you think he was thinking about how inappropriate and offensive his actions were?*

Mother: *Probably not. He was probably hoping it would just end.*

Therapist: *[directed to the father] How do you think your son felt about you during and after the spanking?*

Father: *I don't know? I know he loves me but at the particular moment he was probably angry.*

Therapist: *Have the two of you ever been angry with each other, I mean really angry?*

Mother: *Sure, lots of times.*

Therapist: *When you get to that state of mind, experiencing all of those emotions that leave you feeling really angry, do you hear what the other has to say?*

Mother & Father: *[both nod "no"]*

Therapist: *But you two are still together. How can you become angry with each other "lots of times" and still hold the marriage together?*

Mother: *Well, eventually we get together and talk about our differences. Sometimes it's an hour after we fight, sometimes it's a couple of days later. We take a breather and then deal with the problem.*

Therapist: *Okay. After you spank your son do you return to the issue after a cooling off period - take a breather - and then deal with the problem?*

Mother: *Most of the time. We like to let him know why he got spanked.*

Therapist: *When does this occur?*

Mother: *Depend? Sometimes we just assume he got the message, and we don't talk about it.*

Therapist: *Why not avoid the whole 'getting your son angry' stage and move to the 'dealing with the problem' stage?*

Father: *Huh?*

Therapist: *Sure, sounds like your son does something that requires your intervention - like using the "N" word. You then intentionally get him angry by spanking him, increasing emotional distance between you and your son. You then return later to repair the damage done by the spanking. If that's not enough, you have the task of explaining why you do not want him to use the "N" word. Why not just start with explaining why you do not want him to use that word?*

Father: *Haven't you been listening? That doesn't work with him. Let's say he uses a swear word. I say, "don't use that word." He will certainly use it again. That's the way he is. If we spank him that won't happen.*

Mother: *Why did you ask us if we were spanked as children?*

Therapist: *I think there are other options available that are just as effective as spanking. Perhaps options where you do not have to create emotional distance between you and your son - doing harm - in order to get the same outcome. When parents tell me that nothing else works but spanking, I wonder "what is it they haven't tried?" And "why are the other options not working well for these parents?" More often than not, parents stick with what is familiar and* *known. In your case, that's spanking. Deviating from the familiar can be uncomfortable.*

Father: *What would you suggest?*

Therapist: *There are many options, we'll get to that. But first let's look at why many parents stick with spanking. When parents read about alternatives to spanking - say in a parenting magazine - they may give it a try. Unfortunately, it will not work the first time around. The child will not likely respond in a way that meets the parent's initial expectations. <u>Strike one for the alternative method</u>. Trying something new - especially in regard to parenting - will feel very uncomfortable and unfamiliar to the parent. Parents seem to prefer things that are familiar and known to them. Like spanking. Parents tell me all the time that alternatives to spanking are "just too hard" or that "it just takes too much effort" and that these alternatives " take too much of my time." I interpret these statements to mean "changing how I interact with my child is hard work and at times uncomfortable. I prefer to stick with what I know." <u>Strike two for the alternative method</u>. Finally, I tell parents that the most helpful and healthy alternatives to spanking will only be effective if implemented "more often than not." <u>Strike three for the alternative method</u>. Many parents want to intervene and be done with it. Your son uses the "N" word, you spank him, and the behavior goes away. Unfortunately, he does not really know why he shouldn't use that word and he's angry with you. He doesn't refrain from repeating the "N" word because he gained insight. No, he just doesn't use it around you because he, in some way, is intimidated by you or fearful of what you might do to him.*

Mother: *All right, I understand what you are saying. But we talk to him later about why we spanked him. Well, most of the time.*

Therapist: *Why create the anger and emotional distance? Why not just talk to him about it?*

Father: *Are we talking to him incorrectly? Because, it just doesn't seem to work the way you are suggesting.*

Therapist: *How do you think your son would react to the following input from one of you?:*

"Son, you used that word several times today. I asked you not to earlier. I'm really concerned right now. That

word offends me a lot. I'm really disappointed that you didn't listen to what I had to say earlier, and I'm really concerned that you may not understand why that word may be so offensive to others. What's going on here? What do you think we should do about this?

Father: *I don't know. I haven't taken that approach before. It seems like it gives him too much power.*

Therapist: *What do you mean?*

Father: *Isn't it my job to tell him what to do? What good will come from asking him "what should we do about this?"*

Therapist: *I doubt you are creating emotional distance when you ask your son for his perspective. He's not likely going to be angered or intimidated by this question. He is probably not wanting you to go away as he might after a spanking.*

Father: *Probably not.*

Therapist: *What do you think would be going though his mind?*

Father: *Besides "Dad's acting weird" - he's probably thinking about the situation.*

Therapist: *Exactly. You have his attention, and you can go anywhere from there. You can talk about why the "N" word is offensive to so many people. You can discuss why other kids might use the word - like to get attention, to hurt somebody, and so on.*

I think you will find that if you try this approach "more often than not," your need to rely on spanking will decrease significantly.

Mother: *Do you think it will work?*

Therapist: *Many parents leave out the part about how the child's behavior affected them. Such as "I'm really **concerned** right now. That word **offends** me a lot, and I'm really **disappointed** that you did not listen to what I had to say earlier." For some reason many parents believe they must be the all powerful, all knowing entity in their kid's life. Many seem to think this means they cannot tell their kids how they - the parents - feel. It's a shame. When a parents tells their child how his or her behavior affected them it gets the kid's attention. Children are naturally loyal to their parents. They want to please. When a parent becomes comfortable identifying his or her emotions and can honestly communicate them to the child, it's amazing*

the influence this can have on behavior.
Why don't you give it a try and let's talk about it next
week.

As the incidence of parent to child intimidation increases, so will the emotional gap that exists between parent and child. I have had the opportunity to work with many adults who question why they feel so distanced from their aging parents. These adults report the ability to relate with their parents on an intimate level simply does not exist. Time and time again I find that this inability to relate on an intimate level, the emotional gap, developed over a lifetime. In many instances examples of early parent to child intimidation are easily identified. This may not be the sole reason for the parent-child emotional gap; however, I would not doubt that it was a crucial component.

The couple in the example above were spanking their child because it was familiar, known, and comfortable to them. This was a genuine act they believed to be the most effective and helpful way to raise their son. Yet, after a couple of weeks of trial and error, they were able to arrive at several non–intimidating alternatives that proved to be just as effective without any unhealthy side effects. I would expect that as their son grows, develops, and matures, they will enjoy and benefit from an intimate family relationship. In retrospect, I wish my father had had a similar conversation with a therapist many years ago.

85. Do not attack a child exposing vulnerabilities. This will create further distance. The artful parent will recognize vulnerabilities and address them in a mutually supportive manner.

Rarely do I come across parents who have an actual desire to be mean-spirited toward, or inappropriate with, their children. Yet, one does not have to look very far to see parents acting in ways that may seem mean to the casual observer. Perhaps you have observed a frustrated parent shouting threats or profanity at a misbehaving child. Maybe you have seen a parent slap or spank a screaming child at a grocery store. Are these parents simply mean spirited or are there other processes at work? I believe that most mean-spirited or inappropriate behaviors are almost always rooted in, or can be traced back to, a history of less healthy patterns within the parent's family of origin. I often speak about parents *doing the best they can with the tools they have*. The parent acting in a mean spirited, unhealthy, or inappropriate manner is simply utilizing the parenting tools and concepts that have been passed along from generation to generation. This seems to be true in the case of relatively benign behaviors, such as shouting at your child, as well as the worst cases of abuse and neglect.

I find that parents will usually choose healthier behaviors once these trends are identified, highlighted, and alternatives offered and encouraged. Again, rare is the parent who actually desires to be mean spirited toward or inappropriate with their children. I mention this for a very important reason. Family therapists come across many situations where parents act or react in manners that are simply not very healthy for a child's development or well being. I will present a few examples in the following paragraphs. Understanding these behaviors as *parents doing the best they can with the tools they have* can be very helpful in moving beyond the actual behavior and toward finding healthy and helpful alternatives. Assigning guilt or blame, such as "She's a terrible mother" or "I'm just a horrible father" is easy when observing or confronting these behaviors. However, assigning guilt or blame is simply not very helpful to promoting insight and healthy change. Learning to understand our actions and inactions, both healthy and unhealthy, as the *utilization of the tools that we have* opens the door to greater self-evaluation, growth, and acquisition of additional parenting tools. I first came to realize the importance of this conclusion following a very difficult therapy session.

Years ago I was employed as a therapist within a practice that treated sexual offenders, perpetrators of domestic violence, as well as the victims of this abuse. I had been working with a 14 year-old whom had been sexually abused. He was initially reluctant to process the trauma in therapy. Then, after several weeks he sat before me with tears streaming down his cheeks and told me everything. The abuse had been horrible – probably the worst I had encountered in my practice of family therapy. Just the process of telling the story stimulated a flood of emotional and physical reactions within the boy. His skin lost much of it color. He began having difficulty breathing, he vomited, and looked as if he was going to faint through much of the session. My heart went out to this adolescent as he bared his soul and risked experiencing the uncomfortable emotions associated with processing such terrible trauma. I was pleased that he felt safe enough to begin the difficult process of healing and was confidant that he was prepared for the work we had ahead of us. This session ended with us agreeing to continue meeting, to continue processing this very painful subject, and to do everything we could to help reduce the harmful impact the abuse might wield upon his future.

After this particular session I had about five minutes before the arrival of my next patient. I looked at my schedule and noticed that my next appointment was with a sexual offender, a perpetrator. He was a man in his late 50s who had a history of victimizing boys about the same age of my previous patient. The previous session had had quite an impact on me. I was feeling enraged and without much compassion at that particular moment. These emotions seemed likely to impact my ability to be helpful to this individual. I found myself pacing the office hallways wondering what to do. My first impulse was to cancel the appointment. I believed I owed it the next patient to cancel the appointment face-to-face rather than having the receptionist do it for me. I directed the man to my office and we sat down. While I was attempting to find my words I noticed his genogram.[46]

There was a clear pattern of abuse and neglect throughout this man's family history. He was a victim of childhood sexual and physical abuse at the hands of his father. His early trauma was made worse by the fact that his father was prominent businessman and highly respected within their community. The children in this family felt powerless and without safe harbor. They did not think anybody would believe their accusation of abuse, especially against a man of such prominence, and remained silent for fear of universal rejection. The sexual abuse continued uninterrupted for years. This was the environment in which this man, who was a perpetrator of sexual abuse himself, had been raised. Now, the facts surrounding this man's family and personal history by no means justified his behavior as a sexual offender, however, making a connection between the family patterns and his behavior is important if any therapy is to have any hope of being helpful.

I told this patient that I just witnessed a young man begin the painful process of dealing with sexual abuse and how I had been impacted by the experience. I intended to tell the patient that I did not think I could continue with the session and believed we should reschedule, but chose to ask this perpetrator and victim of sexual abuse if he could relate in any way at all to the trauma experienced by my previous patient. This opened the door to a great deal of clinical progress. This man, this perpetrator, this criminal, had never been asked to explore his own victimization nor how this history might have left him with limited *tools* at his disposal for interacting with others in healthy ways. Acknowledging that he, too, was a victim of sexual and emotional abuse by no means excuses him from the horrible things he did to other human beings. However, neglecting to note, acknowledge, and explore his victimization would certainly hinder any hope of treating the conditions that motivated him to perpetrate sexual offenses.

Eventually, this man came to understand his deviant behaviors. He also came to recognize the deviant behaviors that passed from generation to generation in his family as well as the environment within his community that precluded disclosure, emotional safety, trust, and openness. He eventually came to understand his deviant, harmful, and illegal behaviors as him *doing the best he could with the very limited tools he had.* Over a period of several months, this man learned of subjects such as personal responsibility, empathy, intimacy, thinking errors, emotional processing and safety. These newly acquired skills were absolutely necessary if this man was to rejoin society without re-offending. It was unfortunate for this man, and the numerous victims he created, that *these* tools were not passed from generation to generation in his family.

Now, how does this example relate to this particular Parenting Assumption? Let's briefly return to the parent who slaps her screaming child at a grocery store or that frustrated parent who threatens his misbehaving child. It's easy to conclude that she's just "*a terrible mother*" or that he's "*a horrible father.*" Unfortunately, these conclusions are not very helpful. I prefer to view these parents as human beings managing a difficult situation utilizing the parenting tools that they have. I would prefer to think that if given the opportunity to acquire additional tools these situations would be less likely to recur in the future. I wish I could get these parents into my office to explore the numerous family patterns that leave more helpful and healthier options so elusive.

One particular example surfaces in my interactions with parents that might help clarify this point while returning us to the Parenting Assumption. This example relates to the process of lying. There are few situations in the parent-child relationship where attacking a child's vulnerability will result in such clear consequences. So, let's look at the process of lying for a moment. A person is usually motivated to lie for very specific reasons. The most common reason I come across is that it is simply not emotionally safe to tell the truth. This tends to differ from many people's belief that lying is merely means of getting what one wants at the expense of others or an attempt to cover up one's mistakes. However, if we explore the origins of lying in children, we find its roots fall squarely on the shoulders of how parents address the child's sense of vulnerability.

Children are naturally loyal to their parents. This is a biological aspect of being human. Young children wish to please their parents and for the most part do what they can to obey. Yet, from time to time children make mistakes or are placed in situations that require skills that are beyond their developmental capabilities. What happens when a young child makes a mistake or has an accident – let's say he or she spills a glass of milk. From a child's perspective, this represents a huge issue. Remember, the child is motivated by a biological desire to please his or her parents. From the child's perspective, the spilled milk will likely disappoint the parents. If the child starts to cry it is not because of the "spilled milk," but rather secondary to feelings of disappointment, confusion, and a sense of exposed vulnerability. If the parent responds in a manner that promotes emotional safety – more often than not – the child's sense of vulnerability will not have been assaulted and learning occurs. For example, the child spills a large glass of milk and begins to cry. The parent responds by talking about how difficult it can be to handle such a large glass of milk and engages the child in the clean up process. The parent can further engage the child by asking what he or she can do to help reduce the future spills. The child's desire to please the parent has been supported and perhaps the child has learned something about handling a large glass of milk. Small steps have been taken toward developing greater intimacy in the parent-child relationship.

What happens when a parent responds to the spilled milk with anger or aggression? What happens when the parent scolds the child then angrily rushes to clean up the mess? The experience for this child is significantly different. The child realizes that he or she disappointed the parent yet experienced no emotional resolution to the matter. The child does not have the developmental capabilities to objectively process the information associated with the spilled milk. The young child is unlikely to have the skills to conclude that this accident will probably result in nothing more than a minor inconvenience. The spilled milk can be easily cleaned up. This child experiences the spilled milk as something larger – a failure to please Mom or Dad. The parent's angry reaction leaves the child closer to an understanding that there is no safety in making mistakes. Mistakes and vulnerabilities are shameful, uncomfortable and certainly not something that are processed and explored. Mistakes should be hidden, covered-up, and lied about. Even with an event as minor as a spilled glass of milk we can see the development of a subtle pattern that can be passed from one generation to another. Each time this behavior is reinforced, each time the child's natural vulnerability is criticized or attacked, the child's motivation to lie will become stronger. Again, when there is no safety in processing mistakes the child will fill the void with less helpful skills – such as lying.

The pattern of lying usually starts during early childhood and progresses to a more sophisticated and destructive level during adult years. When I work with adolescents or adults who tend to lie, I always make it a point to explore the motivating processes at work. When I discover a lie I tend to explore why being truthful, or being forthright, is so difficult. This process tends to be very uncomfortable for the person who lied, however, a certain pattern almost always emerges from this line of questioning. More often than not, adolescents and adults will lie to, 1) avoid the emotional discomfort that may be experienced when there is a difference in opinion or perspective and, 2) to avoid disappointing the person to whom the lie is directed. Rarely do I come across lies that, once explored in detail, are motivated by other factors. People tend to lie when there is great discomfort with processing vulnerabilities and differences. A person may be motivated to lie when he or she lacks the skill to create emotional safety when differences of opinion or perspective exist. Persons who lie tend to be doing the best they can with the tools they have – tools that were developed early in their lives.

Do not attack a child exposing vulnerabilities. This will create further distance. The artful parent will recognize vulnerabilities and address them in a mutually supportive manner.

86. Understanding the wide spectrum of relating possibilities is fundamental to the art of parenting.

Let's begin this discussion with a simple statement: We are born with a tremendous capacity to relate with others. I believe this to be a fact and would assert that even a small baby has a built in ability to communicate a majority of the emotions found in Appendix B. That's right, a six month-old baby has the ability to skillfully communicate literally hundreds of emotions. For example, if I were to take all the emotions found in Appendix B and arrange them from the most uncomfortable to the most comfortable, we would have a pretty good example of the broad emotional spectrum. Now, consider a baby's ability to relate to its parents. Are parents able to determine if the baby is feeling *hungry, cold, insecure, frightened*, or *threatened*? Are parents able to determine if the baby is feeling *satisfied, warm, secure*, and *safe*? Can a baby be *grumpy, manipulative*, or *sulky*? How about *lonely, merry, playful*, or *confused*? Of course. When we take the time to think about it, we discover that we are born with an amazing capacity to relate emotionally with others. The baby does not communicate these emotions with words, but rather through very specific body language. There are an infinite number of facial gestures, body movements, and sounds that help the baby let us know these emotions are present, that they are influencing the baby, and also helping the baby interpret his or her environment. Now, my question is, *if we are born with a natural capacity to relate to others through the use of these emotions, what happens as we grow and mature*? Do we lose this capacity?

When a couple comes to my office wanting to work on their marriage, I will often ask them how they feel about a particular subject or event. Other times I will ask one or the other to help me understand their perspective regarding an issue of concern in their relationship. More often than not, I am met with very brief and limited responses. A six month-old baby is able to demonstrate the 16 emotions just cited, yet it seems as if the spectrum of relating possibilities becomes limited or restricted with age. When I ask an adult about their feeling rarely am I met with a response such as, "You know, when she calls me a *stupid jerk* I really feel *hurt, confused, irritated*, and *alone*." A 6 month-old baby is able to communicate his or her emotions to me without inhibition! What happened to the adult's ability to do the same?

A restricted ability to relate with others is what keeps therapists in business and is the central tenant to this Parenting Assumption. We are born with an amazing capacity to relate with others. Unfortunately, this ability can atrophy or fail to develop if the parenting we receive does not leave it well exercised. This is terribly unfortunate, because as our ability to understand the wide spectrum of relating possibilities expands, so does our capacity to excel in so much of what we do

– being a parent, spouse, partner, or significant other, dealing with adversity under a variety of circumstances and contributing to a healthy work environment, to name a few. It is the artful parent who will consider topics such as Basics, History, Balance, Safety, Paradox, Fear, and Skill in an effort to reclaim and expand one's ability to relate with others using the wide spectrum of relating possibilities.

87. Children need not understand the wisdom of parenting when it is just, for they will surely benefit. When unjust, children will neither understand nor benefit from parenting.

History has demonstrated that wars have been waged because political leaders believed they possessed righteous and just thought. History has also demonstrated that entire populations can be repressed if one's political leaders believe they have sole access to undoubted wisdom or superior insight. Leaders who believe they are *just* in their causes and beliefs may feel entitled to keep the citizenry in the dark and ignorant. History has demonstrated over and over again that these conditions result in mass suffering and a perpetuation of subjected populations. Family systems are by no means immune to these same conditions and the resulting consequences. In families, children have suffered because a parent believed he or she was the authority of righteousness.

When there are no checks and balances within a political structure or a family system the subjected – populations of a country or children within a family – are vulnerable. If one's actions are truly *just,* the wisdom behind these actions is less important than the actions themselves. But how do we know our actions, be they political or related to parenting, are *just?* How do we incorporate checks and balances into our consciousness so as to ensure our actions do not leave our children vulnerable? In parenting, **just** should be interpreted and understood to include *empathy, intimacy,* and *emotional process.* If the these concepts are incorporated into one's moral fiber, one's character, and one's interactions, parenting will likely be *just.* When these elements are weak parenting will be *unjust.* These are basic concepts from which both parents and politicians might benefit.

88. Continuity of just rewards and punishments is vital. Evaluation of unjust rewards and punishment is required for artful parenting.

We have explored the concepts of *just* and *unjust* in several previous Parenting Assumptions (see 1, 10, 24, 29, 83, and 87). A *just* reward and punishment distinguishes itself from an *unjust* reward or punishment by the degree to which the parent considers the perspective of the child being punished or rewarded. It is also defined by the degree to which the matter stimulating the reward or punishment is processed between the parent and child. *Just* and *unjust* are therefore influenced by matters of degree and frequency. That is, a parent who only occasionally considers the child's perspective and infrequently processes the thoughts and emotions surrounding rewards and punishments, will likely be less effective than the parent who routinely and frequently engages the child in this manner.

Continuity of parental input ensures the message of *just* rewards and punishments is consistently reinforced. A parent who frequently shifts between *just* and *unjust* rewards and punishments tends to leave the child unsure, resulting in weaker connections between a child's thoughts, emotions, and behaviors. The parental input, rewards, and punishments will have less impact on stimulating desired behavior. The importance of continuity of *just* rewards and punishments is also very important to the overall level of intimacy between parent and child. Rewards and punishments that are *just* promote greater degrees of intimacy in the parent-child relationship. Rewards and punishments that are *unjust* tend to move the parent-child relationship away from greater intimacy.

As a parent becomes increasingly aware of and comfortable with administering *just* rewards and punishments, he or she will likely experience those which are *unjust* as uncomfortable and unsettling. Interactions that fail consider the child's perspective and lack a significant degree of parent-child processing will stand out to the parent as *unjust*.

Identifying and evaluating these *unjust* interactions is an excellent way for parents to improve the overall quality of their parenting while simultaneously working toward greater intimacy in the parent-child relationship. Helpful and healthy parenting trends will emerge as parents risk change and overcome the discomfort that often accompanies this parental self-evaluation. This is an important element in developing and improving crucial parenting skills. The parent who realizes that the brief discomfort often associated with self-evaluation is well worth the benefits passed to one's children, is grasping the idea of artful parenting.

On several occasions I have stated that parents are by no means perfect. Parents are fallible and will, from time to time, make mistakes. Parents will certainly, on occasion, administer rewards and punishments that are *unjust*. This is unavoidable. Luckily, children grow and develop in respect to the parenting trends they experience rather than the individual experiences they encounter. A child who experiences his or her parents as administering *just* rewards and punishments more often than not will be relatively unscathed by the occasional parental mistake or oversight. Children recognize and respond to the trend of *just* rewards and punishments. *Continuity of just rewards and punishments is vital. Evaluation of unjust rewards and punishment is required for artful parenting.*

89. When parenting is weak, the children are without direction, confused and ultimately insubordinate.

This Parenting Assumption speaks of a subject that many parents find very uncomfortable. The subject is *parentificaiton* and the discussion to follow may be tough medicine for some parents. This Assumption was placed near the conclusion of this book for a very specific reason. I hope that by this point in our exploration of *Systemic Parenting*, the reader is able to recognize the significant influence parents have on their child's successes, failures, and overall development. I hope you are able to recognize the strong association between factors such as, the efforts invested into the parenting process and application of parenting skills, to the degree of success and emotional health experienced by a child.

Many family therapists have come to realize that the vast majority of children who act out, who are insubordinate, or who fail to excel often do so as a result of the parenting they receive and the circumstances surrounding their family system. On the other hand, parenting is also to be credited for children who experience healthy relationships, who succeed, and who excel. Unfortunately, many parents tend to shy away from this conclusion. Many parents would rather understand their child's undesirable behaviors as flaws in the child, or as a result of factors external to the family, rather than deficits in their parenting skills and knowledge. This is something few parents will openly admit. However, the truth in this statement becomes strikingly clear when we contrast families who raise healthy and successful children with families whose children struggle and experience lesser degrees of success. An example of one such family was presented in the introduction of this book.

If you will recall, I presented a scenario from my practice that demonstrated the degree to which a parent's actions or inaction will influence whether or not a child succeeds and excels. The parents of a teenage boy asked me to meet with and treat their son. It seemed that his behavior had become quite a problem for the family. He was punching holes in the walls of their house. He was destroying doors and cabinets in fits of rage and he was beginning to experiment with drugs and alcohol. The boy's social network was deteriorating, he was openly insubordinate to his parents, and he was doing poorly in school. These are a few striking characteristics of a child struggling in his efforts to succeed. The parents initially requested that I meet with the boy alone and to fix whatever was ailing him. They made it quite clear that treatment should occur between the boy and a therapist, in the absence of the parents. From the parent's perspective this was the boy's problem. They were resistant to the idea of being present and participating in the therapy process. Connections between their son's behaviors and the parenting he received were just too uncomfortable for these parents to consider.

Family therapists encounter this reaction almost daily in their offices. Parents will place responsibility elsewhere for the problems in the family. Deflection of responsibility may provide parents with a brief sense of relief or a temporary reprieve. However, the process of shifting responsibility for a child's problems or failures external to the parenting he or she receives only results in a continuation or worsening of the undesired symptoms. After a little encouragement, the parents cited in the introduction chose to participate in family therapy and in short order, realized that severe and lingering marital problems were leaving them too preoccupied and distracted to parent well. The boy's troubling behaviors were primarily symptoms of their preoccupation. The child was being destructively parentified.

Destructive parentification occurs when there is an inappropriate reversal in the balance of crucial parenting responsibilities. The primary goal of childhood is to grow, to develop and to become prepared for adult living. It is the responsibility of the parents to ensure that the child has the best possible chance of succeeding and being adequately prepared for the challenges he or she will eventually face. When parenting is weak, or the parents are chronically distracted, children will fill the void by assuming responsibility for their own growth and development. The child is, by default, inappropriately placed in the role of parent. It is unrealistic to expect a child to have the developmental skills and cognitive insight to be successful when burdened with this responsibility. There will always be less healthy and less desirable consequences. The consequences in this example were the boy's destructive behaviors and decreased chances of future success and healthy relationships.

After the boy's parents began the process of addressing their marital problems, he responded in a very predictable manner. As the parents' preoccupation with the rifts in their marriage lessened they were freed to assume their responsibilities as parents. As these responsibilities were shifted back to the parents and off the boy's shoulders, his less desirable behaviors abated. This dramatic change occurred with very little attention being devoted to, or focused on, his troubling behavior. The boy's actions were simply symptoms of his struggles with parentification. The boy had little insight as to why he was acting in such a destructive manner. His cognitive processes and developmental skills were not sufficiently mature for him to formulate sophisticated insight to the problems in the family and the pressure he was encountering. If I were to ask him, *why are you punching walls, why are you destroying the house, why are you experimenting with drugs, and why are you so insubordinate to your parents?* he would probably be at a loss for words. I would likely get a response such as *"I don't know, just seems like the right thing to do. I was frustrated?"* This is why merely working with the child who is symptomatic will usually produce poor results. The child is responding to conditions within the family system over which he had little control. A therapist might assist the child curb some of the undesirable behaviors by working with him individually. However, the underlying and causative conditions resulting in the behaviors will remain and the child will have been inappropriately faulted. The consequences of this particular course of action can be devastating to ones self-esteem and ability to relate to others in an intimate and safe manner.

The example from the introduction showed us a teenager who responded to parentification in a pretty dramatic manner. Most instances of parentification are less obvious and usually go without much notice. However, the consequences of these less dramatic instances of parentification are by no means less severe. A child who is raised in an environment with little emphasis given to promoting intimacy, empathy, and emotional process will be destructively parentified. That is, the child is made responsible for defining and incorporating these very important aspects of human interaction into his or her relationships with others. Without strong parental support and guidance in this undertaking, the child will struggle.

This issue surfaces over and over again in my practice of marriage and family therapy. From time to time I am tasked with helping an adult struggling to establish and maintain healthy relationships in his or her life. My work with these people frequently requires that I help them make connections between early instances of destructive parentification and their current struggles. These adults were, at some point in their earlier lives, tasked with defining for themselves those crucial systemic components, intimacy, empathy and emotional process. In effect, they were self-mentored. My job as their therapist was to assist these individuals reverse the consequences of early parentificaiton by exploring the topics of intimacy, empathy, and emotional process in a safe and supportive manner.

When speaking of parentificaiton it is important to make a distinction between degrees of familial responsibilities and destructive parentification. Remember, destructive parentification results from an inappropriate reversal in the balance of crucial parenting responsibilities. What about families where both parents work? How about families where a parent or sibling has a disability that requires a significant amount of attention? Some children will be called upon to help out with a family business. Are children raised under these conditions being destructively parentified? Not necessarily. Additional family responsibilities can be placed on a child without ill effects. A child may have less time with his or her parents if both work. A child may be tasked with assisting in the care of a disabled sibling or parent. A child may very well be required to help out with a family business after school and on weekends. These circumstances will not result in destructive parentificaiton if the parents support healthy development of those crucial systemic components of intimacy, empathy, emotional process, and safety. In fact, these experiences, these additional responsibilities, can often result in tremendous opportunities for growth if accompanied by a parental emphasis on intimacy, empathy, and emotional process.

A child emerging from a family where both parents work and have less time with their children but emphasize these crucial systemic components is more likely to be healthier than a child emerging from a family with a stay-at-home parent and little emphasis on these components. The same is true in families where a child is tasked with additional responsibilities that accompany owning a family business or if the family has a disabled or special needs member. Children will emerge from these circumstances very healthy if the parenting they receive emphasizes intimacy, empathy, and emotional process in the parent-child relationship.

At the beginning of our exploration of this Assumption I stated that the subject of parentification may be tough medicine for some parents. It is tough for many parents to accept that within the parent-child relationship lies the authority and opportunity to guide a child in the direction of emotional health and happiness or confusion, failure, and conflict. The former direction requires the parent to be skilled in exploration and application of intimacy, empathy, and emotional process. The latter direction requires the parent to externalize problems – blaming the child or factors external to the family for a child's failure disobedience or problems.

Throughout this book I have referred to concepts of *family systems* and viewing a *broader picture* of parenting. That it, I have attempted to communicate that it is the interaction of many variables that influence a child's overall cognitive and emotional development. These variables will, in turn help define the child's ultimate areas of success and failure. Now, in the previous paragraphs I asserted that it is parenting that is the primary determinant of a child's success or failure. I do not believe this assertion is necessarily contrary to the idea of taking a systemic perspective – looking at a larger picture of parenting.

External variables are surely influential to a child's ultimate success. For example, the quality of the school system the child attends will certainly be an important variable. Factors such as opportunities for exposure to cultural diversity and the arts, access to modern technologies, and the level of physical safety within one's community, will all play influential roles in the child's developmental path. However, it is the parent who has the power and authority to take advantage of, and/or respond to, the conditions, strengths and limitations of the larger environment. The parent whose child attends a school with a poor academic record can compensate for this community deficit by spending additional time reviewing homework, reading with, tutoring, and encouraging the child. A parent who resides in an isolated community can enrich a child's life through exposure to creative storytelling and books. The parent is by no means a passive participant to the parenting process. *When parenting is weak, the children are without direction, confused and ultimately insubordinate.*

90. When parenting is repressive, the child will be distressed and placed in a martyrdom role.

I believe this is a fitting Assumption to conclude our exploration of *Systemic Parenting.* We have certainly covered a lot of territory in the previous 8 chapters and 90 Assumptions. We have explored many common challenges facing parents and touched upon ideas that will hopefully help parents see a broader picture, *a systemic understanding of the parenting process.* There are several key elements or concepts that must be embraced and integrated into the parenting process if one hopes to achieve this systemic understanding. These key elements have been mentioned or referenced in nearly every Parenting Assumption. What are these crucial elements and concepts? If you haven't identified them thus far here they are:

* Intimacy

* Empathy

* Emotional Processing

* Emotional Safety

These concepts have been explored from a variety of angles in the preceding chapters. Interwoven in these discussions have been numerous other ideas, points and suggestions – all designed to highlight the importance of the above.[47] The examples, stories and vignettes scattered throughout *Systemic Parenting* were intended to help you explore these concepts from a variety of perspectives. Perhaps a few of the examples may have seemed foreign to you. They may have seemed too dramatic, too severe, or even troubling. Other examples might have seemed as if they were taken directly from your family or parenting experiences. Hopefully, these examples, regardless of how closely they relate to your particular experiences, have helped you recognize the crucial role intimacy, empathy, emotional processing, and emotional safety play in the overall parenting process. These concepts are universally applicable regardless of one's financial status, one's race or religion, where one lives, what political party one may belong to, or the structure of one's family. They are *systemic laws* of healthy parenting and apply to every parent-child relationship.

Many parents will experience a certain amount of discomfort the first time these systemic laws of parenting are considered and explored, especially if these concepts are new to their particular family system. Exploring the connections between intimacy, empathy, emotional processing, and emotional safety and parenting successes or failures requires one to look inward, at how one was parented and how one parents. It requires parents to take responsibility for the parenting process, and to accept the challenges that accompany parenting well. Again, this is not always a comfortable process for parents. At times it just seems easier to look outward – to external or societal variables – to explain parenting successes or failures.

Children from *broken homes* are commonly cited as being more likely to get into trouble than children from *intact* homes. Is it merely the *broken home* that caused the child to go astray or are there other influential variables at work? Does the simple fact that a child lives in an *intact* home guarantee a healthy child? Children living in *single parent households* are also cited as being significantly disadvantaged, vulnerable to behavioral problems, and less likely to succeed. Is it merely the fact that there is *one parent* in the home that results in problematic behaviors and lesser degrees of success or are there other factors to be considered? What about children raised in homes with gay or lesbian parents? What factors truly impact the overall health and success of these children?

Peer influences, the internet, the availability of drugs and alcohol, popular culture, and the state of moral decline in society are also frequently cited as issues that lead to less desirable behaviors from our children as well as failures of parenting. Those who choose to focus on these outward, structural, or secondary variables might be well intentioned. They are seeking explanations and solutions for very real problems. However, when we stand back and look at the larger systemic picture, they are missing the boat.

Examples abound of successful and healthy people emerging from *single parent* or *broken homes*. Many very healthy and successful individuals have been raised in homes with gay or lesbian parents. The majority of children succeed in spite of popular culture, peer pressures, internet influences, the availability of drugs and alcohol, and what some refer to as deteriorating morals within our society. How does one explain this? Why do some children succeed while others struggle? I am by no means stating that the family structures and external influences just mentioned are desirable or beneficial to the parenting process. What I am saying is that the importance and influence of these factors is dwarfed by the influence of the core systemic elements previously mentioned. It is rare for a healthy and successful individual to emerge from a family, regardless of how it is structured, that lacks emotional intimacy, an understanding of empathy, an environment were emotions are freely processed, and where emotional safety is promoted. On the other hand, it is rare to see troubled individuals emerge from families, regardless of how they are structured, that emphasize intimacy, empathy, emotional process, and emotional safety.

This Parenting Assumption is pretty direct and straight forward. An environment that lacks intimacy, empathy, emotional processing, and emotional safety *is repressive* to healthy emotional development in children. The human spirit is not nurtured in the absence of these variables, severely retarding a child's ability to reach his or her emotional and relational potential. The quality of the parenting one receives is the single most important factor in determining how we will interpret and interact with our environment. For example, our parenting will determine if we see the world through cynical or optimistic glasses. Our parenting will determine if we are compassionate and warm or closed-off and emotionally elusive. With such importance placed squarely on the shoulders of the parenting process it is easy to understand how a child can become a *martyr* to his or her parenting.

I have mentioned on several occasions in the preceding pages that children are naturally loyal to their parents. This loyalty can make examining or questioning the parenting we receive difficult, uncomfortable, and highly unlikely. As a result, it can leave us subjected to less healthy patterns of behavior and interaction styles that pass from generation to generation. These patterns become familiar, known, and comfortable. Changing them in ways that would benefit us can be a very difficult process, even when one experiences repetitive failures and unpleasant consequences as a result of these patterns. One is truly a martyr to their parenting when they experience painful consequences or fail to thrive, yet feel prohibited from making healthy and helpful changes.[48]

Having options to improve the quality of one's living and relationships by increasing attention to intimacy, empathy, emotional processing, and creating emotional safety, yet choosing not to is a great misfortune. Healthy and helpful change is possible but tends to be uncomfortable and difficult to implement. *Systemic Parenting* has been structured with this in mind. The 90 Parenting Assumptions contained in *Systemic Parenting* are designed to help parents gradually recognize the importance of these core systemic concepts and to provide a model for making gradual change. It is important to realize that few parents are likely to make changes in their lives that result in *rapid* or profound improvements in their parenting. I am always weary of parents who arrive at new or ultimate truths overnight. Increasing one's understanding of, and ability to promote greater intimacy, empathy, process and safety is a gradual process. Shifts occur ever so slightly.[49] Hopefully, the Assumption format presented in *Systemic Parenting* will plant seeds in the minds of parents then provide them with a helpful resource that can be visited again and again. I hope that, over time, changes will be integrated into your parent-child relationship that will benefit all family members, present and future.

Appendix A

Basics History Balance Safety Paradox Fear Skill Art

1. If you know yourself and the basic needs of childhood, you will likely be successful in your parenting.

2. If you know the basic needs of childhood but not yourself, parenthood will likely be a struggle.

3. If you know neither yourself nor the basic needs of childhood, both the child and parent will likely suffer.

Basics **History** Balance Safety Paradox Fear Skill Art

4. Although most people can see the outward and obvious aspects of parenting, few truly risk change by looking inward and backward. One of the fears associated with this task relates to the certain discomfort likely to be encountered. Both child and parent will greatly benefit from risking change and overcoming fear associated with befriending one's personal, relational, and family histories.

5. A parent examining the relationship he or she had with his or her parents, and the relationship they had with their parents, will likely be confronted with grief and enlightenment. Only then can the parent give to their children by justly replacing the less helpful with helpful.

Basics History **Balance** Safety Paradox Fear Skill Art

6. Parents need emotional alliances. To be isolated or alone in this task weakens the experience for parent and child.

7. *The parent who is emotionally depleted, more often than not, is vulnerable as is his or her child.*

8. *Parents finding themselves short tempered are likely fatigued.*

9. *Too frequent rewards indicate that the parent is at the end of his or her emotional resources; too frequent punishments that he or she is in acute distress.*

10. *Employment of kindness is but half of nurturance. Employment of limits and consequences is but half of discipline.*

11. *Parents finding themselves in conflict with their child without the ability to reflect and flex will often feel fatigued, ineffective, and defeated.*

12. *Parents must trust each other to make decisions that consider both parental perspectives. It is often prudent to delay action until the other parent is present on large matters of parenting. However, on small matters, waiting for the other may be likened to waiting for permission to put out a smoldering fire. When one's permission finally arrives, nothing will remain but ashes.*

A balance between the former and latter is essential.

13. *Too often parents seek outside antagonists rather than focusing inward when faced with a parental challenge. It is often familiar and comfortable to look outward rather than to evaluate one's own influence. Balance between internal and external antagonists is most important.*

14. *The parent distant from the child's educational process, extracurricular opportunities/ accomplishments, and peers will find himself rapidly distanced from the child and always struggling to regain a connection. The child's emotional reservoirs will be depleted attempting to engage the parent. Neither will likely excel.*

15. *There are fair and unfair situations associated with living. Parent and child experience both in a similar manner.*

16. *If your decision is already made, it remains important to consider the child's perspective. For if the child feels his or her perspective has been considered, anger will be accompanied with respect and*

feelings of being cared for vis-à-vis anger and defiance if his or her perspective remain unconsidered.

17. *Anger is a just emotion. A child learns how to manage this emotion solely from the parent(s).*

18. *Pay heed to nourishing the child's intellect, creative forces, and spirit. Yet, in so doing, do not unnecessarily fatigue the child.*

Basics History Balance *Safety* Paradox Fear Skill Art

19. *"Accessible" is when both parent and child can approach each other with near equal ease.*

20. *"Engaging" is when life perspectives are mutually considered.*

21. *"Entrapping" is when the parent portrays accessibility yet is unprepared or unable to be consistent in this manner.*

22. *A "constricted" parent limits the child's exposure to the parent's emotional self. This is a great misfortune.*

23. *When parents become accustomed to the **just role of parent** they will certainly administer rewards and punishments in an enlightened manner. This is but one measure that facilitates safety.*

24. *Children act out for a variety of reasons. The artful parent will distinguish between behaviors attributed to trial and error (growth) and the child's response to unnatural, unjust, and/or incongruent situations. Discerning between the former and latter is paramount for safety.*

25. *Those skilled in parenting realize the child is vulnerable in nearly every respect. The artful parent will support these vulnerabilities in a manner which leaves the child self-assured and safe.*

26. *The skilled parent will address the child's anxieties without threatening his or her sense of safety, security, and well being.*

27. *When a mistake is made and the parent responds by focusing on the negative rather than the growth aspect, the child's sense of safety has been assaulted.*

28. *Parents are the protectors of their children. If this protection is all embracing, is approached with continuity, yet provides for*

maneuverability, flexibility, and individuation the child will grow strong.

29. Parents who are able to unite in matters of parenting will have children who feel secure and able to develop a harmonious existence.

30. A house with fewer resources and clear structure is greater than a house with unlimited resources and loosely defined structure. The former promotes safety and confidence; the latter promotes false security and arrogance.

31. During the occasional uproar associated with parenting, all may seem chaotic, yet those skilled in the art of parenting will find little disorder when knowledgeable about fundamental structure.

32. Continuity in most aspects of parenting is essential for safety to emerge. However, this by no means implies that a parent should avoid evaluating and altering his or her method of relating, for this will be interpreted as honest and genuine by the child of an artful parent.

33. In parenting, trust and safety outweigh respect.

34. Children experiencing their parents as accessible & engaging will feel safe. Children experiencing their parents as distant, constricted, and entrapping will feel unsafe.

35. When there are no consistent rules to guide children, familial disorder will prosper. This sense of disorder will be all-too-common in other aspects of the child's later life.

36. An enlightened parent is cautious to avoid rash actions and reactions. In so doing, the children are made to feel secure, and trust is preserved.

Basics History Balance Safety *Paradox* Fear Skill Art

37. Parents exposing a child to their emotional selves are acting from strength and taking great strides to prepare their son or daughter for adult relationships.

38. Parents who invest themselves by taking emotional risks will likely experience rewarding long-term parent-child relationships.

39. *Before entering parenthood, prospective parents' may benefit from considering the emotional resources required. If the parent's resources are depleted prior to entering this venture the child's resources will likely be exhausted attempting to fill the void. If the parent's emotional reservoirs are frequently replenished through means parallel to that of the child, the child will be better able to challenge living without unnecessary constraint.*

40. *The child who **acts out** is often seeking safety and security. When the parent encounters the "acting out" child, responding in a way that promotes emotional safety may be experienced as paradoxical and unfamiliar.*

41. *Communications are essential and should never be cut off. The angry parent can still communicate in an effective manner. The angry child still has open ears.*

42. *Enhancing development of the child's uniqueness is more helpful than implanting your own. The former leads to individuality, strength, and trusting relationships. Both the child and parent will be rewarded. The latter promotes confusion, dependence and indecision. Initially, the parent may be rewarded yet both child and parent will eventually suffer.*

43. *Seek to find the child's strengths and interests. Encourage those that may differ from your own. Both parent and child will grow together in this process.*

44. *Growth can be promoted in the midst of personal and family tragedy. This should always be remembered as a paradoxical part of living.*

45. *Care for the child by caring for yourself – paradoxical thoughts are often necessary in artful parenting.*

46. *When the child is in a constant state of distress the parent should look inward.*

47. *A loving parent who finds difficulty establishing and enforcing limits, boundaries, and consequences may have a narrow view of love.*

48. *One who only uses favor to show love ultimately finds respect waning.*

49.*The concept of wealth, to children, often varies from the parents' understanding of the same. Often parents can learn from their childhood and children about wealth.*

Basics History Balance Safety Paradox *Fear* Skill Art

50.*In parenting there are no constant conditions. The parent who finds comfort in maintaining the status quo is promoting emotional stagnation. The parent who finds comfort with fluidity is promoting maturation and growth.*

51.*If problems are left un-addressed parental fatigue sets in – greatly hindering the ability to nurture.*

52.*Parents who prepare for life-cycle shifts in advance will be at ease and competent.*

53.*Those who are encouraged to grow during life-cycle shifts will excel. Those encouraged to support or maintain status quo will stagnate and regress.*

54.*War is based upon deception – not parenting. Children recognize deception even when parents do not. Children can handle honesty even when parents cannot.*

55.*When you suspect deceit, allow the child an opportunity to experience consequences that are equitable and fair. In this manner you will not likely fold when there are challenges and you experience anxiety.*

Basics History Balance Safety Paradox Fear *Skill* Art

56.*To understand process without being distracted by content is the acme of parental skill.*

57.*When being engaged with hostility, block the attempt by addressing process.*

58.*If emotionally depleted, do not engage in hostilities. Withdraw, reflect and recompose.*

59.*To recognize the obvious is not the acme of parenting. Rather, it is recognition of the hidden which determines skill.*

60. *The skillful parent rarely misses an opportunity to enrich the child's living.*

61. *A skill of parenting lies in the identification of the unlimited family resource.*

62. *A child is safest when he or she is not required to assume a defensive position more often than not. A skilled parent is able to recognize and shatter the need for defense when it is encountered.*

63. *Parents who avoid entrenchment in emotional reactivity will be wiser when confronted with challenge and more apt to facilitate trust.*

64. *There is no disgrace in modifying parenting tactics that are ineffective.*

65. *Clearly communicate consequences that are to be enforced by the parental hierarchy.*

66. *If children are punished without open process there will be further disobedience and greater distance.*

67. *If threats of punishment are not enforced when called for, later attempts to effectively discipline will grow exponentially more difficult.*

68. *When little attention is devoted to communicating a moral foundation other aspects of parenting will be severely hampered and without enlightenment.*

69. *The parent who is confident in his or her ability to relate unhindered with the child will be a pillar to the child's ascension to adulthood.*

70. *Parents intervene when it is advantageous. However, it is often advantageous to do nothing. The latter is the most difficult to do wisely.*

Basics History Balance Safety Paradox Fear Skill Art

71. *The parent who understands that small interactions are as important as the larger ones will be more effective in all matters of parenting.*

72. *Parenting requires one to follow the "situation of the child."*

73. *The momentum of growth is with the child – this is his or her responsibility. Timing of the experiences he or she encounters is with the parent – this is his or her/their responsibility. Parents need to constantly remind themselves of this.*

74. *The parent who prepares in advance (proactively) will be at ease. The parent who approaches parenting during or after the fact (reactively) will be rushed and weary – making less helpful moves.*

75. *The reactive parent likely finds proactivity foreign and uncomfortable.*

76. *Those skilled in the art of parenting engage their children on difficult matters rather than being engaged on said matters by the child's actions/inaction.*

77. *Children are programmed to grow and challenge. When stagnant, it is the parents' position to promote movement.*

78. *Recognize your child's style of action and reaction. Rather than attempting to change the child, change the methods of acting and reacting in yourself. The child will naturally follow suite. This is tremendously difficult as it is more comfortable (less effective) to look outward for antagonists.*

79. *The artful parent reduces shame associated with weakness while simultaneously reinforcing strengths. This is the essence character development.*

80. *Always be reflective and cognizant of your impact.*

81. *Always turn misfortune to advantage. Not to do so promotes cynicism. To do so promotes optimism.*

82. *Allow space and time to consider and reflect. The impulsive parent seeking immediate gratification will hear what he wishes and experience what he fears.*

83. *There are times when children should not obey their parents – this may be indicative of growth and should be recognized as such. The artful parent recognizes growth from deceit.*

84. *Weak is the parent who intimidates the child – this wearies the child by keeping him constantly anxious and mistrusting his own emotions. This stifles growth and exploration. This parent is powerless in the grand picture of parenting and will eventually*

*lose any hope of receiving the long-term benefits of an intimate
relationship with his or her children.*

85. *Do not attack a child exposing vulnerabilities. This will create
further distance. The artful parent will recognize vulnerabilities
and address them in a mutually supportive manner.*

86. *Understanding the wide spectrum of relating possibilities is
fundamental to the art of parenting.*

87. *Children need not understand the wisdom of parenting when it is
just, for they will surely benefit. When **unjust**, children will neither
understand nor benefit from parenting.*

88. *Continuity of **just** rewards and punishments is vital. Evaluation of
unjust rewards and punishment is required for artful parenting.*

89. *When parenting is weak, the children are without direction, confused
and ultimately insubordinate.*

90. *When parenting is repressive, the child will be distressed and placed
in a martyrdom role.*

Appendix B

A Selected List of Emotions, Feelings, and Reactions

Abandoned
Absent-minded
Absorbed
Abused
Aching
Active
Adamant
Affable
Affectionate
Afflicted
Afraid
Aggravated
Aggressive
Alarmed
Alive
Alone
Ambivalent
Amiable
Angry
Annoyed
Anxious
Apathetic
Appalled
Appealing
Apprehensive
Ardent
Aroused

Ashamed
Assertive
Astounded
Attractive
Avid
Awed
Awkward
Bad
Beaten
Belittled
Belligerent
Betrayed
Bewildered
Bitter
Blah
Blunted
Bold
Bored
Brave
Breathless
Brisk
Buoyant
Burdened
Burnt
Calm
Cantankerous
Captivated
Captive

Carefree
Cautious
Censured
Challenged
Charmed
Cheerful
Choked–up
Churlish
Clammy
Clear
Clever
Close
Closed
Clumsy
Cold
Combative
Comfortable
Compassionate
Complacent
Complete
Concerned
Confident
Confused
Connected
Contemptuous
Content
Contentious
Controlled
Convivial
Cooperative
Courageous
Courteous
Cowardly
Crafty
Creative
Criticized
Cross
Crude

Cruel
Crushed
Curious
Dainty
Daring
Deceitful
Deceived
Defeated
Defiant
Degraded
Dejected
Dependant
Depressed
Desirous
Despair
Destructive
Determined
Dirty
Disappointed
Discarded
Disconnected
Discontent
Discontented
Discouraged
Disenfranchised
Disgraced
Disgusted
Disheartened
Dishonest
Disinterest
Dismal
Dismayed
Displeased
Disrespected
Distant
Distracted
Distraught
Distressed

Distrustful
Disturbed
Divorced
Doubtful
Dreadful
Dreary
Dubious
Dull
Dumbfounded
Dysfunctional
Eager
Earnest
Ecstatic
Edgy
Elated
Electrified
Elevated
Embarrassed
Empty
Encouraged
Energetic
Engrossed
Enraged
Enthusiastic
Entitled
Envious
Euphoric
Evasive
Evil
Excited
Exhausted
Exhilarated
Fascinated
Fastidious
Faulty
Fearful
Fearless
Festive

Fidgety
Firm
Flat
Foolish
Forgiving
Frantic
Friendly
Frightened
Frisky
Frustrated
Fuming
Functional
Funny
Furious
Generous
Genial
Giddy
Glad
Gloomy
Glum
Good
Grateful
Greedy
Gross
Grumpy
Guilty
Gutless
Happy
Hard
Hardy
Heartbroken
Heavy-hearted
Helpless
Heroic
Hesitant
High
Hilarious
Hindered

Hollow
Honored
Hopeful
Hopeless
Horny
Horrified
Humble
Hurt
Hypocritical
Hysterical
Ignored
Ill-at-Ease
Immobilized
Impatient
Imposed Upon
Impulsive
Inadequate
In–a–rut
Indecisive
Independent
Indignant
Infantilized
Inflamed
Informed
Infuriated
Injured
Inquisitive
Insecure
Insistent
Inspired
Insulted
Intent
Interested
In-the-dumps
Intimate
Intimidated
Intrepid
Intrigued

Irate
Irritable
Irritated
Isolated
Jealous
Jittery
Jolly
Jovial
Joyous
Jubilant
Keen
Let-down
Light
Lighthearted
Livid
Lonely
Lovable
Love struck
Lovesick
Loving
Low
Loyal
Lucid
Lustful
Manic
Manipulated
Manipulative
Masochistic
Melancholy
Merry
Mischievous
Miserable
Misled
Mixed-up
Moody
Morose
Mournful
Mystified

Naughty
Nauseated
Nervous
Numb
Obnoxious
Obstinate
Obstructed
Offended
Open
Oppressed
Optimistic
Out-of-sorts
Outraged
Overwhelmed
Pained
Panicky
Paralyzed
Paranoid
Passionate
Pathetic
Peaceful
Perceptive
Perplexed
Personable
Perverse
Pessimistic
Petrified
Phony
Physical
Pitiful
Played-out
Playful
Pleasant
Pleased
Powerless
Preoccupied
Pressured
Prickly

Proud
Provoked
Put-off
Puzzled
Questioning
Quiet
Reassured
Regretful
Rejected
Relaxed
Relieved
Remorseful
Repressed
Repulsed
Resentful
Rested
Right
Risqué
Rude
Sad
Sadistic
Safe
Sarcastic
Satisfied
Secure
Seductive
Selfish
Sensitive
Serene
Serious
Sexy
Shaky
Shameful
Shocked
Shut down
Sick
Silly
Sincere

Skeptical
Slow
Sluggish
Small
Smart
Smug
Sneaky
Soft
Somber
Sorrowful
Sorry
Sparkling
Spirited
Spiteful
Spoiled
Stalled
Startled
Stressed
Stretched
Strong
Stubborn
Stuck
Stultified
Stumped
Stunned
Submissive
Suffering
Sulky
Sullen
Sully
Surly
Surprised
Suspicious
Sweaty
Sympathetic
Tainted
Taut

Tearful
Tenacious
Tender
Tense
Terrified
Threatened
Thrilled
Thwarted
Timid
Tired
Toiling
Torn
Tortured
Tragic
Trapped
Trusted
Trusting
Two-faced
Ugly
Unbelieving
Uncertain
Unclean
Uncomfortable
Understood
Unhappy
Unsatisfied
Upset
Uptight
Used
Useless
Vacant
Violated
Violent
Vivacious
Vulgar
Warm
Wavering

Weak
Weary
Weepy
Weighted
Wicked
Wishy-washy
Worried
Worthless
Wrathful
Wrong
Zealous

|| End Notes

[1] I often encounter many variations of this statement. The most common being "Stop your crying before I give you something to cry about."

[2] *Less Healthy*, *Healthy*, *Less Helpful*, and *Helpful* are phrases commonly used throughout Systemic Parenting. These terms are explored in detail under Parenting Assumptions 59.

[3] *More often than not* is intended to mean that this is a **typical response** from the parent rather than the exception to the rule. This phrase is used throughout *Systemic Parenting*.

[4] Sun Tzu, T*he Art of War* Translated by Samuel B. Griffith Oxford University Press, 1971, New York. Page 84.

[5] A safe manner would be non-judgmental, expressing an interest in understanding the other's position or perspective, even if it differs from their own, and encouraging open processing of emotions.

[6] The son told me during a much later session that he felt as if his parents were attempting to trap him. He initially believe that they were going to use the information they gained through their discussions against him in some way. He realized in short order that this was not the case and relaxed.

[7] See Parenting Assumption 84 for more on spanking.

[8] See Parenting Assumption 36 for more on passive-aggression.

[9] Multidirected partiality is a concept originated by Boszormenyi-Nagy, Ivan. *Between Give and Take*, 1986

[10] Capturing these fleeting thoughts is usually as simple as just making yourself aware that they exist and can be captured. Some people report that occasionally situations "just move too fast to capture those thoughts." Managing anger in a *just* manner takes practice.

One's skill level improves each time one captures and processes these fleeting thoughts and primary emotions. In a relatively short period of time, and with relatively little practice, very few situations will *get the better of you*. More importantly, children absorb this skill as they see their parents working with anger in this manner. It's that simple.

[11] See Parenting Assumption 23 for more detail on intimacy.

[12] See Parenting Assumptions 3, 9, 27, 33, 48, 59 for more on emotional processing.

[13] See Parenting Assumption 36 for more on Aggressive, Passive, Passive-Aggressive interactions.

[14] Several factors will result in one person undermining intimacy, examples would include addictions, some medical, emotional or psychiatric conditions. Also, a long family history of avoiding intimacy is a powerful influence that may result in one person resorting to irrational or less healthy behaviors intended to escape intimacy.

[15] See Parenting Assumption 59 for more on playing with fire.

[16] Note: I only had the opportunity to speak with the father. By far, the healthier way through this situation to have both parents address the child's anxiety. The mother's absence from my conversations with the father made this difficult.

[17] See Parenting Assumption 56 for a more detailed exploration of how a parent might identify underlying anxieties and influences that may affect behaviors.

[18] A *less helpful skill* is just like any skill – it usually comes from training and practice – but is one that results in less healthy and helpful consequences.

[19] There are other ways to systematically address problems such as this (i.e. having both parents initially spend time in the child's bedroom – interacting through play, reading, etc. then reducing the time spent with the child nightly. These parents chose to take a more aggressive approach.

[20] Infantilize: To treat (a child or adult) like an infant or baby or to keep in a dependent, infantile or younger stage of development.

[21] See Appendix B for a copy of this list.

[22] It is important to note that there were no instances of physical or sexual abuse and that neither parent was involved in illegal activities nor drug and alcohol abuse (issues that in extreme situations might justify said actions).

[23] Communications are intentionally severed in some instances of sexual and physical abuse as well as certain psychiatric conditions in order to protect the child's well being.

[24] Note: Spirituality is not intended to mean affiliation with or involvement within religion. See Parenting Assumption 68 for further explanation regarding differentiating the two.

[25] Failing to thrive is a common phrase used by mental health and medical professionals to describe a child who is not developing socially, intellectually, emotionally or physically to his or her full potential. This condition is usually secondary to a adverse environmental or familial conditions.

[26] It was later determined that the 12 year-old girl had been sexually active with a 14 year-old neighbor for several months.

[27] Compartmentalize Uncomfortable Emotions – A means of separating, partitioning, or isolating uncomfortable emotions or situations so as to eliminate them from the forefront of consciousness. An unhealthy means of detaching oneself from uncomfortable emotions or situations.

[28] See Parenting Assumption 5 for an example of how one parent dealt with a relatively minor situation (neglecting to taking out the garbage).

[29] Example of life-cycle shifts include a baby's first words or steps, becoming toilette trained, sexual maturation, shift in focus from family to peers, first boyfriend/girlfriend, getting one's drivers license, graduating from high school, marriage, having a child, the death of one's own parents, retirement, and so on.

[30] The devices that I am referring to are not safety apparatus such as child automobile seats, stairway gates, or high chairs but rather

devices that serve little purpose other than to limit a child's physical activity to the convenience of the parents.

[31] It is important to note that reading to a child and playful verbal games are very beneficial to both **pre** and **post** verbal children.

[32] A vignette is a brief story or sketch that is used to describe or clarify a point.

[33] See Parenting Assumption number 59 for more information on "*right*" vs. "*wrong.*"

[34] Appendix B contains a selected list of emotions, feelings, and reactions for your reference.

[35] See Parenting Assumption 17 for more on differentiating primary and secondary emotions.

[36] See Parenting Assumption 68 regarding moral foundations. Where one decides to place the line between *bad* and *less likely to be helpful* will be determined by each individual and is based upon one's moral foundation.

[37] See Parenting Assumptions 74, 75, 76 for more on preparing in advance. The dangers of fire play is an issue that warrants considerable attention in advance of the behavior.

[38] Other examples might include teaching well, volunteerism, mentoring, etc.

[39] The parents' disabilities were secondary to morbid obesity. Both mother and father weighed in excess of 300 pounds. The father had profound respiratory problems while the mother suffered from diabetes and arthritic knees.

[40] A genogram is essentially a map or diagram of the family tree. It shows many aspects of the family system – (communication pathways, power structures, ethnic influences, religious influences, financial influences, medical histories, addictions, family secrets, and so on).

[41] Most of the sexual offenders I worked with were adults who had been convicted of rape and/or child sexual abuse. I also worked with children and adolescents that were convicted in juvenile court of the same.

[42] The concept of *proactive parenting* is primarily explored in Parenting Assumptions 74, 75, 76. Discussions of *reactive parenting* can be found in Parenting Assumptions 75 and 81. *Parentification* is discussed in Parenting Assumption 89 and *infantilization* is covered in Assumption 37 and 80.

[43] See Parenting Assumption 54 for more on a child's ability to handle the truth.

[44] These thinking errors were adapted from the work of Yochelson, S. and Samenow, S. (1976). *The criminal personality: Vol. 1. A profile for change.* Northvale NJ, Jason Aronson.

[45] It may be helpful to return to Parenting Assumption 42 and to review the definition of self-esteem.

[46] I mention a genogram several times throughout this text. A genogram is an assessment tool commonly used by family therapists to diagram several generations of the family. The genogram helps the therapist and patient identify trends within the family (e.g. history of abuse, addictions, less healthy interaction styles, religious affiliation, race, economic status, medical conditions, mental health histories, family power structures, communication patterns, and so on).

[47] Exploration of self-esteem, individuation, separating process from content, the importance of limits, boundaries and consequences, and thinking errors are all examples of important concepts that play supportive roles to the development of *intimacy, empathy, emotional processing,* and *emotional safety.*

[48] Martyr – a person who suffers great pain or misery for a long time; a person who assumes an attitude of self-sacrifice or suffering.

[49] The phrase *"more often than not"* is used throughout *Systemic Parenting.* This phrase acknowledges that change is a process that best occurs in gradual increments. I recommend parents shift their actions and reactions, from those which are *less likely to be healthy and helpful* to ones that are *more healthy and helpful,* in a gradual manner (e.g. from *rarely,* to *now and then,* to *more often than not*).

Printed in the United States
31442LVS00003B/268-273

9 781593 300852